Pricing and Hedging Interest and Credit Risk Sensitive Instruments

Pricing and Hedging Interest and Credit Risk Sensitive Instruments

Frank Skinner

ELSEVIER

BUTTERWORTH
HEINEMANN

AMSTERDAM • BOSTON • HEIDELBERG • LONDON • NEW YORK • OXFORD
PARIS • SAN DIEGO • SAN FRANCISCO • SINGAPORE • SYDNEY • TOKYO

Elsevier Butterworth-Heinemann
Linacre House, Jordan Hill, Oxford OX2 8DP
30 Corporate Drive, Burlington, MA 01803

First published 2005

British Library Cataloguing in Publication Data
A catalogue record for this book is available from the British Library

Library of Congress Cataloguing in Publication Data
A catalogue record for this book is available from the Library of Congress

ISBN 0 7506 6259 X

Typeset by Newgen Imaging Systems (P) Ltd., Chennai, India
Printed and bound in Great Britain

Contents

Acknowledgements

This book builds upon the discussions with a number of colleagues the author has met over the years. In particular the author wishes to acknowledge David Backus, Laurence Booth, Abhimanyu Chatterjee, Andrew Clare, Cecil Dipchand, Michalis Ioannides and Nicolas Papageorgiou. I owe a debt of gratitude to many former students who read and corrected early drafts of the manuscript, including Dev Kumar Daworaz, Simon Jacobsen, Dilara Moukhomedjanova, R. Ayrton, Kimon Gomozias and Zhihua Chen. I am particularly grateful for the extensive comments from Youssef El Kareh and Spiridon Papalexatos. This project would not have been possible without the love and support of Vesselina.

An introduction to interest and credit risky instruments and their markets

1.1 Bond conventions

It is important to recognize that debt instruments and their derivatives are highly structured contracts that evolved in the past prior to the integration of capital markets. For example, the UK bond market traces its origins to the £1.2 million loan of 1694 used to finance a war with France. Consequently different national bond markets have developed their own conventions for paying coupons, calculating accrued interest and quoting bond prices and yields. This creates a problem for those wishing to learn advanced concepts concerning the debt market because stumbling over the details of, say, day count conventions in measuring accrued interest obscures the important advanced concept at hand. As a result, we have to set the framework conventions. Therefore to lower the barriers we intend to use the following assumptions regarding the bonds that we use to illustrate concepts. These are the 'default' assumptions so without otherwise saying differently, all bonds in this book will have the following conventions.

- *Coupons:* Coupon rates are quoted at annual rates but are paid semi-annually.

  This is the convention followed by many national bond markets such as Australia, Britain, Canada, Italy, Japan and the United States. That is an 8% seminal coupon pay bond would pay $4 per $100 of face value in six months' time and $4 per $100 of face value again at the end of the year. In contrast in most European capital markets, say France, Germany and the Eurobond market, coupons are quoted at annual rates and pay coupons annually. That is an 8% annual coupon pay bond would pay €8 per €100 of face value.

- *Price:* Price is quoted in terms of a hypothetical 100 par value in decimal values.

  Quoting in terms of a hypothetical 100 par value is very convenient since we can interpret the quote as a percentage of par. For example, if we knew that a US Treasury bond was quoted at $90, we would know that the market value of the bond was 90% of its face value so our $20 million face value Treasury bond investment would be worth $18 million. Quoting in terms of decimal values is common, but not universal. For example, US Treasuries are quoted in terms of 1/32 (3.124 cents) and 1/64 (1.5625 cents) so a quote of $90-3 means a price of $90 plus 3/32 or $90.09375 per $100 of face value. If the quote includes a plus sign, for example $90-3+, then one extra 64th is included so the price is $90.109375.

- *Settlement date:* Ownership of the bond is transferred (settled) on the date of trade.

  For the most liquid of bonds, for example UK gilts, there is at least one day between the date of trade and the transfer of ownership of the bond. For the least liquid, for example some types of Eurobonds, settlement is $T + 5$, meaning that the bond is settled five business days from the date of trade. This time is necessary for the back offices of the respective investment banks to complete the necessary paperwork to finalize the trade. The settlement date is important because it is up to this date that the seller is entitled to receive compensation for accrued interest.

- *Accrued interest* is calculated based on the actual/actual day count convention.

  Rarely will we be concerned about this because most of our examples assume that the bond is settled on the day after a coupon date so there is no accrued interest. In other words we use the *clean (flat) price*, which ignores accrued interest, because we assume bonds settle the day after a coupon payment is made. However, we do at certain points explore the consequences of the *dirty (full) price*, which includes accrued interest. The dirty price is the total price a trader must pay when buying a bond that settles part way though a coupon period so it is worthwhile exploring how accrued interest is calculated.

When buying a bond part way into the next coupon period, interest has to be calculated and included in the purchase price. We need to calculate, as of the settlement date, the ratio of the number of days that have elapsed since the last coupon payment has been made, and the number of days that are in the coupon period and then multiply this ratio by the coupon payment to calculate the accrued interest to be paid to the seller of the bond. It is surprising that many bond markets have attempted to 'simplify' this calculation by approximating the number of days in the month as 30, and the number of days in a year as 360. This is the infamous 30/360 day count convention where the ratio needed to calculate accrued interest counts each full calendar month as 30 days and each semi-annual coupon period as 180 days. In contrast the actual/actual day count convention uses the calendar to calculate the actual days that have elapsed since the last coupon has been paid and the actual number of days in the coupon period at hand. The actual/actual calculation is harder to make by hand than 30/360, but the actual/actual calculation is easier to make by computer.

For example, suppose we wish to buy an 8% semi-annual coupon bond for settlement on June 16, 2003 when the next coupon is due on August 16, 2003. Therefore the last coupon has been paid on February 16, 2003. Using the 30/360 day count convention we would say that the seller is entitled to 14 days of interest for February (there are 30 days in February in the 30/360 day count convention), 30 for March, 30 for April, 30 for May and 16 days for June. Therefore the seller is entitled to 120 days of interest. The coupon is semi-annual so the seller is entitled to $120/180 \times €4 = €2.667$ in interest. If we were using the actual/actual day count convention, then the seller is entitled to 12 days of interest for February (there are 28 days in February in the actual/actual day count convention), 31 for March, 30 for April, 31 for May and 16 days for June. Therefore the seller is entitled to 120 days of interest. However, there are 181 days in the coupon period from February 16 to August 16. The coupon is semi-annual so the seller is entitled to $120/181 \times €4 = €2.652$ in interest.

- *Yields:* Yields are quoted at annual rates based on semi-annual compounding. This is sometimes known as bond equivalent yield (BEY).

For example, a 6% semi-annual coupon pay bond that matures in 10 years is quoted at 98.32 and yields 6.228%. The above information means that the above bond costs £98.32 for each £100 face value. In return, the bond pays £3.00 each six months for 10 years, 20 payments in all. The last (20th) payment is £103, as the £100 principal is returned at that time. The yield (internal rate of return) of this investment is 3.114% so its annual bond equivalent yield is $3.114 \times 2 = 6.228\%$.

- *Issue size:* Each bond is understood to have a face value of 1000, so a round lot trade of 100 involves a face value trade of 100 000.

For example, the 6% coupon bond above was quoted at 98.32. This means that if we were to make a round lot trade we would buy 100 bonds of £1000 each for a total cost of £98 320. We would expect to receive a £30 coupon payment in six months' time and another £30 coupon payment at the end of the year. The bond will mature at the end of 20 semi-annual periods when the bond finally pays £1030 representing the return of principal of £1000 and the final coupon payment of £30. However, as noted above, because we price the bond in terms of £100, we will often price the bond using an annuity of 20 £3 coupon payments and a £100 principal. Finally note that we ignore accrued interest as we assume the bond settles on the day after a coupon payment.

1.1.1   Interest and credit risk

Throughout this book we will maintain a clear distinction between 'sovereign' and 'corporate' bonds. The intention is to clarify the issues involved in pricing and hedging interest rate risk only as opposed to the issues involved in pricing and hedging a combination of interest and credit risk. Interest rate risk refers to the possibility of changes in value caused by changes in interest rates whereas credit risk refers to the possibility of changes in value caused by changes in the likelihood that a bond may fail to pay coupons and principal in a timely manner. An investment in a corporate bond always involves both interest and credit risk. So whenever we refer to a 'corporate' bond we have in mind that we are dealing with both interest and credit risk issues. However, sometimes we feel so confident in the credit quality of a sovereign that we assume that an investment in this sovereign bond involves interest rate risk only. That is we assume that there is no possibility that the sovereign will ever fail on its promise to pay coupons and principal in a timely manner. So whenever we refer to a 'sovereign' bond we have in mind that we are dealing with interest rate risk only. Clearly this distinction is false for many sovereigns as they too are subject to credit risk, so whenever we refer to a sovereign bond we really have in mind the debt of nations whose credit risk is very low.

1.2 Bond markets

The Bank of International Settlement reports that as of June 2002, the total world domestic and international debt stood at \$41 256.5 billion. As shown in Figure 1.1, the top six national bond markets, all of whom have more than \$1 trillion face value amounts outstanding, are the United States, Japan, Germany, Italy, the United Kingdom and France. The structure of these markets is generally the same where the domestic market is dominated by their respective national government debt, followed by corporate, semi-government and foreign entity bonds.

In recent years sovereigns have recognized the need to enhance the liquidity of their respective sovereign debt market. Investors value liquidity as a liquid market enables the investor to adjust the size of their position quickly and cheaply. Consequently investors would be satisfied to buy relatively low coupon bonds at par if they expect that these bonds will be easy to sell at the prevailing market price in the future. To save on interest costs by being able to issue relatively low coupon, liquid bonds, sovereigns have taken action to improve liquidity by generally issuing 'plain vanilla' straight bonds concentrated at key maturities. Straight bonds are easier to understand and value and so are easier to trade. By concentrating issues

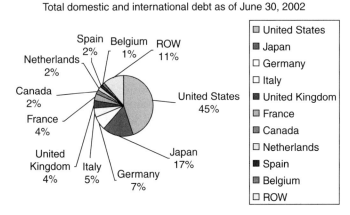

Figure 1.1 World bond markets
Source: BIS. ROW = rest of world

at key maturities, issue size increases. This is thought to improve liquidity since with a larger issue size there is a greater likelihood that active investors will buy these bonds and frequently trade them. Also larger bond issues at key maturities may be perceived as a 'benchmark' issue that can be used to judge the relative attractiveness of non-benchmark issues thereby enhancing the liquidity of even non-benchmark bonds and therefore the entire sovereign bond market.

Typically the second largest segment of the domestic debt market is corporate debt. For most large debt markets the domestic corporate segment is much smaller than the corresponding sovereign debt market. However, the United States is an exception where the domestic corporate debt market is nearly as large as the US Treasury market. Nevertheless all corporate debt markets, even the US corporate debt market, are characterized by a lack of liquidity. This happens because unlike the respective sovereign debt market, corporate debt is issued by a myriad of corporate entities from a wide variety of industries. The average issue size of a corporate bond is much smaller than the issue size of the corresponding sovereign. Furthermore the structure of the bond contract is much more complex. The bond contract contains many detailed bond covenants that are designed to control credit risk and therefore affect the value of the bond. Also there is much more optionality in corporate bonds. Altogether a corporate bond is a complex security making it difficult for traders to quickly assess its value and to agree on its price. Therefore it is no surprise given the relatively small issue size and complexity of corporate bond contracts that corporate bonds are less liquid than the corresponding sovereign bond.

The third segment is the government and semi-government bond market. Here we refer to bond issues of lower levels of government, provinces, states, counties and municipalities rather than the central government, and the agencies of all levels of government. The relative size of this market is variable depending upon how the central government shares governmental responsibilities and revenue. For example, in the UK this segment is so small that it is of little interest because many former government agencies have been privatized (and therefore are more appropriately included in the corporate segment of the bond market) and counties and municipalities are given subsidized financing from the central government (so bond market financing is much more expensive and therefore rarely used). In contrast the US government and semi-government bond market is huge. For example, the municipal (muni) bond market is so large that it deserves a specialist's attention.

The final and typically the smallest segment of the domestic bond market are the bonds issued by foreign entities, corporate or governmental, denominated in the domestic currency. The name of this segment of the domestic bond market is unique to the particular domestic bond market under scrutiny. In the US these bonds are called Yankees, in Japan, Samaria, in the Netherlands, Rembrandt, in the UK, Bulldogs and so on. For example, Hydro Quebec, a Canadian semi-government power utility, has issued a dollar denominated bond in the US bond market and another sterling denominated bond in the UK bond market. In the US, a Hydro Quebec bond would be part of the Yankee bond market whereas in the UK a Hydro Quebec bond would be part of the Bulldog bond market.

Overlaying the domestic bond market is the international bond market. The Eurobond market is by far the largest segment of the international bond market. The centre of trading activity in the Eurobond market is the City of London (the City). Eurobonds are bonds issued by sovereigns, semi-governments and corporations and are sold through many international investment banks and offered to investors of many different countries. This of course creates a problem for traders for if a bond is to be traded in many sovereign jurisdictions at once one would be uncertain as to what set of rules, laws and regulations should be followed in the trading of these bonds. To address this problem ISMA (International Securities Market Association) has been formed. This organization is funded by member investment banks. Upon joining ISMA, an investment bank agrees upon the set of trading rules, conventions and dispute mechanisms set by ISMA that will apply to their trading activities in the Eurobond market.

The attractive feature of a Eurobond is that it is a bearer bond where proof of ownership, like a dollar bill, depends upon possession. In contrast, most domestic bonds are registered bonds where the issuer of the bond knows the name and address of the owner. This means that the taxing authority will be able to tax coupon income at source if the bond is registered, but will find it difficult to tax income at source if the bond is a bearer bond.

It used to be accurate to say that a 'typical' Eurobond is a five-year, annual coupon pay fixed rate high investment grade bond targeted at a Belgian dentist. However, in recent years the Eurobond market has matured so that we cannot say that there is a 'typical' Eurobond. Eurobonds are sold throughout the full maturity and credit risk ranges and incorporate all the variety of coupon payment structures we see in the domestic market. The only commonality among Eurobonds is that they are bearer bonds.

1.3   Trends in the global capital markets

Bonds and their associated interest and credit sensitive instruments are mainly traded 'over the counter'. What this actually means is that international investment banks have their own trading 'floor' where, organized in rows in an open plan setting, each trader has a telephone and computer to be used for communicating their trades. Each trader has access to an information terminal such as Reuters or Bloomberg that keeps them informed of the latest business news and the activity in the market that they are trading in. Typically the investment bank organizes the traders into 'desks' where each 'desk' is responsible for all the trading in a particular market segment. These traders make deals with other traders and investors worldwide with trading activity concentrated in Tokyo, London and New York. Traders work long hours but are correspondingly compensated. Depending upon the instruments they are trading in they may be dealing in any number of currencies. While English is the main business language, increasingly the ability to speak a second language, French, Japanese, German, Spanish and so on, is a desirable attribute. In other words, the over-the-counter market is global.

Moreover the global capital market is a free market. Being lightly regulated by the Bank of International Settlement and the respective national regulatory bodies, investment banks have responded by creating many innovative instruments, like interest rate swaps, floaters, inverse floaters, and zero coupon bonds. A main engine of financial innovation over the last 20 years has been the development of stochastic interest and credit risk pricing models. These models have led to the introduction of interest and credit sensitive derivatives. These derivatives allow investors to separately trade attributes of traditional fixed income bonds to fine tune risk management activities. For example, an early development was the creation of the interest rate swap market. This market allows borrowers to adjust the coupon payment structures of, say, a fixed rate bond sold in the domestic bond market into a synthetic variable coupon rate in response to changing business needs. In other words swaps allow the company to issue bonds with coupon structures that are desired by investors, but then the company can use swaps to adjust the coupon payment structure to suit their own needs. Today there are an astonishing variety of interest rate derivatives that include interest rate caps, floors and collars. Since the early 1990s we have seen the development of the credit derivatives market, which allows investors to separate interest rate risk from credit risk. This allows investment banks to assess counterparty risk by measuring the 'vulnerability' that a counterparty may default on their obligations and allows bond investors to insure their bond from default risk.

1.4   Corporate bonds

Sovereign bonds for the most part are straight bonds. Straight bonds are bonds whose promised cash flows do not change as yield changes. Consequently the structure of sovereign bonds is for the most part simple and easy to understand. Corporate bonds are much more complex for two reasons. First, corporate bonds are subject to credit risk, the possibility that promised cash flows, coupon and principal repayments are not made in full or in a timely manner. Second, as mentioned in section 1.3, a large fraction of all corporate bonds contain optionality. This means that many types of corporate bonds can be viewed as portfolios of more basic straight bonds and options. For this reason many types of corporate bonds are structured securities. Structured securities are bonds whose promised cash flows may change as yields change. Only recently have we made progress in our understanding of credit risk and optionality by applying what we have learned from advanced term structure modelling. Consequently the discussion about credit risk and optionality is best left for later chapters after we have learned how to model credit risk. For now we confine ourselves to a description of how credit risk influences the bond covenants, the clauses that investors impose upon the borrower.

1.4.1   Default risk

The essence of default risk can be seen in Figure 1.2. This figure represents the value of the firm from the point of view of an equity holder when the firm is in financial distress.

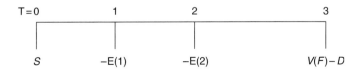

Figure 1.2   Default risk

From the stockholder's point of view, the stock is worth S. For most novices the size of S is puzzling, as it appears to be too high. In our illustration the firm will have *negative* earnings for the next two quarters. Then in three quarters' time, the firm must pay back D, representing the value of principal plus accrued interest of debt maturing at that date. If the value of the maturing debt is greater than the value of the firm $D > V(F)$, then the firm will be bankrupt and most bankers will try to convince you that equity will be worthless.[1] If you try to value this equity using one of the discount cash flow constant growth models, you will probably get values that are much smaller than the market value S. So the size of S appears puzzling.

The key to resolving this puzzle is to recognize that as the firm enters financial distress the nature of the equity claim changes from a claim on a stream of future cash flows to a call option. To see this, look at the terminal payoff. It is

$$S = Max\{V(F) - D; 0\}$$

In other words, if $V(F) > D$, then the equity holders will choose to exercise their call option, pay back debt and, in a sense, buy back the firm. If $V(F) < D$, then equity holders will get nothing, the firm will go bankrupt and the debt holders will take over the firm. Here we see that the face value of debt, including accrued interest D, acts as the exercise price in a call option. This is the essence of limited liability. Limited liability allows the equity holder to view the face value of debt as an exercise price where failure to exercise (i.e. bankruptcy) does not result in further losses to them. Since in the event of financial distress the payoff structure on equity resembles that of a call option it is obvious that you should consider valuing equity as a call option when the firm is subject to financial distress.

But there is more to this fact than may first appear. Equity holders realize that when the firm is in financial distress, their equity transforms from common equity to a call option, so they will be tempted to treat their ownership of the firm as ownership in a limited life option if the firm is in financial distress. The perverse consequence of this can be illustrated by considering how equity holders may select projects.

---

[1] There are violations of the absolute priority rule, that is liquidation payments are first made to secured bondholders, then unsecured debt holders, then preferred shareholders and finally equity. Typically this happens when the firm operates specialized assets where there is no active secondary market so liquidation values are low. Therefore reorganization is carried out where sometimes *bondholders* must pay something to equity holders; otherwise the *stockholders* will force bankruptcy.

Suppose two projects come along. Project A is safe and will make money. In the parlance of corporate finance, we can say that project A is a positive net present value project. However, project A will not improve the value of the firm such that the value of the firm is greater than the value of debt $V(F) > D$ in three quarters' time so the firm will be bankrupt anyway. The only impact project A will have is to increase recoveries by the debt holders. Project B, however, is extremely risky, has virtually no hope of making any money, and most likely will lose the little remaining value of the firm. In the parlance of corporate finance, project B is a negative net present value project. But there is some slight chance that project B will pay off, and if it does, it will make an *enormous* amount. In other words, project B resembles the purchase of a large number of tickets in the national lottery. Further, if project B pays off, then the value of the firm would be much greater than the value of debt so the firm will not go bankrupt and the equity holders will make some money as well. Obviously the equity holders may prefer project B rather than project A. As they control the firm they will instruct management to accept project B and reject project A.

How does it look from the bondholder's point of view? If the project pays off, shareholders make a lot of money. Bondholders get only what was promised prior to financial stress, so they get none of the upside for the enormously risky lottery style gamble. If the gamble does not pay off, then they lose even more than the loss expected prior to the gamble. So they take all the downside risk. It is as if the equity holders are offering to flip a coin with the bondholders, only the deal is 'heads I win, tails you lose'.

Now bondholders are not stupid, they recognize the above problem as an agency conflict. In theory there should be no agency conflict. Senior executives of the firm are to act in the best interests of just one party, specifically a fictitious legal entity called the firm. As management is acting in the best interests of just one entity, there is no agency conflict. They are supposed to act in the best interests of the firm according to the 'prudent man' rule in common law by maximizing the value of the firm. As long as the firm is not in financial stress bondholders and stockholders will agree that management should maximize the value of the firm by accepting all positive net present value projects (type A projects) so there is supposed to be no conflict in their agency relations with debt and equity holders.

But, in the case of financial stress, we can see that equity holders will want one thing (accept B type projects) and debt holders will want something else (accept A type projects). So there will be a conflict, and senior executives are forced to choose to act as an agent for one party at the expense of the other. Since equity holders ultimately employ the senior executives these executives may well resolve the conflict by acting in the best interests of the equity holders and against the best interests of the bondholders.

1.4.2 Bond covenants

Bondholders recognize the above agency conflict, so they protect themselves through bond covenants (or bond indentures). These are clauses designed to either improve recoveries in the event of default or reduce the probability of default.

As an example of the latter kind, we can include a host of clauses that can be described as 'trip wires'. As examples consider accounting ratio-based clauses such as the firm 'must maintain a current ratio (Current assets/Current liabilities) of 2' or 'the total debt ratio (book value of Debt/book value of Equity) must be no more than 1'. These and other similar clauses are designed to catch firms before they get into serious financial difficulty. A company running into trouble will probably start having problems paying off liabilities as they come due (current liabilities increase) since they are running out of cash (current assets decrease) and so the current ratio declines below 2. Similarly as a firm enters financial distress cash flows decrease, so to obtain cash to finance the company's operations the firm borrows more leading to a total debt ratio greater than 1.

While encouraging the firm to stay within the boundaries of accounting ratios reduces the probability of default, this is only part of the solution. For example, what if the firm is experiencing a temporary cash squeeze and as a result violates the current ratio trip wire? Bondholders would like more information, and simply asking for it may not be satisfactory. Forcing immediate foreclosure based on a technical violation of just one covenant is a drastic step where the only winners are the bankruptcy trustee and the legal profession since a significant fraction of the remaining value of the firm is 'eaten up' during the process of bankruptcy. Therefore in tandem with the trip wire covenants the bond indenture agreement might include a clause that, if in the event of a violation of any or all of the above provisions, the bondholders have the right to appoint a representative to the board of directors. If there is no formal bond indenture stating this, then the bondholder's trustee may request representation on the board of directors anyway. Then, with direct representation of the board of directors, the debt holders have a window to see what is going on in the firm. If, for example, the board approves

B type projects, the bondholders can pull the plug and force the firm into immediate liquidation prior to the project B gamble being taken. So these trip wires are very useful for reducing the possibility of default and so are very common particularly when combined with the provision that representation on the board is required if they are violated.

Of course it may prove impossible to prevent bankruptcy. Realizing this bondholders also include provisions designed to improve recoveries in the event of default. This can be done in three basic ways. First, the bond may be secured by specific assets. A mortgage bond is a bond where if bankruptcy occurs the value of the mortgaged asset is pledged against the mortgage bond. Unsecured bonds are riskier since recoveries in the event of default is dependent upon sales of all other unsecured assets and mortgaged assets after the mortgaged bondholders have been satisfied. In this sense mortgage bonds have higher priority in satisfaction of their claim in the event of bankruptcy than unsecured bonds. Second, the bond might be made senior rather than junior so as to reserve a good spot towards the head of the line in the event of bankruptcy. Senior bonds are paid back first and only when their claim is 100% satisfied do junior bonds receive anything. Third, other provisions are designed to preserve their place in the line, such as clauses that prevent issue of more senior debt, or limits to the amount of same priority debt.

The above explanation of how bond covenants work holds true when the 'absolute priority rule' is respected. That is mortgage bonds receive all the proceeds from the sale of pledged assets until their claim is 100% satisfied, senior bonds receive all proceeds from the remaining assets until their claim is 100% satisfied and so on. Very often these absolute priority rules are not respected, particularly when bankruptcy takes the form of administration (chapter 11 bankruptcy in the US) rather than liquidation (chapter 7 bankruptcy in the US). In administration representatives of the creditors and shareholders get together to try to resolve the financial crisis without the involvement of the courts and formal liquidation procedures. In this situation bargaining among all the players often results in agreements that violate the formal absolute priority rules. For instance, senior and junior debtholders' claims maybe satisfied with a new bond with a lower coupon representing a loss for both classes of claims. Therefore junior claims still receive some recovery even though senior claims also suffer a loss.

Nevertheless having a mortgage bond or a senior claim is still useful, as these claims typically will have stronger bargaining power in administration procedures. Consequently we expect that secured bondholders would receive higher recovery amounts in the event of default than unsecured bondholders even though absolute priority is often violated. This holds true in practice. Altman and Eberhart (1994) find that secured bondholders in fact do obtain higher recovery amounts in the event of default on average than unsecured bondholders.

Also, one must be aware that financial contracting is an ongoing process, and that debt holders demand new kinds of covenants to protect themselves against adverse (from their point of view) financial innovations. The clearest example of this is event risk covenants.

The idea here is that if some pre-specified event were to occur, say a leveraged buyout was approved, a major plant was suddenly destroyed, a parent guarantee is invalidated by the bankruptcy of the parent, the event risk covenant would be triggered. The bondholders would then have some pre-specified right to reset the coupon at a higher rate, or require the immediate repayment of debt. Since the quality of the event risk covenant varies Standard and Poor's rank event risk covenants from E1 (strong) to E5 (weak).

1.4.3   Adverse selection

One may be tempted to argue that bond covenants are not really necessary since lenders could simply charge more by requiring a higher coupon rate for the more credit risky borrowers. Unfortunately, using the coupon rate only to compensate for credit risk will fail absolutely because of adverse selection.

The idea here is that borrowers know more about the likelihood that they may go bankrupt and the consequences should they do so. Therefore if the lender charges a higher rate of interest for those borrowers they think are more credit risky without resorting to restrictive covenants to control for credit risk, the lenders will respond by borrowing from the lender only when the lender does not charge enough for the credit risk. If the borrower charges too much, the lender will borrow from another lender that requires restrictive covenants but in return offers a lower interest rate. In other words by attempting to charge for credit risk through the coupon rate rather than attempting to control for the amount of credit risk through restrictive bond covenants, the lender will be picked off by the borrowers. The lender will inadvertently select only borrowers that require an even higher coupon rate and they will lose all the safer credit risks to their competitors who require restrictive covenants, but offer lower coupon rates as well. Therefore lenders must also use bond covenants to control for credit risk as well as charge higher rates for more risky lenders.

1.5   Scope of this book

This book is for those who wish to gain knowledge of the pricing and hedging of all sorts of 'fixed income' instruments and their derivatives. By 'fixed income' we mean those securities that promise a schedule of payments according to some formula. This would include not only fixed coupon bonds, but also instruments such as floaters where the coupon is not fixed, but varies according to some defined relationship with an index interest rate such as libor (London Inter-Bank Offer Rate).

Therefore we will examine the pricing and hedging of fixed income bonds; sovereign, variable rate (floaters), and inverse variable rate (inverse floaters) bonds, and their associated derivatives; interest rate swaps, caps, floors and collars. Recognizing that a large and growing portion of fixed income bonds are subject to credit as well as interest rate risk we examine the pricing and hedging of corporate bonds and their associated derivatives, vulnerable options and credit default swaps. Moreover corporate bonds, particularly those of low credit ratings, have options embedded in the bond contract so we will concern ourselves with the pricing and hedging of callable, putable and sinking fund corporate bonds as well.

We will concentrate on pricing these instruments using binomial stochastic interest rate methods starting with the simplistic Ho and Lee (1986) model and build up to the Black Derman and Toy (1990) model employing Excel spreadsheets to demonstrate how to implement these models. The objective here is to lower the barriers making the understanding and implementation of these binomial stochastic interest rate models accessible to anyone with even a rudimentary knowledge of algebra. Moreover starting from basic principles we extend the binomial stochastic interest rate models to include credit risk by implementing the Jarrow and Turnbull (1995) interest and credit risk model that neatly extends Black Derman and Toy (1990) for credit risk. Later we go one step further and implement the Duffie and Singleton (1999) model for interest and credit risk as an extension of Jarrow and Turnbull (1995). In order to implement these models we must measure the existing sovereign and corporate term structure of interest rates. Consequently we will explore how to interpolate sovereign and corporate yield curves using spline and parsimonious techniques. In other words, we intend to build up the knowledge and skills of the novice to the point where they are able to employ intermediate level models to price all of the fixed income instruments and their derivatives discussed in this book.

The above models are all examples of the term structure consistent approach to modelling the sovereign and corporate term structure of interest rates. There is an alternative class of models that attempts to generate a sovereign or corporate term structure without reference to the sovereign or corporate term structure of interest rates that exists in the capital markets. We describe this alternative approach as the evolutionary approach. For reasons explained later, practitioners tend to prefer the term structure consistent approach, so we pay much more attention to this approach rather than the evolutionary modelling approach. However, we feel we would be negligent if we did not mention this alternative modelling approach at all, so we will briefly discuss and implement two famous early examples of the evolutionary term structure modelling approach, specifically Vasicek (1977) and Cox Ingersoll and Ross (1985).

Another important objective of this book is to explain how to manage the risk inherent in forming positions in fixed income securities. We will review standard hedging practices in detail explaining how modified duration and regression hedge ratios can be applied using interest rate futures contracts. We will explore alternative technologies including extensions of modified duration, Fisher Weil (1971) and key rate durations and the hedge ratios implied by the binomial trees of the interest rate and credit risk models employed earlier in the modelling chapters. We will show how these hedging techniques can be applied to all of the instruments that we explore in this book.

We emphasize that the focus is on learning so we intend to reinforce learning by implementing all models introduced in the book via Excel spreadsheets. The attraction of doing this is that Excel is the simplest possible programming technique available that nevertheless demonstrates the use and applicability of the candidate model. Once the novice appreciates the Excel spreadsheet implementation, then it is much easier to implement the model in a practical setting using a more sophisticated programming language such as Visual Basic, Gauss or C++.

In summary this book is for those who wish to learn how to price and control the risk inherent in holding all sorts of debt instruments. We will maintain this focus throughout all the book.

1.6 Exercises

Question 1

You buy an 8%, semi-annual coupon pay bond for settlement on December 16, 2002. The bond matures on February 15, 2010.

(a) What is the accrued interest using the 30/360 day count convention?

(b) What is the accrued interest using the actual/actual day count convention?

Question 2

About the most complicated financial instrument is a bond contract. Included in many bond contracts are a number of contract terms called bond covenants. In general, these contract terms are designed to control the bondholder's risk. Why do bondholders rely on these contract terms rather than increase the coupon rate to compensate them for higher risk?

Question 3

The following is a list of three bond covenant terms.

1. Minimum Current Ratio (Current Assets/Current Liabilities)
2. Seniority Clause
3. Event Risk Covenant

Describe each term in enough detail to convey your understanding of the covenant and provide a rationale as to why a bondholder would desire each covenant.

The sovereign term structure and the risk structure of interest rates

2.1 Objectives pricing and hedging

What we want to do is to measure the existing sovereign term structure of interest rates and to measure the existing credit risk structure
of interest rates. We wish to do this for two reasons, pricing and
hedging. We wish to price debt claims in relative and absolute terms.
By constructing the term and risk structure of interest rates we
obtain a pan global representation of the risk return trade-off in the
fixed income market that allows us to make a 'quick and dirty' assessment of the relative value of any bond that is available for trade. We
also need these yield curves to price any bond (not included in the
yield curve) and interest rate derivative in absolute terms.

We wish to price these bonds and derivatives in absolute terms
not only for its own sake, but also because we can hedge our bond
and derivative positions. We wish to hedge so that we can control
the amount of risk we accept in our investments. Once we know the
valuation equation that prices a given security, we know how it will
behave if the unexpected happens. For example, suppose we believe

that the only factor that causes the value of a security to change is its yield. Then we can construct a 'delta' as the first partial derivative of the securities price B_0 with respect to a change in yield i. That is

$$\frac{\Delta B_0}{\Delta i} = \text{'the delta'}$$

This expression tells us the change in the bond's price ΔB_0 that occurs due to a change in the yield Δi. Now we can control the risk of our position by forming a hedge portfolio V_H. Here we protect a long position in, say, a bond B_0 with a short position in a certain number N of a 'hedge' security V_h.[1]

$$V_H = B_0 - NV_h$$

The trick is to realize that if we have sold the right number N of hedging instruments V_h then in response to an unexpected rise in yields, losses on the cash instrument B_0 are exactly offset by gains on hedge position and we experience no net loss. A hedge ratio that does this is called the *perfect hedge ratio*.[2] We call this hedge ratio 'perfect' because it eliminates all possible downside risk.

To observe how the above perfect hedge ratio works, we look at how the above hedge portfolio will behave due to an unexpected change in yield Δi. In equation form the change in value of our hedge portfolio with respect to a change in yield is the sum of changes in value of our cash and hedging instruments with respect to the same change in yield.

$$\frac{\Delta V_H}{\Delta i} = \frac{\Delta B_0}{\Delta i} - N\frac{\Delta V_h}{\Delta i} = 0 \qquad (2.1)$$

Intuitively as yields rise the value of all instruments decreases. We have a loss on our cash bond B_0 because we hold it long. However, we have a gain on the hedge asset V_h because while the value of this asset also declines, we hold it short. Specifically we borrow this asset and sell it at a high price, and then buy it back after yields have risen, and then replace our borrowings at a low price. As you can see the critical parameter in the above equation is the perfect hedge ratio N, the number of hedging instruments we need to short in order to hedge

---

[1] I am being purposely vague here as to what this 'hedge' security is as I do not want to obscure the basic point being made above. Later we will use futures contracts as hedge securities in Chapter 7.

[2] As you may well guess, a 'perfect' hedge ratio occurs only in the extremely restrictive case where you hedge a bond by shorting a futures contract where the underlying item is the same bond and the hedge is to terminate at the same date that the futures contract matures. That way we have no basis risk. In general this is not the case. See section 7.9 for a discussion of basis risk.

our cash asset. We can appreciate what this number really represents by solving (2.1) for N.

$$N = \frac{\Delta B_0}{\Delta i} \bigg/ \frac{\Delta V_h}{\Delta i}$$

In other words, the perfect hedge ratio is nothing more than the price sensitivity of the cash instrument relative to the price sensitivity of the hedging instrument. *All* hedge ratios have this interpretation, so this fact is well worth remembering.

2.1.1 *Imperfections in perfect hedge ratios*

Beware of value laden terms. If you were to hedge, how can you ever use any other hedge ratio other than the perfect one? The fallacy of this can be seen if we look at what happens if yields were to fall rather than rise. As yields fall, the value of our cash bond that we wish to hedge will rise in value. We gain on our cash bond because we hold it long. Of course, our hedging instrument will rise in value too, and since we hold it short we will lose on the hedging instrument. Then our 'perfect' hedge ratio will 'successfully' eliminate any net gain, a disappointing result. Surely you will not always want to use a perfect hedge ratio all the time since you will not only eliminate all downside risk, but also all upside potential. In effect, by using a perfect hedge ratio you are not in the market.

A more intelligent use of hedge ratios is to recognize that what you want to do is to control risk, taking on the amount of risk you judge to be appropriate given the circumstances of the market. From this point of view, we can think of the perfect hedge ratio as a benchmark. If we wish to make no bet on the direction of interest rates then we would hedge using the above perfect hedge ratio. If we believe that interest rates are about to rise, and we feel very strongly about this, then why not overhedge? That is we would short more hedging instruments than indicated by N so that in response to the expected rise in interest rates, losses on our cash bond will be more than just offset by gains on our hedge position so we end up with a gain overall. Conversely if we strongly believe that yields will fall, so normally we would not hedge, why not go *long* in the hedging instrument? That way as yields fall, you gain on both the cash bond and the 'hedging' instrument thereby doubling your gain. Of course, if the unexpected happens, and interest rates unexpectedly rise rather than fall, then you would double your loss.

Considering all the above scenarios, you can probably see yourself looking at the perfect hedge ratio as a benchmark, and making limited bets on the direction of interest rates. For example, if you think interest rates are likely to increase, but you are not sure, you will short a number of hedging instruments that are less than N. That way if interest rates do rise, you will lose more on your cash asset than you will gain on your hedging instrument, but at least you get some reduction in the loss. But, of course, yields might also unexpectedly fall, and you will experience an overall gain since gains on the cash bond are not fully offset by losses on the hedging instrument. You would go to the extremes and make large bets by deviating from the perfect hedge ratio by large amounts only when you have a very strong belief in the direction of future yields. In this way, you can see yourself controlling the amount of risk that you accept in your investments.

2.2   Introduction to the term and risk structure of interest rates

The term structure of interest rates is the schedule of sovereign interest rates organized by term to maturity. Note that the interest rates contained in the sovereign term structure are not risk free; they are subject to interest rate risk. That is a sovereign bond investor will experience losses if interest rates unexpectedly increase. If the bond investor actually sells a sovereign bond once sovereign interest rates increase then the loss will be realized. But even if they do not sell the bond once interest rates have increased, an opportunity loss is experienced since they now have a bond that is not worth as much as they had hoped earlier. Hence we can say that sovereign interest rates are risky, and so we wish to model this risk recognizing that sovereign interest rates are stochastic (have a variance).

Similar to the definition of the term structure of interest rates, the risk structure of interest rates may be defined as a series of term structures, each of which is composed of a series of yields on corporate bonds of the same credit risk class, organized by term to maturity. Typically we group bonds in risk classes according to credit rating as given by Standard and Poor's or by Moody's. Most will immediately note that corporate bond yields are subject to credit and interest rate risk.

Losses due to interest rate risk are precisely the same for corporate bonds as they are for sovereign bonds, so we will pay more attention here to credit risk. Of course, one important element of credit risk is the possibility of default, that the bond may not pay coupon and principal in a timely manner. Then it is possible that the company that issued the bond may be forced into administration (chapter 11 bankruptcy in the US) or even liquidation (chapter 7 bankruptcy in the US). In these cases the corporate bond will decrease dramatically in price, and may even turn out to be worthless.

However, there is another, equally important aspect to credit risk, namely credit quality changes. For example, a bond's rating may decrease signalling that the credit quality of the bond has deteriorated, and that the possibility of future default is more likely. As you would expect, the price of the bond will decrease and the yield correspondingly increases. Losses are experienced by corporate bond investors as the yield rises in the same way that sovereign bond investors experience losses as sovereign bond yields rise, the only difference is the reason why the corporate bond yield rose. So losses due to credit risk may be experienced even though no bankruptcy event has yet occurred.

In summary, we note that for corporate bonds there are two sources of risk (or variance). We can say that corporate interest rates are risky, and so we wish to model this risk recognizing that corporate interest rates are stochastic (have a variance) from two sources of risk, interest rate risk and credit risk.

2.3   The uses of the term structure and risk structure of interest rates

The first purpose of the term and risk structure of interest rates may be gleaned by simply examining a graph of these yield curves. A stylized graph of the term and risk structure of interest rates is shown in Figure 2.1.

Note that we have an upward slope to sovereign term structure of interest rates as is typical in a normal market. These graphs show us the pan global representation of the risk return trade-off in the fixed income market. They can be used for relative pricing. In other words, these yield curves enable traders to quickly decide at what price and yield a bond should trade in relative terms. For example, if the yield on 10-year sovereigns is, say, 6%, then we would expect that if someone was to offer to sell a 10-year bond then negotiations concerning price should start somewhere near to a price

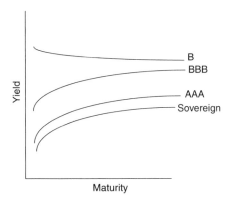

Figure 2.1 Term and risk structure of interest rates

that corresponds to a yield of 6%. Similarly we would note that, say, 10-year BBB bonds are priced to yield 155 basis points above the sovereign, then we would expect offers in the range of 7.55%. Deviations from these targets should reflect the differential characteristics of the particular bond offered for sale when compared to the average of the bonds used to construct the term and risk structure of interest rates.

A second, less obvious use of the term and risk structure of interest rates is to act as the starting point to model interest rate and credit risk. These models are then used to price all sorts of fixed income instruments and their interest rate sensitive derivatives in absolute terms. A large fraction of this book will be devoted to showing how information embedded in these curves is added to interest rate and credit risk models to assure that the output of these models is at least reasonable. Once we have estimated these models and have assured ourselves that the output is consistent with these curves, then we can price all sorts of bonds with embedded options such as callable bonds and sinking fund bonds, all sorts of interest rate derivatives such as caps and floors, and all sorts of credit derivatives such as vulnerable derivatives and credit default swaps.

A third use of the term and credit risk structure of interest rates is to discover and use information embedded in these yield curves. For example, it has long been thought that the sovereign term structure of interest rates includes investors' expectations concerning the future rate of inflation. Therefore if we measure the sovereign term structure of interest rates accurately, we may be able to forecast the market's expectation of inflation. If we believe that the market is on average correct, then we may be able to act upon expected changes in inflation before the change occurs. Similarly changes in the *credit spread*, that is the difference in yield between a given credit risky bond, say triple B that underlies the triple B yield curve less the corresponding maturity sovereign yield, may indicate changes in the expectation of the likelihood of recession.

2.3.1 Which yield curve?

Because the term structure of interest rates can be used for a variety of purposes there are three different types of sovereign yield curves each of which is specially suited for a particular purpose. The three types of yield curves are the benchmark yield curve, the par coupon yield curve and the zero coupon yield curve.

The first two are used for relative pricing. The benchmark yield curve, as the name suggests, is composed of the most frequently traded bonds in the sovereign bond market. You can readily identify the benchmark yield curve as there are only a few observations, and the points between these observations are linearly interpolated. In other words, the benchmark yield curve is a piece-wise linear curve that looks something like Figure 2.2.

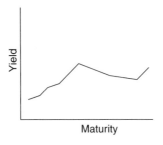

Figure 2.2   The benchmark yield curve

Here we see that there are about eight observations, and points between are simply straight lines that join them up. Obviously the interpolation is very crude and the yields indicated are not very reliable. This yield curve will be useless for pricing bonds and other securities because the discount rates obtained from this curve will be crude and inaccurate and inevitably this will lead to crude and inaccurate prices. However, that is beside the matter, because it is the few benchmark yields that are of interest. This yield curve is for those who are interested in trading in the benchmarks.

Benchmarks attract a lot of interest because they are the most frequently traded bonds, so much of the activity of bond traders is concentrated in these few bonds. Small movements in the yield of a benchmark represent huge changes in the value of positions, so traders need a benchmark yield curve to keep track of what is happening. Additionally, since benchmarks represent the bonds that most frequently trade, they are the bonds that will first reflect new information as it arrives in the bond market. Anyone wishing to know how the latest events have impacted the sovereign bond market should look at the benchmark yield curve.

The second relative pricing yield curve is the par coupon yield curve. As the name suggests it is composed of bonds whose coupons are the same as the yield to maturity, so the bond is priced at par. Obviously there are rarely enough par value bonds to construct an entire yield curve, so actually this yield curve is carefully estimated from the yields of non-par value bonds. As a result, the par coupon yield curve will look very smooth like the sovereign yield curve shown in Figure 2.1. How we go about measuring the par coupon yield curve is a topic we will explore in some detail in Chapter 3. For now note that the attraction of the par coupon yield curve is that it provides a relative pricing benchmark for non-benchmark bonds. This is in contrast with the benchmark yield curve where in between the benchmarks the interpolation is very crude.

The third type of yield curve is the zero coupon yield curve. Like the par coupon yield curve it is an estimated yield curve. In fact, once you have estimated a par coupon yield curve you can simply transform it into the corresponding zero coupon yield curve. This happens because the par and zero coupon yield curves are often estimated from the same underlying statistical technique. The attraction of the zero coupon yield curve is that it can be used for absolute pricing. In other words, it is used to price all sorts of fixed income instruments and their corresponding interest sensitive derivatives. Additionally we use it to extract information that we believe is contained in the structure of yields in the sovereign bond market. You should note that it is this yield curve that we will be talking about by default. In other words, throughout the rest of this book, the 'yield curve' is understood to be the zero coupon sovereign yield curve unless otherwise specified.

2.4 Theories of the sovereign term structure of interest rates

What governs the shape of the sovereign zero coupon term structure? There have been three hypotheses proposed over the years, specifically the expectations, the preferred habitat and the liquidity preference hypothesis. We can conceptualize these three hypotheses according to how we believe that investors view interest rate risk.

2.4.1 The expectations hypothesis

The simplest is the expectations hypothesis. Here investors are risk neutral in the degenerate sense, investors simply want the highest possible return regardless of risk. From this starting point, investors view the following two investment strategies as equivalent. Strategy A is to buy a long-term, say, 10-year bond. Strategy B is to buy a one-year bond today, let it mature in one year, then buy another one-year bond, and let it mature and so on until 10 years have elapsed. Since investors do not care about risk, the expected returns from both strategies are the same. Therefore we can say

$$(1 + {}_0R_{10})^{10} = (1 + {}_0R_1)^1(1 + E[{}_1f_2])^1(1 + E[{}_2f_3])^1$$
$$\times (1 + E[{}_3f_4])^1 \cdots (1 + E[{}_9f_{10}])^1 \qquad (2.2)$$

In other words, if we buy a 10-year bond today 0 and let it mature in 10 years' time we would earn an annual yield of R for 10 years, building up to a cash amount of $(1 + {}_0R_{10})^{10}$ in 10 years' time. The cash amount thereby returned at the end of 10 years would be equivalent to the amount received by strategy B. That is, the amount received from the 10-year bond would be equivalent on average to the amount received from the following procedure. First, buy a one-year bond today 0, let it mature in one year's time 1 earning the known one-year interest rate of ${}_0R_1$. Then reinvest the entire proceeds in a new one-year bond one year later 1 to earn an unknown, but expected E one-year interest rate (the one-year forward rate) of ${}_1f_2$. When this one-year bond matures two years from today, again reinvest the entire proceeds in a new one-year bond one year later (year 2) to earn an unknown, but expected E one-year interest rate (the one-year forward rate, two years from now) of ${}_2f_3$. Again we reinvest the entire proceeds in the same manner as above, and continue to do so until 10 years have elapsed.

The expected earnings from strategy B must equal the expected earnings from strategy A because the risk neutral investor would always take the strategy that pays the highest expected return. For example, if the expected earnings from investing in a sequence of one-year bonds implied by strategy B was greater than the earnings expected from strategy A then the investor would follow strategy B. Then the price of the short-term bond would increase, depressing yields on one-year bonds $_0R_1$, so that the expected returns on strategy B once more equal the expected returns from strategy A.

There is a problem with (2.2); we have on the RHS one known (today's one-year rate of interest) and nine unknowns (nine unknown, but expected one-year rates of interest). Therefore we cannot solve (2.2). It is only descriptive; it is an empty mathematical shell. To make progress we generalize (2.2) such that we have only one unknown on the RHS. This is done below.

$$(1 + {_0R_2})^2 = (1 + {_0R_1})^1 (1 + E[{_1f_2}])^1 \tag{2.3}$$

Here strategy A involves investing in a two-year bond at an annualized interest rate $_0R_2$, and strategy B involves investing in a known one-year bond $_0R_1$, letting it mature and reinvesting the full proceeds at an unknown, but expected E one-year interest rate $_1f_2$ one year from today. Now we have one equation and one unknown, $E[{_1f_2}]$, so we can solve for this unknown. From Figure 2.1, we have measured the sovereign term structure of interest rates, so we know that the one-year rate of interest $_0R_1$ is 4% and the two-year rate of interest $_0R_2$ is 4.25%. Therefore the one-year rate of interest one year from now $_1f_2$ must be 4.5%. We can see that is true by working out the numbers using (2.3).

$$(1 + 0.0425)^2 = (1 + 0.04)^1 (1 + 0.045)^1$$

$$1.0868 = 1.0868$$

Rather than try to work out the unknown but expected one-year rate of interest one year from now by trial and error, we can solve (2.3) for the unknown.

$$E[{_1f_2}] = \left\{ (1 + {_0R_2})^2 / (1 + {_0R_1})^1 \right\} - 1$$

$$= \left\{ (1 + 0.0425)^2 / (1 + 0.04)^1 \right\} - 1 = 0.045$$

But notice that we can make further progress and find the one-year rate of interest, two years from now by comparing a three-year strategy A with a three-year version of strategy B as done below.

$$(1 + {_0R_3})^3 = (1 + {_0R_2})^2 (1 + E[{_2f_3}])^1$$

In other words, strategy A is to invest in a three-year bond, and strategy B is to invest in today's two-year bond, let it mature and then reinvest in a one-year bond, two years from now $_2f_3$. Again we have one equation and one unknown, the one-year rate of interest two years from today. If the three-year rate of interest read off from the sovereign term structure of interest rates is 4.75%, then the one-year rate of interest two years from now must be,

$$E[_2f_3] = \left\{(1 + {_0}R_3)^3/(1 + {_0}R_2)^2\right\} - 1$$

$$= \left\{(1 + 0.0475)^3/(1 + 0.0425)^2\right\} - 1 = 0.05757$$

Now notice I could always work out what the one-year rate of interest is expected to be at any arbitrary date in the future. For example, the one-year rate of interest nine years from now can be found from the two strategies.

$$(1 + {_0}R_{10})^{10} = (1 + {_0}R_9)^9(1 + E[_9f_{10}])^1$$

Then solving for the unknown.

$$E[_9f_{10}] = \left\{(1 + {_0}R_{10})^{10}/(1 + {_0}R_9)^9\right\} - 1$$

To be completely general, we can always find the *forward rate*, the expected, but as yet unknown rate of interest at some date in the future from the *spot rates*, the known interest rates that we can read off the sovereign term structure of interest rates. If we note L as the long date, and S as the short date, we can write the formula that determines the unknown forward rate as

$$E[_Sf_L] = \left[\left\{(1 + {_0}R_L)^L/(1 + {_0}R_S)^S\right\}\right]^{1/(L-S)} - 1 \qquad (2.4)$$

For example, suppose we want to solve for the two-year rate of interest, one year from now. From our sovereign term structure of interest rates, we know the spot rates. They are ${_0}R_1 = 0.04$, ${_0}R_2 = 0.0425$ and ${_0}R_3 = 0.0475$. According to (2.4), the expected E two-year annualized rate of interest one year from now $_1f_3$ is

$$E[_1f_3] = \left[\left\{(1 + {_0}R_3)^3/(1 + {_0}R_1)^1\right\}\right]^{1/(3-1)} - 1$$

$$= \left[\{1.154321\}/\{1.0425\}\right]^{1/2} - 1 = 0.0513$$

The above example demonstrates that one can find one-year, or multiple-year annualized forward rates at any date in the future as long as you can read off the corresponding long and short spot rates of interest from the sovereign yield curve.

The most interesting, and potentially useful, aspect of the expectations hypothesis is that the forward rate forms an estimate of future spot rates of interest. It is a prediction of what interest rates are expected to be, an extremely useful piece of information. For example, notice that our spot rates in the above examples were increasing. If we were to plot these spot rates we would have an upward sloping term structure. What would this shape of the yield curve imply about future spot rates of interest? Looking at our forward rates, we find that the forward rates were larger than the spot rates. We can now see that the reason why the sovereign term structure is increasing is because interest rates are expected to increase as the forward rates are increasing. Similarly we can say that if the sovereign term structure of interest rates were decreasing, then the expectations hypothesis would suggest that future rates of interest would be lower as the forward rates would be lower.

2.4.2 The liquidity and preferred habitat hypotheses

I hope you never took the expectations hypothesis too literally, as it does depend upon a very strong assumption, namely that investors do not care about risk. This cannot be true! So the liquidity and preferred habitat hypotheses attempt to extend the expectations hypothesis by relaxing the risk neutral assumption. How they do this can be seen if we review strategy A and B and ask which strategy is the more risky. What you shall see is that if the liquidity hypothesis is correct, then the forward rate estimated from the spot rates is too high. If the preferred habitat is correct, you will see that the forward rate is biased, but we will be unable to suggest whether the predicted future interest rate is too high or too low. For completeness, note that if the expectation hypothesis is correct, and investors are risk neutral, then the forward rate is an unbiased forecast of future rates of interest, being neither too high nor too low on average.

The liquidity hypothesis suggests that strategy A is the more risky strategy. That is long-term bonds are more risky than short-term bonds. Here investors are concerned about preservation of capital, since if interest rates were to increase, then the value of long-term bonds would decrease more than short-term bonds. It is easy to see why this happens. For a given increase in interest rates, investors in long-term, say, 10-year bonds would bear the impact of this increase for 10 years, whereas investors in one-year bonds would bear the increase for only one year. As a result 10-year bonds would decrease in price by more than the decrease in price of one-year bonds, hence 10-year bonds are more risky.

Bearing this in mind, now consider our two strategies. If the long-term bond were more risky, then risk adverse investors would demand a risk premium. In the parlance of the liquidity premium hypothesis, the risk premium is the liquidity premium. In other words, the expected returns from investing in the long-term bond (strategy A) is greater than the expected cash returns from investing in a sequence of short-term bonds (strategy B) because long-term yields include a liquidity (risk) premium. In equation form we can say,

$$(1 + {}_0R_L)^L > (1 + {}_0R_S)^S(1 + E[{}_Sf_L])^{L-S}$$

Then solving for the forward rate we rewrite (2.4) as

$$\left[\left\{(1 + {}_0R_L)^L/(1 + {}_0R_S)^S\right\}\right]^{1/(L-S)} - 1 > E[{}_Sf_L]$$

In other words, when one calculates the forward rate using the short and long spot rates read off the sovereign term structure of interest rates, one obtains an estimate of the forward rate that is, on average, too high.

The preferred habitat hypothesis suggests that strategy B may be the more risky strategy. In other words, short-term bonds may be more risky than long-term bonds. Here investors are concerned about preservation of income, since if interest rates were to decrease, then the income from short-term bonds would decrease more than the income from long-term bonds. It is easy to see why this happens. For a given decrease in interest rates, investors in short-term, say, one-year bonds would upon reinvestment in at most one year's time, earn income at the new, lower coupon rate. On the other hand, investors in 10-year bonds would continue to enjoy the now relatively high 10-year fixed coupon rate for the full 10 years. Only upon reinvestment would long-term bond investors then bear the new, low, fixed coupon rates implied by a decrease in interest rates. Hence 10-year bonds are less risky than one-year bonds since the income on 10-year bonds is more stable.

The preferred habitat goes a little further and considers the investor's objective in investing in bonds. Life insurance companies, for example, sell insurance products where the maturity of policies is known. They intend to fund this liability by investing in bonds such that the maturity of the bonds matches the maturity of the liabilities on the insurance product.[3] The objective is to fund the liability and make a profit. From the insurance company's point of view, if, say, seven-years is the date the liability is due, then they will prefer to invest in seven-year securities. Shorter-term, say, six-year bonds have more income risk than seven-year bonds, and

---

[3] For those who know better, I apologize for the above little lie. We know that actually insurance companies match Macaulay duration rather than maturities of the bond investment and liability portfolios when running the above portfolio immunization strategy. However, we know that Macaulay duration is closely associated with maturity, so the text motivation for preferred habitat is accurate. More on portfolio immunization later.

longer-term, say, eight-year bonds have more capital risk than seven-year bonds. Therefore we see that seven-year bonds are the preferred investment or preferred habitat in the parlance of the preferred habitat hypothesis.

In our example, the life insurance company can only be lured out of the preferred habit if they are offered a risk premium. Notice this means that if the life insurance company is lured into investing in eight-year bonds, they in effect earn a positive liquidity premium just as the liquidity hypothesis would suggest. That is, the longer-term bond is more risky so the liquidity premium increases as maturity increases. However, if the life insurance company is lured into a shorter term, say six years, then the life insurance company is obtaining a 'negative' liquidity premium. That is the life insurance company is earning a risk premium by investing in a shorter-term bond because the shorter-term bond is more risky than the longer-term preferred habitat bond.

Now consider the impact the preferred habitat hypothesis has on the forward rate. There are different insurance products and there are different insurance companies that have different profiles of insurance products, so there is no one overall preferred investment horizon. This means that there is no one preferred habitat or preferred investment horizon in the bond market. This suggests that when we examine strategy A and strategy B, we have no idea which strategy is the more risky overall, so we cannot claim to know if a risk premium is required to lure the investor into the long-term bond, or if a risk premium is required to lure the investor into the short-term bond. In other words,

$$(1 + {}_0R_L)^L >^?< (1 + {}_0R_S)^S (1 + E[{}_S f_L])^{L-S}$$

So

$$\left[\left\{(1 + {}_0R_L)^L / (1 + {}_0R_S)^S\right\}\right]^{1/(L-S)} - 1 >? < E[{}_S f_L]$$

This means we suspect that the forward rate is a biased forecast of future rates of interest, but we have no idea whether the forecast is too low, or too high, on average.

2.4.3 The Fisher effect

An idea related to the expectations theory is that sovereign interest rates are composed of just two elements. The first element is the real rate of return. This represents the return investors require to induce them to postpone consumption rather than to consume today. The real rate does not include any risk premium and is thought to reflect the average long run growth rate of the economy. The second element is an inflation adjustment that reflects the average investor's expected rate of inflation. This amount is meant to compensate the investor for expected inflation and therefore to protect the real return from inflation. This inflation adjustment may include an inflation risk premium if investors are sufficiently uncertain as to what the future rate of inflation may be. These ideas may be expressed in a simple formula, as shown below.

$$(1 + {_0}R_N) = (1 + r)(1 + I) \tag{2.5}$$

Where ${_0}R_N$ represents the nominal (observed) annualized yield on a sovereign bond sold today 0 and matures in N years from now, r is the real, constant annualized rate of return and I is the inflation adjustment that may or may not be more than the true expected annualized inflation rate expected from date 0 to N depending on whether investors require an inflation risk premium. For example, if the one-year sovereign yield is 4.0% and we believe that the long run growth rate of the economy is 2.5% then the nominal yield implies an inflation adjustment of 1.46%. To show this we can solve (1.5) for the inflation adjustment.

$$I = (1 + {_0}R_N)/(1 + r) - 1 = (1 + 0.04)/(1 + 0.025) - 1 = 1.46\%$$

If we believe that investors do not require an inflation risk premium then 1.46% is a forecast of next year's rate of inflation. Otherwise this forecast is biased upwards and the actual expected rate of inflation is somewhat lower.

2.4.4   Cox Ingersoll and Ross (1981)

So far we have shown that the unbiased expectations theory is consistent with the idea that the forward rate is an unbiased predictor of future rates of interest but only if investors do not care about risk. Cox Ingersoll and Ross (1981) point out that since investors are risk adverse there is no hope that unbiased expectations can hold in its most general form, that expected returns on all bonds are the same over all possible time horizons. They show that the only possible form of unbiased expectations that can hold in equilibrium when investors are risk adverse is the 'local expectations hypothesis'. That is the expected returns on all bonds are the same over the shortest possible investment time horizon.

2.4.5   Information in the sovereign term structure of interest rates

Over the years economists have had a busy time investigating whether one term structure hypothesis or the other holds in practice. The end result of this process is inconclusive. However, some recent progress has been made concerning extracting information contained in the term structure of interest rates and using this information to make forecasts of future economic conditions. This work is mildly support- ive of the expectations hypothesis implying that while there may be risk premiums embedded in the sovereign term structure of interest rates, it appears that at least in part the term structure of interest rates is set in accordance with investors' expectations concerning future possible economic conditions. More interestingly, it looks as though we can extract this information and use it to make forecasts.

Fama (1984), Mishkin (1988) and Hardouvelis (1988) all find that forward rates can predict the future direction of short-term interest rates. In other words, while the expectations theory may not be able to predict the *level* of future rates of interest, there appears to be some validity to the expectations hypothesis since changes in the forward rate appear to have some forecasting ability to predict the direction in future rates of interest. Papageorgiou and Skinner (2002) build upon this work by showing that changes in the forward rate are able to predict directional changes in interest rate one month ahead with rather more than 60% success.

Estrella and Hardouvelis (1991) find that increases in the slope of the term structure foreshadow improvements in real economic activ- ity while Estrella and Mishkin (1998) find that decreases in the slope of the term structure can indicate an increased likelihood of future recessions. Also, Estrella and Mishkin (1997) find that increases in the slope of the term structure are associated with increases in inflation as long as five years ahead.

The idea here is that the monetary authority (e.g. European Cent- ral Bank in the Eurozone, the Fed in the US) attempts to adjust interest rates to control inflation and maintain sustainable economic growth. These monetary authorities have a greater influence on short-term rather than long-term interest rates, so changes in the monetary policy stance are reflected in changes in the slope of the sovereign term structure. For example, if the monetary authority is worried about inflation, they raise short-term interest rates, which decreases the slope of the term structure. Evidently this decreases future inflation, but at the risk of increased likelihood of future recessions. Conversely, if the monetary authority is more worried about low economic growth, they lower short-term interest rates, which increases the slope of the sovereign term structure. Evidently this increases future economic growth, but at the risk of increased likelihood of future inflation.

2.5 Theory of the risk structure of interest rates

In contrast to the sovereign term structure of interest rates, we have not studied the risk structure extensively. This lack of attention is not due to a lack of interest. Rather it is because it is difficult to estimate a structure of credit risky yield curves, a topic we will turn to later in Chapter 3. However, we have made some progress.

The major question is whether credit risk increases or decreases with maturity. Johnson (1967) was the first to study this question, finding that the answer depends in part upon the credit class and in part upon the time period we are examining. For high investment grade bonds, triple, double and single A, corporate yield curves are more or less parallel curves that lie above the sovereign yield curve. He finds that the *credit spread* (the difference between a corporate bond yield and the corresponding sovereign bond yield of the same maturity) tends to increase with maturity. This makes sense since all corporate bonds are subject to at least the same amount of interest rate risk as sovereign bonds, so for that reason they should have at least the same yield. But since corporate bonds have an additional source of risk, credit risk, their yields should lie above the sovereign yield curve. Finally, since credit spreads for these high credit quality bonds tend to increase with maturity then it appears that credit risk increases with maturity. Again this makes sense since while we know that a bond deserves a double A rating today, we do not know whether this bond will be double A in five years' time. Therefore we may view a 10-year double A bond as more credit risky than a five-year double A bond simply because it is more likely that the double A bond may experience an adverse credit event in 10 years rather than five years.

However, examining below investment grade bonds Johnson (1967) found that sometimes the below investment grade yield curve, say single B, was downward sloping when the underlying sovereign term structure was upward sloping like we show in Figure 2.1. We think this happens because of the *crisis at maturity* problem. The explanation is as follows. The issuers of original issue single B bonds do not plan to pay back the debt borrowed because the issuer does not have the financial resources to do so. This is one reason why the bond of the issuer was rated single B. Instead they plan to 'roll over' the bond as it matures. That is as the bond approaches maturity, the issuer issues a new bond, the proceeds of which are used to pay back the retiring issue. Therefore the issuer's ability to retire its single B bonds depends upon its ability to issue new single B bonds.

The crisis at maturity problem occurs when credit conditions deteriorate because of an increased likelihood of recession. Then most investors would be unwilling to buy new issue single B bonds because these are the most likely bonds to default when credit conditions deteriorate. This means that existing issuers of single B bonds may not be able to issue new bonds to retire existing debt. Because they cannot pay back the debt from the resources of the company, these bonds will likely default. Investors know this, so the price of these maturing single B bonds falls, and the promised yield rises. For longer-term single B bonds, the crisis at maturity is less of an issue because they have, say, three years or more before the problem of paying back the debt occurs. In three years' time credit conditions are likely to be better so it is likely that these longer-term bonds will not experience a crisis at maturity problem. Investors know this so these bonds are more valuable having a higher price and lower yield. This creates the observed downward sloping single B yield curve because maturing single B bonds have high yield as they are subject to the crisis at maturity problem, and longer-term single B bonds have lower, more normal yields as they are not immediately subject to the crisis at maturity problem. Therefore we end up with a downward sloping single B yield curve.

This still leaves unresolved the question why below investment grade yield curves often appear downward sloping when the underlying sovereign term structure is upward sloping. It could be that the crisis at maturity problem occurs even when the sovereign term structure is upward sloping. This is a bit doubtful since a crisis at maturity problem should be evident when a recession looms and then we would expect a downward sloping sovereign term structure as well. The latter would occur as the monetary authority raises short-term interest rates to reduce inflation but also increases the risk of a recession. Helwege and Turner (1999) suggest that below investment grade yield curves are too often downward sloping because of a selection bias. Helwege and Turner (1999) measure the slope of a sample of term structures for below investment grade bonds and find that they are most often downward sloping. When they correct for selection bias by selecting matched pairs of bonds from the same firm with the same seniority in the liability structure, the previously downward sloping below investment grade bond yield curves often become upward sloping.

2.5.1 The relationship between changes in the sovereign term structure and the credit spread

Recent evidence by Papageorgiou and Skinner (2003), Kiesel, Perraudin and Taylor (2002), Collin-Dufresne, Goldstein and Martin (2001), Duffee (1998) and others shows that the relation between the level and slope of the sovereign term structure and the credit spread is negative. Specifically as the level of interest rates, and as the slope of the sovereign yield curve rises, the credit spread narrows. These results are consistent with financial theory. The Cox Ingersoll and Ross (1985) model shows a positive covariance with wealth so a rise in sovereign yields is associated with increasing wealth. Increasing wealth should be associated with an improvement in economic conditions and a reduction in the likelihood of recessions and a narrowing of the credit spread. Similarly a rise in the slope of the sovereign term structure signals a likely rise in future interest rates and an improvement in future economic conditions. This would lead to a reduced probability of future recessions and a lowering of the credit spread. The later result is also supported by the empirical findings of Estrella and Hardouvelis (1991) and Estrella and Mishkin (1998) as outlined in section 2.4.4.

2.6   How sovereign bonds are issued

Unlike corporate bonds, sovereign bonds are not issued in the same way as equity securities. Therefore in this section we discuss how sovereign bonds are issued, an important aspect of any nation's bond market. There are two stylized types of auctions, the American auction and the Dutch auction. Just as European and American options have no geographic implications, so too American and Dutch auctions have no geographic meaning. In fact the US sovereign employs both types of auction for different maturities of US Treasury bonds.

The objective of the sovereign is to obtain funds for government spending while minimizing funding costs. What is a suitable method for the US sovereign may not be suitable for another sovereign so we will later discuss some variations from these two stylized types of auctions that have been pioneered by other sovereigns in response to their needs.

2.6.1 American auction

There are two types of bidders, competitive and non-competitive. Competitive bidders specify the *amount* and *price* they are willing to pay. In contrast non-competitive bidders specify only the amount they are willing to buy. In this case the price the non-competitive bidders pay and the yield they will receive will be determined as the average of the successful competitive bids. The maximum amount non-competitive bidders can bid for is usually low. For example, in the US the maximum amount a non-competitive bidder can bid for is $1 million. Obviously the intention is to restrict non-competitive bids to relatively small investors.

The best way to illustrate the workings of an American auction is by way of example. Suppose the sovereign needs $12 billion in 90-day T-bills and prior to the auction they receive $1.5 billion in non-competitive bids. This means $10.5 billion ($12−$1.5) remains to be sold at auction to the competitive bidders. Suppose the competitive bids are as outlined in Table 2.1.

Table 2.1   American auction

Bids	Treasury bill	Cumulative bids accepted
Non-competitive bids of 1.5 billion	Accept 1.5 billion	1.5 billion
(A) 2 billion @5.2%	Accept 2.0 billion	3.5 billion
(B) 4.0 billion @5.3%	Accept 4.0 billion	7.5 billion
(C) 6.0 billion @5.4%	Accept 4.5 billion	12.0 billion
(D) 1.0 billion @5.5%	Reject bids	

As Table 2.1 illustrates, the sovereign ranks all bids and places them in classes from the most to the least desirable from their point of view. They will accept bids according to this pecking order until the full $12 billion needed is raised. Notice that bids in class C are only partly filled. Individual bids in this class receive a pro rata share, that is if you bid for $100 million Treasury bills at 5.4%, only $75 million would be accepted. Notice also that class D bidders were 'shut out' as all of their bids were rejected.

The *stop yield* is the highest yield received by the competitive bidders. In this case the stop yield is 5.4%. As mentioned earlier, the non-competitive bidders will receive the average yield that the competitive bidders obtained. In this case it is 5.3% calculated as follows.

$$\frac{2}{10.5}(5.2\%) + \frac{4}{10.5}(5.3\%) + \frac{4.5}{10.5}(5.4\%) = 5.3\%$$

Finally the *tail* is the difference between the stop and average (non-competitive) yields. This represents the maximum a competitive bid could have obtained over a non-competitive bid. In this case it is 10 basis points (5.4 − 5.3). Assuming the distribution of the competitive bids is symmetrical, the tail can be interpreted as a measure of *winner's curse*, the idea that you surely will 'win' if your bid price is too high. In other words, it suggests that some hapless competitive bidders 'won' their bids by paying too much and receiving a yield of only 5.2%, 10 basis points less than average.

The disadvantage of the American auction is winner's curse. This creates caution and discourages aggressive bidding and even creates the incentive to collude. However, there are some legitimate strategies to avoid the worst of winner's curse. The first strategy is to bid at low prices. Then it would be unlikely that you pay too much. The disadvantage is that you may be shut out like the bidders in class D in our example or end up with a small pro rata share if you bid a little more aggressively and end up at the stop yield. The second strategy is to bid at low prices, but for larger than really wanted amounts. The risk is that you still may be shut out, but if you turn out to be at the stop yield, your pro rate share will leave you with a reasonable amount. Of course, if you end up at the stop yield you may also receive more than expected but it should be no problem to finance the investment in Treasury bills or to sell off the excess amounts. As we shall explain later, the repo market allows traders to finance excess investments in Treasury securities cheaply. The problem with the second strategy is that there are restrictions on the amount you can bid. In the US, no dealer can bid for more than 35% of the issue.

2.6.2 Dutch auction

There is one key difference between American and Dutch auctions. Unlike an American auction, in the Dutch auction, the lowest price (highest yield) necessary to sell the entire offering becomes the price at which all accepted bids, both competitive and non-competitive, are sold. Otherwise the Dutch auction is the same as an American auction. The competitive bids are allocated according to classes A, B, C and so on. Some bids are shut out, others receive a pro rate share, and so it still makes sense for small bidders to submit a non-competitive bid. It is just that all *accepted* bids receive the 'stop' yield. Using the last example, the yield on all accepted bids would be 5.4%.

The *disadvantage* of the Dutch auction from the sovereign's point of view is that they may end up paying a higher interest rate. The *advantage* is that it encourages more aggressive bidding as it reduces the likelihood of winner's curse. To appreciate why, consider the bidding strategies you would follow in a Dutch auction. If you suspect your competitors are bidding low prices, you have an incentive to bid high because you will get *your entire* bid at the *higher* yield. On the other hand, if you suspect that your competitors are bidding high prices, you have an incentive to submit a low bid as this may lower the price for you (and everyone else), but of course you may be shut out. As you can see, the dominant strategy is to bid at what you think is the right price since there is no incentive to bid at more cautious lower prices. If you are wrong in bidding too high, you will likely be protected as your price is above the minimum accepted price and so you too will receive the higher price.

From the sovereign's point of view it is not obvious that the Dutch auction is more expensive. Using our previous example, at first glance the Dutch auction might look like it is more expensive since the stop yield was 5.4% but the sovereign was paying only 5.3% on average in the American auction. According to the rules of a Dutch auction, the sovereign would pay 10 basis points more, 5.4% rather than an average of 5.3%. This is a fallacy since these figures are from an American auction where cautious bidding is the rule rather than the exception. It is possible that if the example was from a Dutch auction, more aggressive bidding may obtain a stop yield of 5.2%, and result in a 10 basis point saving when compared to the results of the corresponding American auction. It is interesting to note that the US Treasury now employs the Dutch auction for most of its auctions.

2.6.3 Variations

In the US there are regularly scheduled auctions of sovereign debt all along the yield curve. They can (have to?) do this since their debt requirements are so huge. But other sovereign debt markets have developed variations that are more suited to their needs.

2.6.3.1 Ad hoc (or tap) system

The UK does not always follow a regular auction cycle. Instead they sometimes raise funds when, in the opinion of the sovereign, there is an excess demand for their debt and there is a need for funds. The attempt here is to smooth the demand for sovereign debt and to minimize the disruptive effects that sudden excess demand for sovereign debt may create.

2.6.3.2 Linear bond

For Belgium (prior to the Euro), the overall need for funds is small relative to most sovereign markets. Belgium debt issues tend to be small and closely held. This leads to a problem with liquidity, so yields are higher than what they could be if only the sovereign could make their debt market more marketable.

To solve the liquidity problem, Belgium (and more recently, Canada, France, Netherlands and the UK) began to reopen old issues when new funds were needed. The reissues have exactly the same covenants, coupons and remaining maturity as the old issue, and so to prevent arbitrage, they must have identical yields as the old issue. This means that instead of having many small illiquid issues, Belgium has fewer, but larger and more liquid issues. These 'linear bonds' should sell at lower yields because the premium required by the market for liquidity problems should be lower, thereby reducing interest costs for the sovereign.

2.6.3.3 Shrinking sovereign debt markets

In recent years some sovereigns have enjoyed budget surpluses. Rather than having to raise additional funds in their respective debt markets, they began to buy back old Treasury issues. This creates a challenge to debt markets for now the Treasury market is not only smaller, but also less liquid and consequently individual Treasury issues are difficult to price.

It is interesting to note that the UK Debt Management Office (DMO) has recently responded to this problem. The DMO occasionally makes a tender offer for old illiquid issues and then sells a new tranche of a linear bond or even sells an entirely new issue. For example, when a long-term UK Treasury bond's maturity fell below 15 years, it was no longer suitable for inclusion in bond indexes as the benchmark bond. It was unlikely that this bond would trade very frequently, and the UK sovereign did not need additional funds to allow them to sell a new long-term bond to play the role of the long-term UK Treasury bond benchmark. So the DMO made a tender offer for the old benchmark bond and replaced the funds used in the tender offer by selling a new long-term bond that was suitable to use as a benchmark. In this way the DMO is able to maintain large, liquid benchmark bonds even though the new amounts issued by the UK sovereign are declining.

2.7 Repos

An important problem in dealing with Treasury securities is financing. The fact is that bonds in most markets trade in round lots of 100 bonds. For US Treasuries, each bond has a face value of $1000 (in the UK it is £1000) so just one round lot buy order represents an investment of $100 000 in terms of face value. For EuroMTS, a Eurozone-wide electronic bond market that specializes in trading the most liquid Eurozone bonds, €5 or €10 million is a common minimum trade size. It does not take long before a position of several hundreds of millions is built up. How can investors finance these positions?

This is why we have repo markets for sovereign securities. A repo is a sale and repurchase agreement. Here if a bond trader was to 'do a repo', they will sell their Treasury security while simultaneously agreeing to buy it back a few days later at a higher price. Notice that the trader is still long the Treasury security. Since they are committed to buy back the Treasury security at an agreed price on the second leg of the transaction any increase in value caused by an interest rate decrease would accrue to them. But in the meantime they have sold the security so now they do not have to use any of their own cash to finance this long position.

Of course, there is a price to pay for this transaction. The trader sells at a low price and must buy the Treasury security back at a higher price. Now the truth comes out, the trader is borrowing money to purchase the Treasury security and is paying interest, the amount of which is the difference between the relatively low sale and higher repurchase price. For the trader doing the repo, this is still a good deal because the implied interest rate, called the *repo rate*, is very low. To appreciate why this is the case, we need to look at the repo from the other side, from the point of view of the trader that is 'buying a repo'. In other words, the lender who agrees to buy the Treasury security at a low price but agrees to sell the security back at a higher price later.

From the lender's point of view, the loan has very little credit risk. First, the transaction passes title to the lender. If for some reason the borrower was to default and fail to repurchase the bond as agreed, then there is no question that the lender can keep the security. In effect, the Treasury security that has been 'repoed' is collateral for the repo transaction. Second, the quality of the collateral is excellent. The collateral has no credit risk (it is a Treasury security) and repos are usually done with Treasury securities that are reasonably easy to sell.[4] Finally, the repo is usually done for a short time, a few days is most common, and terms as long as two weeks are uncommon. So there is not much time for things to go wrong. For these reasons, the spread between the relatively low purchase price and the higher sell price (from the lender's perspective) is quite modest implying a low interest rate is charged on the loan implied by the repo.

In summary, to 'do a repo' (or sell collateral as it is sometimes called) is a cheap loan used to finance capital intensive long positions in Treasury securities. To 'buy a repo' (or buy collateral as it is sometimes called) is a useful way to temporarily park money in a safe, interest bearing transaction.

However, things can go wrong, even in a few days, and the loan implied by buying collateral does involve some credit risk. For example, if interest rates were to rise, the value of the collateral may fall below the amount advanced. Now the lender has some credit exposure, the value of collateral is less than the amount of the loan. If the borrower was now to default, the lender will experience default losses.

Recognizing this, lenders in the repo market may protect themselves in two ways. First, the lender may impose a margin requirement, in effect advancing a smaller amount than the value of the treasury security being bought. In other words, the amount advanced is set below the value of the Treasury security, so that even if interest rates rise, it is less likely that the value of the collateral will be less than the amount loaned. Second, the lender may 'mark to market'. Here the value of the collateral is calculated, say, daily, and if the value of the collateral approaches the amount loaned, the borrower is required to make additional payments to the lender to maintain a margin of safety. If the borrower fails to meet this margin call, the lender is free to sell the collateral at a price that is still above the loan amount. The lender then deducts the promised interest and remits the remainder to the borrower.

2.8 Summary

In this chapter we have set out the objectives for this book, namely we wish to learn how to price and hedge all sorts of interest sensitive instruments. We covered the theory of the sovereign and credit risk structure of interest rates, and have discussed two important operational aspects of sovereign bond markets, specifically how sovereign

---

[4] Just as you would expect, if the underlying security in the repo was not very marketable the implied interest rate would be higher.

bonds are issued and how traders can finance their position in sovereign bonds.

2.9 Exercises

Question 1
Consider the following zero coupon spot rates.

Maturity (years)	Zero coupon spot rate (%)
0.5	3.00
1.0	3.15
1.5	3.25
2.0	3.40
2.5	3.60
3.0	4.00

(a) Calculate the six-month forward rates implied by the above zero coupon spot curve.
(b) Under what conditions can we claim that the above forward rates are unbiased forecasts of future rates of interest?

Question 2: An experiment
Find the current T-bill rate for your sovereign in your national newspaper. If your sovereign does not have one, look for the UK T-bill rate in the *Financial Times*. If the real rate is 2%, find the predicted inflation rate according to the Fisher relation. Is the prediction realistic?

Question 3
You have just been assigned to manage an emerging market's mutual fund. Part of your job involves reading extensive information about economic conditions in other countries in order to assess the likelihood of earning superior returns in a country's nation stock and bond markets. This time around you are looking at Brazil. Below is the Federal Government of Brazil's term structure based on coupon bonds.

World bank forecasts made at the beginning of the year projected annual inflation at 10% while real growth should continue at 5% per year.

Time to maturity	Yield (%)
One year	18
Two years	19.5
Three years	20.75
Five years	21.00
Ten years	22.00
Fifteen years	22.25
Twenty years	22.50

Answer the following questions.

(a) If the annual inflation rate is truly expected to remain at 10%, what will be the projected real rate of return on one-year sovereign bonds? (Assume the maturity premium is zero.)

(b) Since in most G7 countries real rates of return are more in the range of 3–4%, is this a good place to invest? (Note exchange risk can be eliminated through currency futures contracts and assume that inflation is really going to be 10%.)

(c) What would be the expected one-year rate of interest next year according to the forward rate? What would be the rate of interest on a four-year bond sold next year according to the forward rate?

Question 4
In the first few years of this decade, the US Treasury used Dutch auctions much more frequently than American auctions. Why do you suppose this is the case?

Question 5
The resulting competitive bids received for the auction of a 4.75% gilt maturing in 2015 are contained in the following table. The sovereign needs to raise £2.75 billion from competitive bids.

Bid class	Amount (million)	Yield
A	£1500	4.67
B	£2660	4.68
C	£3000	4.69
D	£300	4.70

1. Under the rules of an American auction, answer the following questions.
   (a) Which bids will be accepted?
   (b) What will be the yield for non-competitive bids?
   (c) What is the stop yield?
   (d) What is the tail?
2. If instead the Dutch auction is used, answer the following questions.
   (a) Which bids will be accepted?
   (b) What will be the yield for non-competitive bids?
3. Generally speaking, is the American auction cheaper for the sovereign than the Dutch auction?

Measuring the existing sovereign term structure and the risk structure of interest rates

3.1 Measuring the sovereign term structure of interest rates

To measure yield curves we require the following information. First, we need frequently traded bonds all along the yield curve. Second, we need zero coupon interest rates. Third, we need a continuous yield curve. No matter which yield curve we are trying to estimate, sovereign or corporate, domestic or foreign, we will always have difficulties in satisfying these three requirements. We illustrate strategies for overcoming problems in satisfying these requirements by using the US Treasury market as an example. We use the US Treasury bond market to illustrate that even in the largest, most liquid bond market we still have problems in satisfying these three requirements. The strategies we use to overcome these problems in the US Treasury market are precisely the same strategies we would follow to estimate, say, the Indian sovereign yield curve. Below we discuss these three requirements in detail and the strategies we will follow to satisfy these requirements.

3.2 Frequently traded bonds

To estimate an accurate sovereign yield curve you need accurate bond prices. In order to obtain accurate bond prices, you must deal with two problems, stale prices and tax bias.

Many countries have few bonds that actively trade. This creates a stale price problem. If a bond has not traded recently, we must rely on quotes, if available, as an estimate of the bond's price and yield. These quotes may not be accurate because the trader quoting the bond may not be aware of all the latest information concerning developments for the sovereign and its associate debt market. The bond trader is not necessarily punished for posting inaccurate quotes since quotes are indicator prices only and there is no firm commitment on behalf of the bond trader to trade at posted quotes. This means that the quote may not reflect all relevant information concerning the bond issue. These stale prices are therefore inaccurate, and so if we construct a yield curve using inaccurate information, we will obtain inaccurate yield curves.

This is the reason why benchmark yield curves are desirable. Since the benchmark is composed of bonds that frequently trade, the data points representing the yield of benchmarks are not subject to the stale pricing problem. These yields are as accurate as you are going to get so they can be used in some confidence as the basis for trading in the benchmarks.

That was the good news. The bad news is that for non-benchmark bonds you may not even get quotes at all or almost as bad, you may get matrix prices. Matrix prices are obtained by referring to a bond whose yield is known. The trader then adds a few basis points according to some formula that adjusts for differential features of the bond to be priced. For example, the bond to be priced might be callable whereas the known bond is not, so the trader may matrix price the unknown bond as the known bond yield plus 50 basis points as compensation for the unattractive call feature. Then the yield is translated into the price for the bond. So what you end up with is a crudely estimated price and yield for the bond. Sarig and Warga (1989) and Warga (1991) show that the use of matrix priced information may lead to serious errors.

The second problem is tax bias. Many sovereigns offer concessionary tax rates on capital gains. In the bond market, it often happens that coupon income is taxed at ordinary tax rates, but price appreciation caused by buying a discount bond and holding it to maturity and having it redeemed at par is taxed at concessionary capital gains rates. From the investor's point of view, this makes discount bonds more valuable than bonds that are sold at par, because at least some of the return from the discount bond is taxed at concessionary tax rates. For example, if the capital gain was $10, and the ordinary tax rate and the capital gains tax rate were 40% and 20% respectively, the investor pays $2 rather than $4 in tax. Therefore the overall tax burden on discount bonds is less than the tax burden on par bonds because all income from par bonds is received in the form of coupons and is taxed at ordinary tax rates. Investors will bid up the price of these discount bonds and lower their yield below what it would have been in the absence of capital gains tax treatment.

Of course, premium bonds also receive capital gains tax treatment, but investors find this feature unattractive. Here the coupon on the premium bond is too large given current market yields so the bond is priced above par. Of course, the bond will be redeemed at par at maturity, so just like the discount bond, the premium bond's price will be 'pulled to par' as the bond moves through time towards maturity. This means that investors will experience a loss by buying the bond above par and having it redeemed later at par. This loss is often treated as a capital loss. The unpleasant consequence of this is that this loss attracts tax relief at the same low capital gains tax rate. That is if the capital loss was $10, and the ordinary tax rate and the capital gains tax rate were 40% and 20% respectively, the investor would be able to reduce taxes otherwise payable by $2 rather than $4. Since the premium bond is unattractive, investors would buy the premium bond only if its price was below and its yield is above what it would have been in the absence of capital gains tax treatment.

We would like to avoid tax bias in constructing our sovereign yield curve because we would like to use this yield curve to price instruments that are not subject to capital gains tax treatment. If, for example, we were to use bonds whose price is affected by tax bias, then the discount rates that we extract from the yield curve may be too low (yields on discount bonds are too low) or too high (yields on premium bonds are too high). When we use these discount rates to price other instruments, it would be difficult to understand how accurate our prices are since the price we obtain from these discount rates is affected by some unknown and complex mixture of tax bias that is not relevant for the instrument that we are attempting to price.

This is the attraction of the par coupon yield curve. Since this yield curve represents yields on bonds whose price is par, there are no discounts or premiums; 100% of the income from these bonds comes from coupons that attract ordinary income tax treatment. Therefore par coupon yield curves do not have tax bias. Then it is easy to see whether or not a given bond is incorrectly priced. For example, a bond may have a yield above the par coupon yield curve not because it is underpriced, but because it is a premium bond. If you were comparing this bond with a coupon yield curve not adjusted for tax bias, it would be difficult to decide if the bond is mispriced or not because you must compare the tax bias in the yield curve with the tax bias included in the bond at hand.

The solution to the stale price problem is to select those bonds that trade most frequently. They can be identified as the 'on the run' issues. These are the most recently issued bonds at key maturities all along the yield curve. This happens because there are always two types of investors in the bond market, passive and active investors. Typically there are more passive than active investors. Say, for example, 70% of all investors are passive and the remaining 30% are active. Then when a new bond is issued we can expect that active investors would hold approximately 30% of the bonds. These investors will occasionally trade so we can obtain up-to-date prices for these bonds. Over time some of these bonds would be sold to a passive investor and so will no longer trade. This means that the percentage of the bond issue that actively trades will gradually decline from 30%, and the bond will be increasingly subject to the stale price problem. Then after a few months, a new bond of the same original maturity is issued and all active investors would realize that this brand new issue will be much more marketable since approximately 30% of these bonds would actively trade. They will shift from the previous on the run bond to the new bond. Since the old bond is now much less marketable, we call it 'off the run' and the brand new bond is now called 'on the run'. Therefore we can identify the 'on the run' bonds as a class of bonds that we can be reasonably sure are actively traded and therefore accurately priced. For the countries that do not regularly issue bonds at key maturities, we can identify the 'on the run equivalent' as the bonds that have been most recently issued at key maturities.

However, selecting only on the run bonds is rarely sufficient to resolve the stale price problem as you will probably be able to identify only a handful, perhaps six to eight, data points in this way. You fill in the gaps by accepting 'large' bonds where what is large is defined by your chosen minimum amount outstanding. For example, you may decide initially to accept all bonds with an amount outstanding of, say, £1 billion, only to find that this adds only five more bonds to your data. Then you would lower your standards and accept all bonds with a minimum size of £750 million in order to increase sample size. You would continue this process until you decide that you have enough data to estimate the sovereign yield curve. Large bonds are more attractive because we expect that there will always be some active investors that are interested in trading these bonds, so if we cannot always get trade prices we will at least get good indicator quotes. By the way, if the quotes are identified as being determined by matrix pricing methods, you are well advised to eliminate these prices from your sample.

Similarly you would handle the tax bias problem by judicious selection of data. On the run bonds tend to be priced close to par so tax bias is slight. Then as you apply the size filter to select additional data you would also apply an additional filter rule to select bonds that are priced within, say, £95 to £105. The idea here is that bonds priced only slightly away from par will have only slight tax bias. If these filter rules do not obtain enough data points, you relax the criteria once more to, say, bonds that are priced in the £92.5 to £107.5 range. Notice that these strategies do not eliminate the stale price and tax bias problems. Rather, these strategies are designed to minimize the impact these problems may cause and so these strategies can be used to select the most accurately priced bonds in any sovereign bond market.

3.2.1   Other data problems

In general, the objective is to obtain as 'clean' a sovereign yield curve as possible. What we mean by clean is that we do not want the yield curve to be influenced by special features of the individual bonds that comprise the yield curve that is not also generally influential in pricing all other interest sensitive instruments. In practice this means we want the bonds that we use to estimate the sovereign yield curve to be influenced by interest rate risk only. We want bonds that have no optionality or special features like inflation protection. To avoid special features we extend our stale price and tax bias filters to include a filter that eliminates all bonds with call and put features, inflation protection, adjustable coupons and so on.

3.2.2 Estimating corporate yield curves

Problems in estimating yield curves are more severe in the case of estimating yield curves that are subject to credit risk. The primary reason for this is that unlike sovereign yield curves, there is no one issuer that issues bonds all along the yield curve. To obtain a reasonable sample size one must group bonds in some way, and one must be convinced that the group of bonds one selects has homogeneous credit risk.

One obvious grouping is to select all bonds of a given credit rating, say AA. But this is not sufficient because from as long ago as Hickman (1958) we know that bonds of the same credit rating may not have the same sort of credit risk. For example, can you seriously claim that an AA Disney bond and an AA Ford Motor Corporation bond have the same credit risk? But both have been rated AA. The solution is to select within the AA credit class bonds within the same industry class, say all financial or all utility or all industrial bonds. The latter, of course, will group Disney and Ford again, so if the sample size permits, you could select bonds with a smaller range of SIC codes.

A related issue is whether credit risk is significantly different as we move through shades of credit ratings within the same broad rating class. For example, AA financial bonds can be subdivided into AA−, AA and AA+, but is this refinement important? Elton et al. (2001) find that for investment grade bonds grouped by broad rating category, pricing errors are modest, although the variance of the errors did increase as credit rating decreased. Also, Diaz and Skinner (2001) find that the differences in pricing errors obtained by grouping AA financial bonds by broad rating category rather than by shades of credit ratings were trivial. However, this conclusion only pertains to investment grade bonds, so we are unsure whether we can group bonds by broad rating category, thereby increasing sample size for below investment grade bonds.

Finally, there is one documented case where the credit rating itself is not reliable as a selection criterion for constructing corporate yield curves. Helwege and Turner (1999) find that within below investment grades some bonds are long term and some are short term and these two types of bonds are not equally credit risky. They show that within, say, the BB rating category, only the safer BB rated bonds are issued at long-term maturities while the riskier BB rated bonds are issued at shorter maturities. Therefore, the longer-term bonds are the more creditworthy bonds and the shorter-term bonds are the less creditworthy bonds. This is the reason why they suggest that below investment grade bond yield curves tend to be downward sloping more often than one would expect if solely caused by the crisis at maturity problem.

Now consider the fact that since there is no one issuer, it is not immediately obvious which bond is 'on the run'. A way around this is to look at the issue date and select only those bonds that have been recently issued. Of course, you should be willing to lengthen the time horizon of your definition of what is 'recent' in order to select enough bonds to estimate your corporate yield curve. Also, the average issue size is smaller than the sovereign bond market, so stale price problems are more serious.

Considering the above factors, and noting that there is a lot more optionality in the corporate bond market, one realizes that estimating corporate yield curves is more challenging than estimating sovereign yield curves. In fact Diaz and Skinner (2001) show that investment grade corporate yield curves are indeed less accurate than the corresponding sovereign yield curve. My own view is that at least for the investment grade categories for the large economies we can collect enough information by applying issue size, recent issue, near par price and optionality filters to same industry and broad rating categories of bonds to estimate corporate yield curves. I am much more pessimistic about our ability to estimate below investment grade yield curves.

3.3 Zero coupon yields

We need the term structure of zero coupon yields because we wish to price instruments whose cash flow may be paid at any arbitrary date in the future. If we were to use yields constructed from coupon bonds, then the discount rates thereby obtained will be relevant only for cash flows that have the same structure of payments as the coupon bond. This happens because all yields to maturity assume that intermediate cash flows are reinvested at the yield to maturity. This implies that the yield to maturity of a bond is a weighted average of the periodic interest rates expected to hold in the future.

To see this, reconsider bond valuation. Suppose we value an 8% semi-annual coupon pay, 6.5-year Treasury bond with a YTM of 8.5%. Diagrammatically, Figure 3.1 shows the valuation equation.

Notice that we are using the same discount rate (the yield to maturity of 8.5%/2) for all cash flows, so if we were to 'go the other way' and future value, we are implicitly assuming that future coupon payments are reinvested at a constant 8.5%. For example, the total future value from this bond is composed of the future value of the coupon

Figure 3.1 Standard bond valuation using yield to maturity

payments and the return of $100 principal. That is

$$Coupon \left[\frac{(1 + i/m)^{nm} - 1}{i/m} \right] + Principal$$

$$= \$4 \left[\frac{(1 + 0.085/2)^{(6.5)2} - 1}{0.085/2} \right] + \$100 = \$167.564$$

Therefore the total future value, including repayment of $100 principal, is $167.564. The realized compound yield would be that annualized interest rate which, when used as a discount rate, will present value this amount in m times n periods to equal today's price. This realized compound yield would be the average annual rate earned over the 6.5-year life of the bond. In other words

$$RCY = M \left(\left[\frac{FV}{PV} \right]^{1/(MN)} - 1 \right)$$

$$= 2 \left(\left[\frac{167.564}{97.542} \right]^{1/(6.5 \times 2)} - 1 \right) = 8.50\%$$

Notice that the realized compound yield is the yield to maturity, so indeed the yield to maturity is a weighted average of interest rates expected in the future.

3.3.1 Zero coupon yields and coupon bias

Sometimes we wish to have a schedule of *reinvestment rates* at all points along the yield curve. The idea here is that we may want to forecast future rates of interest from the yield curve using the forward rate believing that the bias from liquidity or preferred habitat risk premiums is small. Or we may want to model the term structure of interest rates so we can price interest rate derivatives. If we were to use the par coupon yield curve, our interest rate forecast and/or reinvestment rate will be biased due to coupon bias.

The idea here is that the reinvestment yield curve we wish to establish is the schedule of *true* interest rates that we can expect to earn for money invested today until some point in the future. The par coupon yield curve does not give this information, because the par coupon yield curve is a YTM curve. That is the interest rate at each point in time represents a weighted average of interest rates from today to that future point in time, the weights being determined by the size of the par coupon.

To see what the problem is more clearly, consider the par yield (say it's 10%) on a 10-year bond. Ask yourself, is 10% the interest rate on 10-year money? Well no, the 10-year bond will pay $5 per 100 every six months, which is assumed to be reinvested at the 10% rate. This is true only if the yield curve is flat. Since this is almost never true, the true reinvestment rates will be something else. For the 10-year semi-annual coupon pay bond, we can think of 19 reinvestment rates, one for each coupon paid prior to maturity, and each one will be different. Of course, there *are* true reinvestment rates, and this does have an impact on the value and therefore yield on our 10-year bond. But how do we find these true reinvestment rates?

The solution is zero coupon bonds. This is the solution because a zero coupon bond pays no intermediate cash flows, all of the investment is invested till maturity, so the yield on the zero is not influenced by yields at other points in time. Zero yields are pure rates of interest and they represent true reinvestment rates on money invested for the life of the zero. So we simply construct our yield curve using the yields on zero bonds rather than par coupon bonds. If we were to use coupon bonds instead we would have coupon bias. To see the difference coupon bias makes, consider Figures 3.2 and 3.3.

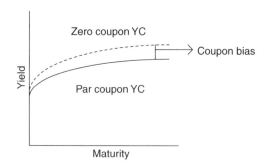

Figure 3.2   Coupon bias–upward sloping yield curve

Notice that the true reinvestment rates lie above the par yield curve. This happens since coupons from the par bond are reinvested at a lower than final maturity interest rate. The par coupon yield or weighted average return is pulled down, forcing the YTM to a point below the corresponding reinvestment rate.

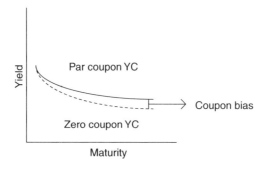

Figure 3.3   Coupon bias–downward sloping yield curve

In Figure 3.3 notice that the true reinvestment rates lie below the par yield curve. This happens since coupons from the par bond are reinvested at a higher than final maturity interest rate. The par coupon yield or weighted average return is pulled up, forcing the YTM to a point above the corresponding reinvestment rate. Also, the longer the term to maturity, the more important will be the reinvestment income in determining the value of the bond and so the greater will be coupon bias.

Clearly this means that in general the yield to maturity represents an *average* of what the series of future short-term rates of interest, some higher and some lower than the yield to maturity, are expected to be, and this average is dependent upon the size of the coupon payments that are paid on the bond. Since in general we will be valuing all sorts of instruments that have all sorts of cash flow structures, it follows that each of these instruments will have a different yield to maturity as they have different weights (payment structures) that are used to determine the weighted average of future rates of interest (yield to maturity). What we need is a measure of yield that is not dependent on the cash flows structure of the particular bond at hand. But where are we going to get these zero coupon yields?

3.3.2 Bootstrapping

The solution is to 'strip' coupon bonds into a series of 'mini bonds' that we call zero coupon bonds. The theoretical basis for doing this is Modigliani and Miller's proposition I. Specifically the value of the firm is independent of the way it is financed in the absence of market imperfections. What this actually means is that values must add up, the value of debt plus equity equals the value of the firm. This is the principle of *value additivity*. In this case, the value of all the coupon payments plus principal (mini bonds or zero coupon bonds) must equal the value of the coupon bond.

This means we can view an ordinary coupon bond as composed of a series of zero coupon payments, each of which entitles the owner to one payment at the coupon date, and nothing otherwise. So for a 30-year Treasury bond, we can sell 60 zero coupon payments (coupons on Treasury bonds are paid semi-annually do not forget) to 60 different investors. The process of doing this is called *coupon stripping* and it is common practice to do this in the respective sovereign bond markets of Germany, Spain, the United States and the United Kingdom among others. We know the price of the sum of these 60 zero coupon bonds, as they must add up to the value of the underlying 30-year Treasury bond.

Now we can obtain these underlying zero coupon rates by a process of bootstrapping. It is best to illustrate by example. Imagine that the six-month Treasury bill is priced as $97.36. Note that a six-month Treasury bill is a zero coupon bond since it is sold on a discount basis, one buys the bond today at a price below par, receives no coupon, but the bond is redeemed at par six months later. The difference between the discount (below 100) price and the redemption value of 100 represents the interest earned on investing in six-month T-bills. Now ask yourself, what is the value of 1/100th of a T-bill? Numerically it is 97.36/100 or 0.9736. But what does this represent? It is a *discount factor*, as it represents the value today of the certain receipt of $1 in six months' time, and you receive nothing otherwise. This is our first mini bond price that we call a zero coupon bond. We can find the corresponding zero coupon yield by the following two-step process. First, find the total return, and then annualize the total return. For example, our total return for our six-month T-bill is

$$TR = \left[\frac{FV}{PV}\right] = \left[\frac{1}{0.9736}\right] = 1.027116$$

Of course, this is earned in six months so we need to convert this six-month return into its annual equivalent or bond equivalent yield (*BEY*).

$$BEY = ([TR]^{1/(NM)} - 1)M = ([1.027116]^{1/(0.5 \times 2)} - 1)2 = 5.4232\%$$

Notice that for zero coupon bonds, the *BEY* formula *is* the *RCY* formula. This makes sense since in both cases you are trying to work out the annualized return given today's price and the future value of the investment.

The above *BEY* gives us the six-month zero coupon yield. The next step is to find the one-year zero coupon yield. Unlike in the US, there is no one-year T-bill in many countries, but do not despair, we can now obtain the one-year zero coupon yield from a one-year coupon bond. Suppose a one-year, 10% semi-annual coupon pay bond exists that is currently priced at \$103.83. We can represent the one-year bond as a package of \$1 face value zero coupon bonds; five that mature in six months, and 105 that mature in one year.

According to value additivity, the price of each of the five six-month zeros is \$0.9736. If it was not, let's say it was \$0.98, then you should be delighted. You should be delighted because you are going to strip the coupon bond and sell the first six-month stripped coupon at \$0.98 per \$1 face value and simultaneously reinvest in six-month T-bills for only \$0.9736 per \$1 face value. This delightful venture will net you \$0.0064 per \$1 face value zero coupon bond, and you are going to do this for millions of zeros. Notice that these transactions *pay you*, yet you have no obligations or risk. These are Treasury securities so there is no default risk. You are buying and selling at the same time, so interest rates do not have a chance to change, so there is no interest rate risk. To put it another way, these transactions do not require you to invest your own money, they do not require you to take any risk, and they still pay you. It is money for nothing. This is what is meant by *pure arbitrage*. Obviously this kind of opportunity will not last long because *you* (you do not need to rely on anybody else) in the very process of exploiting this opportunity will cause it to disappear. As you buy the T-bill, you will drive its price up. As you sell the stripped coupon you will saturate the market and drive its price down. Very quickly the price of the stripped coupon will equal the price of the six-month T-bill. Therefore we can be sure that the price of the first six-month zero coupon will be \$0.9736, the same price, per \$1 of face value, as the six-month T-bill.

So now the price of the one-year Treasury note can be seen as an equation with only one unknown because we know the price of the package of zero coupon bonds (the one-year Treasury note) and the price of the six-month zero coupon bond d_1 but we do not know the price of the second zero coupon bond d_2.

$$103.83 = 5d_1 + 105d_2$$

We have one equation and one unknown, so we can solve for the price of the one-year zero d_2 as

$$d_2 = \frac{103.83 - 5d_1}{105} = \frac{103.83 - 5(0.9736)}{105} = 0.9425$$

As before we can convert this zero coupon price into its corresponding zero coupon yield using the *BEY* formula. First, we work out its total return.

$$\frac{1}{d_2} = \frac{1}{0.9425} = 1.061 \text{ or } 6.1\%$$

Its *BEY* is then found.

$$BEY = ([TR]^{1/(NM)} - 1)M = ([1.061]^{1/(1 \times 2)} - 1)2 = 5.9126\%$$

Now we can continue to bootstrap. That is we now look at an 18-month Treasury coupon bond, write its price as a package of zero coupon bonds, note that we know the price of the first d_1 and second d_2 coupons and that we do not know the price of the third coupon and principal payment d_3, solve the resulting equation for the one unknown d_3, convert the price d_3 into its corresponding zero coupon yield by using the *BEY* formula. For example, suppose we have an 18-month, 4% semi-annual pay coupon bond that is worth $96.454. We can write the value of the bond as a package of zeros.

$$96.454 = 2d_1 + 2d_2 + 102d_3$$

Then solve for the price of the third zero.

$$d_3 = \frac{96.48 - 1.9472 - 1.8855}{102} = 0.9081$$

Now we convert this price into its zero yield.

$$\frac{1}{d_3} = \frac{1}{0.9081} = 1.1012$$

$$BEY = ([TR]^{1/(NM)} - 1)M = ([1.1012]^{1/(1.5 \times 2)} - 1)2 = 6.5311\%$$

Here is a simple exercise for you. Suppose you now have a 10% semi-annual coupon pay bond that matures in two years that is priced at $107.43. What is the price of the fourth zero d_4 and what is its zero yield? The answers are $0.88657 and 5.99%.

To summarize, we can obtain the zero coupon yield curve from the prices of coupon bonds by 'bootstrapping' and relying on the principle of value additivity. These zero coupon rates are unique. There is only one, say, 18-month zero coupon rate and all 18-month cash flows are valued correctly by using this 18-month rate as the discount rate. All bonds regardless of coupon size are valued by the same structure of zero coupon rates. These zero coupon yields must be correct, because otherwise this would imply a pure arbitrage opportunity. If coupon bonds were underpriced, then investors would be able to buy the coupon bond and then strip the coupons from coupon bonds and sell them at higher prices to earn money but take no risk or invest none of their money for doing so. Alternatively, if the coupon bond was overpriced, the investor can reverse the transaction by buying the zeros (they exist at least in Germany, Spain, the US and the UK) and reforming the coupon bond and selling the package at the higher coupon bond price. Again the investor earns money but takes no risk or invests none of their money for doing so.

3.3.2.1 Bootstrapping arbitrage and corporate bonds

Unfortunately the above pure arbitrage argument does not apply for corporate bonds because the failure to pay one mini bond implies that the underlying corporate bond has defaulted so all subsequent mini bonds will default as well. For example, if an investor believes that a corporate bond is underpriced then the investor should buy the bond at a relatively low price and then sell the strips at a higher price. If the corporate bond defaults, the investor will not receive subsequent coupon and principal payments from the corporate bond to satisfy their strip obligations. This implies that the investor may also default if they cannot pay the strip obligations from their own resources.

Therefore the pure arbitrage argument behind the bootstrapping method breaks down as the risk of default remains. In other words, the investor may earn money by bootstrapping over- or undervalued corporate bonds but they must take on risk in doing so. Consequently the above arbitrage argument holds only to the extent that we can ignore bankruptcy. Nevertheless it is common practice to apply bootstrapping methods to estimate a corporate zero coupon yield curve as it is thought that the possibility of default, at least for investment grade bonds, is small.

3.3.3 STRIPS are not the answer

The above procedure for estimating the zero coupon yield curve looks clumsy, is there an easier way? It is tempting to suggest that we should use the zero coupon yield curve implied by STRIPS (for what it is worth, these are Separate Trading of Registered Interest and Principal Securities). These securities are formed by stripping the coupons and principal from ordinary sovereign coupon bonds. As mentioned previously they exist in the sovereign bond markets of Germany, Spain, the US and the UK. These securities are sold separately on a discounted yield basis. In other words, they are like any ordinary three-month T-bill, but say US investors have a range of at least 60 maturities to choose from, every six months up to 30 years. The BEY of these securities would form an estimate of the zero coupon yield curve.

But the STRIPS' yield curve will be inadequate because STRIPS do not trade very often. Passive investors just love these securities because these securities have wonderful 'duration' (more on this in Chapter 7) properties that help 'portfolio immunization' (more on this in Chapter 8) strategies run more effectively. Therefore the prices of STRIPS are subject to severe stale price and matrix price problems discussed earlier. To put it bluntly, STRIPS prices are usually inaccurate, so you would obtain inaccurate zero coupon yield curves from them.

3.4   Measuring continuous yield curves

After selecting our sample in accordance with sections 3.2 to 3.2.2, we now need to interpolate among the data points to estimate a continuous yield curve. We need a continuous yield curve because we wish to price all sorts of fixed income instruments, derivatives and embedded options for instance, where cash flows from these securities need to be valued and may occur at any point in time. As noted above, the bootstrap method for estimating the zero coupon yield curve is clumsy. This routine is paper and pencil intensive, all you get is a series of data points and we still need to interpolate between them to obtain a continuous yield curve. What we want to do is to find a method that we can program into a computer to estimate a continuous zero coupon yield curve. Below we will discuss two types of techniques, splines and parsimonious methods.

3.4.1   Natural splines

Natural splines are designed to model the *discount function* from which we obtain the zero coupon term structure. We estimate the yield curve in three steps. First, we strip the cash flows, the coupons and principal payments for the bonds in our sample and treat them as mini bonds. We will assume a particular form for the discount function that determines the observed price of each mini bond that makes up a given coupon bond. This discount function will be used to calculate the *discount factor* for each mini bond. A discount factor represents the value today of the guaranteed receipt of $1 of each mini bond at some specified date in the future. Second, we sum the observed values of this discount function for each of the mini bonds to find the total value of this discount function for each coupon bond. Third, after collecting these observations of the value of the discount function for each coupon bond we will run an OLS (ordinary least squares) regression that will estimate a continuous discount function that applies to all coupon bonds in our sample. Once we have this discount function we are finished, for it is a simple matter to compute specific discount factors from this continuous discount function and convert these discount factors into the corresponding zero coupon yield.

It is best to illustrate how this is done using some numerical examples. First, let bond one be an 8.875% coupon bond that matures in 17 months. Since this is a semi-annual coupon pay bond, and it pays its last coupon at maturity in 17 months, it must pay its second to last coupon six months earlier in 11 months from now, and its third to last coupon only five months from now. So we know there are three coupon payments remaining. Notice that the bond pays its first coupon in only five months, so anybody buying this bond today must pay for the interest accrued since the last coupon payment, one month ago. Therefore we need to know its full (or dirty) price. This is the flat (or clean price) plus accrued interest, which in this case is $106.40.

Now we use two equations, the pricing equation and the discount function. The pricing equation we get from the idea, covered in the previous section, that we can view a coupon bond as a portfolio of zero coupon mini bonds. With three payments remaining, the pricing equation is,

$$c_1 d_1 + c_2 d_2 + (c_3 + 100)d_3 = B \tag{3.1}$$

where c_1 is the first coupon, c_2 is the second coupon etc., d_1 is the value today of $1 of the first coupon payment, d_2 is the value today of $1 of the second coupon payment etc., 100 is the redemption amount and B is the full (or dirty) price.

The second equation is our discount function.

$$d(t) = 1 - a(t) - b(t^2) - c(t^3) \tag{3.2}$$

Here $d(t)$ is the discount factor (just like d_1, d_2 and d_3 above) and t is calendar time. The letters a, b and c are constants that we are going to estimate via OLS in the third step.

We can choose any type of discount function. We chose the one above because it looks like it may work well in practice. To see why, just imagine if we have a zero that promises to pay $1 immediately. Then all the ts in the above discount function are zero, so the $d(t) = 1$. This makes sense; the value today of the receipt of $1 today is worth $1. Encouraged, let's go on. Suppose we have a zero that promises to pay $1 at some time in the future. Obviously this zero should be worth less than $1, hence the minus sign for all the remaining terms in (3.2). If we have only minus $a(t)$ and set $b(t^2)$ and $c(t^3)$ to zero, then the value of the zero would decease linearly as the date of payment of $1 is extended into the future. We believe this to be unreasonable if for no other reason because of the effect of compound interest. We know that an investment today of $1 grows at an increasing rate because we earn compound interest, which is interest earned on interest. Discounting (finding today's value of a payment in the future) is just the reciprocal, so we know that discounting would cause the value of the zero to decrease at a decreasing rate. By including the second term $b(t^2)$ we are forcing a quadratic relation, now the value of the payment of $1 in the future decreases at a decreasing rate as the term of the payment is increased. However, we still have a problem. If we convert the quadratic discount function into its corresponding yield curve we would always have a smoothly upward (or downward) sloping yield curve. We know that this is often not the case, where yield curves have a 'humped' or even 'U' shape. Therefore to add additional flexibility, we incorporate a third term $c(t^3)$ that allows for extra flexibility in the structure of discount factors and the corresponding yield curve such that the yield curve can accommodate 'humped' or 'U' shapes. As you may well guess, we could add additional terms to add even more flexibility. For example, *Datastream*'s 401N program measures sovereign yield curves where a fifth order natural spline is used. This is simply our discount function (3.2) with two additional terms subtracted, $d(t^4)$ and $e(t^5)$.[1]

Now we substitute the discount function (3.2) into the pricing equation (3.1) to obtain,

$$4.4375 \left[1 - a\left(\frac{5}{12}\right) - b\left(\frac{5}{12}\right)^2 - c\left(\frac{5}{12}\right)^3 \right]$$

$$+ 4.4375 \left[1 - a\left(\frac{11}{12}\right) - b\left(\frac{11}{12}\right)^2 - c\left(\frac{11}{12}\right)^3 \right]$$

$$+ 104.4375 \left[1 - a\left(\frac{17}{12}\right) - b\left(\frac{17}{12}\right)^2 - c\left(\frac{17}{12}\right)^3 \right] = 106.4$$

Notice that the first line above is the coupon 4.4375 multiplied by the discount function (3.2). Since the first coupon is paid five months from now, $t = 5/12$. Similarly the second and third lines are the cash flows from the bond multiplied by the discount function for the relevant dates (second coupon at $t = 11/12$, and the third coupon and principal at maturity in 17 months or 17/12 years) that this cash flow is to be received. Finally, the value of the function equals the full or dirty price of the bond, $106.40 in this instance.

---

[1] Tragically, Datastream's 401N interpolates yield to maturity so these yield curves are at best interpreted as par coupon rather than zero coupon yield curves. However, Datastream has recently added another section that gives historical estimates of zero coupon yield curves for several sovereigns.

Now it is just a matter of basic numeric calculations. We multiply the cash flows through the left-hand side, organizing them in columns and adding up the columns we obtain,

$$
\begin{array}{llll}
4.4375 & -1.8490a & -0.7704b & -0.3210c+ \\
4.4375 & -4.0677a & -3.7287b & -3.418c+ \\
104.4375 & -147.9531a & -209.6003b & -296.9337c = 106.4 \\
\hline
113.31 & -153.87a & -214.10b & -300.67c = 106.4
\end{array}
$$

Placing the strait numbers (dependent variable) all on the left-hand side and all the independent variables on the right-hand side we obtain the first observation of the discount function that we will estimate by OLS.

$$6.91 = 153.87a + 214.10b + 300.67c$$

To avoid confusion, recognize that a, b, and c coefficients are *not* dependent upon the number of coupons. For example, on December 13, 1996 a 24-month T-note with $C = 5.125$, $B = 98.84375$ and $Y = 5.743$ exists. The data point can be represented as

$$2.5625[1 - a(0.5) - b(0.5^2) - c(0.5^3)]$$
$$+ 2.5625[1 - a(1) - b(1^2) - c(1^3)]$$
$$+ 2.5625[1 - a(1.5) - b(1.5^2) - c(1.5^3)]$$
$$+ 102.5625[1 - a(2) - b(2^2) - c(2^3)] = 98.84375$$

And grind through as before to obtain

$$11.4062 = 212.81a + 419.22b + 832.03c$$

In this manner we collect our data points. We collect 10 bonds that trade for settlement on July 29, 2002. The schedule of data points and the corresponding estimates of the parameters a, b and c that we obtain is reported in Table 3.1.

We now run OLS regressions on these 10 data points to obtain least squares estimates of the parameters a, b and c. This can be easily done in Excel. See the spreadsheet NaturalBo2.xls. Choose 'data analysis' under the 'tools' sub menu.[2] Then select 'regression' and click OK. Following the instructions you will obtain an estimate of the regression and find that the values of these coefficients are, $a = 0.066562$, $b = -0.00371$ and $c = 0.000119$. We then work out

---

[2] It is possible that data analysis is not installed in your version of Excel. You need to select 'add ins' under the 'tools' sub-menu, and then tick off 'analysis tool pack'. While you are at it, make sure 'solver' is ticked off too; you are going to need it soon.

Table 3.1   Data points for natural spline interpolated yield curve

Raw data			Observations for OLS regression			
Data	Coupon	Dirty price	Y	a	b	c
Oct. 31, 2002	0	99.56917	0.430833	25.54348	6.524693	1.666633
Oct. 31, 2003	2.75	102.0163	2.108696	128.6596	160.6532	201.2076
May 31, 2004	3.25	102.6489	3.851093	190.957	347.8546	636.7549
Nov. 15, 2005	5.75	110.2188	9.28125	369.9093	1184.761	3847.187
Oct. 15, 2006	6.5	114.6723	14.57775	486.0451	1967.046	8119.145
Aug. 15, 2008	8.375	110.7671	52.04538	927.4476	6048.853	40912.35
Feb. 15, 2011	5	107.5933	37.40668	1048.022	8438.201	69903.24
Feb. 15, 2012	4.875	106.2554	42.49456	1226.106	11251.13	106518.4
May 15, 2018	9.125	144.391	101.609	2755.165	37533.76	545677.5
Feb. 15, 2019	5.25	99.44095	92.43405	2489.899	38112.94	612788.2

the discount function for t from 0.25 years until 20 years as $d(t) = 1 - 0.066562(t) + 0.00371(t^2) - 0.000119(t^3)$ for the range of t that we select. Next we convert the discount factors into zero coupon yields using the BEY formula. Finally, we plot the resulting zero coupon yield curve and for good measure, the forward curve as estimated from these spot rates. These yield curves are reported in Figure 3.4.

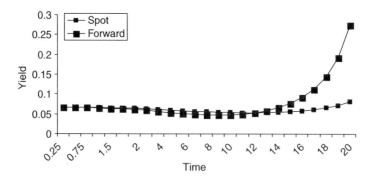

Figure 3.4   Zero coupon spot and forward yield curve on July 29, 2002 as estimated by natural splines

3.4.2   The problem with splines

The above is an example of a 'natural' spline in the sense that the underlying discount function from which we obtain the zero coupon yield curve is assumed to have only one functional form that applies to the entire yield curve. The problem with natural splines is that the technique is too inflexible. Sometimes the yield curve takes on unusual shapes, perhaps having more than one hump. In these cases, natural splines will be unable to provide a good fit. One quick fix is to add additional parameters to the discount function. Unfortunately this is unlikely to solve the problem. The root cause of the technique's inflexibility is that it has only one functional form to the discount function, parameters a, b, c (and any other parameters that you care to add) apply to the whole maturity range.

It might be thought that different forms of the discount function should apply to different maturity ranges. That way, the first set of parameters a, b and c may be estimated via OLS for coupon and principal payments up to and including five years' maturity and then a second set of parameters a', b' and c' may be estimated via OLS for coupon and principal payments beyond five years' maturity. The resulting yield curve would be much more flexible as different sets of parameters of the discount function apply to different maturity ranges.

This is what McCulloch's (1975) cubic splines attempt to achieve. He suggests that we use a number of 'basis functions', essentially different functional forms for the discount function, each of which apply to different maturity ranges. He constrains the 'knot points', the points along the estimated yield curve where a new discount function takes over, to be smooth so there are no discontinuities at the knot points. The main difference between the natural spline that we have shown you and McCulloch's cubic spline is that we have used only one 'basis function'.

However, there are still three problems with this technique. First, there is a danger that the more basis functions that you include in the cubic spline, the more likely you are overfitting the data. In other words, cubic splines are too flexible. Second, the cubic spline tends to be unstable at the long maturity range. Sometimes you can see this clearly where you will see the yield curve fly off at the long end. Take a look at the zero yield curve in Figure 3.4 and you will see that the natural spline suffers from the same problem. Another diagnostic check to see if your zero yield curve is reasonable is to look at the corresponding forward curve. The forward curve is a term structure of forward rates implied by the zero coupon term structure of interest rates. It is measured by the forward rate formula (see Chapter 2) the inputs of which are the interest rates from the zero coupon term structure of interest rates.[3] Since the forward curve is dependent upon the spot curve we can see that what appears to be

---

[3] Notice that the forward rate formula in Chapter 2 assumes that unbiased expectations hold.

a small problem in the zero spot curve can then often be seen as a more serious problem in the forward curve.

As an illustration, look at Figure 3.4, and you will see that the apparently modest upward slope in the spot curve is actually a more serious problem than it first appeared because the implied forward curve is exploding upwards. This cannot be right. Third, and most importantly, cubic splines sometimes require more data points to estimate the functions than you have. This is particularly evident when you are trying to estimate corporate yield curves or non-G7 sovereign yield curves where the bond market is characterized by a lack of liquidity so there are few good data points available. Because of these problems, we have been turning more and more towards parsimonious yield curve methods.

3.4.3   Parsimonious yield curve estimates

Since the most rigorous challenge for an estimate of a spot yield curve is a reasonable forward yield curve, parsimonious yield curve methods start by assuming an asymptotic form for the zero forward curve. Then we derive the corresponding spot curve. When we estimate the spot curve, the corresponding forward curve is then guaranteed to be asymptotically smooth. The first to suggest this approach are Nelson and Siegel (1987).

They assume that the forward curve has the following asymptotic shape.

$$F = B_0 + B_1 \, exp\left(-\frac{t}{\tau_1}\right) + B_2\left(-\frac{t}{\tau_1}\right)exp\left(-\frac{t}{\tau_1}\right) \qquad (3.3)$$

The parameters B_0, B_1, B_2 and τ_1 are estimated and t is the time to maturity. We derive the spot curve by integrating (3.3) over the term to maturity t.

$$r_t = B_0 + B_1\left[\frac{1 - exp(-t/\tau_1)}{(t/\tau_1)}\right] + B_2\left[\frac{1 - exp(-t/\tau_1)}{(t/\tau_1)} - exp\left(-\frac{t}{\tau_1}\right)\right]$$

$$(3.4)$$

The parameter t is the maturity measured in years and fraction of a year, and the parameters B_0, B_1, B_2 and τ_1 are parameters to be estimated by the minimization process. The dependent variable r_t is the zero coupon spot yield given the maturity that it relates to.

Equation (3.4) gives you a schedule of zero yields. For each bond, you find the implied price using the zero coupon spot yields r_t from

(3.4), as shown in (3.5) below.

$$Estimated\ price = \sum_{t=1}^{N} \frac{C_t}{(1+r_t)^t} + \frac{FV}{(1+r_t)^t} \tag{3.5}$$

Next you find the error yield i for each bond by finding the implied yield i that sets the value of the below equation to zero.

$$\left(Market\ price - \left[\sum_{t=1}^{N} \frac{PV\ of\ coupon_t}{(1+i)^t} + \frac{PV\ of\ principal_N}{(1+i)^N}\right]\right) = 0 \tag{3.6}$$

Notice that the *PV of coupon* and *PV of principal* are the present value of the coupons and principal as estimated in (3.5). If your estimate of the zero coupon yield curve is accurate, the estimated price and the market price should be nearly the same, so the yield error would be very small. Then you square these yield errors and add them up. Therefore you estimate (3.4) for your observations by minimizing the sum of squared yield errors from (3.6).

In other words, you minimize the sum of squared yield errors of all the bonds in the sample. You estimate the model by iterating between (3.4) and the sum of the squared errors from (3.6) until updates of B_0, B_1, B_2 and τ_1 in (3.4) no longer significantly improve the sum of squared yield error from (3.6).

You need to see this in a spreadsheet. An example of how to estimate Nelson and Siegel (1987) is included in workbook NSB02.xls. See the spreadsheet NS (1). Procedurally you first collect the dirty price and write down all the coupon payments (in one column) and the precise number of years and fraction of a year for each coupon payment (in another column) for each bond in your sample. For the third column, you will write in equation (3.4) where you will refer to different blank cells for B_0, B_1, B_2 and τ_1. 't' will refer to the corresponding exact time of payment of the coupon in the first column. At the top of column four you type in the dirty price. We enter the dirty price here as a negative number. You fill in the rest of the fourth column by finding the present value of each coupon payment where the interest rate to be used as the discount rate will refer to the adjacent cell in column three. Now you find the internal rate of return in the cell just above the dirty price (entered as a negative number) in the fourth column. This is the yield error that you want to minimize. Next you sum the squared yield errors for all bonds in your sample. Then find the square root of the mean of the squared yield errors. This is cell D24 in spreadsheet NS (1). We will refer to this cell as the target cell.

Now you place some starting values for B_0, B_1, B_2 and τ_1. A disadvantage of Nelson and Siegel (1987) is that the estimation technique is highly non-linear and in some cases the results are sensitive to the starting values. A good way to guess the starting values is to appreciate the intuitive meaning of the parameters.

- B_0 is the asymptotic (long-term) value of the forward rate. It must be positive.
- B_1 is the short-term value of the forward curve that determines the speed at which the curve trends towards its long-term value. Together B_0 and B_1 determine the vertical intercept in the resulting zero coupon yield curve.
- τ_1 specifies the inflection point that determines the hump or U shape in the yield curve, if any. This parameter must be positive as well.
- B_2 determines the magnitude and direction of the curve at the inflection point τ_1.

We use the observations contained in Table 2.1. Since the yield on the first coupon bond is only 1.694%, we choose $B_0 = 1.5$ and $B_1 = 1$ as starting parameter values since they add up to 2.5, slightly above the three-month T-bill yield to maturity in our sample. Since we know that zero curves should lie above yield to maturity yield curves when the term structure is upward sloping, we are hopeful that these are good starting values. Then we arbitrarily choose $\tau = 7$ and $B_2 = 7$. Then we go to the tools menu and choose solver.[4] In solver we set as the target cell the cell that we earlier referred to as the target cell. This is the cell that contains the root mean squared yield error for all bonds in our sample as calculated from (3.6). We set this cell to be minimized. The change cells are the row of cells that contain B_0, B_1, B_2 and τ_1. Now we click on solve. Hopefully the resulting yield curve would appear to be reasonable. If not, you have to try new starting values for B_0, B_1, B_2 and τ_1. However, this problem is somewhat unusual as the underlying function is robust with respect to reasonable starting values.

As an internal check, we can examine the yield errors for each bond in the sample. These errors, measured in basis points are reported in cells C14 to C23. Notice that the 8.375% coupon bond that matures on August 15, 2008 is particularly badly priced; the error, highlighted in red is more than 100 basis points. This may be due to bad data, so we delete this observation and re-estimate the Nelson and Siegel function again without including this bond in our sample. This is

---

[4] See footnote 2.

done in the second worksheet NS (2). Now notice that no one bond is particularly badly priced, so we decide to go with these estimates. The results we obtain are reported in Figure 3.5.

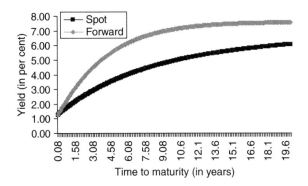

Figure 3.5 The zero coupon and forward yield curve of July 29, 2002 as estimated by Nelson and Siegel

Since the spot and forward yield curves estimated by natural splines (Figure 3.4) and parsimonious methods (Figure 3.5) come from the same data set, the results are directly comparable. First, comparing Figures 3.4 and 3.5, it is evident that since Nelson and Siegel (1987) is much more flexible than natural splines, the NS spot yield curve is able to show much more curvature than the natural spline spot yield curve. Notice that short-term rates start at much lower rates and then rise to around 6%, whereas the natural spline models remain much closer to 6% throughout. Since the three-month redemption yield is almost 2%, the NS spot curve looks much more realistic. Second, notice that the NS forward curve, in contrast with the natural spline forward curve, does not 'fly off' at the long end. Again this indicates the superiority of the NS spot curve since a diagnostic test for a good spot curve is a believable forward curve.

Of course, Nelson and Siegel (1987) has its problems too. As already mentioned, sometimes the NS spot curve is difficult to estimate and the final result is sensitive to the starting values. Sometimes it is even impossible to get NS's spot curve estimates to converge. This happens when the underlying spot curve is unusual, having two inflection points rather than only one.

This is the motivation for Svensson (1995), a slightly more complex parsimonious model. The Svensson (1995) model is essentially an extension of Nelson and Siegel (1987) where Svensson simply adds an additional term to the assumed asymptotically flat forward curve that enables the forward curve and the resulting spot curve to fit two rather than one hump or 'U' shape. The spot curve is derived in the same manner as Nelson and Siegel (1987) and is shown below.

$$R_t = B_0 + B_1 \left[\frac{1 - exp(-t/\tau_1)}{(t/\tau_1)} \right] + B_2 \left[\frac{1 - exp(-t/\tau_1)}{(t/\tau_1)} - exp\left(-\frac{t}{\tau_1}\right) \right]$$

$$+ B_3 \left[\frac{1 - exp(-t/\tau_2)}{(t/\tau_2)} - exp\left(-\frac{t}{\tau_2}\right) \right] \tag{3.7}$$

Notice that the first three terms in (3.7) form Nelson and Siegel (1987). The fourth term in (3.7) adds two new parameters, a second inflection point τ_2 and a measure of curvature of the yield curve B_3 at the second inflection point. These additional terms add flexibility and so allow the Svensson (1995) model to incorporate a wider variety of yield curve shapes. Note that (3.7) is implemented in the same way as (3.4) where we use starting values for the parameters B_0, B_1, B_2, τ_1, B_3 and τ_2 respectively to minimize root mean square yield error.

3.4.4   Which yield curve fitting technique is best?

The weight of empirical evidence seems to favour the parsimonious yield curve fitting techniques, although much of the evidence is anecdotal, and sometimes spline techniques turn out to be best. Anderson et al. (1996) present evidence that suggests Nelson and Siegel (1987) performed poorly relative to Svensson (1995) and McCulloch (1975), but the latter two models performed equally well. However, Elton et al. (2001) report that Nelson and Siegel (1987) fitted investment grade corporate and Treasury yields as well as McCulloch (1975) and opt to use NS.

When it comes to fitting yield curves to small data sets, parsimonious methods seem to come out on top. When attempting to measure the on the run US Treasury yield curve, Jordan and Mansi (2000) find that parsimonious methods are more accurate than spline methods. Similarly Subramanian (2001) finds that parsimonious methods are more accurate than spline methods when attempting to estimate the Indian yield curve.

3.5   Par coupon yield curves

Once we have an estimate of a zero coupon yield curve, it is trivial to convert this curve into the corresponding par coupon yield curve.

As discussed earlier, you may wish to use a par coupon yield curve to assess the relative attractiveness of a non-benchmark bond.

Lutz (1940) was the first to consider the required coupon necessary to price a bond at par given a zero coupon yield curve. Of course, for a par coupon bond, the coupon is its yield. The solution is

$$_0C_n = \frac{\prod_{t=1}^{N}(1+r_t) - 1}{1 + \sum_{t=2}^{N}\prod_{j=t}^{N}(1+r_j)}$$

Where C is the coupon rate (par yield) and r is the zero coupon rate.

No doubt an example will help. In the workbook NS02.xls, spreadsheet NS (3) you will find in cells K11 to K250 estimates of the par coupon yield curve for July 29, 2002 given the Nelson and Siegel (1987) estimates of the zero coupon yield curve. A graph comparing the zero and par coupon yield curves is shown in Figure 3.6. Notice that the zero coupon yield curve is rising and the par coupon yield curve lies below the zero coupon yield curve. This observation agrees with the predictions of coupon bias contained in section 3.3.1.

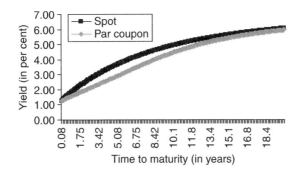

Figure 3.6 The zero coupon yield curve and par coupon yield curve of July 29, 2002 as estimated by Nelson and Siegel (1987)

3.6 Summary

In this chapter we have learned how to estimate sovereign and corporate yield curves. In doing so we have highlighted the importance of data selection, of estimating zero coupon yield curves and of accurate interpolation techniques. We discussed the yield curve interpolation techniques that are commonly employed and demonstrated in detail the Nelson and Siegel (1987) parsimonious zero coupon yield curve interpolation scheme.

3.7 Exercises

Question 1

A problem facing traders in any debt market is to estimate a 'true' sovereign yield curve. Discuss problems that typically arise when attempting to construct a sovereign yield curve and suggest strategies to overcome them.

Question 2

Consider the following information on gilt securities that trade for settlement on April 3, 2002.

Inst_Name	Mat_Date	Price	Acc_Int	Full price
7 Treasury 2002	07/06/02	100.53	2.25	102.78
6 1/2 Treasury 2003	07/12/03	102.42	2.089285714	104.5092857
5 Treasury 2004	07/06/04	99.82	1.607142857	101.4271429
8 1/2 Treasury 2005	07/12/05	110.42	2.732142857	113.1521429
7 1/2 Treasury 2006	07/12/06	108.75	2.410714286	111.1607143
7 1/4 Treasury 2007	07/12/07	108.98	2.330357143	111.3103571
5 3/4 Treasury 2009	07/12/09	102.44	1.848214286	104.2882143
8 Treasury 2015	07/12/15	125.97	2.571428571	128.5414286
8 Treasury 2021	07/06/21	133.41	2.571428571	135.9814286
6 Treasury 2028	07/12/28	113.26	1.928571429	115.1885714

Apply the natural spline method to estimate the sovereign yield curve up until a maturity of 10 years. Also, calculate the forward curve from the spot curve. In answering this question adapt the spreadsheet ycdataB02.xls to suit the above data.

Question 3

The table below contains the prices of a series of bonds.

Maturity	Coupon (%)	Price	YTM
0.5 years	0	€98.522	?
1.0 years	8	€104.738	?
1.5 years	4	€101.089	?
2.0 years	5	?	3.40%
2.5 years	10	?	3.60%
3.0 years	6	?	4.00%

(a) Calculate the yield to maturity for the first three bonds in the above table.
(b) Calculate the price for the last three bonds in the above table.
(c) Using the bootstrap method, extract the zero coupon term structure of interest rates implied by all six bonds in the above table.
(d) Why is the bootstrap method correct?

Question 4

Using the bond data from question 2, apply the Nelson and Siegel method to estimate the sovereign yield curve up until a maturity of 10 years. Use the values of 1.5, 1, 7 and 7 for B_0, B_1, B_2, and τ_1 respectively. Also, calculate the forward curve from the spot curve. What do the resulting yield curves look like?

Question 5

Compare the spot and forward yield curves from questions 3 and 4.

Modelling the sovereign term structure of interest rates: the binomial approach

4.1 The binomial approach

We intend to model the sovereign term structure and risk structure of interest rates using the binomial stochastic interest rate approach. We do this for four reasons. First, the binomial approach is easy to implement via spreadsheets. This means those with only modest mathematical and computer programming skills can not only understand stochastic interest rate modelling, but can implement these models as well. This helps strip away some of the mystery that surrounds modelling stochastic interest rates and helps us appreciate some of the strengths and limitations of recent advances in interest rate modelling. Second, the binomial approach establishes a framework than can be easily extended. In Chapter 5 we will extend the simple binomial approach introduced here to three different stochastic interest rate models showing how one can add additional layers of complexity and, hopefully, realism in the model.

In Chapter 6 we will extend the binomial approach again to incorporate credit risk. Third, this approach enables us to incorporate information from the term structure of interest rates. Specifically, we will adjust or 'fine tune' our binomial stochastic interest rate (and much later, credit risk) process to ensure that the results from our model agree with the term structure (and much later the risk structure) of interest rates. This adds an important 'reality check' to our models giving us confidence that the results from our model are sensible. Fourth, this approach can obtain believable results in just a few steps. In other words, one can implement the binomial stochastic interest (and credit risk) models on a modest sized PC and so these models are easily accessible.

4.2 The simple model

We wish to describe how interest rates are expected to evolve over time. Our first candidate model is the 'simple model', which as the name suggests is not at all realistic. The purpose of this model is to introduce the binomial approach, showing how it works and pointing out its potential that we will exploit in Chapters 5 and 6.

The simple model describes the evolution of the short-term (say six-month T-bill) interest rates as follows.

$$R_{t+1} = R_t + \varepsilon_{t+1}$$

where $\varepsilon_{t+1} = +\sigma$ with probability 0.5 and $-\sigma$ with probability 0.5

$$(4.1)$$

In other words, next period's six-month T-bill rate R_{t+1} will be today's six-month T-bill rate R_t plus some random jump next period ε_{t+1}. This random jump is a binomial meaning that next period's six-month T-bill rate must either rise or fall, there is no third possibility. Specifically, one half of the time the six-month T-bill rate may experience an uptick of σ basis points and one half of the time the T-bill rate may experience a downtick of σ basis points. For example, if today's T-bill rate is 5%, and the jump size σ is 100 basis points, then next period's T-bill rate will either be 6% or 4% and these two outcomes are equally likely.

The binomial stochastic process (4.1) is a multiperiod model as it describes the evolution of six-month T-bill rates over time. Consider the evolution of the six-month T-bill rate when we start with today's rate of 5%, a constant jump size of 100 basis points and a time step (the time interval between jumps) of six months. Figure 4.1 shows all

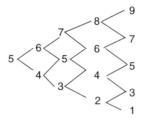

Figure 4.1　The binomial interest rate tree

possible six-month T-bill rates and all possible paths the six-month T-bill rate may follow over the next two years or four time steps.

To appreciate what Figure 4.1 represents we have to introduce some new notation. Let $r(t,i)$ be the rate of interest that arrives in time period t and interest level i. For example, $r(0,0)$ is today's rate of interest 5% because today is $t = 0$, and there is only one six-month T-bill interest rate. In one time step, six months later in our example, there are two possible rates of interest, 6% or 4%. Then $r(1,0)$ is 4% and $r(1,1)$ is 6%. This reveals that we count the interest rate level i as the number of upticks in interest above the lowest possible interest rate that may arrive at that date. Continuing until the fourth time step, $r(4,2)$ is 5% and $r(4,4)$ is the highest possible interest rate that may arrive at the fourth time step, 9% in our example.

There are two important details to note in the above tree. First, the interest rate is revealed at the *beginning* of the period. For example, the current 5% is the rate that will be earned over the next six months, so $r(0,0)$ refers to the interest rate that exists as of today and lasts for six months. Then, say, $r(1,0)$ is the lowest possible interest rate that may be revealed in six months, similarly $r(2,0)$ is the lowest interest rate that may be revealed in one year and so on. This is important to keep in mind because later we will look at other trees where cash flows arrive, like in your first course in finance, at the *end* of the period. Second, i is never greater than t. For example, $r(2,3)$ does not exist.

Notice that the above tree represents all possible evolutions of the six-month T-bill rate. That is one path might be 5% on 30 April 03, 6% on 31 Oct. 03, 7% on 30 April 04, 6% on 31 Oct. 04 and 5% on 30 April 05, or $r(0,0)$, $r(1,1)$, $r(2,2)$, $r(3,2)$ and $r(4,2)$. In other words, this interest rate tree represents all possible scenarios of the evolution of the six-month rate of interest over the next two years. This means that we are not only modelling the six-month T-bill rates, but implicitly we are modelling the whole sovereign term structure of interest rates. The latter is true because we know that, say, a 30-year

T-bond rate is nothing more than a sequence of 60, six-month T-bill rates.

To appreciate how we are going to use this information, consider the way we used to value, say, an 8% semi-annual coupon pay, two-year T-note as shown in Figure 4.2.

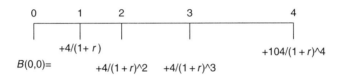

Figure 4.2   Standard bond valuation

We choose *not* to use the two-year sovereign yield as the discount rate r. If we do use a constant discount rate we are assuming that interest rates remain constant and we *know* that is not true. Also, we choose not to use the sequence of six-month forward rates (replace r with $_t f_{t+1}$ in Figure 4.2) that we can extract from the existing sovereign term structure of interest rates. If we do use the forward curve as the discount rates, we are assuming that the existing term structure of interest rates will remain constant and we *know* this is not true. Instead we choose to find the value of this bond by accounting for all possible interest rate paths that may evolve for the six-month T-bill rates over the next 24 months. If we do this then we are explicitly recognizing the stochastic (non-constant) nature of interest rates.

The above binomial tree has two important characteristics. First, you will notice that in tracing out all possible paths the six-month T-bill rate may follow, certain levels of interest reoccur. This happens because the above tree is 'recombining', that is an uptick in interest rates followed by a downtick gives you the same result as the reverse order, a downtick followed by an uptick in interest rates. This is in contrast to a non-recombining tree where a downtick in interest rates followed by an uptick gives us a different interest rate than the reverse order. A recombining tree has an important advantage. Later we will see that in order to price American style derivatives, we have to determine the payoff from the option at all possible interest states (nodes in the interest rate tree). For N time steps, a recombining tree has $N + 1$ possible interest rate states at date N, but a non-recombining interest rate tree has 2^N possible interest rate steps. It will be impossible to evaluate all possible payoffs on an American option when employing a non-recombining tree as the number of calculations that needs to be done at maturity date N and all prior dates will be too large. In this case Monte Carlo simulations need to be employed. In contrast, a recombining tree will have a greatly reduced number of interest rate states to examine, and so ordinary calculations may be employed.

Second, the binomial probability that a particular interest rate may evolve in N periods can be made to be very believable. We have used a large time step (six months) and a large interest rate jump (100 basis points) but this was done only for illustrative purposes. We could have just as easily used, say, a 10 basis point jump and a one-week time step. Intuitively we would guess that the likelihood that an extreme event, say that interest rates will rise by 100 basis points in 10 weeks, would be extremely unlikely, but not impossible. The binomial will measure the likelihood of that extreme event. The probability of 10 consecutive 10 basis point upticks in interest rates from a starting value of 5% to an ending value of 6% will be 0.5^{10} or 0.09%. In other words, the binomial model agrees that this event is not impossible, but very unlikely.

In contrast, most would agree that interest rates would likely be about the same in 10 weeks. The binomial would conform to this expectation as well since the recombining tree will give many paths to the 5% interest rate level, so the total probability of remaining at 5% in 10 weeks will be fairly high. For example, we can see this by looking at Figure 4.1 and realizing that we can obtain an interest rate of 5% from any path that gives as many upticks as downticks in four time steps. Noting U as an uptick and D as a downtick, we can see that there are six different paths, namely UUDD, UDUD, UDDU, DUUD, DUDU and DDUU, that lead to the 5% level in four time steps. Each of these paths will occur with 6.25% probability (0.5^4), so in total the probability that we will end up at 5% in four time steps is 37.5% $(6 \times 6.25\%)$. In fact, as the number of time steps is increased, the binomial probability distribution converges into the normal probability distribution. In other words, the binomial model is not as unrealistic as it may first appear.

4.3 Which short rate of interest should we model?

So far we have used the six-month T-bill rate to represent the stochastic nature of interest rates. As explained, since a long, say 30-year, Treasury rate is simply the evolution of 60 six-month interest rates we are in effect modelling the whole sovereign term structure of interest rates. However, most can think of many other candidate interest rates such as one-week, or one-month T-bill rates or even short-term libor rates. So why choose to use six-month T-bill rates?

Duffee (1996) looks at this issue and finds that the correlation between one- and two-month US T-bill rates with longer-term Treasury rates declined dramatically since 1983, to approximately $+0.3$. This is quite low. He suggests that the demand for very short-term T-bill rates is determined by some kind of preferred habitat where corporate America needs to park excess cash in very liquid and safe assets where the yield is only of secondary importance. This means that the demand for very short-term T-bills does not have all that much to do with its yield, so yields on very short-term T-bills do not have all that much to do with longer-term Treasury yields. The upshot of all this is that we are trying to model the whole yield curve through our choice of the short-term interest rate. We would be reluctant to attempt to model the whole yield curve based on an interest rate that does not have much to do with the rest of the yield curve, so we avoid very short-term T-bill rates.

Another possible candidate is very short-term libor rates. The problem with libor rates is that they represent interest rates that are subject to credit risk. Remember, libor rates represent the interest rate that one international bank will lend to another international bank that has a nominal credit rating of AA/A. Again we would rather model the term structure of interest rates that is not subject to credit risk with an interest rate that is itself not subject to credit risk. While this may seem rather obvious, sometimes we may have no choice. For example, when you need to price a short-term interest rate option, say it matures within 30 days, it is difficult to see how you can justify using a model that starts with the six-month T-bill rate. In this case, you have a difficult choice to use either a short-term Treasury rate that has only a low correlation with longer rates, or a libor rate that is subject to credit risk.

4.4 Pricing a bond using the interest rate tree

This section describes the mechanics of how to find the value of any cash (non-derivative) interest sensitive security. The method we use is called *backward induction*, because as the name suggests we start the valuation process by considering the value of the security at maturity. Then we find the value of the security one period prior to maturity, then two periods prior to maturity and so on until we find the value of the security as of today. To illustrate we consider the two-year 8% semi-annual coupon pay bond introduced in Figure 4.2.

At maturity this bond will surely be worth $100 since it is a sovereign bond. The clean price is $100 because there is no possibility that the sovereign will default and fail to pay the amount promised. However, we do not know the value of the bond at any other time and interest rate state. To illustrate the problem, we write the bond price tree in Table 4.1.

Table 4.1　Backward induction: the problem setup

$t = 0$	$t = 1$	$t = 2$	$t = 3$	$t = 4$
				100
			B(3,3)	
		B(2,2)		100
	B(1,1)		B(3,2)	
B(0,0)		B(2,1)		100
	B(1,0)		B(3,1)	
		B(2,0)		100
			B(3,0)	
				100

The first step is to find the value of the bond at one period prior to maturity at all possible interest rate states that may evolve in three periods from today given that we expect interest rates to evolve according to the simple model as illustrated in Figure 4.1. We simply show you the mechanics first, and then explain some of the concepts we are using. We use the following formula.

$$B(n,i) = \frac{P_U B_U + P_D B_D + C}{(1 + r_{n,i}/2)} \tag{4.2}$$

Note that $B(n,i)$ is the value of the bond at the beginning of period n when interest rates have experienced i upticks (above the lowest possible interest rate that may evolve in period n), P_U and P_D represent the probability that next period interest rates may experience an additional uptick or downtick in interest rates respectively, B_U and B_D represent the value of the bond should interest rates experience an additional uptick or downtick respectively and finally, $r_{n,i}$ is the rate of interest that has already evolved at the time and state where you are trying to value the bond. So in this case the value of the bond at node $B(3,3)$ is

$$B(3,3) = \frac{0.5(100) + 0.5(100) + 4}{(1 + 0.08/2)} = 100$$

That is, we ask what would be the value of the bond $B(3,3)$ if in three periods' time interest rates experience three upticks (above the lowest possible interest rate that may evolve in period three), all the while knowing that the bond will mature in one more period and during that last period interest rates may yet again rise or fall? To make progress, we assume interest rates are equally likely to rise to 9% or fall to 7%, so we assign 50% probabilities to these interest rate events. We know that at the end of the third period, the bond will pay $100 regardless of the interest rate that evolves at the beginning of period 4 and it will pay a semi-annual coupon of $4, so in this case we know the clean price of the bond at nodes $B(4,4)$ and $B(4,3)$ will be $100. Therefore it is just a matter of discounting the value of the bond backwards one period, recognizing that we are uncertain as to which interest rate may evolve, 9% or 7%, so we assign equal probabilities to these interest rates. Note, however, that since the bond will mature in one more period, the clean price of the bond will be $100 next period whether interest rates rise to 9% or fall to 7%. Such is not the case in earlier time steps, so for completeness we retain the use of the 50/50 probabilities. The value of the bond at bond price state $B(3,3)$ found using (4.1) is $100.

Similarly the value of the bond at nodes $B(3,2)$ and $B(3,1)$ are

$$B(3,2) = \frac{0.5(100) + 0.5(100) + 4}{(1 + 0.06/2)} = 100.971$$

$$B(3,1) = \frac{0.5(100) + 0.5(100) + 4}{(1 + 0.04/2)} = 101.961$$

We leave it to you to work out that the value of the bond at $B(3,0)$ is $102.970.

The next step is to continue to solve backwards, and find the value of the bond at two periods prior to maturity at all possible interest rate states that may evolve in two periods from today. The problem is a little more involved now since we cannot be sure that the clean price of the bond next period, which is one period prior to maturity, is $100. But we have worked out what the clean price of the bond will be at all possible interest rates next period (at one period prior to maturity) from the previous step. So now the process of finding the value of the bond at all possible interest rates as of two periods prior to maturity is simply the same mechanical procedure as in the prior step. The only difference is that B_U and B_D are not necessarily $100. To illustrate

$$B(2,2) = \frac{0.5(100) + 0.5(100.971) + 4}{(1 + 0.07/2)} = 100.952$$

$$B(2,1) = \frac{0.5(100.971) + 0.5(101.961) + 4}{(1 + 0.05/2)} = 102.894$$

We leave it to you to work out that the price of the bond at state $B(2,0)$ is $104.892.

Now we continue according to the above backward induction procedure to find that the price of the bond is $105.666 as illustrated in Table 4.2.

Table 4.2 The value today of an 8% coupon, two-year Sovereign Bond

$t = 0$	$t = 1$	$t = 2$	$t = 3$	$t = 4$
				100
			100	
		100.952		100
	102.838		100.971	
105.666		102.893		100
	105.777		101.961	
		104.892		100
			102.970	
				100

Notice that we slipped a subtle point past you in the above example. The problem setup in Table 4.2 requires us to find the value of the bond at the beginning of the period when payoffs from the bond actually occur at the end of the period. Meanwhile the interest rate tree outlined in Figure 4.1 gives us the interest rate that evolves at the beginning of the period. This should cause no confusion once you realize that interest rates that evolve at the beginning of the period still apply until the end of the period. For example, interest rate $r(3,3)$ or 8% is the interest rate we use as the discount rate to find the value of the bond at $B(3,3)$. Once one of these interest rates actually evolves at the beginning of period three, they hold right to the end of period three when the bond pays off, $100 plus the semi-annual coupon of $4 in this case. Therefore we can find the value of the bond according to (4.1). Technically it is always a matter of matching up the same time and state interest rate to be used as the discount rate to value the same time and state bond price.

4.5 The problems with the simple model

The simple model is not only useful for illustrating the mechanics of valuation by backward induction, but also for illustrating the four main challenges of interest rate modelling. The first and most obvious problem for interest rate modelling can be seen if you look at the interest rate that will evolve in $r(6,0)$ in Figure 4.1, it will be a *negative* 1%. This cannot happen, for if interest rates were negative it will imply that the lender will *pay* the borrower to borrow money. Nevertheless, the simple model allows for negative interest rates, so this is a serious flaw.

The second problem is similar. Consider what happens to interest rates at the other extreme as they continue to follow the highest possible interest rate path. For example, suppose we actually reach interest rate state $r(15,15)$ where the six-month T-bill rate is 20%. Can we seriously entertain the notion that interest rates are equally likely to rise to 21% or fall to 19% in the next, 16th period? We would expect that interest rates would be more likely to fall rather than rise if for no other reason than we would enter a recession. Together, the fact that we cannot have negative interest rates, nor can our model continue to generate extremely high interest rates, suggests that our model should incorporate *mean reversion*. In other words, there should be some central tendency to the interest rates that are generated by our model. To put it another way, there should be something in our model that forces interest rates generated by the model away from the extremes towards some long run mean or central tendency. This central tendency is lacking in the simple model so it allows for extreme and ridiculous interest rate states.

A third problem is that the simple model has a constant volatility of 100 basis points. In other words, if interest rates were to change they will jump by 100 basis points, either up or down, regardless of the interest rate level or which interest rate along the yield curve the interest rate volatility pertains to. We know that interest rate volatility is not constant. In fact we do observe a term structure of volatility where at the short end, volatility rises sharply and then later decreases at a decreasing rate.

The fourth problem is the most serious of all. The above simple model prices securities at the expected value. In other words the simple model assumes investors are risk neutral in the degenerate sense. Evidently investors are assumed to care about expected returns only and do not care about risk. Given a choice between a risky and a riskless alternative, they will choose the risky alternative if it offers even an infinitesimally small amount more. We know this is not true and that investors care a great deal about risk.

To see where the simple model assumes risk neutrality and to determine how the model might be corrected for risk aversion, reconsider our valuation model in the above example at, say, $B(2,2)$.

$$B(2,2) = \frac{0.5(100) + 0.5(100.971) + 4}{(1 + 0.07/2)} = 100.952$$

Notice that we are assuming 50/50 probabilities of an uptick and downtick in interest rates. This suggests that we are working with an efficient market where all information regarding the likelihood of future interest rate movements is already incorporated in current interest rates. Having no proprietary information regarding future interest rate movements, we assume up- and downticks in interest rates are equally likely and so we are pricing the bond at its expected value given the price of the bond next period if interest rates do go up or down. Risk averse investors would never price a risky security at its expected value. Instead they would price the security below its expected value thereby gaining, on average, a risk premium. This suggests that one way we can incorporate risk aversion is to adjust the 50/50 probabilities to some other combination. For example, if it is true that interest rates will go up with 50% probability next period, then risk averse investors will price the bond *as if* the likelihood of interest rates rising next period was 60% rather than 50%. This will reduce the value of the bond below its expected value and as long as interest rates do indeed rise on average with a 50% probability next period the investor will earn a risk premium on average.

Alternatively we can incorporate risk aversion in another way. We can continue to use the 50/50 probabilities as long as the price of the bond next period if interest rates rise or fall incorporates risk aversion. In other words the price of the bond that we use in our valuation process in the up- or downtick states next period is below the price that will evolve should interest rates actually experience an up- or a downtick. Notice in our simple model the interest rate process (4.1) does not include a term that incorporates risk aversion. If it did, however, we could lower the price of the security next period in the up and down interest rate states so that the bond will be priced below the expected value even though we still use the 50/50 probabilities.

In summary we know that the simple model has four main flaws. It allows for negative interest rates, it does not incorporate mean reversion, it assumes constant volatility in interest rates and, most seriously, it assumes risk neutrality. However, it looks as though we can incorporate risk aversion either by adjusting the probabilities of interest rate upticks and downticks next period, or by adjusting the interest rate process to include risk aversion. Which method should we choose? This is the topic of the next section.

4.6   Incorporating risk aversion

The trick is to realize that we can price any derivative security by portfolio replication. That is you can replicate the cash flow pattern of any derivative instrument by using two (or more) other instruments. Since you know the value of these other instruments, you know the value of the replicating portfolio. Since you know the value of the replicating portfolio and since it replicates the cash flow pattern of the derivative instrument, then the replicating portfolio's price must be the same as the derivative security's price.

In other words, since the replicating portfolio *is* the derivative instrument (a synthetic derivative), the price of the derivative instrument and the replicating portfolio is the same. This is simply an application of the law of one price. The fact that one investor may be more risk averse than another is irrelevant since the law of one price will ensure that the two instruments (the derivative and the replicating portfolio) giving the same cash flow pattern must have the same price.

To make these concepts more concrete we will illustrate using a simple numerical example.

Suppose we know that the six-month interest rate tree is as follows.

$T = 0$	$T = 1$
	6.587
6.036	4.587

Given that we 'know' these interest rates, we can work out the price of a 12-month zero coupon bond using our backward induction method.

$T = 0$	$T = 1$	$T = 2$
		100
	96.8115	100
94.4347	97.7579	100

Suppose we can buy an option to call this bond at 97 in six months. How much is it worth?

First, we determine the option's cash flows, and then replicate the cash flows by investing in a combination of zero coupon bonds. Since we know the price of the zero coupon bonds, we know the value of the replicating portfolio. Since the replicating portfolio is the call option, the call option must have the same price as the replicating portfolio. Otherwise we will have a violation of the law of one price. If we have a violation, we can arbitrage and make money for free. As we do so, our own actions will force the value of the call option and the replicating portfolio of zeros to be the same.

Here are the cash flows we will obtain from the call option.

$T = 0$	$T = 1$
	0
0	0.7579

We can replicate these cash flows with six-month and 12-month zeros as of today, when the prices of these underlying securities are known.

$$\text{Six-month zero: } \frac{100}{(1 + 0.06036/2)} = 97.0704$$

12-month zero (as above): 94.4347

We can replicate the cash flows of the six-month call option to call the 12-month zero at 97 by employing the correct mixture of six-month and 12-month zeros. The following portfolios are designed to replicate the value of the option in six months' time.

Portfolio replicating $T = 1$ (up):   Portfolio replicating $T = 1$ (down)
$F_{0.5} + 0.968115F_1 = 0$ $F_{0.5} + 0.977579F_1 = 0.7579$

where $F_{0.5}$ is how many £1 (face value) in six-month zeros, and F_1 is how many £1 (face value) in 12-month zeros we need to replicate the call option's cash flows at $T = 1$. Note that 0.968115 and 0.977579 are the per £1 price of the one-year zero in the up and down states respectively as found by our 12-month zero coupon bond price tree. We have two equations in two unknowns, so this system is easy to solve. The solution is to buy 80.0824 of face value of the one-year zero and short 77.5290 of face value of the six-month zero.

To check:

$$-77.5290 + 0.968115(80.0824) = 0 \ldots \text{the up state}$$

$$-77.5290 + 0.977579(80.0824) = 0.7579 \ldots \text{the down state}$$

This replicates the call's cash flows.

Therefore what is the value of the portfolio today?

$$B_{0.5}F_{0.5} + B_1F_1 = -0.970704(77.5290) + 0.944347(80.0824)$$

$$= 0.3679$$

where $B_{0.5}$ and B_1 are the per £1 prices of the six-month and 12-month zeros as of today already priced by our interest rate process above.

Therefore the price of *any* security that has the cash flow pattern

$T = 0$	$T = 1$
	0
0	0.7579

is worth £0.3679. This must be correct, irrespective of the degree of risk aversion of different investors since any violation is also a violation of the law of one price. A violation of the law of one price means that investors can make money by investing nothing and by taking no risk.

To demonstrate pure arbitrage, consider the case where the call is (mis)priced at £0.45. To see what you should do, compare the market price with the portfolio-replicating price, and remember to buy cheap and sell dear. In this case,

Market > Replicating portfolio

£0.450 > £0.3679

Therefore you will sell (actually short) the market call at £0.450 and use the proceeds to buy the replicating portfolio at £0.3679. Notice that per transaction, you are left with £0.0821. Since you have been paid to take on this position, what are your obligations that will occur in six months' time?

If interest rates go up in six months' time ($r = 6.587\%$), the value of the market call is 0, and the value of the replicating portfolio is 0. So you keep the £0.0821 you got six months ago.

If interest rates go down in six months' time ($r = 4.587\%$), the value of the call you have shorted is £0.7579, but the value of the replicating portfolio is also worth £0.7579, so you can net the two and leave yourself with no net obligation. But you still keep the initial £0.0821.

So you see, you end up being paid £0.0821 (per transaction) for no obligation under all possible interest rates scenarios. This is a money tree. You got money for nothing. Investors like something for nothing, no matter what their degree of risk aversion happens to be. When they spot opportunities of this kind, arbitrage will occur, driving up the price of the replicating portfolio and driving down the price of the market call until the law of one price is no longer violated. Since risk aversion is irrelevant in pricing the call *relative* to the replicating portfolio, we call this *risk neutral* pricing. Notice that this does not mean that investors are risk neutral, it just means that the degree of risk aversion is irrelevant in pricing the call, *relative to* the replicating portfolio. Of course, the replicating portfolio is priced according to the degree of risk aversion of investors because the price is determined by the price of component zeros that trade in the market by risk adverse investors. Naturally, the price of the call reflects the same degree of risk aversion as the replicating portfolio. All risk neutral pricing says is that once you know the price of the replicating portfolio, you know the price of the call.

But there is more! So far all we have done is to describe risk neutral pricing as it relates to standard binomial option pricing. But there is another 'wrinkle' used when pricing bonds and bond options using binomial theory.

Notice that we have priced the option using the replicating portfolio, the 'known' interest rate tree and the known zero coupon prices. We could not care less about the probability of an up or down interest rate movement. Since the actual numbers we use for these probabilities are irrelevant, why not make it computationally easy and assume the probabilities are 50/50? That way we can price the one-year zero using backward induction as before, and we do not have to work with replicating portfolios (as above) to price the call. That is:

$$T = 0 \quad T = 1$$
$$0$$
$$0 \qquad 0.7579$$

So $P_c = \dfrac{0.5(0) + 0.5(0.7579)}{(1 + 0.06036/2)} = 0.3679.$

However the problem is that we do not 'know' the interest rate tree. There are two ways to fix this problem. One is to find the correct probabilities and assume our interest rate tree is correct. In this case, the probabilities will reflect the investor's degree of risk aversion. Another is to use the 50/50 probabilities and stop assuming our model that generates our interest rate tree is correct. We can use market information that 'fine tunes' our model to calibrate our model generated interest rate tree to agree with market rates. In this case, our fine tuned interest rates will reflect the investor's degree of risk aversion. So we have a choice. Which is the preferred method of incorporating risk aversion? First, let's look at adjusting probabilities.

Let's look again at our two period zero. We know that at maturity our zero will be worth £100 as it is a sovereign zero. We generate our interest rate tree, but it is only approximately correct, generating an up tick in interest rates next period of 6.5506% rather than 6.547% and a down tick of 4.4107% rather than 4.547%. Today's six-month interest rate is observable so it remains the same. Since we 'know' the interest rate tree, we 'know' that the value of the zero in six months' time will be £96.82857 (previously it was £96.8115) in the 'up' interest rate state, and £97.84224 (previously it was £97.7579) in the 'down' state. We do know that the market value of the zero today is £94.4347. So the question becomes, what probability of an up or down state in six months will replicate the market price of £94.4347 that we observe today? Since the probability of an up and a down state must necessarily add to one, we can write the problem in terms of only one unknown. This is done below.

$$\frac{(1 - P_d)(96.82857) + P_d(97.84224)}{(1 + 0.06036/2)}$$

$$= 94.4347$$

Solving for P_d, the probability of a down movement in interest rates is 0.45 and the probability of an up interest rate movement $(1 - P_d)$ is 0.55.

To check, we can substitute the above probabilities to replicate the zero price.

$$\frac{(1 - 0.45)(96.82857) + 0.45(97.84224)}{(1 + 0.06036/2)}$$

$$= 94.4347$$

And we can use these correct probabilities to find the value of the call option.

$$P_c = \frac{(1 - 0.45)(0) + 0.45(0.84224)}{(1 + 0.06036/2)} = 0.3679$$

Notice that investors 'underprice' the call option below that of its expected value (£0.4088 would be the price if we used the 50/50 rule) in order to obtain a risk premium.

But you may notice that adjusting the probabilities is computationally awkward. Further, to assume your interest rate model is correct, even when it is inconsistent with the market, seems a bit dangerous. Therefore, you will find most market participants assume the up and down probabilities are 50/50 for computational convenience, but then incorporate market risk aversion by fine tuning their interest rate model to assure their interest rate tree agrees with market rates. This style of calculating bond and bond option prices is also called *Risk Neutral Pricing*, which is of course a misnomer. Again, risk aversion is still incorporated by adjusting the discount rates to reflect market determined risk aversion. Precisely how we 'fine tune' our interest rate process is covered in the next chapter.

4.7 Exercises

Question 1
Use the following interest rate tree to find the value of a 2.5-year 6% coupon semi-annual coupon pay bond.

```
                9
              8 7
            7 6 5
          6 5 4 3
        5 4 3 2 1
```

Question 2
What interest rate should we be using in a one-factor model?

Question 3
Consider an option to purchase a one-year zero with a face value of £100 000, one year from today at an exercise price of £96 000. The one-year spot rate of interest r_1 is 0.04 and this short rate will evolve in the next year as:

$$r^u = r + \sigma = 0.06$$

$$r^d = r + \sigma = 0.02$$

Use a one year time step to answer the following questions.

1. Calculate the second period spot rate $_0R_2$ using one period discount factors and risk neutral pricing methodology.
2. Construct a portfolio of one-year and two-year zeros that replicates the payoffs of the option.
3. Price the option.
4. State whether the risk neutral pricing methodology used above gives the correct price when investors are risk adverse. Then explain your answer. (Note: the best answers will include a simple numerical illustration in the explanation.)

Interest rate modelling: the term structure consistent approach

5.1 Desirable features of an interest rate model

In this chapter we explore how we are going to model interest rates. There are a variety of approaches but we will emphasize the development of the term structure consistent approach because these models can be implemented by those of modest mathematical and computer programming skills. We will make some comments considering alternative approaches to modelling the term structure of interest rates in Chapter 6.

From Chapter 4, we understand that there are four desirable features that we would like to include in our simple binomial model. They are

- No negative interest rates
- Mean reversion (central tendency)
- Interest rate volatility curve
- Risk aversion

We intend to explore how we can extend the simple binomial to include all four desirable features but as you shall see, no one model is able to accomplish this satisfactorily. All models seem to have their flaws. Therefore we do not intend to resolve all issues in interest rate modelling. Rather our purpose is to give the reader a clear idea of the issues involved by going through the early development of interest rate modelling. We will, however, implement Black Derman and Toy (1990), an interest rate model commonly employed by practitioners.

5.2 Ho and Lee (1986)

Ho and Lee (1986) employ the following interest rate process.

$$r(n,i) = r(0,0) + \sum_{j=1}^{n} u_{t+j} + (2i - n)\sigma \tag{5.1}$$

The parameters $r(n, i)$ represent the short-term interest rate (say the six-month T-bill rate) that arrives at time n and interest state i, $r(0,0)$ is today's observed short-term interest rate, u is a calibration factor that applies at time $t + j$, and σ is the interest rate volatility measured as a standard deviation. The special feature of this model is the calibration factor u. This parameter is used to calibrate or fine tune the model such that the resulting binomial interest rate tree is forced to agree with the existing term structure of interest rates that we have learned how to measure in Chapter 3.

Notice that we have only constant volatility in Ho and Lee. We shall see later that Ho and Lee allows for negative interest rates and includes no mean reversion. In other words, Ho and Lee (1986) *is* the simple model with the sole exception of the calibration factor u. However, this innovation is important, for this factor enables the Ho and Lee model to incorporate risk aversion. Therefore Ho and Lee deals with the fourth desirable feature only.

One question often asked is what is the strange term $(2i - n)\sigma$? This term describes the volatility structure. It is best to describe the role this term plays by example where in this case we ignore the role of u, setting it to be zero in all cases. As just explained, this means the Ho and Lee model collapses to the simple binomial model, so with a constant volatility of 100 basis points and a starting short-term interest rate of 5%, Figure 4.1 will be replicated by (5.1). For illustrative purposes Figure 4.1 is shown below as Figure 5.1.

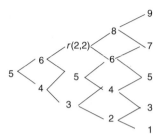

Figure 5.1 Ho and Lee with $u = 0$

We start with $r(0,0) = 5\%$. Next period, $n = 1$ and for $i = 0$, $(2i - n)\sigma = (2 \times 0 - 1) \times 1\% = -1\%$. Therefore (5.1) is 4% as shown below.

$$r(1,0) = r(0,0) + \sum_{j=1}^{n} u_{t+j} + (2i - n)\sigma$$

$$= 5\% + 0 + (2 \times 0 - 1) \times 1\% = 4\%$$

Similarly, $r(1,1)$ is 6% because for $i = 1$, $(2i - n)\sigma = (2 \times 1 - 1) \times 1\% = 1\%$. As another example, consider $r(2,2)$. We have two upticks in two periods, so $i = 2$ and $n = 2$. Then $(2i - n)\sigma = (2 \times 2 - 2) \times 1\% = 2\%$ or 2% above $r(0,0)$. This is 7% just like in Figure 4.1. Therefore we recognize that the term $(2i - n)\sigma$ generates the binomial structure of the interest rate tree.

Of course, this also implies that Ho and Lee will generate negative interest rates, for given enough downticks the term $(2i - n)\sigma$ will be such a large negative number that it will be greater than the sum of the calibration factors u and the initial interest rate $r(0, 0)$. This volatility structure also implies that interest rates can become arbitrarily high and so Ho and Lee does not include any mean reversion in interest rates as well.

5.2.1 State prices

In order to appreciate the role of the calibration factor u in Ho and Lee, we have to introduce a new theoretical concept called the *state price*. The state price $S(n,i)$ is the value today of £1 received at a particular interest rate state i and time n in the future, otherwise it pays nothing. For example, $S(1,0)$ represents a state security that will pay £1 next period, but only if interest rates experience a downtick. If instead interest rates experience an uptick, then this state security will pay nothing.

The interesting point of state securities is that the prices of these securities incorporate the *risk* of reaching a particular interest rate state and the *time value* of money received in the future. Specifically, the state security $S(1,0)$ may not pay off because interest rates next period may go up rather than down. For that reason investors will find this security unattractive. The price of $S(1,0)$ must incorporate interest rate risk. Also, investors have to wait one period before the security pays off, because interest rates will not experience any movement until one time step (six months in our example of Chapter 4) has elapsed. Therefore the cash flow from this security must be discounted back one period. The price of $S(1,0)$ must incorporate the time value of money.

These state securities are an extremely useful construct that we will use in two ways. First, we will use them to price state contingent claims. State contingent claims are securities that pay off in some interest rate states, but not in others. We will use state security prices to price some types of interest rate state contingent claims, such as zero coupon bonds and European interest rate options, more efficiently than our backward induction method. Second, these state securities are also used to reconcile model generated interest rate trees with the existing term structure of interest rates.

To understand how we are going to price state securities, we have to reconsider discount factors. As you will recall, a discount factor is the price of a £1 face value zero. In other words, a discount factor represents the value today of the receipt of £1 at some specified date in the future. We can convert our interest rate tree into a discount factor tree where each discount factor is the price today of the receipt of £1 at the end of the very next period. In other words, our discount factor tree is a tree of one period discount factors or one period zeros. To find these one period discount factors, we simply find the reciprocal of each state contingent interest rate from Figure 5.1. These discount factors are found as

$$d(n,i) = \left[\frac{1}{(1 + r(n,i)/200)} \right]$$

Note we divide by 2 because we have a six-month time step and we divide by 200 because the state contingent interest rates are quoted as whole numbers (for example, 5 instead of 0.05) when we want to have our discount factors priced in terms of a £1 face value zero. Our discount factor tree is shown in Table 5.1.

We use the discount factor tree to recover the state price tree. To start, ask yourself what is the value today of the certain receipt of £1? Obviously it is £1, but ask yourself why that is the case. It is true because there is no time value to consider (the £1 is paid today) and there is no interest rate risk (the £1 will be paid today before interest rates have a chance to change in the next time step, six months away).

Table 5.1 Discount factor tree

	Time step				
	0	1	2	3	4
Interest rate					0.956938
state				0.961538	0.966184
			0.966184	0.970874	0.975610
		0.970874	0.975610	0.980392	0.985222
	0.975610	0.980392	0.985222	0.990099	0.995025

Remembering this, consider the value today of the guaranteed receipt of £1 next period (six months from today) *if* interest rates rise $S(1,1)$ otherwise you get nothing. Here we must consider time value and interest rate risk.

If we happen to *know* that interest rates will rise, then the value of $S(1,1)$ is simply $1/(1+5/200) = 0.97561$. This is the discount factor $d(0,0)$ as shown in Table 5.1. This shows that we use the discount factor to measure time value because we are certain to receive £1 next period from $S(1,1)$. There is no interest rate risk. On the other hand, $S(1,0)$ is worth nothing, we know interest rates will not fall, so this state security will not pay off.

Now consider the case where we are not certain if interest rates are going to rise or fall next period. What would be the value of $S(1,1)$ then? Here we have both interest rate risk and time value to consider. We adjust for interest rate risk by multiplying the payoff from the security by the probability that this payoff will occur. We use 50/50 'risk neutral' probabilities because as we shall see later, we will adjust the interest rate tree in Figure 5.1 for interest rate risk. Therefore the value of $S(1,1)$ is found as follows.

$$S(1,1) = 0.5 \times d(0,0) = 0.5 \times 0.97561 = 0.487805$$

Similarly the value of $S(1,0)$ is 0.487805 because there is a 50% probability that interest rates may fall to 4% next period, and if indeed interest rates do fall, we must wait one time step where the applicable discount rate is 5%, and the value of £1 next period is 0.97561.

We can now build up a state price tree by *forward induction*. Unlike backward induction, the calculations for forward induction start at the present time and move forward in time. We can use forward induction because all the information we need to know how to calculate the value of the state price is known at the beginning of the period. Specifically the interest rates and therefore discount factors are revealed at the beginning of the period. Additionally we know the payoffs from the state security that occur at the end of the period and the likelihood of receiving them at the beginning of the period as well. To see the difference between forward and backward induction, note that we can find the value of S(1,1) by either forward or backward induction. This is demonstrated below.

$$S(1,1) = \frac{0.5(\pounds 1)}{(1+0.025)} = \pounds 0.487805 \qquad (5.2)$$

$$S(1,1) = 0.5(\pounds 0.975601) = \pounds 0.487805 \qquad (5.3)$$

Equation (5.2) finds the value of the state security that pays £1 if interest rates rise next period by the familiar backward induction method and (5.3) finds the value of the same security by forward induction. Jamshidian (1991) shows that forward induction is much more computationally efficient than backward induction and appreciably reduces the time necessary to run interest rate models.

Figure 5.2 shows the results of calculating the state prices via forward induction using the discount factor tree as shown in Table 5.1, which in turn was derived from the simple interest rate process as shown in Figure 5.1.

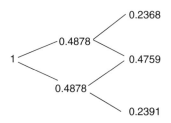

Figure 5.2 The state price tree

To start, note that there is only one path for S(2,2) and S(2,0) to pay off. For example, S(2,2) will pay off only if we experience two consecutive upticks in interest rates in the next two time steps. Similarly S(2,0) will pay off only if we experience two consecutive downticks in interest rates. Therefore we have only one path of interest rates to consider. For S(2,2) we have the following.

$$S(2,2) = 0.5(0.9756) \times 0.5(0.9709) = 0.2368$$

To appreciate this calculation, follow through the state price path depicted in Figure 5.2. There is a 50% probability that interest rates may rise next period, and if they do, any payments must be discounted back one period. This moves us to the state price S(1,1). From here interest rates may experience another interest rate rise with a probability of 50% and then any payments must be discounted back another period. In sum, the £1 payoff must be discounted back two periods (0.9756 × 0.9709) and must experience two favourable interest rate movements with a probability of 0.25 (0.5 × 0.5). This can be clearly seen if we calculate the value of S(2,2) via backward induction.

$$S(2,2) = 0.5 \left[\frac{£1}{(1+0.03)} \right] \times 0.5 \left[\frac{£1}{(1+0.025)} \right] = £0.2368$$

While the backward induction is more intuitive, forward induction is more computationally efficient because the results of prior calculations can be used to continue further calculations. For example, we have already calculated the value of $S(1,1)$ in (5.3) and we can use this intermediate result for our calculation of the value of $S(2, 2)$. That is $S(2, 2) = S(1,1) \times 0.5 \times d(1,1)$. This is demonstrated numerically below.

$$S(2,2) = S(1,1) \times 0.5 \times d(1,1) = 0.4878 \times 0.5(0.9709)$$
$$= 0.2368$$
$$S(2,0) = S(1,0) \times 0.5 \times d(1,0) = 0.4878 \times 0.5(0.9804)$$
$$= 0.2391$$

Similarly we find the value of S(2,0) as S(1,0) × 0.5 × d(1,0).

The power of forward induction is more clear when we consider S(2,1). Here there are two paths that may lead to S(2,1) paying off, interest rates may go up then down, or vice versa. When using forward induction, S(2,1) is found as

$$S(2,1) = S(1,1) \times 0.5 \times d(1,1) + S(1,0) \times 0.5 \times d(1,0)$$
$$= (0.4878) \times 0.5(0.9709) + (0.4878) \times 0.5(9804)$$
$$= 0.2368 + 0.2391 = 0.4759$$

In other words we count both interest rate paths that may lead to S(2,1) and add them up. In general, we can always find the value of any state security as

$$S(n,i) = S(n-1,i) \times 0.5 \times d(n-1,i)$$
$$+ S(n-1,i-1) \times 0.5 \times d(n-1,i-1) \qquad (5.4)$$

Note that for $i > n$, the interest rate state does not exist (just like $r(2,3)$ in section 4.2) so the corresponding discount factor is defined as zero.

In contrast if we were to find the value of $S(2,1)$ by backward induction, we have to go though the following process.

$$\frac{0.5 \times \left\{ 0.5 \times \left[\dfrac{0}{1+r(1,1)} \right] + 0.5 \times \left[\dfrac{1}{1+r(1,1)} \right] \right\}}{1+r(0,0)}$$

$$+ \frac{0.5 \times \left\{ 0.5 \times \left[\dfrac{1}{1+r(1,0)} \right] + 0.5 \times \left[\dfrac{0}{1+r(1,0)} \right] \right\}}{1+r(0,0)}$$

$$= \frac{0.5 \times \{0.5 \times [0] + 0.5 \times [0.9709]\}}{1.025}$$

$$+ \frac{0.5 \times \{0.5 \times 0.9804 + 0.5 \times [0]\}}{1.025} = 0.4759$$

This is an awkward procedure that requires many more calculations for the computer to perform.

These state securities are used to recover the zero coupon BEY. To see how, consider what is the value today of a portfolio of state securities, one each of $S(2,2)$, $S(2,1)$ and $S(2,0)$? This portfolio will pay off £1 no matter which interest rate state occurs in two time steps and will pay nothing in the meantime. This is a synthetic zero coupon bond because this is precisely the pay off structure we get if we buy a two period zero coupon bond. To put it another way, the portfolio of $S(2,2) + S(2,1) + S(2,0)$ is our replicating portfolio that replicates the cash flow structure of a two period zero coupon bond. To prevent arbitrage, this replicating portfolio must have the same price and yield as the two period zero coupon bond.

We can find the *BEY* of this replicating portfolio in the usual way. The price of the two period zero is

$$B_2 = S(2,2) + S(2,1) + S(2,0) = 0.2368 + 0.4759 + 0.2391$$

$$= 0.9518$$

Then the total return and *BEY* are found as

$$TR = \left[\frac{FV}{PV} \right] = \left[\frac{1}{0.9518} \right] = 1.050641$$

$$BEY = ([1.050641]^{1/(1\times2)} - 1) \times 2 = 5\%$$

Notice that we can find the zero coupon *BEY* for any date in the future because the portfolio formed by buying all of the state securities that mature at a particular date is a synthetic zero coupon bond. We can find its price, then its total return and corresponding *BEY*. For example, if we were to buy one each of $S(1,1)$ and $S(1,0)$, then we would have bought a synthetic one period zero coupon bond because no matter what happens next period, whether interest rates go up or down, our portfolio will pay £1. The price, total return and *BEY* of this one period zero are

$$B_1 = S(1,1) + S(1,0) = 0.4878 + 0.4878 = 0.9756$$

$$TR = \left[\frac{FV}{PV}\right] = \left[\frac{1}{0.9756}\right] = 1.02501$$

$$BEY = ([1.02501]^{1/(0.5\times2)} - 1) \times 2 = 5\%$$

5.2.2 Calibration

To assure our model is consistent with the existing term structure, our model generated interest rate tree should generate state contingent prices that agree with the zero coupon spot curve. This is precisely what the calibration factor 'u' in Ho and Lee sets out to achieve. To see how this is done, refer to the flow chart in Figure 5.3.

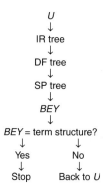

Figure 5.3   Flow chart for calibrating Ho and Lee

We start with the simple model by setting the calibration factor to zero. We generate an initial interest rate tree from (5.1) where $u = 0$. From this initial tree we generate the discount factor tree, essentially the reciprocal of one plus the corresponding interest rate in our initial interest rate tree. From the discount factor tree we calculate the state prices as outlined above. Then we calculate the price of our replicating portfolio for the first period, say six-months, as the sum of all possible state security prices that pays off at the end of the first six-month period. Then we calculate the implied *BEY*.

We now compare the *BEY* from our replicating portfolio with the six-month zero coupon yield from our estimate of the zero coupon yield curve that we previously estimated via Nelson and Siegel in Chapter 3. Are they the same? If they are not, then we adjust the factor *u* in Ho and Lee to a non-zero value. In sequence this changes the interest rate tree, the discount factor tree, the state security price tree, the replicating portfolio price and finally the *BEY* implied by our replicating portfolio. Again we compare the *BEY* from our replicating portfolio with the six-month zero coupon yield from our estimate of the zero coupon yield curve that we previously estimated via Nelson and Siegel in Chapter 3. If they are still not the same we go through the above process once more by adjusting the calibration factor u. We continue to do this until the *BEY* from our replicating portfolio agrees with the six-month zero coupon yield from our estimate of the zero coupon yield curve. Once this happens we do precisely the same for the second and all other later time steps. We always adjust the calibration factor u until the *BEY* implied by any given period's replicating portfolio of state securities agrees with our estimate of the corresponding maturity zero coupon *BEY* implied by our estimate of the existing sovereign zero coupon yield curve.

The justification for this calibration procedure is pure arbitrage. The portfolio consisting of one of each of all the state securities that mature at a particular date is our replicating portfolio. This replicating portfolio replicates the payoff on a zero coupon bond that matures at a given date. The price and therefore the yield on this replicating portfolio must agree with the price and therefore the yield on the zero coupon bond that underlies our estimate of the zero coupon yield curve at that point along the zero coupon yield curve. If, say, the replicating portfolio's price was too high, then we should sell the replicating portfolio and simultaneously buy the zero coupon bond that underlies the term structure. By definition, this position pays us money, yet we have no risk since any gains or losses on our short replicating portfolio are offset by gains or losses on our zero coupon bond. As we attempt to conduct this pure arbitrage, we will drive the price of the zero coupon bond up. We would saturate the market for the replicating portfolio and drive its price down. Very quickly, the price of the replicating portfolio would decrease and the price of the zero coupon bond will increase until both prices are the same.

This means that the Ho and Lee will incorporate market determined risk premiums in the interest rate tree. This happens because the prices of zero coupon bonds are determined from our estimate of the term structure of interest rates. Recall that we estimate the zero coupon yield curve by stripping coupon bonds, and coupon bonds are priced by risk adverse investors who trade in the bond market. If the coupon bond price includes risk premiums, then so do the zero coupon bonds and the corresponding zero coupon yield curve that we estimate using the methods of Chapter 3. Since we calibrate the state security price tree to this zero coupon yield curve, then the structure of state securities also includes these risk premiums.

Finally, since the state security prices are directly determined by the discount factors, and the discount factors are in turn determined by the interest rate tree, it follows that the interest rate tree also incorporates risk premiums. We can say that the interest rate tree is determined by 'risk neutral' methods, not because investors are truly risk neutral, but because relative to our estimate of the zero coupon yield curve, all investors, no matter what their degree of risk aversion, will agree that the interest rate tree is correct. Again, otherwise the investors can pure arbitrage.

5.2.3   Implementing Ho and Lee

To aid us in implementing Ho and Lee refer to Tables 5.2 and 5.3 and the spreadsheet HLB02.xls. Table 5.2 shows us the results from the calibrated Ho and Lee spread sheet given the sovereign term structure as reported in row 30. These are annualized sovereign yields observed at six-month intervals until 2.5 years' maturity. In sequence Table 5.2 shows the calibration factors u in row 5, the calibrated interest rate tree in block A7 to E11, the calibrated discount factor tree in block A13 to E17 and the calibrated state security price tree shown in block A19 to E23. Row A26 finds the value of the replicating portfolio as the sum of all possible state securities that mature in the next period (or column). Then row 27 finds the implied yield from the replicating portfolio that agrees with the sovereign term structure as reported in row 30.

Table 5.3 shows the formulas that underlie the calculations shown in Table 5.2. The formula sheets (Table 5.3) follow the same layout as the numerical sheet (Table 5.2) except that we show only the first four semi-annual time steps. The objective is to calibrate the implied zero coupon yields from our replicating portfolio of state securities (row 27) to equal the term structure as estimated via the methods of Chapter 3 (row 30).

We obtain the implied yields from our replicating portfolios that are in turn ultimately obtained from our estimates of the interest rate tree. Our interest rate tree, contained in block A7 to D11, contains the Ho and Lee interest rate process (5.1). For example, look at cell D11. $A$11 is the current six-month interest rate $r(0,0)$ and the next term SUM ($A$5:C5) is the sum of the calibration factors u contained in row 5. The next term $(2*\$A\$6-D6)*\$B\$3$ is our volatility structure $(2i - n)\sigma$.

The formulas for cells above row 11 in the interest rate tree are simply the interest rate generated in the lower interest rate state plus two times volatility σ. We can do this because Ho and Lee generates the interest rate tree in an additive manner like the simple model.

Table 5.2 Numerical spreadsheet – Ho and Lee

	A	B	C	D	E
1	Parameters		Ho and Lee		
2	r(0,0) =	6.036			
3	sigma =	1			
4	u1	u2	u3	u4	
5	−0.4488857	0.2814684	0.0445739	0.3496129	
6	0	1	2	3	4
7					10.26277
8	I.R. Tree			8.9131566	8.2627695
9			7.8685827	6.9131566	6.2627695
10		6.5871143	5.8685827	4.9131566	4.2627695
11	6.036	4.5871143	3.8685827	2.9131566	2.2627695
12					
13					0.9511907
14	D.F. Tree			0.9573356	0.9603253
15			0.9621464	0.9665891	0.9696369
16		0.9681146	0.9714935	0.9760232	0.979131
17	0.9707041	0.9775787	0.9810241	0.9856433	0.9888127
18					
19					0.0541002
20	State Price Tree			0.1130225	0.2195701
21			0.2349382	0.342379	0.3341868
22		0.4853521	0.4721731	0.3457232	0.2260649
23	1	0.4853521	0.2372349	0.1163666	0.057348
24					
25	E[D.F.] & E[Y]				
26	0.9707041	0.9443463	0.9174913	0.8912701	0.8644118
27	6.036	5.809	5.824	5.839	5.91399
28	Spot Rates				
29	1	2	3	4	5
30	6.036	5.809	5.824	5.839	5.914

The discount factor tree contained in block A13 to D17 is essentially the reciprocal of the corresponding interest rate generated by
the above interest rate tree. For example, D17 is $1/(1 + D11/200)$
where D11 is the interest rate $r(3,0)$. We divide the interest rate by
200 because we need to convert the interest rate quoted as a percentage (2.91) into a real number (0.0291) on a semi-annual basis
(0.0146). Next we obtain the state prices in block A19 to D23 by
forward induction. Notice that these state prices depend upon the

Table 5.3 Formula spreadsheet – Ho and Lee

	A	B	C	D
1	Parameters		Ho and Lee	
2	r(0,0)=	6.036		
3	sigma=	1		
4	u1	u2	u3	u4
5	-0.448885743161502	0.281468446690973	0.044573911545717	0.349612931380064
6	0	= A6 + 1	= B6 + 1	= C6 + 1
7				
8	I.R. Tree			= D9 + 2*$B$3
9			= C10 + 2*$B$3	= D10 + 2*$B$3
10		= B11 + 2*$B$3	= C11 + 2*$B$3	= D11 + 2*$B$3
11	= B2	= $A$11 + SUM(A5) + (2*$A$6 – B6)*$B$3	= $A$11 + SUM($A$5:B5) + (2*$A$6 – C6)*$B$3	= $A$11 + SUM($A$5:C5) + (2*$A$6 – D6)*$B$3
12				
13				
14	D.F. Tree			= 1/(1 + D8/200)
15			= 1/(1 + C9/200)	= 1/(1 + D9/200)
16		= 1/(1 + B10/200)	= 1/(1 + C10/200)	= 1/(1 + D10/200)
17	= 1/(1 + A11/200)	= 1/(1 + B11/200)	= 1/(1 + C11/200)	= 1/(1 + D11/200)
18				
19				
20	State Price Tree			= C21*0.5*C15
21			= B22*0.5*B16	= C21*0.5*C15 + C22*0.5*C16
22		= A23*0.5*A17	= B22*0.5*B16 + B23*0.5*B17	= C22*0.5*C16 + C23*0.5*C17
23	1	= A23*0.5*A17	= B23*0.5*B17	= C23*0.5*C17
24				
25	E[D.F.] & E[Y]			
26	= B22 + B23	= C21 + C22 + C23	= D20 + D21 + D22 + D23	= E19 + E20 + E21 + E22 + E23
27	= 200*((1/A26)^(1/A29) – 1)	= 200*((1/B26)^(1/B29) – 1)	= 200*((1/C26)^(1/C29) – 1)	= 200*((1/D26)^(1/D29) – 1)
28	Spot Rates			
29	1	= A29 + 1	= B29 + 1	= C29 + 1
30	6.036	5.809	5.824	5.839

discount factors, which in turn depend upon the interest rates generated by the Ho and Lee interest rate process. For example, cell D23 is the state price $S(3,0)$. It is calculated as $C23*0.5*$ C17 or $S(2,0)*0.5*d(2,0)$.

Therefore it is clear that as the Ho and Lee interest rate process changes, the discount factor and state price trees correspondingly change as well.

The prices of the replicating portfolios which represent the value today of a portfolio that is guaranteed to payoff £1 no matter which interest rate actually arrives at that date are contained in row 26. They are simply the sum of all the state security prices that may pay off as of a particular date. We find the *BEY* for these replicating portfolios in row 27. This yield must equal the zero yield from our estimate of the zero coupon yield curve as supplied by row 30 in the absence of arbitrage. The yield on the replicating portfolio and the zero yield from our exogenously supplied term structure must be equal because both represent the yield on a zero coupon bond of the same maturity.

To calibrate the model, we click on 'solver' under the tools menu. We choose cell B27, the second implied zero yield from our state security price tree as the target cell.[1] The target cell is set to equal 5.809, the corresponding interest rate from our estimated yield curve. The change cell is the first calibration factor u, which is cell A5 in our spreadsheet. Now we click on solve. As the change cell A5 adjusts, the interest rates in cells B10 and B11 change, which in turn change the discount factors B16 and B17 and the state security prices C21, C22 and C23. This obtains a new price for the replicating portfolio in cell B26 and a new *BEY* for the replicating portfolio in cell B27. The factor u in A5 continues to change until cell B27 equals 5.809. Then we continue this calibration, period by period. For example, the next calibration chooses C27 as the target cell, the target is 5.824 and the change cell is B5 and the next calibration after that chooses D27 as the target cell, the target is 5.839 and the change cell is C5 and so on.

5.2.4 Using the calibrated interest rate tree

The discount factor tree in block A13 to D17 in Table 5.2 is used to price all sorts of securities by backward induction. Table 5.4

---

[1] Notice that the first zero yield implied by our state security price tree cell A27 already equals the exogenously supplied term structure yield in cell A30. This happens because the first interest rate is the risk-free rate and if you buy it today you will indeed earn that rate of return for six months. Such is not the case for the second zero yield, for interest rates will change in six months and if they go up, you would be disappointed that you locked yourself in for one year.

shows the numerical calculation for pricing a five period (2.5-year) 6% coupon sovereign bond and Table 5.5 shows the formulas. Note that the bond we price is not a bond we have used to estimate the yield curve. To do so is useless for by construction the model will replicate the market price very closely, and any difference is simply a measure of the error of the yield curve interpolation scheme, say Nelson and Siegel, that we have used to estimate the existing yield curve.

Table 5.4   The price of a 6% coupon, 5 period bond

	A	B	C	D	E
33	Bond price tree (6% 5 period bond)				
34	coupon =	6.0000			97.9726
35				97.1151	98.9135
36			97.2187	98.9720	99.8726
37		98.3664	99.9935	100.8833	100.8505
38	100.2059	102.0938	102.8772	102.8510	101.8477

5.3   Black Derman and Toy: constant volatility

A useful stepping-stone to understanding Black Derman and Toy (1990) is the constant volatility version of this model. The interest rate process employed by the constant volatility version of the Black Derman and Toy model (hereafter BDTCV) is shown in (5.5) below.

$$r(n,i) = r(0,0) \times exp \left[\sum_{j=1}^{n} u_{t+j} + (2i - n)\sigma \right] \qquad (5.5)$$

Notice that (5.5) *is* Ho and Lee (1986) except that the latter two terms are multiplied rather than added, and these latter two terms are carried to the exponent. Performing exp operations always returns positive values so this transformation forces the volatility structure always to return positive numbers. In other words, the BDTCV prevents negative interest rates. Also, this operation transforms the limiting distribution of generated interest rates from the normal to the log normal distribution. Otherwise the model shares the advantages and disadvantages of Ho and Lee in that it has constant volatility

Table 5.5 Formulas for pricing a coupon bond

	A	B	C	D	E
33	Bond Price Tree (6% 5 Period Bond)				
34	Coupon =	6			= (100 + $B$34/2)*E13
35				= 0.5*D14*(E34 + E35 + $B$34)	= (100 + $B$34/2)*E14
36			= 0.5*C15*(D35 + D36 + $B$34)	= 0.5*D15*(E35 + E36 + $B$34)	= (100 + $B$34/2)*E15
37		= 0.5*B16*(C36 + C37 + $B$34)	= 0.5*C16*(D36 + D37 + $B$34)	= 0.5*D16*(E36 + E37 + $B$34)	= (100 + $B$34/2)*E16
38	= 0.5*A17*(B37 + B38 + $B$34)	= 0.5*B17*(C37 + C38 + $B$34)	= 0.5*C17*(D37 + D38 + $B$34)	= 0.5*D17*(E37 + E38 + $B$34)	= (100 + $B$34/2)*E17

but it also is able to incorporate information from the existing term structure of interest rates.[2]

Since the only difference between the Ho and Lee (1986) and BDTCV is the interest rate tree, we highlight this difference by reporting the BDTCV interest rate tree formulas in Table 5.6.

Notice that the formulas in block A8 to D11 are the interest rate process (5.5). For example, in D11, A11 is $r(0,0)$. This is multiplied by the sum, taken to the exponent, of the calibration factors u(A5 to C5) and the binomial volatility structure $(2i - n)\sigma$ $(2 * \$A\$6\text{-}D6) * \$B\$3$.

Because the constant volatility version of Black Derman and Toy (1990) is so close to the Ho and Lee (1986) model, the calibration procedure is precisely the same. We leave it to the reader to calibrate the model as an exercise. However, we would like to point out that the solver routine can be used more efficiently and we encourage readers to try out this slightly different calibration procedure. The constant volatility version of Black Derman and Toy is contained in workbook BDTCVB02.xls. Choose the discount factor $d(1,0)$ in cell B17 as the target cell. Select maximize. Then choose the row of calibration factors, cells A5 to D5, as the change cells. Finally, add a constraint where row 27 (A27 to E27) is equal to row 30 (A30 to E30). Click on solve. Then the entire five period model is calibrated in just one step, a considerable convenience.

As a final point, note that since the BDTCV model employs a slightly different interest rate process than Ho and Lee, it also obtains slightly different prices. To see this, Table 5.7 reports the BDTCV price for the same 2.5-year, 6% coupon sovereign bond that was priced by Ho and Lee in Table 5.4. Notice that the BDTCV model prices the bond at $100.205818, which is very slightly lower than the Ho and Lee price of $100.20586. This difference is not due to rounding but differences in price will remain generally modest for most cash (non-derivative) securities. However, for derivatives the difference in price obtained by the two models may be substantial. This happens because the value of a derivative is critically dependent upon the payoffs at only a relatively few states, so small differences in the interest rates generated by the two models will result in larger differences in payoffs in the critical payoff states for the derivative.

---

[2] Tuckman (1995) points out that actually the constant volatility version of Black Derman and Toy does allow for an implied volatility curve but the curve changes very slowly and in a very restrictive manner.

Table 5.6 Interest rate tree for Black Derman and Toy (constant volatility)

	A	B	C	D
1		Parameters Black, Derman and Toy, Constant Volatility		
2	r(0,0)=	6.036		
3	sigma =	1		
4	u1	u2	u3	u4
5	-7.8198125	4.7491688925204	0.50757825774907	5.45672224659311
6	0	=A6 + 1	=B6 + 1	=C6 + 1
7				
8		I.R. Tree	=$A$11*EXP((SUM($A$5:B5) + (2*$C$6 − C6)*$B$3)/100)	=$A$11*EXP((SUM($A$5:C5) + (2*$D$6 − D6)*$B$3)/100)
9			=$A$11*EXP((SUM($A$5:B5) + (2*$C$6 − C6)*$B$3)/100)	=$A$11*EXP((SUM($A$5:C5) + (2*$C$6 − D6)*$B$3)/100)
10		=$A$11*EXP((SUM(A5) + (2*$B$6 − B6)*$B$3)/100)	=$A$11*EXP((SUM($A$5:B5) + (2*$B$6 − C6)*$B$3)/100)	=$A$11*EXP((SUM($A$5:C5) + (2*$B$6 − D6)*$B$3)/100)
11	=B2	=$A$11*EXP((SUM(A5) + (2*$A$6 − B6)*$B$3)/100)	=$A$11*EXP((SUM($A$5:B5) + (2*$A$6 − C6)*$B$3)/100)	=$A$11*EXP((SUM($A$5:C5) + (2*$A$6 − D6)*$B$3)/100)

Table 5.7   Price obtained by the BDTCV model

	A	B	C	D	E
33	Bond Price Tree (6% 5 Period Bond)				
34	Coupon =	6			99.773921
35				99.780323	99.835839
36			99.857582	99.898058	99.896606
37		100.1205032	100.0283	100.01367	99.956241
38	100.205818	100.3395555	100.19602	100.12718	100.01476

5.4 Black Derman and Toy (1990)

The special feature of Black Derman and Toy (1990) is that it allows for non-constant volatility. The interest rate process is

$$r(n,i) = u_t \left[exp(v_t(2i - n)\sqrt{dt}) \right] \qquad (5.6)$$

Here v_t is the *local volatility* which is calibrated to a volatility curve that you input from external sources. The local volatility refers to a one period forward volatility that applies to a given future time step. The relationship between a volatility curve and the term structure of local volatilities is analogous to the yield curve and the term structure of one period forward rates. Specifically the sequence of local volatilities implies the volatility curve. The term dt is the time step, 0.5 years in our examples. It is taken to the square root because the time step is multiplied by the local volatility that is measured in standard deviation units. The term u_t is a second calibration factor that calibrates the interest rate process to an input zero coupon term structure of interest rates. This means that to fully calibrate the model you need to calibrate it to both an input yield using u_t and a volatility curve using v_t as the calibration factors.

Other than including a volatility curve, Black Derman and Toy (1990) (hereafter BDT) shares all the advantages and disadvantages of the BDTCV model. Specifically it does include information from the term structure of interest rates by calibration and since the volatility structure is carried to the exponent it prevents negative interest rates. However, it does not specifically model mean reversion. This is a serious problem because there is a relationship between the volatility curve you include in a given term structure model and the rate of mean reversion that this implies. Specifically, if your input volatility curve implies a local volatility structure that is too high you underestimate mean reversion and if your input volatility curve implies a local volatility structure that is too low you overestimate mean reversion. The danger is that in order to match the model to the term structure of volatilities you may inaccurately model both local volatility and mean reversion. You would rather have a model that allows for flexibility in determining both the local volatility structure and the degree of mean reversion.

In fact Backus, Foresi and Zin (1998) show that if your local volatility structure does not imply the correct amount of mean reversion, then the prices you obtain from the interest rate model are not arbitrage free, even though the prices you obtain from the model are calibrated to the existing term structure of interest rates. For example, if the volatility curve you input into BDT implies that mean reversion is underestimated then this implies that future local volatility is overestimated. As we know, if volatility is overestimated all options, both calls and puts, will be overpriced. Although prices today are calibrated to the existing term structure, it will turn out that next period the price you sold the option for last period was too high since volatility turned out to be lower in the second period. Backus, Foresi and Zin (1998) suggest this is a real possibility for models like BDT that do not allow for a specific model of mean reversion.

If this were the case with BDT, what would you be tempted to do? Sell options! The idea is that you would be selling options that may appear to be fairly priced today, but next period when the stronger mean reversion actually occurs, and volatility is lower than anticipated, then you would buy back the options you sold last period at a cheaper price. While this may look like a good deal, beware. The above strategy is not pure arbitrage. Instead we can call it *risk arbitrage* because while you buy cheap and sell dear as in pure arbitrage you also take on some risk in doing so.

For example, suppose you do sell call and put options and collect premiums for doing so. At this point you are terribly exposed. If there is one thing we can be certain about is that given enough time disaster will strike. Next period the unexpected may happen, the central bank may unexpectedly cut interest rates by a large amount or maybe a liquidity squeeze may occur that raises interest rates. In other words, if the unexpected happens either the calls or the puts will be in the money and there is almost no doubt that you will lose much more than the premiums you have cumulatively earned up until that point. The moral of the story is that to risk arbitrage intelligently on a day in day out basis you cannot simply leave yourself fully exposed, you must control the amount of risk you accept by hedging. This is a key point of this book that we will return to in Chapter 7.

5.4.1   Implementing BDT

BDT requires you to input a volatility curve that you think is reasonable. One possible source is the implied volatilities from cap and floor 'prices'. These are estimates of interest rate volatilities found by solving Black's option price model (a variation of the more famous Black-Scholes option pricing model) for volatility rather than price. These are readily available from many information sources. For example, Datastream has at the money implied cap and floor volatilities for many countries and for a range of maturities.

We choose to include the time step in our interest rate process at this stage because we intend to add much more flexibility in our model. An awkward feature of our previous version of the BDTCV model was that if we were to choose another time step length, say one month rather than six months, we would have to adjust entire parts of our spreadsheet, the discount factor tree for example, to accommodate the time step change. By including the time step as a parameter in the interest rate process, we can then rewrite our spreadsheet such that by just changing the value of this parameter, we can adjust our spreadsheet to any arbitrary time step.

However, this also implies we have to adjust our discounting from semi-annual compounding to the corresponding compounding of our chosen time step, monthly for example. It is easier to program this change in compounding by using continuous time compounding because the functional forms available in continuous compounding allow us to make the transition from, say, a semi-annual time step into a monthly time step easier.

To aid us in understanding how this is done, we include the continuous compounding case of the constant volatility version of Black Derman and Toy (1990) in the first spreadsheet BDTCV in our Black Derman and Toy workbook BDTB02.xls. Notice that our interest rate process now directly includes the time step D3. For example, look at $r(3,0)$ or cell D11 and you will see that this interest rate process formula is $A$11 * EXP((SUM($A5:C5) + (2 * $A$6-D6) * $B$3 * $D$3^0.5)/100) where $D$3 is the time step. Then our discount factor tree is adjusted by dividing the interest rate from our interest rate tree by 100 times the time step rather than by dividing by 200. For example, the discount factor formula for $d(3,0)$ in cell D17 is EXP $(-D11/100 * $D$3)$. There is no need to adjust the state price tree or the price of the replicating portfolio. Finally, the continuously compounded three period yield 'BEY' is calculated according to the following formula.

$$y = \left[\frac{-LN(d_t)}{M \times t} \right] \tag{5.7}$$

Note that y is the continuously compounded yield, d_t is the zero coupon bond price per $1 face value, M is the time step size and t is the number of time steps. The equivalent expression in the worksheet is (-LN (C26)/($D$3 * C29)) * 100. Taking the negative log of the replicating portfolio price obtains the total return, and dividing the total return by the number of time steps converts the total return into its annual equivalent return. The advantage of this formulation is that if you wish to adjust the time step to, say, one month, then all you need to do is to change the parameter in cell D3 from 0.5 to 0.0833. Of course, your estimated yield curve in row 30 must also contain monthly observations, and you will need to recalibrate the model as well. But then again you do not have to adjust the rest of the spreadsheet by hand.

Now we turn to the main BDT spreadsheet, BDT. Table 5.8 shows the spreadsheet layout while Table 5.9 shows the formulas for the first five columns.

Rows two and three of Table 5.8 report the zero coupon yield curve and the volatility curve respectively. Rows four and five report the interest rate and volatility calibration factors that have been used to calibrate the model to the zero coupon yield and volatility curves. Row eight is the zero coupon bond price implied by our zero coupon yield curve, and row ten is the local volatility curve implied by our calibration. Notice that the local volatility curve rapidly declines as most practitioners claim it should.

The next block, from cell D12 to H17, are the results from a number of equations that are used to calibrate the model to the yield and volatility curves. A detailed discussion of this block is left until we discuss the calibration procedures. The remaining rows are the familiar interest rate, discount factor and state security price trees. However, you will notice that the main difference in the layout of BDT when compared to the previous models for this latter part of the spreadsheet is that we split the state price tree into an 'up' or $QU(n,i)$ in block C35 to I41 and 'down' or $QD(n,i)$ state price tree in block C43 to I49. Later these two state security price trees are added together in the main state security price tree in block C51 to I57. We do this to add a second degree of freedom so we can calibrate the model to the volatility and term structure of interest rates.

It is best to explain the logic of the formulas in Table 5.9 by explaining how we go about calibrating the model. This is done in a two-step procedure. In the first step we go to solver and select cell D13 as our target. We set it equal to the value of cell D14 and set cell D12 as our change cell and then click on solve. We continue to do this for the remaining cells in these rows. For example, the next calibration

Table 5.8   BDT numerical results

	A	B	C	D	E	F	G	H
1	dt	0.5						
2	InitialYield	0.06036	0.05809	0.05824	0.05839	0.05914	0.05989	0.061
3	InitialSigma	0.01	0.005025	0.003367	0.002538	0.00204	0.001709	0.001472
4	U(i)	0.06	0.055819	0.05854	0.058839	0.06214	0.06364	0.06766
5	sigma(i)	0.01	0.005025	0.001786	0.000926	0.000654	0.000483	0.000426
6	Time	0	1	2	3	4	5	6
7								
8	Bond_Price	1	0.970271	0.943565	0.916347	0.889781	0.86256	0.835546
9								
10	Volatility		0.003553	0.001263	0.000655	0.000462	0.000341	0.000301
11								
12	Bu			0.97238	0.944295	0.916901	0.888839	0.860991
13				1.944952	1.888848	1.834088	1.777979	1.722294
14				1.944952	1.888848	1.834088	1.777979	1.722294
15	Bd			0.972572	0.944553	0.917187	0.88914	0.861303
16	EQ_Bu		1	0.97238	0.944295	0.916901	0.888839	0.860991
17	EQ_Bd		1	0.972572	0.944553	0.917187	0.88914	0.861303
18								
19								0.067783
20							0.063749	0.067742
21						0.062255	0.063706	0.067701
22	r(n,i)				0.058955	0.062198	0.063662	0.06766
23				0.058688	0.058878	0.06214	0.063619	0.06762
24			0.056018	0.05854	0.058801	0.062083	0.063575	0.067579
25		0.06036	0.055621	0.058393	0.058724	0.062025	0.063532	0.067538
26								
27								0.966677
28							0.968628	0.966696
29						0.969352	0.968649	0.966716
30	d(n,i)				0.970953	0.96938	0.96867	0.966736
31				0.971082	0.97099	0.969408	0.968691	0.966755
32			0.97238	0.971154	0.971028	0.969436	0.968712	0.966775
33		0.970271	0.972572	0.971226	0.971065	0.969463	0.968733	0.966795
34								
35								
36	QU(n,i)							0.026902
37							0.055546	0.134517
38						0.114604	0.222196	0.269051
39					0.236065	0.343829	0.333314	0.269069
40				0.48619	0.472148	0.34387	0.222223	0.134543
41			1	0.48619	0.236083	0.114621	0.055559	0.0269
42								
43								
44	QD(n,i)							0.026911
45							0.055565	0.134565
46						0.11464	0.222272	0.269148
47					0.236129	0.343936	0.333428	0.269166
48				0.486286	0.472276	0.343954	0.222298	0.134592
49			1	0.486286	0.236147	0.114657	0.055578	0.02692
50								
51								
52	State Price Tree							0.026947
53							0.055598	0.134752
54						0.114524	0.22242	0.269535
55					0.235868	0.34361	0.333668	0.269566
56				0.485135	0.471783	0.34365	0.222471	0.134798
57			1	0.485135	0.235915	0.114563	0.055624	0.026963
58								
59		Zero		0.970271	0.943565	0.916347	0.889781	0.862561
60	Implied Yield			0.06036	0.05809	0.05824	0.05839	0.05914
61	Observed Yield			0.06036	0.05809	0.05824	0.05839	0.05914

chooses E13 as the target, the value of cell E14 is the value the target cell is set equal to and cell E12 is the change cell.

What does this initial calibration do? It ensures that the value of the structure of zero coupon bonds one period forward in time if interest rates rise next period $B_u(i)$ is found by calibration and is consistent with the following two equations.

$$B_d(i) = B_u(i)^{exp(-2\sigma(i)\sqrt{t})} \tag{5.8}$$

$$B_u(i) + B_u(i)^{(exp(-2\sigma(i)\sqrt{t}))} = 2B(i)[1 + r(0,0)t] \tag{5.9}$$

Equation (5.8) establishes the relationship between the price of a given zero coupon bond in the up interest rate state and the down interest rate state next period. It says that the price of the bond in the down interest rate state is two times the exponent of volatility less than the price of the bond in the up interest rate state. Then (5.9) forces this structure between the price of the bond in the up and down interest rate states next period to be consistent with observed zero coupon bond prices and the known one period spot rate as of today.

In the second calibration step we target $S_u(1,0)$ which is the price of the state security that pays off £1 next period should interest rates fall according to the 'up' state security price tree in cell D41. We choose to maximize this cell and the change cells are the block of calibration factors C4 to H5. Note that row four represents the one period rates of interest and row five represents the one period local volatilities. In other words, we are attempting to calibrate the BDT model to both the yield curve *and* the volatility curve. We now apply two constraints. First, row 12 (D12 to I12) is set equal to row 16 (D16 to I16) and second, row 15 (D15 to I15) is set to equal row 17 (D17 to I17). Row 12 represents the price of the zero coupon bonds that under-lie the current term structure should interest rates rise next period. This second calibration forces these bond prices to agree with the replicating portfolio of up state prices. Similarly row 16 represents the price of the zero coupon bonds that underlie the current term structure should interest rates fall next period so this second calib-ration forces these bond prices to agree with the replicating portfolio of down state prices. In other words, this second step calibrates the up and down state price trees to the observed zero yield and volatility curves. Simultaneously the interest rate process, the discount factor tree and the corresponding combined state price tree are calibrated.

You can assure yourself that BDT is indeed calibrated to both the term structure of interest rates and the volatility curve. First, you will notice that the yields implied by the replicating portfolio of state security prices from the combined state security price tree (row 60) are indeed equal to the estimated term structure (row 61). Second, you will notice that the implied volatility as calculated from

Table 5.9 BDT formula spreadsheet

	A	B	C	D	E
1	dt	0.5			
2	InitialYield	0.06036	0.05809	0.05824	0.05839
3	InitialSigma	0.01	= $B$3/10/(1 − 0.99^D6)/10	= $B$3/10/(1 − 0.99^E6)/10	= $B$3/10/(1 − 0.99^F6)/10
4	U(i)	0.06	0.0558194223626875	0.0585402740769533	0.0588394982945269
5	sigma(i)	0.01	0.00502512562749665	0.00178572756451539	0.000926431918806675
6	Time	0	= B6 + 1	= C6 + 1	= D6 + 1
7					
8	Bond_Price	1	= EXP(−B2*C6*$B$1)	= EXP(−C2*D6*$B$1)	= EXP(−D2*E6*$B$1)
9					
10	Volatility		= 0.5*LN(C24/C25)	= 0.5*LN(D23/D24)	= 0.5*LN(E22/E23)
11					
12	Bu			0.972379557808096	0.944295434392062
13				= D12 + D12^(EXP(−C3*2*SQRT($B$1)))	= E12 + E12^(EXP(−D3*2*SQRT($B$1)))
14				= 2*D8*EXP($B$2*$B$1)	= 2*E8*EXP($B$2*$B$1)
15	Bd			= D12^EXP(−C3*2*SQRT($B$1))	= E12^EXP(−D3*2*SQRT($B$1))
16	EQ_Bu		= SUM(C38:C41)	= SUM(D35:D41)	= SUM(E35:E41)
17	EQ_Bd		= SUM(C46:C53)	= SUM(D43:D49)	= SUM(E43:E49)
18					
19					
20					
21					
22	r(n,i)				= E$4*EXP(E$5+(2*$E$6−E$6)*SQRT($B$1))
23			= C$4*EXP(C5+(2*$C$6−C$6)*SQRT($B$1))	= D$4*EXP(D$5+(2*$D$6−D$6)*SQRT($B$1))	= E4*EXP(E$5+(2*$D$6−E$6)*SQRT($B$1))
24			= C$4*EXP(C5+(2*$B$6−C$6)*SQRT($B$1))	= D$4*EXP(D5+(2*$C$6−D$6)*SQRT($B$1))	= E4*EXP(E5+(2*$C$6−E$6)*SQRT($B$1))
25		= B2	= C$4*EXP(C5+(2*$B$6−C$6)*SQRT($B$1))	= D$4*EXP(D5+(2*$B$6−D$6)*SQRT($B$1))	= E$4*EXP(E5+(2*$B$6−E$6)*SQRT($B$1))

	B	C	D	E
26				
27				
28				
29				
30	d(n,i)			= EXP(-E22*$B$1)
31			= EXP(-D23*$B$1)	= EXP(-E23*$B$1)
32		= EXP(-C24*$B$1)	= EXP(-D24*$B$1)	= EXP(-E24*$B$1)
33	= EXP(-B25*$B$1)	= EXP(-C25*$B$1)	= EXP(-D25*$B$1)	= EXP(-E25*$B$1)
34				
35				
36	QU(n,i)			
37				
38				
39			= 0.5*D40*D31	
40		= 0.5*C41*C32	= 0.5*D41*D32 + D40*D31	
41		= 0.5*C41*C32	= 0.5*D41*D32	
42	1			
43				
44	QD(n,i)			
45				
46				
47			= 0.5*D48*D32	
48		= 0.5*C49*C33	= 0.5*D49*D33 + D48*D32	
49		= 0.5*C49*C33	= 0.5*D49*D33	
50	1			

Table 5.9 Contd.

	A	B	C	D	E
51					
52		State Price Tree			
53					
54					
55			= 0.5*(C41 + C49)	= 0.5*D56*C32	= 0.5*D56*C32 + 0.5*D57*C33
56				= 0.5*C57*B33	= 0.5*D57*C33
57				= 0.5*C57*B33	
58					
59		Zero		= (SUM(D51:D57))	= (SUM(E51:E57))
60	Implied Yield			= −LN(D59)/(C6*$B$1)	= −LN(E59)/(D6*$B$1)
61	Observed Yield			= B2	= C2
62					
63					
64					
65					
66					
67					
68					
69					
70					
71					
72					
73					
74					

our calibrated interest rate tree (row 10) is equal to the local volatility (row 5). The implied volatility is found using the following formula.

$$Local\ vol(t) = d(t) \left[ln\left(\frac{r(n,1)}{r(n,0)}\right) \Big/ \sqrt{d(t)} \right] \qquad (5.10)$$

We find the local volatility from the two lowest interest rates $r(n,1)$ and $r(n,0)$ in the calibrated interest rate tree because the local volatility is the same for all interest rates at a particular time step. Notice also that we need to divide the log ratio of the one period interest rates by the standard deviation of the time step size $d(t)$ to annualize the measure of local volatility because volatility is measured in standard deviation units.

For what it is worth, you can also assure yourself that the interest rate trees are consistent with your input volatility curve. For example, you can recover the one-year volatility by first finding the price of a three period zero (1.5 years) and then calculate the yield on this zero next period should interest rates rise Y_u or fall Y_d. Then apply (5.10) using Y_u and Y_d in place of $r(n,1)$ and $r(n,0)$. This obtains the one-year volatility since one six-month period later, the 1.5-year zero is a one-year zero and the volatility implied by the (now) one-year up and down yields is the one-year volatility. To replicate the three period volatility, you again calculate Y_u and Y_d as above, only from a two-year zero. Again since one six-month period later the two-year zero is a 1.5-year zero so the volatility implied by the (now) 1.5-year up and down yields is the 1.5-year volatility. You can continue in this manner to recover the input volatility curve, always first calculating the price of a zero one time step longer than the desired volatility because next period, the zero has the same maturity as your target volatility. See the spreadsheet Lvol in BDTB02.xls for the numerical example.

5.5   Some other one factor term structure consistent models

It is evident that Black Derman and Toy still has a flaw because it does not incorporate a specific model or function for mean reversion. In fact, the degree of mean reversion in the model is implied by the volatility curve, so this model is inflexible with regard to the degree of mean reversion. Some other models have attempted to incorporate independent mean reversion and volatility curves. Of these, we mention Black and Karasinski (1991) and Hull and White (1990).

The problem is that we must find some way to incorporate another degree of freedom to add flexibility in incorporating both mean reversion and volatility curves. Black and Karasinski (1991) accomplish this by varying the size of the time step from time step to time step. The unattractive consequence of this is that the resulting model is non-recombining. As mentioned earlier, this means that it is impossible to price American options within the model as there are too many interest rate states that need to be evaluated. Monte Carlo methods must be employed instead. Hull and White (1990) add another degree of freedom by employing a trinomial rather than a binomial tree. In other words, next period interest rates may increase, decrease or remain the same, or increase at three different rates, decrease at three different rates or any other combination that you could possibly imagine. Unfortunately the model does allow for negative interest rates, which can be a serious problem when valuing interest rate options with a large number of time steps. In short, there does not appear to be a simple one factor interest rate model that allows us to incorporate all the desirable features as outlined in section 5.1.

5.6　Summary

We have reviewed the early development of term structure consistent interest rate modelling. We have studied the implementation of Ho and Lee and two variations of Black Derman and Toy (1990) and have discussed the advantages and disadvantages of these and two other models, Black and Karasinski (1991) and Hull and White (1990).

5.7　Exercises

Question 1
We have reviewed a number of one factor interest rate models, including 'Black and Karasinski', 'Black Derman and Toy' and 'Ho and Lee'. Describe each of them in detail, highlighting their advantages and disadvantages as opposed to what would be the characteristics of an ideal model.

Question 2
Why should we *not* calibrate our interest rate model to the par yield curve?

Question 3

The following two questions use the following sovereign term structure of interest rates.

Maturity	Interest rate	Volatility
$_0r_1$	0.0350	0.1000
$_0r_2$	0.0363	0.0503
$_0r_3$	0.0373	0.0337
$_0r_4$	0.0382	0.0254
$_0r_5$	0.0391	0.0204
$_0r_6$	0.0401	0.0171
$_0r_7$	0.0410	0.0147

Find the price of an 8% coupon bond 3.5-year bond using Black Derman and Toy (constant volatility version). Volatility is constant at 10%. Use a step size of six months. To accomplish this task, adjust the spreadsheet BDTCV in workbook BDTB02.xls.

Question 4

Price the same bond as in question 3, but now use the Black Derman and Toy (1990) model as implemented in BDTB02.xls. Use the term structure of volatility as given in the above table.

Question 5

Consider the following interest rate tree that has been calibrated to the existing sovereign yield curve using the Black Derman and Toy model (constant volatility version). Note that we use a one-year time step.

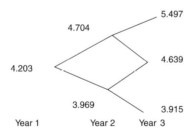

(a) Recover the two-period annualized volatility from the above interest rate tree.
(b) Would you expect the true term structure of volatility to be the same as you would recover from the BDT (constant volatility)? If not, in what way would it differ?
(c) What impact would you expect this BDT (constant volatility) volatility bias (if any) to have in pricing an interest rate call option?
(d) What impact would you expect this BDT (constant volatility) volatility bias (if any) to have in pricing a floater?

6

Interest and credit risk modelling

6.1 Evolutionary interest rate models

In contrast to term structure consistent models, evolutionary interest rate models are based on continuous time processes that are designed to describe how interest rates are to evolve. These evolutionary models are also arbitrage free. Like Black and Scholes (1973) these models are based on continuously adjusting replicating portfolios such that risk is eliminated. What remains is a partial differential equation that can either be solved explicitly or numerical methods can be employed to price zero coupon bonds and interest rate derivatives of any maturity. Of course, this means that the model obtains a zero coupon yield curve but one that is estimated without reference to an input yield curve. Two famous early evolutionary models are Vasicek (1977) and Cox Ingersoll and Ross (1985).

The main difference between these evolutionary models and the term structure consistent models is that the term structure consistent models are calibrated to an estimate of the existing term structure of interest rates whereas the evolutionary models output an estimate of the term structure without reference to a term structure estimated by market prices. However, this distinction is more of a continuum than an absolute distinction for there are interest rate models that combine elements of both. For example, Hull and White (1990) is a term structure consistent model as it is calibrated to an estimate of an existing term structure but the underlying interest rate process is Vasicek (1977), a classic evolutionary model. Similarly,

Heath Jarrow and Morton (1992) is calibrated to an estimate of the forward curve but the underlying interest rate process is evolutionary in nature. So it is best to think of interest rate modelling as a continuum with Ho and Lee (1986) at the extreme end of the term structure consistent approach, Hull and White (1990) in the middle and Vasicek (1977) at the extreme end of the evolutionary approach.

6.2 Vasicek (1977)

The stochastic model of interest rates proposed by Vasicek is as follows.

$$dr = \alpha(\gamma - r)dt + \sigma dz \tag{6.1}$$

The term dr refers to an infinitesimally small change in the short rate of interest. The first term is the drift, referring to the amount by which the short rate will change in an infinitesimally small unit of time dt. It is measured as the distance between the long run mean or central tendency of the short rate γ and the current (known) short rate of interest r multiplied by the speed of mean reversion α. The second term is the volatility structure. Rather than being generated by a binomial structure, the model generates constant volatility σ as increments in a Wiener process dz.

After proposing this process, Vasicek applies the standard mathematical routine to find the pricing equation for zero coupon bonds. First, he assumes the existence of two assets, a risk-free asset whose return is perfectly correlated with the interest rate as described by (6.1) and a default-free bond. He then applies Ito's lemma to transform the stochastic differential equation for the default-free bond and to isolate terms containing the mean and the variance. Weights are then chosen for a portfolio of the risk-free asset and the default-free bond such that terms containing the only source of risk dz for both instruments are eliminated. The economic intuition is that the source of risk dz is eliminated by continuously adjusting hedge portfolios such that losses on long positions are offset by gains on short positions. Therefore the portfolio is risk free and must yield the instantaneous risk-free rate to avoid arbitrage. The resulting differential equation applies to all securities whose value is dependent upon the short rate of interest as otherwise investors can conduct pure arbitrage. However, we can identify the pricing equation for a given interest rate sensitive instrument by solving the differential equation given the boundary conditions (i.e. a zero coupon bond is worth £1 at maturity) that apply to that instrument.

The resulting expressions for zero coupon bond prices and the resulting continuously compounded yields are

$$d(t,T) = A(t,T)exp^{-rB(t,T)} \tag{6.2}$$

$$Y(t,T) = -\frac{ln[A(t,T)]}{T-t} + \frac{B(t-T)}{T-t} \tag{6.3}$$

The above terms for the zero coupon bond price $d(t,T)$ and yields $Y(t,T)$ that apply from date t to a later date T are equations. Specifically,

$$Ln[A(t,T)] = \frac{R}{\alpha}(1 - exp^{-\alpha(T-t)}) - (T-t)R$$

$$- \frac{\sigma^2}{4\alpha^3}(1 - exp^{\alpha(T-t)})^2 \tag{6.4}$$

$$R = \gamma - \frac{\sigma^2}{2\alpha^2} \tag{6.5}$$

$$B(t,T) = \frac{1}{\alpha}(1 - exp^{-\alpha(T-t)}) \tag{6.6}$$

Note that by taking the exponent of (6.4) gives the value of the function $A(t,T)$ needed to find the value of the discount bond $d(t,T)$ in (6.2). Finally, the local volatility $\sigma(t,T)$ is determined by the volatility parameter σ and the speed of mean reversion α.

$$\sigma(t,T) = \frac{\sigma}{\alpha(T-t)}(1 - exp^{-\alpha(T-t)}) \tag{6.7}$$

The advantage of this approach is readily apparent. The model explicitly incorporates mean reversion and is consistent with no arbitrage. However, the stochastic process (6.1) does allow for negative interest rates because, like Ho and Lee, the volatility structure is additive. For a wide range of parameter values, a negative volatility value will be larger than the drift term resulting in a negative interest rate overall. This is the underlying reason why Hull and White (1990) may also generate negative interest rates since Hull and White (1990) incorporates Vasicek's interest rate process. Vasicek also contains a local volatility curve as represented by (6.7). A non-constant volatility term structure will result, albeit this volatility term structure will change in a restrictive manner. Specifically the model ignores empirical evidence that the volatility term structure should shift upwards as the level of interest rates rises. In fact the term structure of volatility implied by Vasicek does not change as the level of interest rates changes. Many of the parameters, specifically the central tendency of the short rate γ and the speed of mean reversion α, must be estimated from the historical behaviour of interest rates and only the short rate r and volatility σ can be obtained by market traded instruments.

6.2.1 Implementing Vasicek

Refer to workbook EvolB02.xls, spreadsheet Vasicek for our implementation of Vasicek. We show the numerical results in Table 6.1 and the formulas in Table 6.2. To start we need estimates for the short rate r, the volatility σ, the central tendency of the short rate γ and the speed of mean reversion α. We choose to implement Vasicek on July 29, 2002. The short rate r is the one-month rate of 1.3822% that we estimated via Nelson and Siegel in Chapter 3. We use the one-year cap volatility, which is the shortest quoted at the money volatility on July 29, 2002, of 4.48% as our estimate of the short rate volatility. We use the 20-year interest rate of 6.0618% as estimated by Nelson and Siegel on the same day as our proxy for the central tendency of the short rate γ. We could not easily estimate the speed of mean reversion, so we simply 'calibrated' the Vasicek model by minimizing squared error between the yields implied by Vasicek and our Nelson and Siegel estimated yield curve. This is not very fair to Vasicek but this should not matter, as the purpose of this exercise is simply to illustrate the workings of the model. Of course, better parameter estimates will give you better results.

To start, refer to Table 6.1.

Table 6.1 Vasicek – numerical example

	A	B	C	D	E	F	G	H	I
1	Parameters			Pure Discount	Bond Price				
2	γ	0.060618	dt	0.083333					
3	α	0.51156	t	0	0.083333	0.166667	0.25	0.333333	0.416667
4	σ	0.0448							
5	r	0.013822		B(t,T)	0.081582	0.159759	0.234674	0.306462	0.375254
6				R	0.056783	0.056783	0.056783	0.056783	0.056783
7				Ln[A(t,T)]	−0.000106	−0.000417	−0.000924	−0.001618	−0.00249
8				d(t,T)	0.998767	0.997378	0.995841	0.994163	0.992353
9				σ(t,T)	0.043859	0.042943	0.042054	0.041189	0.040347
10				Vasieck	1.480365	1.575314	1.667221	1.756206	1.842382

Table 6.1 shows the zero coupon bond price $d(t,T)$ and the corresponding zero yield curve (Vasicek) implied by our parameter choices for the first five months. The block E3 to I10 shows the calculations. Rows 5, 6 and 7 are the subsidiary equations (6.6), (6.5) and (6.4) whereas rows 8 and 9 are the prices of the zero coupon bond (6.2)

and the term structure of volatility (6.7). Finally, the last row is the zero coupon yield curve implied by Vasicek that is found using (5.7).[1]

In Table 6.2 we show the details of the calculations.

Table 6.2 Vasicek – formulas

	A	B	C	D	E
1	Parameters				
2	γ	0.06061800	*dt*	= 1/12	
3	α	0.51155983	*t*	0	= D3 + (1∗$D$2)
4	σ	0.0448			
5	r	= E12/100		$B(t,T)$	= (1/$B$3)∗(1 − EXP(−$B$3∗E3))
6				R	= $B$2 − 0.5∗(($B$4^2)/$B$3^2)
7				$Ln[A(t,T)]$	= ($E$6/$B$3)∗(1 − EXP(−$B$3∗(E3 − $D$3))) −(E3 − $D$3)∗$E$6 − (($B$4^2)/(4∗$B$3^3)) ∗(1 − EXP(−$B$3∗(E3 − $D$3)))^2
8				$d(t,T)$	= EXP(E7)∗EXP(−$B$5∗E5)
9				$\sigma(t,T)$	= ($B$4/($B$3∗(E3 − $D$3))) ∗(1 − EXP(−$B$3∗(E3 − $D$3)))
10				Vasieck	= (−LN(E8)/(E3))∗100

6.3 Cox Ingersoll and Ross (1985)

Cox Ingersoll and Ross (1985) proposed the following interest rate process.

$$dr = \alpha(\gamma - r)dt + \sigma\sqrt{r}dz \qquad (6.8)$$

Notice that the Cox Ingersoll and Ross (hereafter CIR) interest rate process *is* the Vasicek process except that the volatility σ is multiplied by the square root of the short rate. Therefore the parameters have the same interpretation. Specifically, the term dr refers to an infinitesimally small change in the short rate of interest. The first term is the drift, referring to the amount by which the short rate will change in an infinitesimally small unit of time dt. Again, it is measured as the distance between the long run mean or central tendency of the short rate γ and the current (known) short rate of interest r multiplied by the speed of mean reversion α. The second term is the volatility structure. Rather than being generated by a binomial structure, the model generates constant volatility σ, multiplied by the square root of the short rate, as increments in a Wiener process dz.

---

[1] We use (5.7) rather than (6.3) to measure the spot zero coupon yield curve as they generate the same results but (5.7) is simpler. However, (6.3) is more general. For example, (6.3) can be used to compute the Vasicek generated forward curve. We include (5.7) and (6.3) in the workbook EvolB02.xls.

After proposing this process CIR, just like Vasicek, applies the standard mathematical routine to find the pricing equation for zero coupon bonds.

The resulting expressions for zero coupon bond prices and the resulting continuously compounded yields are

$$d(t,T) = A(t,T)exp^{-rB(t,T)} \qquad (6.2)$$

$$Y(t,T) = \frac{ln[A(t,T)]}{T-t} + \frac{B(t-T)}{T-t} \qquad (6.3)$$

Notice that we have simply repeated the Vasicek equations for the zero coupon bond price and its corresponding continuously compounded yield. The differences between CIR and Vasicek show up in the sub-equations that define the terms in (6.2) and (6.3).

$$A[(t,T)] = \left(\frac{\phi_1 \, exp^{\phi_2(T-t)}}{\phi_2(exp^{\phi_1(T-t)} - 1) + \phi_1} \right)^{\phi_3} \qquad (6.9)$$

$$B[(t,T)] = \left(\frac{exp^{\phi_1(T-t)} - 1}{\phi_2(exp^{\phi_1(T-t)} - 1) + \phi_1} \right) \qquad (6.10)$$

$$\phi_1 \equiv \sqrt{\alpha^2 + 2\sigma^2} \qquad (6.11)$$

$$\phi_2 \equiv \frac{(\alpha + \phi_1)}{2} \qquad (6.12)$$

$$\phi_3 \equiv \frac{2\alpha\gamma}{\sigma^2} \qquad (6.13)$$

Finally the term structure of local volatility $\sigma(t,T)$ is determined by the constant volatility σ, the square root of the short rate r and the subsidiary equation (6.10).

$$\sigma(t,T) = \frac{\sigma\sqrt{r}}{T-t}B(t,T) \qquad (6.14)$$

The main advantage of CIR is that by multiplying the constant volatility by the square root of the short rate in the stochastic process (6.8), the generated short rate can never go negative. Unlike Vasicek this innovation forces the volatility term structure to shift upwards as the short interest rate increases. Otherwise the model shares the same advantages and disadvantages of Vasicek. Specifically, the model explicitly incorporates mean reversion and is consistent with no arbitrage. However, it still contains a constant volatility as represented by the constant parameter σ so the term structure of local volatilities changes in a restrictive manner. Like Vasicek, the central tendency of the short rate γ and the speed of mean reversion α must be estimated from the historical behaviour of interest rates and only the short rate r and volatility σ can be obtained by market traded instruments.

6.3.1 Implementing CIR

Refer to workbook EvolB02.xls, spreadsheet CIR for our implementation of CIR. We show the numerical results in Table 6.3 and the formulas in Table 6.4. To start we need estimates for the short rate r, the volatility σ, the central tendency of the short rate γ and the speed of mean reversion α. Like Vasicek we choose to implement CIR on July 29, 2002. We use the same short rate of interest, one-year cap volatility and the central tendency of the short rate of 1.3822%, 4.48% and 6.0618% respectively. Again we could not easily estimate the speed of mean reversion, so we simply used the same mean reversion estimate that we used for Vasicek. This is not very fair to CIR but this should not matter, as the purpose of this exercise is simply to illustrate the workings of the model. Of course, better parameter estimates will give you better results.

We first look at the numerical results in Table 6.3.

Table 6.3   CIR – numerical example

	A	B	C	D	E	F	G	H	I
1	Parameters			Pure Discount	Bond Price				
2	γ	0.060618	dt	0.083333					
3	α	0.51156	t	0	0.083333	0.166667	0.25	0.333333	0.416667
4	σ	0.0448							
5	r	0.013822		theta1	0.515468	0.515468	0.515468	0.515468	0.515468
6				theta2	0.513514	0.513514	0.513514	0.513514	0.513514
7				theta3	30.90097	30.90097	30.90097	30.90097	30.90097
8				$B(t,T)$	0.081582	0.159758	0.234669	0.306452	0.375235
9				$A(t,T)$	0.999894	0.999581	0.999071	0.998372	0.997493
10				$d(t,T)$	0.998767	0.997376	0.995836	0.994152	0.992333
11				$\sigma(t,T)$	0.005156	0.005049	0.004944	0.004842	0.004743
12				CIR	1.480587	1.576173	1.669094	1.759431	1.847266

Table 6.3 shows the zero coupon bond price and the corresponding zero yield curve implied by our parameter choices for the first five months. The block E3 to I12 shows the calculations. Rows 5 to 9 are the subsidiary equations (6.11), (6.12), (6.13), (6.10) and (6.9) whereas rows 10 and 11 are the prices of the zero coupon bond (6.2) and the term structure of volatility (6.14). Finally, the last row is the zero coupon yield curve implied by CIR that is found using (5.7).

In Table 6.4 we show the details of the calculations.

6.4 Other evolutionary models

Vasicek (1977) and Cox Ingersoll and Ross (1985) are representative of the best of the one factor evolutionary models that give us

Table 6.4 CIR – formulas

	A	B	C	D	E
1	Parameters				
2	γ	0.06061800	*dt*	= 1/12	
3	α	0.51155983	*t*	0	= D3 + (1*$D$2)
4	σ	0.0448			
5	r	= E15/100		theta1	= ($B$3^2 + 2*$B$4^2)^0.5
6				theta2	= ($B$3 + $E$5)/2
7				theta3	= (2*$B$3*$B$2)/$B$4^2
8				$B(t,T)$	= (EXP($E$5*(E3 − $D$3)) − 1) /($E$6*(EXP($E$5*(E3 − $D$3)) − 1) + $E$5)
9				$A(t,T)$	= (($E$5*EXP($E$6*(E3 − $D$3))) /($E$6*(EXP($E$5*(E3 − $D$3)) − 1) +$E$5))^$E$7
10				$d(t,T)$	= E9*EXP(−E8*$B$5)
11				$\sigma(t,T)$	= ($B$4*($B$5^0.5)/(E3 − $D$3))*E8
12				CIR	= (−LN(E10)/E3)*100

a flavour for the potential of this approach. Following component analysis studies which seek to discover the number of factors necessary to describe the variation of yields included in the term structure (see Nelson and Schaefer 1983, Litterman and Scheinkman 1991 and Steely 1997), a consensus emerged that two and possibly three factors are required to model the term structure of interest rates. This led to the development of two and three factor evolutionary models of interest rates. An example of a two factor model is Brennan and Schwartz (1979) who propose a two factor model where the first factor is the short rate and the second factor is the long rate of interest. An example of a three factor model is Ioannides (2000) who proposes a model where the first and second factors are the short and long rate of interest and the third factor is the stochastic market price of risk. There are many more models.

6.5 Comparing the term structure consistent and evolutionary models

Evolutionary models have not been popular with practitioners. Instead they show much more interest in the term structure consistent approach. This begs the question why and the answer turns on the practitioner's judgement as to which approach has the 'worst' flaw.

Evolutionary models attempt to model the behaviour of the term structure through time. However, it is unable to replicate the existing zero coupon term structure of interest rates. This means that evolutionary models cannot agree with known prices of market traded bonds. As an illustration, consider Figure 6.1, which plots the estimated term structure of interest rates as of July 29, 2002 with the term structures generated by our examples of Vasicek and CIR.

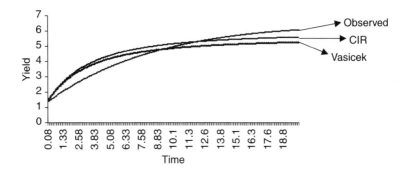

Figure 6.1   'Calibrated' CIR and Vasicek yield curves: mean reversion = 51.2%

Notice that in this case Vasicek and CIR are almost identical where Vasicek is the lower curve of the two, but both cannot replicate the term structure of interest rates that we estimated from actual bond prices using the Nelson and Siegel interpolation scheme. This is the best we can do, because we 'calibrated' the mean reversion parameter to minimize squared errors between the generated Vasicek yields and the actual term structure yields. Again we note that this is hardly fair to Vasicek and CIR but the point being made is that in general evolutionary models generate their own yield curves without reference to actual market price generated yield curves. Therefore in general evolutionary models do not agree with the actual market yield curve.

Meanwhile term structure consistent models replicate the existing sovereign term structure of interest rates. However, it does not match the term structure next period. This is because the model is calibrated to today's sovereign term structure but makes no attempt to model how the term structure may change next period. In the very next period the calibrated model will not price market traded bonds correctly. The model has to be recalibrated period by period.

Therefore the main difference between an evolutionary and a calibrated term structure consistent model is this. The calibrated model uses information from the existing sovereign term structure to price securities but does not explicitly model the evolution of the term structure of interest rates. Evolutionary models model the evolution of the term structure of interest rates, but cannot replicate the existing term structure of interest rates.

6.5.1 The seriousness of these problems from the practitioner's perspective

Suppose you price a bond option based on the term structure consistent approach. Let's say the model underestimates mean reversion, which has the effect of overestimating future volatility. The bond option will be priced correctly *today*, but by the next period when the incorrectly modelled mean reversion results in lower actual volatility, the bond option will turn out to have a lower than modelled price. This will become evident when you recalibrate the model in the next period. In other words, it is likely that the derivative prices you obtain from term structure consistent models are biased. However, if you know the direction of this price bias and we think there is an upward bias, then at least you can correct for the worst of this bias in the prices you quote based on accumulated trading experience.

The main problem with evolutionary models is that they replicate existing bond prices only approximately. But what is worse is that when you attempt to price options written on these bonds, these errors are magnified. Remember that a position in an option is a highly levered position on a portion of the payoff from the underlying security. Therefore small errors in pricing the underlying translate into large errors in pricing the derivative.

Practitioners, in the main, have favoured the term structure consistent approach. Practitioners favour these models because they ask themselves, how can I trust an evolutionary model to give me the correct price for a derivative (say an interest rate cap) when I can see that the model gives me the wrong price for the underlying security (a bond)? Meanwhile there is some hope that the term structure consistent approach is useful since it is at least consistent with today's known sovereign term structure. So they look for a term structure consistent model that has all the desirable characteristics, mean reversion (central tendency), a term structure of volatility, no negative interest rates and so on.

But that is not to say that the evolutionary model approach is useless, for each model has a purpose. Therefore we need to examine the advantages and disadvantages of the term structure consistent and evolutionary models in some detail.

6.5.1.1 Data availability

The advantage goes to the term structure consistent models on this point. From Chapter 3, we realize that the term structure consistent models use market data as inputs so at least in well-developed debt markets we should be able to implement these models. For evolutionary models we have a problem here because the model requires historical information for the value of parameters such as mean reversion. Often historical information only proxy for the 'true' factor that you wish to measure. This leads to two problems.

1. Historical data in general and proxy variables in particular may be subject to measurement error. Given that evolutionary models are typically implemented via regression techniques, this means you may have biased and inconsistent coefficient estimates.
2. You will always have a trade-off between choosing a longer time series of historical information (the longer the time series, the better the efficiency of estimates) and the concern that the older the data, the less relevant it is for future use. For example, you would have met this trade-off before when you were concerned with estimating betas in CAPM. Typically it is suggested that if you are using monthly data, a time series of 60 data points is about right.

6.5.1.2 Errors in market data

Obviously this is a problem for term structure consistent models rather than evolutionary models since evolutionary models do not rely much on market data. However, recall that in Chapter 3 we were careful to develop strategies to reduce the likelihood and severity of errors in estimating sovereign (and corporate) yield curves. Therefore a careful application of these strategies should allow for reasonably accurate implementation of calibrated models at least for well-developed debt markets.

6.5.1.3 Strategies

It is on this dimension that we see the practical trade-off between term structure consistent and evolutionary models. When attempting to make 'yield curve bets', you are essentially looking for incorrectly priced bonds. Ideally the incorrectly priced bond should be a reasonably liquid bond so that you can easily buy and sell according to whether your model signals that the bond is under- or overpriced. Unfortunately, the term structure consistent models are useless for this type of strategy because it is precisely these bonds that are used to estimate the sovereign yield curve. Our model is then calibrated to this yield curve so the model will, by construction, very closely replicate the bond's price. The calibrated model will then be incapable of signalling that the bond is incorrectly priced.

In contrast, evolutionary models are ideally suited for yield curve bet strategies. First, these models do not take the existing yield curve, and therefore the prices of reasonably liquid bonds, as given. Therefore they are capable of finding incorrectly priced bonds.

However, term structure consistent models should be more reliable in finding incorrectly priced interest rate derivatives. Recall that calibrated models make sure that the model closely replicates the value of the underlying bond, so it can say that relative to the value of the underlying, the interest rate derivative price is wrong. Clearly you can take advantage of this by delta hedging and the model will give you the appropriate hedge ratios.

In contrast the evolutionary model cannot clearly signal that the derivative is incorrectly priced. Rather, quite often the evolutionary model will signal that both the underlying and the derivative are incorrectly priced. It would take a leap of faith to hedge (say delta hedge) in this context because essentially you would be betting that the derivative is not correctly priced so you should attempt to buy or sell the derivative, but the underlying is correctly priced so you can delta hedge. In a sense you are making two bets, first that the model is correct in signalling that the derivative is incorrectly priced, and second that the model is wrong in signalling that the underlying is incorrectly priced.

6.6 The problem with interest rate (and credit risk) modelling

One point that should be made clear is that finance has not settled on one model of stochastic interest rates that serves as a standard upon which all other models are judged. Such is not the case in equity option pricing where the Black-Scholes model serves as a kind of benchmark. This is happening for debt instruments because interest rates are a 'non-traded asset'. What precisely does this mean? We need to look more carefully at the replicating portfolios that underlie the 'arbitrage-free' arguments that drive the term structure consistent and evolutionary models.

The 'non-traded asset' nature of interest rates can be most clearly seen if we look at the replicating portfolio that underlies the term structure consistent approach. Recall that the replicating portfolio consists of all possible state securities that pay off at a particular date in time. Each state security pays off only if a unique interest rate occurs at that date, and all other state securities will not pay anything. However, we are guaranteed that one of the state securities in the replicating portfolio will pay off because each state security is associated with a particular interest rate level and the replicating portfolio has all possible state securities and therefore all possible interest rates that may occur at maturity of the replicating portfolio. Since the replicating portfolio replicates the cash flow structure of a £1 face value zero that matures at the same date, the price and therefore the yield of the replicating portfolio must equal the price and therefore the yield of the zero coupon bond. The empirical weakness in this argument is that these state securities do not trade, so we do not have any observable state security prices.

The practical importance is that each model will generate its own unique set of state security prices. For example, compare the Ho and Lee and BDTCV state security prices. They are different. This cannot be right because the two models will give different prices to the same interest rate sensitive security and there can be only one price. The state security price trees are different because each model has a different interest rate process that will in turn generate a different interest rate and the corresponding state security price tree. This suggests that the replicating portfolio is unique only with respect to a particular interest rate process. So which interest rate process should we use? We need to empirically test the models to see which one agrees with actual state security prices. Only the problem is, these state securities do not exist so we have no direct test of the interest rate model.

A second line of attack is to see whether the interest rate model can replicate the price of market traded interest rate derivatives. Here the problem is that these derivatives trade over the counter wherever stale prices and inaccurate quotes, even if prices are available, are the rule rather than the exception. Hence it is very difficult to empirically verify the 'best' interest rate model.

Overall this means that we cannot work out precisely the true stochastic process that the underlying risk variable, the term structure of interest rates (not just the short interest rate), follows. This is not a problem for regular equity options since the equity of a particular firm represents just one asset that, if it trades frequently, is easy to track and model and then empirically verify that the model replicates market prices.

Consequently we have to make our guess as to what the stochastic process that governs the term structure of interest rates should look like. Perhaps just a one factor model is sufficient where the single factor is the short-term rate of interest since long rates are nothing more than the evolution of a sequence of short rates. Maybe the short rate has stochastic volatility caused by the absorption of new information, so we need a two factor model where the short rate plus stochastic short rate volatility are the two factors. Or may be we should try to model the whole yield curve via a three factor model where the extra third factor is the long-term (10 years?) interest rate. And of course we can think of other candidates for factors in a one factor, two factor or three factor model. So it should come to you as no surprise that we have developed *dozens* of interest rate models. Each and every one of them is equally theoretically valid as they are all arbitrage free. But they are arbitrage free only with respect to the assumed underlying stochastic process.

6.6.1 So which model is best?

Here is a hard truth. All models are false; some are useful. Obviously the best way to judge a model's usefulness is how accurate are the prices obtained by the model. What we would like to do is to test the model to see how well it replicates prices next period. However, this is difficult to do since interest rate derivatives are traded over the counter, so we do not have a reliable time series of information that we can use to test the models. For the testing that has been done, we see that most models do perform well under one set of circumstances, but in another, they perform poorly. For example, for short-term interest rate derivatives, Ho and Lee (1986) performs reasonably well, even though this is the most primitive of models. In other words, we cannot say which model is 'best'. Interest rate modelling is an active area of research in finance, so determining the 'best' model is very much 'work in progress'. Welcome to the frontier.

6.7 Non-stochastic credit risk models

In this section we intend to review the early development of credit risk modelling starting with the simple, non-stochastic credit risk models of the 1970s. In the next section this will lead up to Jarrow and Turnbull (1995), the first term structure consistent credit risk model, and Duffie and Singleton (1999). It is hoped that this approach will expose the reader to the challenges of and potential solutions to the modelling of credit risk. We will end this chapter with a brief review of alternative academic and practitioner credit risk models.

6.7.1   Bierman and Hass (1975)

To start, let us consider a zero coupon corporate bond that *promises* to pay \$1 next period. At maturity, the bond may survive with probability P but then again it may default with probability $(1 - P)$. These events are mutually exclusive, so the probabilities must add up to 1. That is $P + (1 - P) = 1$.

Consider the case that the probability of survival P is constant but each period represents a new trial where the zero may default, or survive. This means that the probability of survival declines with time. For example, say the probability of survival in any one period is 90%, then in two periods the probability of survival is 81% ($P^2 = 81\%$) and for 40 periods it is 1.48% ($P^{40} = 1.48\%$). Meanwhile the probability of default (or hazard rate) is increasing. For two periods the probability of default is 19% ($1 - P^2 = 19\%$) and for 40 periods it is 98.52% ($1 - P^{40} = 98.52\%$). In other words, given enough time (or trials) a corporate bond *will* default. Notice that the above structure suggests that credit risk increases with time, which is in accordance with the empirical findings of Johnson (1967) for at least high credit quality bonds (see section 2.5).

The above suggests that we can find the value of a corporate bond in two ways, discount promised values using a default risk adjusted discount rate (6.15) or discount default risk adjusted cash flows using a default risk-free discount rate (6.16).

$$b_c = \frac{1}{(1 + r_c)} \tag{6.15}$$

$$b_c = \frac{1 \times P}{(1 + r)} \tag{6.16}$$

Note that b_c is today's value of a corporate zero, r_c is the default risk adjusted discount rate and r is the default risk-free sovereign zero coupon yield. Since these two expressions are equivalent, we can equate them and solve for the implied probability of survival.

$$\frac{P}{(1 + r)} = \frac{1}{(1 + r_c)}$$

So

$$P = \frac{(1 + r)}{(1 + r_c)} \tag{6.17}$$

Equation (6.17) suggests that as the credit spreads, the positive difference between r_c and r increases, the above ratio declines so the probability of survival declines. This is what we would expect. If we observe that the credit spread between, say, the AA yield curve and the Treasury yield curve was increasing, we would expect that credit risk is increasing because the likelihood of default was increasing and therefore the probability of survival was decreasing.

Note that the probability of survival P above is actually a downwardly biased estimate of the true probability of survival. This happens because default risk is a systematic risk so investors require a risk premium. To obtain this they 'underprice' the corporate zero below its true expected value by underestimating the probability of survival. Fons (1987) solved the credit spread for the implied probability of default and found that the implied probability of default was larger than actual default experience, implying that investors demand and receive a risk premium for accepting credit risk. More recently Elton et al. (2001) find that investment grade credit spreads can in part be explained by a credit risk premium.

Equation (6.17) presumes that in the event of default, the amount recovered is zero. This is rarely the case. Over long periods of time (25 years or more) Altman and Kishore (1999) find that there is tremendous variation among recovery rates δ for different defaulted bonds. As we would hope, they find that bonds with higher original ratings and bonds that are secured and/or senior rather than unsecured/junior tend to have higher recovery rates. However, the average recovery rate of all domestic US corporate bonds is approximately 40%. This of course means that the amount lost given default (intensity of default, $1 - \delta$) averaged 60%.

Bierman and Hass (1975) were the first to consider the impact of recovery rates as determinates of the credit spread. Their one period model incorporates the recovery rate δ in (6.16) above such that the expected value from a one period $1 face value zero is $P + (1 - P)\delta$. In other words, if the bond survives with probability P, the bond investors receive the promised $1. If, however, the bond defaults with probability $(1 - P)$, then the bond investor receives a fraction δ of the promised $1. Then this expected value is discounted back to the present using the pure interest rate r. Mathematically this expression is

$$b_c = \frac{P + (1 - P)\delta}{(1 + r)} \tag{6.18}$$

As in (6.17) above, this means we have two ways to value the corporate zero, either discount promised cash flows using a credit risk adjusted interest rate or discount credit risk adjusted expected cash flows, specifically $P + (1 - P)\delta$, at a credit risk-free interest rate. Mathematically this statement is as follows.

$$\frac{1}{(1 + r_c)} = \frac{P + (1 - P)\delta}{(1 + r)} \tag{6.19}$$

Solving (6.19) for the corporate interest rate we have

$$r_c = \frac{(1 + r)}{P + (1 - P)\delta} - 1 \tag{6.20}$$

We can see that (6.20) makes sense if we evaluate the behaviour of the model as key parameters change. If $P = 1$, then the corporate bond is not subject to credit risk. Notice the denominator collapses to 1 since $(1 - P) = 0$ and the plus and minus 1 cancel so we are left with $r_c = r$. This is what we should expect, for if the corporate bond was not subject to credit risk it should have the same yield as the sovereign bond. Similarly, if the recovery rate was 1 (or 100%), the denominator collapses to 1 since $P + (1 + P) = 1$ and the ones cancel, so we are again left with $r_c = r$. Again this makes sense, for if the bond defaults yet the bondholder receives the full \$1 promised amount then default is really a non-event. This means that Bierman and Hass models credit risk only and gives no consideration to other factors such as liquidity or reinvestment risk. Specifically there is no adjustment for the fact that upon default the investors are forced to reinvest recovery amounts at possibly low interest rates and pay transactions costs in the process of doing so.

We also find that the behaviour of the model is reasonable as, one by one, the recovery rate δ and then the probability of survival P decreases from 1. Notice that as P decreases, the denominator becomes smaller so the corporate yield r_c must become larger. This is what we should expect because as the probability of survival decreases, the bond is more credit risky and should require a higher promised yield to compensate for the higher credit risk. Similarly as the recovery rate decreases the denominator becomes smaller, so the corporate yield r_c must become larger. Again this is what we should expect because as the recovery rate decreases more is lost if the bond defaults. Therefore the bond is more credit risky and should require a higher promised yield to compensate for the higher credit risk.

6.7.2 Jonkhart (1979)

Bierman and Hass (1975) is extremely simple as it is a one period, non-stochastic credit risk model. Jonkhart (1979) makes an important contribution as he extends Bierman and Hass in a multiperiod framework. From our perspective, the Jonkhart model is interesting because the framework he establishes points the way for us to incorporate stochastic interest rates and stochastic credit risk in a multiperiod framework. The Jonkhart model finds the value of a coupon bearing, $1 face value corporate bond as follows.

$$B_c = \sum_{t=1}^{n} \left[\frac{[P_{t0}R_n + (1 - P_t)\delta_t] \left(\prod_{j=n-t}^{n-1} P_j \right)}{(1 + {}_0r_t)^t} \right] + \frac{\prod_{t=1}^{n} P_t}{(1 + {}_0r_n)^n} \quad (6.21)$$

Note that B_c is the value today of the $1 face value bond that pays a fixed coupon of ${}_0R_n$ each date t. At date t the bond may survive with probability P_t and pay the coupon. Then again, the bond may fail to pay the coupon with default probability $(1 - P_t)$. In that case the bond will default and the bond will terminate early. The investor will recover a fraction of the $1 promised face value δ_t instead where the recovery fraction may differ period by period. Notice that the probabilities of survival and default are conditional probabilities because default is an absorbing state. That is, if the bond defaults all subsequent coupons are not paid since the bond is terminated early. Therefore in order for the bond to default, say in the third period, it must have survived in the first two periods. So what we need is a probability of survival at date t conditioned upon its ability to survive all prior periods $t - 1$. This is the reason why we include the multiplicative expression at the end of the first term in (6.21). This means that the probability of survival at date t inside the second square brackets of the first term P_t is multiplied by all prior probabilities of survival as shown in the multiplicative term, so in total the probability of receiving a given coupon ${}_0R_n$ at date t depends upon the ability of the bond to survive the current period and all prior periods. The final term in (6.21) recognizes that the bond may survive all dates until maturity and pay the final redemption amount of $1. Again notice that this $1 amount is multiplied by the sequence of one period probabilities of survival because in order to make the final redemption payment the bond must survive the current period and all prior periods.

No doubt a numerical example will help. Suppose we have a three-year, 12% annual coupon pay single B bond. The bond may survive the first period with probability $P_1 = 0.995$, the second period $P_2 = 0.99$ and the third period $P_3 = 0.985$. If the bond defaults, we assume that the recovery fraction δ is constant at 40%. The underlying zero coupon yield curve is flat at 5%, that is ${}_0r_1 = {}_0r_2 = {}_0r_3 = 5\%$. Substituting the appropriate values into (6.21) we obtain a value of $1.17.

$$B_c = \left[\frac{[(0.995)(0.12) + (1 - 0.995)0.4](1)}{(1 + 0.05)^1}\right]$$

$$+ \left[\frac{[(0.99)(0.12) + (1 - 0.99)0.4](1 \times 0.995)}{(1 + 0.05)^2}\right]$$

$$+ \left[\frac{[(0.985)(0.12) + (1 - 0.985)0.4](1 \times 0.995 \times 0.99)}{(1 + 0.05)^3}\right]$$

$$+ \frac{1 \times 0.995 \times 0.99 \times 0.985}{(1 + 0.05)^3}$$

$$B_c = 0.115619 + 0.110826 + 0.105685 + 0.838159$$

$$= \$1.170289$$

Another way to appreciate how the Jonkhart model works is to simply count up all possible scenarios, value them and then add them up. This is what the above numerical example does. Notice that in the first period, the bond may survive or default. In any event, the bond must have survived the earlier period, which must be with a probability of 1 because when the bond was issued, it was not in default. Then we add together the survival and default values, multiply the result by all possible prior probabilities of survival (1 in this case) and discount the result back at the one-year zero coupon rate, 5% in this case. Then we do precisely the same for the second period. The bond may survive or default in the second period. In any event, the bond must have survived the earlier period, which must be with a probability of 1 times 0.995 because when the bond was issued, it was not in default and it must have survived the first period in order to survive (or default) in the second period. Then we add together the survival and default values, multiply the result by all possible prior probabilities of survival (1 × 0.995 in this case) and discount the result back at the two-year zero coupon rate, 5% in this case. We do the same for the third period. Finally, the only remaining scenario is whether the bond pays back its final redemption amount of $1. This depends upon the bond's ability to survive all three periods, so we multiply $1 by all prior probabilities of survival (1×0.995×0.99×0.985 in this instance) and then discount this value back three periods at the prevailing three-year zero coupon interest rate. Notice that at this last stage we do not need to worry about the possibility that the bond may not pay back the final redemption amount for earlier periods as all the default scenarios are accounted for in the earlier period-by-period scenarios.

Perhaps the most interesting aspect of Jonkhart is that it sets a framework that helps us understand a large fraction of the credit risk models that have been developed in recent years as it exposes the issues those interested in modelling credit risk must face. First, we note the potential of extending the Jonkhart model by recognizing that the zero coupon term structure $_0r_t$ can be modelled and inserted directly from any given stochastic interest rate model, be it Vasicek or Black Derman and Toy. Therefore it should be possible to generalize a Jonkhart type model to incorporate stochastic interest rates. Once this is done, however, a generalized (for stochastic interest rates) version of (6.21) raises the following issues.

1. Is credit risk stochastic? In other words, do one or both of the parameters P_t and δ_t have a variance? If they do have a variance then we need to insert some stochastic process be it a binomial or some evolutionary Wiener generated process for P_t and/or δ_t, in the generalized form of (6.21).
2. If credit risk is stochastic then what is the relationship between credit risk as summarized by the parameters P_t and δ_t and interest rate risk as summarized by the parameters $_0r_t$? We need to add some degree of correlation between the credit risk parameters and the interest rate parameters.
3. The Jonkhart model suggests that a bond either defaults or survives and there are no intermediate states. However, we may argue that the default process is more complex where the bond moves through a series of credit downgrades as unfavourable information is released before the bond defaults. This suggests that we can extend the non-stochastic binomial process suggested by Jonkhart into a transition matrix type stochastic process where we could have a number of intermediate credit rating states prior to the absorbing default state.
4. Is default an absorbing state? If not then this suggests that we should use a default process where the recovery fraction paid in the event of default could be in the form of another defaultable security where further defaults are possible.

Finance has only recently begun to explore these issues. One of the first models that started this process is Jarrow and Turnbull (1995).

6.8 Jarrow and Turnbull (1995)

Jarrow and Turnbull (1995, hereafter JT) can be implemented as a term structure consistent credit risk model that can use any underlying pure (credit risk-free) interest rate process. Default risk is modelled as a residual from the credit spread. Specifically they assume that the recovery rate δ is constant and the probability of survival P is calibrated to the credit spread. In other words, there is no specific credit risk process since the probability of survival is simply a calibration parameter. The correlation between credit risk as summarized by the probability of survival P and the sovereign term structure of interest rates is zero. There are no intermediate credit risk states as the bond either survives or defaults and default is an absorbing state. Nevertheless the model they establish can be, and indeed soon after was, extended to relax many of these restrictive assumptions.

For the binomial implementation of the JT, we insert credit risk as a second binomial within the pure interest rate process. To see precisely what this means refer to Figure 6.2.

Figure 6.2   JT credit and interest rate process as a double binomial

In the first period, interest rates may rise or fall. This is depicted in Figure 6.2 as the two main branches emanating from the first node. Since survival S or default D has no correlation with interest rates, then either credit event can happen no matter which branch the interest rate process follows. This is depicted in Figure 6.2 as the two sub-branches, one that ends in survival S and another that ends in default D, that each emanate from the two main (interest rate) branches. In other words, JT superimposes a credit risk event binomial onto the interest rate binomial process.

Furthermore note that the double binomial forms a recombining tree. For example, if the bond experiences an up- and then a downtick in interest rates and survives both periods, the result is the same if the bond experiences a down- and then an uptick in interest rates and again survives both periods. Although not obvious in Figure 6.2, the same is true in the default states. That is the bond will have the same value if it experiences an up- and then a downtick in interest rates and then defaults in the second period when the bond experiences a down- then an uptick in interest rates and defaults in the second period.

We can write the JT version of the corporate state security price $C(n,i)$ that *promises* to pay $1 at maturity if a particular interest rate evolves, otherwise it pays nothing, as

$$C(n,i) = \left[\sum_{t=1}^{n} [(1 - P_t)\delta] \left(\prod_{j=1}^{n} P_j \right) + \prod_{t=1}^{n} P_t \right] \times S(n,i) \qquad (6.22)$$

Here the term $S(n,i)$ is the value of the credit risk-free state security price that will pay \$1 if interest rate state i occurs at date n and pays nothing otherwise. This term adjusts the corporate state security $C(n,i)$ for interest rate risk and the time value of money. Notice that the term in square brackets is the numerator of Jonkhart (6.21) adjusted for zero coupon bonds and so this is the term that adjusts the corporate state security for credit risk. This separation between the credit risk adjustment and the interest and time value of money adjustment terms is possible because JT assumes that the correlation between credit and interest rate risk is zero.

Equation (6.22) shows that an easy way to implement JT is to take the state security prices generated by any pure interest rate process be it BDT, Ho and Lee or Hull and White, and then adjust these state securities for credit risk via a Jonkhart type credit risk process. This is what we intend to do. Procedurally the first step is to calibrate the pure interest rate process, say BDT, to the sovereign term structure of interest rates. Then we calibrate the one period probability of survival P_t such that the price and therefore the zero yield of replicating portfolios of corporate state securities agree with the zero yields included in the corporate yield curve that we estimate via the methods of Chapter 3. This is possible because in (6.22) the recovery fraction δ is constant. This means that there is only one unknown time dependent parameter P_t, so with one additional piece of information, namely the corporate zero coupon yield, we can solve for that survival rate P_t that generates a replicating portfolio of corporate state securities that replicates the yield included in the corporate yield curve.

6.8.1 Implementing JT

The workbook that we use to implement JT is JTB02.xls. The first spreadsheet is BDT which is the same spreadsheet contained in the workbook BDTB02.xls that we used to implement BDT in Chapter 5. We will not discuss this spreadsheet as a complete discussion is contained in section 5.4.1.

A numerical example of JT is reported in Table 6.5 and the formulas are contained in Table 6.6. The first three rows report the time step dt, recovery fraction δ and the calibrated one period probabilities of survival P. Rows 5, 7 and 9 are building blocks that build up to the default risk adjusted expected values reported in row 11. These expected values are the separable credit risk adjustment contained inside the square brackets of (6.22). The block A12 to F18 is the corporate state security tree. Notice that replicating portfolios of corporate state securities add up, in row 19, to corporate zero coupon bond prices the yield of which, reported in row 20, agrees with the zero yields that underlie the corporate yield curve reported in row 21.

Table 6.5　Jarrow and Turnbull – numerical example

	A	B	C	D	E	F
1	*dt*	0.5				
2	δ	0.6				
3	*P*	0.979715	0.98621	0.992307	0.993509	0.998858
4		Survival Vector				
5	$P \times P$	0.979715	0.966205	0.958771	0.952548	0.951461
6		Maturity Default-expected values				
7	$P + (1 - P)\delta$	0.991886	0.994484	0.996923	0.997404	0.999543
8		Default Tree-Expected Values				
9	$(1 - P)\delta$	0.012171	0.008274	0.004616	0.003894	0.000685
10	Expected values					
11	$P \times P + \Sigma(1 - P)\delta \times P \times P$	0.991886	0.986482	0.983509	0.981019	0.980584
12		State Price Tree				
13						0.026424
14					0.054543	0.132135
15				0.112635	0.218198	0.264301
16			0.232679	0.337944	0.327335	0.264332
17		0.481199	0.465405	0.337983	0.218248	0.132181
18	1	0.481199	0.232726	0.112674	0.054568	0.026439
19		0.962398	0.93081	0.901235	0.872892	0.845813
20	Implied Yield	7.665428	7.170021	6.932602	6.797146	6.698265
21	Observed Yield	7.665428	7.170021	6.932602	6.797146	6.698265
22	Time Step	1	2	3	4	5

The JT spreadsheet formulas contained in Table 6.6 show that once the expected values are calculated it is trivial to calculate the corporate state security price. All that is necessary to calculate the corporate state security price is to multiply the pure interest state security price $S(n,i)$ generated by BDT in spreadsheet BDT! by the expected value generated in row 11. This procedure is in strict accordance with (6.22). Therefore key to the understanding of the implementation of JT are the expected values reported in row 11.

It is best to understand the calculation of the expected values by recognizing that all this calculation does is to add together the payoffs from all possible survival and default scenarios. For example, look

Table 6.6 Jarrow and Turnbull-Formulas

	A	B	C	D	E
1	dt	0.5			
2	δ	0.6			
3	P	0.979714895789365	0.986210047971719	0.9923066403741	0.993509440892295
4		Survival Vector			
5	P×P	=B3	=B5*C3	=C5*D3	=D5*E3
6		Maturity Default-expected values			
7	P + (1 − P)δ	=(B$3 + (1 − B$3)*$B$2)	=(C$3 + (1 − C$3)*$B$2)	=(D$3 + (1 − D$3)*$B$2)	=(E$3 + (1 − E$3)*$B$2)
8		Default Tree-Expected Values			
9	(1 − P)δ	=(1 − B$3)*$B$2	=(1 − C$3)*$B$2	=(1 − D$3)*$B$2	=(1 − E$3)*$B$2
10		Expected values			
11	P × P + ∑(1 − P)δ × P × P	=+B7	=(C$7*B$5 + $B$9)	=(D$7*C$5 + $B$9 + $C$9*$B$5)	=(E$7*D$5 + $B$9 + $C$9*$B$5 + $D$9*$C$5)
12		State Price Tree			
13					
14				=D$11*BDT!F54	=E$11*BDT!G53
15			=C$11*BDT!E55	=D$11*BDT!F55	=E$11*BDT!G54
16		=B$11*BDT!D56	=C$11*BDT!E56	=D$11*BDT!F56	=E$11*BDT!G55
17		=B$11*BDT!D57	=C$11*BDT!E57	=D$11*BDT!F57	=E$11*BDT!G56
18	1	=B18 + B17	=C18 + C17 + C16	=D18 + D17 + D16 + D15	=E$11*BDT!G57
19					=E18 + E17 + E16 + E15 + E14
20	Implied Yield	=−LN(B19)/($B$1*B22)*100	=−LN(C19)/($B$1*C22)*100	=−LN(D19)/($B$1*D22)*100	=−LN(E19)/($B$1*E22)*100
21	Observed Yield	=0.0766542793621718*100	=0.0717002145033969*100	=0.0693260223678709*100	=0.067971464784957*100

at the formula in cell F11 that reports the expected payoff from a corporate zero in five periods' time. The first term is F$7*E$5. F$7 is the one period expected value found in the numerator of Bierman and Hass $P + (1-P)\delta$ in (6.18). But we know from Jonkhart that in a multiperiod context, in order to make payoffs in five periods' time, the corporate zero must have survived the prior four periods. Therefore F$7 is multiplied by E$5, which is the survival vector that represents the sequence of the four prior periods' probability of survival, multiplied together. But this first term F$7*E$5 represents only one possible scenario, that the bond may survive the first four periods to default or pay off at maturity in five periods' time. The other possibilities are that the bond may default in four, three, two and one period's time. The remaining four terms in F11 are the expected payoffs from these four prior period default scenarios. For example, the next term is B$9. This is $(1 - P_1)\delta$, the payoff in period one should the bond default at the end of the first period. Notice that this term is not multiplied by the prior probability of survival (it is 1). Then the third term is $C$9*$B$5 which is the payoff in the event of default at the end of the second period $C$9 or $(1 - P_2)\delta$ multiplied by all prior probabilities of survival $B$5 or P_1. We do the same to calculate the expected values should the bond default at the end of the third $D$9*$C$5 and at the end of the fourth $E$9*$D$5 period. Therefore we see that F11 contains all possible expected payoffs from a five period corporate zero.

Similarly we calculate the expected value of the promise to pay $1 at the end of each period as the sum of the values of the expected amounts paid in the event of survival or default at maturity and in the event of default at all prior dates. The expected value for each time step is reported in row 11.

Once we have this expected value we multiply it by all pure interest rate state securities that mature at the end of the fifth period. We use the same credit risk adjustment F11 for all possible states at the end of the fifth period because there is zero correlation between the interest rate state that arrives and the credit event (default or survival at $t = 5$, or default in any prior time step) that occurs by the fifth time step. We do the same for all prior time steps. For example, E11 is multiplied by all the BDT generated state security prices that exist at the end of the fourth time step.

Therefore to calibrate the JT model, we first input a corporate yield curve that we estimate according to the methods of Chapter 3. We choose the solver routine found under the tools sub-menu. Select B18 as the target cell and click on maximize. The row B3 to F3 are the change cells. We add a constraint that row 20, cells B20 to F20, equals row 21, cells B21 to F21. This ensures that the corporate state security price tree outputs an implied yield curve that agrees with the actual market corporate yield curve. Then we click on solve. The probability of survival row 3 changes the expected values row 11 and the corporate state security price tree block B13 to F18. This continues until columns of corporate state security prices add up to a value of the synthetic corporate zero row 19 that obtains a zero yield row 20 that agrees with the input yield curve row 21.

6.8.2 Using the calibrated JT model

We can find the value of a corporate bond by backward induction using the credit risk adjusted discount factor tree. The latter is easily obtained by multiplying the underlying interest rate process's (BDT in this case) discount factor tree by the corresponding time period expected value. This will obtain the credit risk adjusted discount factor tree that we use to price a corporate bond by backward induction.

We employ the credit risk adjusted discount factor tree to price a 2.5-year 6% semi-annual coupon pay corporate bond when the corporate yield curve is as reported in row 21 in Table 6.5. The numerical results are reported in Table 6.7 and the formulas are reported in Table 6.8.

Table 6.7 The price of a 6% coupon, five-year corporate bond obtained by the JT model

	B	C	D	E	F	G
50	Corporate Price Tree (6% 5 Period Bond)					
51	Coupon	6				
52		0	1	2	3	4
53						97.90471
54					97.91977	97.90753
55				97.95652	97.92629	97.91034
56			98.13522	97.97009	97.93279	97.91316
57		98.12078	98.16787	97.98364	97.93929	97.91597

Notice that the price of this bond reported in Table 6.7 is much lower than the sovereign bond reported in Table 5.7. This is what we should expect given that this bond is subject to credit risk and so must offer a higher yield.

In Table 6.8 column F all the promised cash flows are multiplied by the expected value as well as the BDT discount factor. The former adjusts for credit risk and the latter for interest rate risk and the time value of money. For example, in cell F57 the promised cash flow of

Table 6.8 Formulas used to Price a Corporate Bond using JT

	B	C	D	E
50	Corporate Price Tree (6% 5 Period Bond)			
51	Coupon	6		
52	0	= B52 + 1	= C52 + 1	= D52 + 1
53				
54				=((F53 + F54)*0.5 + ($C$51/2)*E$11)*BDT!E30
55			=((E54 + E55)*0.5 + ($C$51/2)*D$11)*BDT!D31	=((F54 + F55)*0.5 + ($C$51/2)*E$11)*BDT!E31
56		=((D55 + D56)*0.5 + ($C$51/2)*C$11)*BDT!C32	=((E55 + E56)*0.5 + ($C$51/2)*D$11)*BDT!D32	=((F55 + F56)*0.5 + ($C$51/2)*E$11)*BDT!E32
57	=((C56 + C57)*0.5 + ($C$51/2)*B$11)*BDT!B33	=((D56 + D57)*0.5 + ($C$51/2)*C$11)*BDT!C33	=((E56 + E57)*0.5 + ($C$51/2)*D$11)*BDT!D33	=((F56 + F57)*0.5 + ($C$51/2)*E$11)*BDT!E33

principal 100 and the semi-annual coupon ($B$51)/2 is multiplied by the expected value F$11 and the BDT discount factor BDT!F33. In contrast in the next period column E only the promised coupon is multiplied by the expected value. The value of the bond next period found using the 50/50 rule is *not* multiplied by the expected value because the value of the bond next period has already been adjusted for credit risk in column F.

6.9 Duffie and Singleton (1999)

This model employs a different approach to modelling recoveries in the event of default than Jarrow and Turnbull (1995). Rather than defining the recovery rate as a fraction of a Treasury zero, Duffie and Singleton (1999) suggest that we model recovery amounts as a fraction of next period's *survival contingent* value of the corporate zero. The advantage of doing this is that then we can conveniently adjust the sovereign discount factor tree to the corresponding corporate discount factor tree where the credit risk adjustment enters as a multiplicative term. That way we can employ the credit risk adjusted discount factor tree to find the value of credit risky instruments using backward induction. Moreover, this formulation allows us to model corporate interest rates in the same way that we model sovereign interest rates.

Duffie and Singleton (1999) define the loss rate L as one minus the recovery amount. In turn this recovery amount is a fraction ω of the end of period survival contingent value of a $1 face value zero.[2] We describe this recovery amount as the return of market value. In contrast in Jarrow and Turnbull the recovery amount is a fraction of the promised amount reinvested in a Treasury zero for the remaining promised maturity. As an illustration, the loss rate for Duffie and Singleton for a two period corporate zero is

$$L_{t+1} = 1 - \{1 - (h_1 + h_2)\}\omega V_t \tag{6.23}$$

---

[2] Duffie and Singleton (1999) also propose a 'return of face value' (RF) recovery assumption. In this case the fractional loss L_t is simply a fraction of next period's promised amount or $(1 - \omega_t V_{t+1})$. There is little difference between the results obtained whether we use the RF or return of market (RM) recovery assumption because the amount recovered in the event of default under RM is simply the RF recovery amount multiplied by the probability of survival that usually is a number very close to 1. Therefore for the sake of brevity we omit mention of this in the main text.

Where h_1 and h_2 are the probabilities of default at the end of the first and second periods respectively, one minus the sum of these probabilities is the probability of survival, ω is the fraction of the corporate zero recovered in the event of default and V_t is the value of what the corporate zero would have been worth had it not defaulted or \$1 at $t = 2$. Together these terms measure the recovery amount as a fraction ω of the end of period survival contingent amount or $\{1 - (h_1 + h_2)\}V_t$. Then one minus this term is the amount lost in the event of default.

The main advantage of this formulation of the loss rate is that we can define a discount factor subject to credit risk as the sovereign discount factor multiplied by a credit risk adjustment. Assuming a zero correlation between interest rates and credit risk the corresponding one period state contingent corporate discount factor is

$$d_C(n,i) = (1 - h_t)e^{-r(n,i)} + h_t e^{-r(n,i)}(1 - L_t)$$

The above expression says that in the event of survival $(1 - h_t)$ at time n and interest level i the promised \$1 payment is discounted back at the corresponding state contingent sovereign interest rate $r(n,i)$. In the event of default h_t at time n and interest rate state i the recovery amount which is one minus the loss rate L_t is discounted back at the corresponding state contingent sovereign interest rate $r(n,i)$. Collecting terms we simplify the above expression.

$$d_C(n,i) = (1 - L_t h_t)e^{-r(n,i)} \tag{6.24}$$

Taking the negative of the natural logarithm of (6.24) and continuing to assume that there is a zero correlation between the sovereign and corporate rate of interest, we obtain the corresponding state contingent corporate interest rate.

$$r_C(n,i) = -Ln[e^{-r(n,i)}(1 - h_t L_t)] \tag{6.25}$$

6.9.1   An example of Duffie and Singleton (1999)

The workbook that we use to implement DS is DSB02.xls. Like Jarrow and Turnbull (1995) Duffie and Singleton (1999) is first calibrated to a sovereign and then is calibrated to a corporate term structure. Therefore the first spreadsheet is BDT which is the same spreadsheet contained in the workbook BDTB02.xls that we used to implement BDT in Chapter 5. We will not discuss this spreadsheet as a complete discussion is contained in section 5.4.1. The second calibration is contained in the second spreadsheet DS.

A numerical example of DS is reported below in Table 6.9 and the formulas for the corporate interest rate process are contained in

Table 6.10. As Duffie and Singleton (1999) models corporate interest rates in the same way that we model sovereign interest rates only the corporate interest rate process is new, all other formulas and the structure of the spreadsheet are the same as, say, the constant volatility version of Black Derman and Toy.

The first three rows of Table 6.9 report the time step dt, recovery fraction δ and the calibrated one period probabilities of survival P. The next block from cell B5 to F9 is our corporate interest rate tree. To illustrate how these interest rates are obtained, consider cell F9 in Table 6.10. The formula in cell F9 is $-LN$ (EXP $(-BDT!\ F25)*(1-(1-F\$3)*(1-\$B\$2*F\$3)))$. The term EXP $(-BDT!\ F25)$ is the pure interest discount factor using the Black Derman and Toy generated sovereign interest rate from state S(4,0). This discount factor is adjusted by multiplying it by the term $(1-(1-F\$3)*(1-\$B\$2*F\$3))$. Since $\$F\$3$ is the calibrated probability of survival, $(1-F\$3)$ is the hazard rate h_4. The hazard rate is then multiplied by the loss rate L_4, which is one minus the recovery

Table 6.9 Duffie and Singleton

	A	B	C	D	E	F
1	*dt*	0.5				
2	δ	0.6				
3	P	0.961785	0.973858	0.985277	0.987592	0.99779
4						
5		R(n,i)				0.063142
6					0.064024	0.063085
7				0.064726	0.063946	0.063027
8			0.066945	0.064578	0.063869	0.06297
9		0.076654	0.066548	0.06443	0.063792	0.062913
10		0	1	2	3	4
11						0.968922
12		dc(n,i)			0.968495	0.96895
13				0.968155	0.968533	0.968978
14			0.967082	0.968227	0.96857	0.969006
15		0.962398	0.967274	0.968298	0.968607	0.969033
16						
17	QU(*n,i*)					0.026424
18					0.054543	0.132135
19				0.112635	0.218198	0.264301
20			0.232679	0.337944	0.327335	0.264332
21		0.481199	0.465405	0.337983	0.218248	0.132181
22	1	0.481199	0.232726	0.112674	0.054568	0.026439
23		0.962398	0.93081	0.901235	0.872892	0.845813
24	Implied Yield	7.665428	7.170021	6.932602	6.797146	6.698265
25	Observed Yield	7.665428	7.170021	6.932602	6.797146	6.698265
26	Time Step	1	2	3	4	5

Table 6.10 Duffie and Singleton (1999) corporate interest rate process

	B	C	D	E
5	R(n,i)			
6			=−LN(EXP(−BDT!D23)*(1 − (1 − D$3)*(1 − $B$2*D$3)))	=−LN(EXP(−BDT!E22)*(1 − (1 − E$3)*(1 − $B$2*E$3)))
7			=−LN(EXP(−BDT!D24)*(1 − (1 − D$3)*(1 − $B$2*D$3)))	=−LN(EXP(−BDT!E23)*(1 − (1 − E$3)*(1 − $B$2*E$3)))
8		=−LN(EXP(−BDT!C24)*(1 − (1 − C$3)*(1 − $B$2*C$3)))		=−LN(EXP(−BDT!E24)*(1 − (1 − E$3)*(1 − $B$2*E$3)))
9	=−LN(EXP(−BDT!B25)*(1 − (1 − B$3)*(1 − $B$2*B$3)))	=−LN(EXP(−BDT!C25)*(1 − (1 − C$3)*(1 − $B$2*C$3)))	=−LN(EXP(−BDT!D25)*(1 − (1 − D$3)*(1 − $B$2*D$3)))	

rate. The recovery rate is a constant fraction $B$2 of next period's survival contingent F$3 value. Note that this is a one period interest rate so next period's promised value is $1, which we neglect in this expression. Finally, one minus the product of the hazard rate and the loss rate $(1 - h_4L_4)$ is multiplied by the one period sovereign discount factor thereby obtaining the one period corporate discount factor. Taking the negative of log of the one period corporate discount factor obtains the one period corporate interest rate as outlined in expression (6.25).

The remainder of the spreadsheet DS follows precisely the same structure of the usual pure interest rate modelling spreadsheet, namely the next block from B11 to F15 is the corporate discount factor tree, followed by the corporate state security tree in block B17 to F22. Columns of corporate state securities are added up in row 23 where each sum represents the replicating portfolio. That is a portfolio of one each of all possible corporate state securities that may arrive in, say, time period 4 represents the promise to pay $1 no matter which corporate interest rate state arrives in time period 4. Therefore this is a synthetic corporate zero, the yield of which (row 24) is forced to agree with the corporate zero coupon term structure of interest rates (row 25) as estimated using the methods of Chapter 3. Accordingly the calibration procedure for the corporate spreadsheet is the same as when we calibrated Ho and Lee and Black Derman and Toy, constant volatility version.

6.9.2 Using the calibrated DS model

We can find the value of a corporate bond by backward induction using the credit risk adjusted discount factor tree. Unlike Jarrow and Turnbull we need not multiply the sovereign discount factor by the expected value of each promise to pay $1 at some future date in time. Instead we employ the corporate discount factor tree in the same way that we employ the sovereign discount factor tree when finding the value of a sovereign bond. We employ the credit risk adjusted discount factor tree to price a 2.5-year 6% semi-annual coupon pay corporate bond when the corporate yield curve is as reported in row 25 in Table 6.9. Notice that we use the same corporate yield curve that we used for the Jarrow and Turnbull (1995) model as reported in row 21 of Table 6.5. The numerical results are reported in Table 6.11 and the formulas are reported in Table 6.12.

Notice that the price of the 6% semi-annual coupon pay bond is the same as the price we obtained for the same bond when we used Jarrow and Turnbull. However, this happens only because we have

Table 6.11   Price obtained by the Duffie and Singleton model

	B	C	D	E	F	G
55	Straight Corporate Price Tree (5 Period Bond)					
56	Coupon	6				
57		0	1	2	3	4
58						99.79896
59					99.56169	99.80183
60				99.29885	99.56832	99.8047
61			98.938	99.31261	99.57493	99.80757
62		98.12078	98.97093	99.32634	99.58154	99.81043

a short-term bond. In general Diaz and Skinner (2003) and Delia-nedis and Lagnado (2002) find that Jarrow and Turnbull will obtain lower values because given the same recovery fraction δ (60% in our example) the recovery assumption that underlies Jarrow and Turnbull implies higher hazard rates.

In Table 6.12, column G all the promised cash flows are multiplied by the DS discount factor. For example, in cell G62 the promised cash flow of principal 100 and the semi-annual coupon (\$E\$56)/2 are multiplied by the DS discount factor F15. Stepping one period backwards, the value of the bond in state $S(3,0)$ is 50% each of next period's value in state $S(4,0)$ and $S(4,1)$, plus the coupon payment all multiplied by the corresponding DS corporate discount factor $d(3,0)$ or E15. In other words, we employ the same mechanical procedure to value a corporate bond via backward induction that we used to value a sovereign bond. In contrast as shown in section 6.8.2 we have to adjust our backward induction methods somewhat when we use Jarrow and Turnbull.

6.10   Other credit risk modelling approaches

There are two stylized approaches to credit risk modelling, the structural and the reduced form approach. The structural approach originates with Merton (1974). One idea expressed in this paper is that the firm's debt and equity can be viewed as options written on the value of the firm's assets just as we discussed in section 1.4.1. For example, bondholders implicitly sell a call option to the equity holders because if the value of the firm should fall below the amount

Table 6.12 Formulas used to Price a Corporate Bond using DS

	B	C	D	E	F	G
56	Coupon					
57		6				= F57 + 1
58		0			= E57 + 1	= (100 + $C$56/2)*F11
59				= D57 + 1	= ((G58 + G59)*0.5 + ($C$56/2))*E12	= (100 + $C$56/2)*F12
60			= C57 + 1	= ((F59 + F60)*0.5 + ($C$56/2))*D13	= ((G59 + G60)*0.5 + ($C$56/2))*E13	= (100 + $C$56/2)*F13
61			= ((E60 + E61)*0.5 + ($C$56/2))*C14	= ((F60 + F61)*0.5 + ($C$56/2))*D14	= ((G60 + G61)*0.5 + ($C$56/2))*E14	= (100 + $C$56/2)*F14
62		= ((D61 + D62)*0.5 + ($C$56/2))*B15	= ((E61 + E62)*0.5 + ($C$56/2))*C15	= ((F61 + F62)*0.5 + ($C$56/2))*D15	= ((G61 + G62)*0.5 + ($C$56/2))*E15	= (100 + $C$56/2)*F15

owed the equity holders would declare bankruptcy rather than contribute even more capital to a failing enterprise. This is a long call
option from the shareholder's point of view because if on the other
hand the value of the firm's assets are above the value of debt, the
shareholders will instruct the firm to redeem the debt and in effect
buy back the firm thereby exercising the call option. One can see that
the value of debt plays the role of the exercise price in the implied
call option. Therefore one can model default as the first time some
stochastic process that models the value of the firm's assets generates
an asset value that is below the value of the firm's debt.

There have been many extensions of the structural modelling
approach that have improved our theoretical understanding of capital structure issues.[3] However, it soon became generally recognized
that it is difficult to implement the structural modelling approach
because it requires a frequently observed time series of the value of
the firm's assets. This information is not available. To overcome this
difficulty, the reduced form approach models default as the result of
a default process not directly tied to the value of the firm's assets.
In principal one can implement a reduced form model as it does not
require observations of the unobservable asset values.

The reduced form approach itself may be classified into two categories, hazard (default) rate models and transition matrix models.
Jarrow and Turnbull (1995) and Duffie and Singleton (1999) are two
examples of the hazard rate approach where default occurs as a surprise realization of some default process not directly related to the
value of the firm's assets, otherwise the bond survives. Hazard rate
models can be implemented as an evolutionary or as a term structure consistent model. For example, we have already implemented
Jarrow and Turnbull (1995) as a term structure consistent model.
To implement Jarrow and Turnbull (1995) as an evolutionary model
one assumes that the underlying stochastic hazard process takes
some continuous form and then one derives closed form expressions
for the value of debt based on arbitrage arguments similar to Vasicek
(1977) and Cox Ingersoll and Ross (1985).

In contrast transition matrix models take up point 3 in
section 6.7.2 where the bond must pass through several intermediate credit risk states, say a series of credit downgrades prior to
default. This approach then models the process of default where a
bond may experience improvements as well as deterioration in credit
quality. Therefore we can say that the transition matrix approach is

---

[3] The capital structure issue refers to questions concerning the optimal portion of the
firm's assets that should be financed by debt and equity.

more comprehensive as it models credit risk, unexpected changes in credit quality, rather than simply default risk. A classic example of a transition matrix model is Jarrow Lando and Turnbull (1997). Schönbucher (1998) takes up point 4 by extending the transition approach by allowing for multiple defaults.

Like interest rate risk modelling the distinction between the structural and the hazard rate modelling approaches is more of a continuum than an absolute distinction for there are credit risk models that combine elements of both. Recent hybrid models have been proposed that promise to combine the conceptual insights offered by structural models with the tractability of reduced form models. For example, Zhou (1997) places a hazard rate jump diffusion process for the value of the firm.

Under pressure from the Bank of International Settlements investment banks have been implementing one version or another of the above credit risk modelling approaches. Practitioners unwilling to develop their own in-house credit risk model can choose among three commercially available credit risk models. JP Morgan's CreditMetrics is a credit rating triggered transition matrix model whereas Crédit Suisse's Credit Risk+ is a hazard rate model. Meanwhile the KMV model is an application of the structural modelling approach.

6.11 Summary

In this chapter we have explored alternative approaches to modelling interest rate and credit risk. We explored two classic evolutionary interest rate models and have discussed the advantages and disadvantages of the evolutionary models when compared to the term structure consistent models of Chapter 5. We then reviewed non-stochastic credit risk models as a platform to help us understand recent stochastic credit risk models. Along the way we implemented Jarrow and Turnbull (1995), one of the earliest stochastic credit risk models, and Duffie and Singleton (1999).

6.12 Exercises

Question 1
Discuss the differences between the 'term structure consistent' and the 'evolutionary' approach to valuing debt securities and their derivatives.

Question 2

An inspection of Figure 6.1 reveals that Vasicek's yield curve is slightly lower than the CIR yield curve and at five years' maturity, both are higher than the observed yield curve. Are these differences substantial? Find the price of a five-year 5% annual coupon pay bond using the observed Vasicek and CIR yield curves.

Question 3

Consider the following sovereign discount factor tree, sovereign state price tree and one period survival vector. The sovereign discount factor and state price trees are calibrated to the Treasury yield curve and the survival probabilities are calibrated to a triple B corporate yield curve according to Jarrow and Turnbull (1995). A one-year time step is used. I suggest that you round all intermediate steps to four digits.

Sovereign discount factor tree

				0.9415
			0.9410	0.9437
		0.9388	0.9432	0.9459
	0.9342	0.9411	0.9454	0.9480

Sovereign state price tree

				0.0486
			0.1032	0.1949
		0.2192	0.3102	0.2934
	0.4671	0.4390	0.3110	0.1963
1.0000	0.4671	0.2198	0.1039	0.0492

Corporate one period probabilities of survival vector
0.9787   0.9878   0.9845   0.9817

What is the value today of a 5% annual coupon pay three-year non-callable corporate bond? This bond will recover 60% of its value should it default.

Question 4

Find the value of the 5% annual coupon pay three-year bond contained in question 3, only now use Duffie and Singleton. Continue to use the values of the parameters contained in question 3.

Hedging sovereign bonds: the traditional approach

7.1 Introduction

We now turn our attention to hedging positions in interest sensitive instruments. We start by reviewing the traditional duration approach to hedging long positions in sovereign securities. In order to appreciate the strengths and weaknesses of this approach, we need to fully understand duration and convexity. After reviewing these concepts we will use them to construct hedge ratios and then to demonstrate the most common methods of hedging long positions in sovereign bonds.

7.2 Macaulay duration

During Chapter 2, you were introduced to the concept of interest rate risk. That is, the price of a bond would decline if interest rates were to increase unexpectedly. Macaulay duration is a measure of this risk. It measures how sensitive a bond's price is to an unexpected change in its yield. Formally

$$D = -\frac{\Delta B}{B_0} \bigg/ \frac{\Delta(1+Y)}{(1+Y_0)} \tag{7.1}$$

Equation (7.1) shows that Macaulay duration D is a ratio of the percentage change in a bond's price $\Delta B/B_0$ to the percentage change in the bond's yield $\Delta(1+Y)/(1+Y_0)$. The bond price B_0 and yield Y_0 subscripts indicate that the percentage change is calculated from today's price and yield respectively prior to the unexpected movement in price. You will note that Macaulay duration is a price elasticity measure so it is an 'instantaneous' measure, derived from calculus. Also note that (7.1) contains a minus sign. This represents the fact that as yield rises, bond price falls. Since this is such a fundamental concept all market information providers such as Reuters and Bloomberg neglect this sign. In this book we will often follow this practice.

To implement (7.1) we use the following approximation.

$$D = \sum_{T=1}^{M} \frac{T \times C(T)}{(1+Y_0)^T/B_0} \tag{7.2}$$

In (7.2) T refers to the time step measured in units of years and $C(T)$ is the cash flow paid by the bond at date T. Meanwhile Y_0 and B_0 are the bond's current yield and price. The most accurate measure of Macaulay duration D uses the dirty price and a yield based on the dirty price although the difference between using parameters based on their respective clean values is very often small. Table 7.1 shows the calculation of Macaulay duration for an annual coupon pay 15% Eurobond with five full years left to maturity and priced to yield 12%.

Table 7.1 Macaulay duration – calculation

Year	1	2	3	4	5
CF	15	15	15	15	115
CFXT	15	30	45	60	575
PV of CFXT	13.393	23.916	32.030	38.131	326.270

The first row of Table 7.1 writes in the year and the second writes in the payment the bond makes in the corresponding year. As instructed by the numerator of (7.2), the third row multiplies the payment by the year in which the payment occurs. Then we find the present value of this time-weighted cash flow in row 4. Finally, we add together the sum of the time-weighted present values of the cash flows and divide by the bond's initial price to find that Macaulay duration for this bond is 3.91 years. In other words $\sum PV$ of $CFXT/B_0 = 4337.46/110.815 = 3.91$.

What does 3.91 years mean? It is a relative measure of the sensitivity of a bond's price to a change in its yield. That is, a bond with duration of five years will have greater price sensitivity than a bond with duration of four years. When the yield increases the price of a bond with duration of five will decline more than the price of a bond with duration of four. Duration is a measure of interest rate risk.

Duration has a nice intuitive interpretation. It is a time-weighted average of the present value of the cash flow from the bond. To make the interpretation more concrete, consider Figure 7.1.

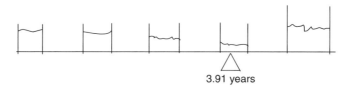

3.91 years

Figure 7.1   Visual diagram of duration

Figure 7.1 depicts a seesaw that is just balanced when the fulcrum is placed at the point noted as 3.91 years. To appreciate what this diagram is telling us note the following. The line is a time line segmented into years. At each year we place a container. The volume of the container corresponds to the nominal cash flow paid by the bond at that point in time. Therefore the first four containers are of equal size having a volume of 15 because the bond pays a coupon of $15 at these points in time. The last container is far larger since the bond pays the final redemption amount and the last coupon in five years, so the last container has a volume of 150. Next we partially fill these containers with water. The amount of water we place in each container corresponds to the present value of the cash flow paid by the bond at that point in time. That is the reason why the first container is nearly full and the next three equal sized containers are successively less full. As the date of payment of the coupon of $15 recedes into the future its present value is less. Notice that the payment of the principal and the last coupon payment occur the longest in time, so a lot of discounting occurs. Nevertheless there is still a lot of water in the last container because the nominal cash flow paid at that point in time is so huge. Finally, we note that when we place the fulcrum at the point along the time line that balances the seesaw so that one half of the present value of cash flows paid by the bond occurs prior to that point, and one half of the present value of the cash flows occur after that point, we find Macaulay duration. So it is in this sense that Macaulay duration represents a time-weighted average of the present value of the cash flow from the bond and Macaulay duration is measured in time units.

Using Figure 7.1, we can make the following observations about the characteristics of duration.

1. The Macaulay duration of a zero coupon bond is the same as the maturity of the zero coupon bond.

Imagine we remove all the coupon containers in Figure 7.1. Then the seesaw will tilt to the right. To maintain balance the fulcrum will have to move to the right until it is under the principal repayment container that is paid at maturity. Therefore the Macaulay duration of a zero is its maturity.

2. For coupon bonds, Macaulay duration is less than maturity.

Imagine we now add coupon containers to our balanced seesaw for zero coupon bonds in point 1. Now the seesaw will tilt to the left, so to maintain balance the fulcrum must shift to the left. This means that coupon bonds have a Macaulay duration that is less than maturity.

Notice the important implication of this. Since a coupon bond has a lower Macaulay's duration than a corresponding maturity zero the coupon bond is less interest sensitive than the zero. In other words, the coupon bond has less interest rate risk than the corresponding maturity zero.

3. As the coupon rate increases, Macaulay duration decreases.

Imagine we increase the size of the coupon containers for our balanced seesaw for the coupon bond above in point 2. All containers will get larger. The amount of present value (water) in each container will also increase simply because the nominal value of the coupons is now larger. However, more nominal value is added to the left of the fulcrum because there are more containers there. Therefore as more present value is added to the left of the fulcrum the seesaw will tilt to the left. In order to maintain balance we must move the fulcrum to the left. This means that as the coupon rate increases, Macaulay duration decreases.

Notice the important implication of this. Since a low coupon bond has a higher Macaulay duration than a corresponding maturity high coupon bond, the low coupon bond is more interest sensitive than the high coupon bond. In other words, the low coupon bond has more interest rate risk than the corresponding maturity high coupon bond. To put points 1 to 3 together, in rank order of risk from highest to lowest are zero coupon, low coupon and high coupon bonds, all else equal.

4. As the yield to maturity increases duration decreases.

Imagine we increase the yield for the bond in Figure 7.1. The amount of present value (water) will decrease for all containers because more discounting is being applied. However, we know that the last containers will lose the most present value because more discounting is applied to later cash flows than earlier cash flows due to compounding. This means that more present value (water) is taken away from the principal and last coupon payment container than any other coupon only container. This will cause the seesaw to tilt to the left. In order to maintain balance we must move the fulcrum to the left. This means that as the yield to maturity increases, Macaulay duration decreases.

Notice the important implication of this. As yields increase, Macaulay duration decreases, so interest rate risk decreases. The startling revelation is that when we have low interest rate environments we have high interest rate risk.

5. Long-term bonds have higher Macaulay duration than short-term bonds.

Look again at our seesaw in Figure 7.1 and imagine we increase the length of the time line and add more intermediate single coupon containers. If we leave the fulcrum at 3.91 years the seesaw will tilt to the right. In order to maintain balance we must move the fulcrum to the right. This means that as the maturity of a bond increases, Macaulay duration increases.

Notice the important implication of this. Long-term bonds have higher Macaulay duration than short-term bonds so long-term bonds have more interest rate risk than short-term bonds. Putting points 1 to 5 together, the most risky bond is a low yield long-term zero coupon bond in a low interest rate environment and the least risky bond is a high yield short-term high coupon bond in a high interest rate environment.

7.3 Modified duration

Although useful as a relative measure of interest rate risk Macaulay duration does not suit the purpose of those wishing to hedge a long position in a bond. What bond traders really need in order to control for the amount of risk they accept is a measure of price sensitivity. In other words, what is required is a measure of the price response of a given bond to a change in its yield. This is what modified duration does. As the name suggests, it is a modified version of Macaulay duration. To see this reconsider Macaulay duration defined as an elasticity measure in (7.1) below.

$$D = -\frac{\Delta B}{B_0} \bigg/ \frac{\Delta(1+Y)}{(1+Y_0)} \tag{7.1}$$

We can rewrite (7.1) in another way.

$$D = -\frac{\Delta B}{B_0} \frac{(1+Y_0)}{\Delta Y} \tag{7.3}$$

Written in this way (7.3) reveals that Macaulay duration measures the percentage change in a bond's price with respect to an inverse percentage change in its yield. In other words, it is a relative risk measure, but what bond traders need is a measure of the percentage price response of a bond to an absolute change in the bond's yield. From the trader's perspective what is 'wrong' with (7.3) is the term $(1 + Y_0)$, for this term converts the change in yield to an inverse percentage change in yield. So modified duration gets rid of this extra term by dividing through (7.3) by $(1 + Y_0)$ as shown in (7.4) below. This measure of duration (noted as D^*) is called modified duration to distinguish it from Macaulay duration.

$$\frac{D}{(1+Y_0)} = -\frac{\Delta B}{\Delta Y} \frac{1}{B_0} = D^* \tag{7.4}$$

In other words, modified duration D^* is the change in price ΔB of a bond given a particular change in yield ΔY scaled by the bond's original (before the change in yield) price B_0. We can clearly see that modified duration is a measure of price volatility and that it is expressed as a percentage (rather than as units of time like Macaulay duration) if we note that

$$\frac{\Delta B}{B} = -D^* \Delta Y \tag{7.5}$$

$$\Delta B = -D^* \Delta Y B \tag{7.5a}$$

Equation (7.5) says that the percentage change in a bond's price is equal to its modified duration multiplied by a given change in yield. Meanwhile (7.5a) is very useful as it tells us the price change of the bond in response to a given change in yield ΔY. This is precisely what bond traders would like to know. Since we are dealing with true fixed income securities (bonds whose cash flows do not change with changes in yield), we can obtain a closed form solution to modified duration. As suggested by (7.4) all we need to do is to take the first partial derivative of the bond's price with respect to its yield dB/dY and then divide through by the bond's price.

To show how we obtain a closed form solution to modified duration we first take the first partial derivative of the bond's price with respect to its yield.

$$\frac{-dB}{dY} = \frac{1}{(1+Y)}\left[\frac{C}{(1+Y)} + \frac{2C}{(1+Y)^2} + \cdots + \frac{n(FV+C)}{(1+Y)^n}\right] \quad (7.6)$$

Then we apply annuity formulas to obtain a closed form solution to the above partial derivative. Finally we divide through the result by bond price B_0 to obtain the closed form solution for the modified duration of the bond.

$$D^* = \frac{-dB}{dY}\frac{1}{B_0} = \frac{\dfrac{C}{Y^2}\left[1 - \dfrac{1}{(1+Y)^N}\right] + \dfrac{N\left(100 - \dfrac{C}{Y}\right)}{(1+Y)^{N+1}}}{B_0} \quad (7.6a)$$

where $C = \$$ coupon, $Y =$ yield, $N =$ number of coupon payments, B_0 is the current price of the bond in terms of 100 and FV is set to 100. Note that if coupons are paid annually, C, Y, N and the resulting D^* are annual measures. If coupons are paid semi-annually, then these are semi-annual measures. Also the most accurate calculation of D^* uses the dirty price and a yield based on the dirty price.

No doubt an example will help. Consider a 4% semi-annual coupon pay bond, maturing in 20 years' time, priced at $64.036 (par value £100) and yielding 7.5%. This means that $C = £2$, $Y = 0.0375$ and $N = 40$. Then

$$D^* = \frac{\dfrac{2}{(0.0375)^2}\left[1 - \dfrac{1}{(1+0.0375)^{40}}\right] + \dfrac{40\left(100 - \dfrac{2}{0.0375}\right)}{(1+0.0375)^{40+1}}}{64.036}$$

$$= \frac{14\,222.2222[0.77066] + 412.62397}{64.036}$$

$$= 23.55977 \text{ semi-annually}$$

The correct answer converts this to an annual measure by dividing by 2. The final answer is 11.78.

Another example is a 12% semi-annual coupon pay bond maturing in 20 years, priced at 146.24 and yielding 7.5%. You should be able to confirm that modified duration is 9.43.

Finally, note that from (7.4) there is a direct correspondence between Macaulay duration D and modified duration D^*. This has two important implications. First, if one wishes to find D then it can be found simply by calculating D^* using (7.6a) and then multiply the result by one plus one period yield $(1 + Y)$. If the bond yielding 8% pays coupons annually, Y is the full years yield or 8%; if the coupons are paid semi-annually, Y is divided by 2, so Y is 4%; if the coupons are paid monthly then Y is divided by 12, so Y is 0.667%.

Second, Macaulay duration behaves just like modified duration with respect to changes in maturity, coupon, yield and so on. So if you were to rank a group of bonds using modified duration from the highest modified duration (and highest risk) bond to the lowest, Macaulay duration will always agree with these rankings.

7.4   Other measures of interest rate sensitivity

Because interest rate risk is such an important aspect of bond investments there are still other measures of interest rate risk. The price value of a basis point (*PVBP*) is the price response of a bond for a *one basis point* change in yield. The relation between modified duration and the *PVBP* is as follows.

$$PVBP = \frac{D^*}{100} \times \frac{Price}{100}$$

If one wishes to use *PVBP* it is more simple to calculate it directly rather than calculating D^* and then applying the above formula. That is, first note the bond's current price and yield combination, then re-price the bond using just one basis point less than the current yield for the new yield. The difference in price from the current value and the recalculated value would be the *PVBP*.

Similarly we can calculate yet a fourth measure of interest rate sensitivity, the yield value of a price change *YVPC*. This is the analogue of the *PVBP*. The *YVPC* is the yield response of a bond to a one cent change in price. Again it is best to calculate the *YVPC* directly by noting the current price yield combination for the bond and then recalculating the yield based on a new price that is just one cent less than the current value. The difference between the current yield and the recalculated yield is the *YVBP*.

7.5 Convexity

Duration is only an approximation of the actual change in bond price given any small change in yield. It is an approximation because duration assumes that as yields change, the bond price changes at a constant rate. This of course ignores the non-linearity caused by compounding. So how good is this approximation? See Figure 7.2.

The non-linear curve reports the *actual* price change of a bond with respect to a change in yield, whereas the linear curve reports the *modelled* (by modified duration) price change of a bond with respect to a given change in yield. Notice that for large decreases in yield, say moving from A to B on the *x*-axis, modified duration (straight line) will underestimate the actual rise in price. This can be seen by noting the distance between the modelled price as indicated by the point P_B on straight line and the actual price as indicated by the point P_T on the curved line. For large increases in yield, say moving from A to C on the *x*-axis, modified duration will overestimate the actual fall in price of a bond. However, for small yield changes, there is hardly any difference between the prices as reported by the straight and curved lines. This indicates that modified duration is a reasonably accurate measure of the price response of a bond for a small change in yield.

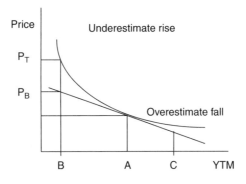

Figure 7.2 Convexity

7.5.1 Properties of convexity

You have probably heard about convexity and how complex it is. Actually it is very easy to understand it if you will allow me to put it in a very simple (and rather dumb) way.

First, there are two types of convexity, positive convexity and negative convexity. As you may guess, positive convexity is 'nice' and you will like it. Negative convexity is not 'nice' and you will not like it.

Also, all straight bonds have positive convexity whereas structured securities may have negative convexity.

7.5.1.1 *Positive/negative convexity*

To explain positive convexity, imagine you are long the bond depicted in Figure 7.2. Currently the yield is at point A. Now yields fall by a large amount to B. Rubbing your hands with glee (you know the bond price will rise and since you are long the bond you know you made a lot of money) you use modified duration to work out that the bond's price will rise to point P_B. Chuckling with delight, you look up the bond on the Reuters screen only to find that the bond price is now *even higher*. This is nice. This is positive. This is positive convexity.

But what happens if yields fall? How many times have you heard things like 'I have good news for you and bad news'? Well, this is one of those rare cases where we can say 'I have good news for you, and I have more good news for you'. So enjoy it.

Let's say you hold the bond depicted in Figure 7.2, and now yields rise from A to point C. Now you are worried. You know that as yields rise, bond prices fall. You have lost a lot of money. You use modified duration to work out that you lost a lot of money according to the straight line as depicted in Figure 7.2. Depressed, you peek at the Reuters screen just to confirm your worst fears. To your surprise and relief, you find that the price decrease (as indicated by the curved line) was not as bad as you had anticipated. This is nice. This is positive. This is positive convexity.

But let's sit back a second and think about what all this means. The more non-linear the curve in Figure 7.2 is, the more positively convex the bond will be. What this means is that the more positively convex a bond is, the more upside potential it offers in response to a decrease in yield and less of the downside risk in response to an increase in yield. That is, I have good news for you, and I have more good news for you.

Buy what is negative convexity? As promised, you will not like it. It is the possibility that in response to a decrease in yield, the price of a structured security will be less than what you would expect if you were using modified duration to estimate the expected increase in price. This is disappointing. This is negative. This is negative convexity. However, since negative convexity only occurs with structured securities, and this is a topic covered well in later chapters, this is all that will be said about negative convexity in this chapter.

7.5.1.2 *The price of convexity*

By now you will agree that positive convexity is a nice property for bonds to have. Suppose you look at two bonds, bond A and bond B.

Suppose that both are identical in all respects but one. Bond A is more positively convex than bond B. Which one would you prefer? Everybody will prefer bond A. This of course means that bond A is more valuable than bond B, so bond A will have a higher price. In other words, positive convexity is valuable and this will be included in the price of bond A. But would you expect that the price of convexity would always be the same?

Typically you would not expect the price of convexity to be constant. In particular, when interest rate volatility is high, you are more likely to benefit from high positive convexity. That is, with a large increase in interest rates the price of a bond will decrease by a large amount, and the more positively convex a bond is, the less of the downside you get in response to an increase in yields. If, on the other hand, interest rates are very stable, then it is not likely that interest rates will move very much, so it is unlikely that you will benefit much by positive convexity. In other words, the price of convexity (the price spread between high convex bond A and low convex bond B) will increase with increases in interest rate volatility.

This gives us a trading strategy. Suppose you hold the low convex bond B. Imagine you are able to forecast interest rate volatility. Your forecast suggests that interest rate volatility will increase yet the high convex bond A is only a few pennies more than bond B. So you do a bond swap, selling the low convex bond B and replacing it with the high convex bond A. You do this because you expect that you will benefit from the extra positive convexity offered by bond A by more than the few extra pennies that it cost you to do the bond swap. In other words you believe that positive convexity is underpriced.

Now imagine six months or so later, you forecast that interest rate volatility will decrease in the near future. You notice that bond A is now much more valuable than bond B since the effects of the last bout of high interest rate volatility is still included in bond A's price. In other words, positive convexity is overpriced according to your forecast. So now you do another bond swap, selling the high convex bond A and replacing it with the cheaper, but lower convex bond B, taking the difference in cash.

Notice that we are buying and selling bonds not based on a forecast of interest rates, but on a forecast of interest rate volatility.

7.6 Hedging

Recall from Chapter 2 that the hedge ratio is the ideal number N of the hedging instrument that you wish to short in order to protect your long position in a bond from unanticipated increases in yield. There are two types of traditional hedge ratios that can achieve this result, the regression based hedge ratio and the duration hedge ratio. Below we will discuss each in turn.

All hedge ratios N represent the number of hedging instruments one should short in order to minimize the change in value of a hedge portfolio V_H. The hedge portfolio consists of a long position in a cash asset that you wish to have hedged B_0 and a short position in a hedging instrument V_h. That is, you wish to minimize changes in the value of the following equation.

$$\Delta V_H = \Delta B_0 + N \Delta V_h$$

7.7   Regression-based hedge ratios

The simplest hedge ratio is the response coefficient β from the following equation that is estimated via OLS regression.

$$\Delta B_{0,t} = \alpha + \beta \Delta V_{h,t} + \varepsilon_t \tag{7.7}$$

The term $\Delta B_{0,t}$ refers to a time series of observations of changes in the value of the bond you wish to hedge and $\Delta V_{h,t}$ is a time series of simultaneously observed changes in the value of the instrument that you wish to use as a hedging instrument. Meanwhile α and β are parameters that you estimate via OLS and ε refers to a time series of errors produced by your regression.

The above regression equation attempts to answer the question, when the cash instrument changed in value, by how much did the value of the candidate hedging instrument respond, on average? Obviously the hope is that there was a close relationship, ideally every time the cash instrument increased by, say, $1, the hedging instrument increased by, say, $0.25 and if the cash instrument decreased by $1 the hedging instrument decreased by $0.25. If this was indeed the case then graphically the above equation will be a straight line and the OLS estimate of this line would be perfect. The OLS regression will achieve an R^2 of 1 representing a perfect fit. The slope coefficient β would be 4 meaning that to hedge a $100 investment in the cash asset B_0 you need to short $400 of the hedging instrument. In other words, the slope coefficient β is the hedge ratio N. If (and this is a big if) the relation between the cash and hedging instrument continues to hold in the future, then losses on the long cash asset will be fully offset by gains on the hedging instrument held short.

For example, suppose we wish to hedge a $100 investment in a bond with a $400 short position in a, say, bond futures (more on this later) because our OLS regression (7.7) estimated a slope coefficient β of 4. Then if the past relation holds perfectly in the future and the value of the cash bond decreases by $1, then the value of our hedge portfolio will remain unchanged. That is

$$\Delta B_0 + N \Delta V_h = \Delta V_H$$

$$\$1 - 4 \times \$0.25 = 0$$

This of course is too good to be true. The correlation between the cash and hedging instrument will not be $+1$ as the above illustration assumes. This means that on average the most effective hedging instrument will be the one that has the highest correlation with the cash instrument that you want to hedge and the closer to $+1$ it is, the better. Hedging necessarily involves some unexpected losses and gains, but hopefully these gains and losses will be less than the gains and losses that would have occurred had you not hedged at all. Therefore we look for an *optimal* hedge ratio, which is the number of hedging instruments that is held short that results in a minimum variance of unexpected gains and losses on the hedge portfolio.

The R^2 from the OLS regression is an (optimistic) measure of hedge effectiveness, the closer to one the better. To appreciate why, recall that the R^2 is the ratio of 'one minus the ratio of the error sum of squares divided by the total sum of squares'. To put it in economic terms, the total sum of squares TSS is the total squared unexpected gains and losses on the cash instrument without the benefit of hedging. In other words, TSS is a target that we wish to reduce as much as possible. Then the error sum of squares ESS is the total squared unexpected gains and losses that occur on the hedge portfolio. In other words, the ESS is a measure of disappointment and ideally you wish this number to be zero. Finally the regression sum of squares RSS is the amount by which the hedge was able to reduce the total squared gains and losses on the cash instrument that would have occurred had you not hedged. In other words, the RSS is a measure of success and you wish this number would be as high as possible. Since $TSS = RSS + ESS$ we can divide through this equation by the TSS to obtain a measure of the percentage by which the regression sum of squares reduced the total sum of squares R^2

as shown below.

$$R^2 = 1 - \frac{ESS}{TSS} = 1 - \frac{\sum (\textit{Hedge gains and losses})^2}{\sum (\textit{Cash gains and losses})^2}$$

Ideally you would like the ESS to be zero so the R^2 would be 1 meaning that the hedge ratio used to form the hedge portfolio was 100% effective since it was able to eliminate all unexpected gains and losses on the hedge portfolio. Of course, this will never happen, so what you look for is an optimal hedge ratio that produces the highest R^2, the closer to 1 the better, of the available hedging instruments.[1]

In contrast the *perfect* hedge ratio is one that completely eliminates all possible unexpected gains and losses from the hedge portfolio. It has a minimum variance of zero but this is only a theoretical construct as in practice the relationships among asset prices are never perfectly correlated and the R^2 from OLS regression estimates of the hedge ratio is never 1.

7.7.1   An example of regression-based hedging

Suppose we wish to hedge a long $30 million position in the 5.25% semi-annual coupon pay US Treasury bond maturing on February 15, 2029. Today's date is September 7, 2002. Since the US Treasury bond is more than 26 years to maturity, we choose to hedge the bond with the Treasury bond futures contract that trades on the Chicago Board of Trade (CBT). We choose this contract because we suspect that the bond we want to hedge and the bond that underlies the futures contract is similar, so we expect a high correlation between the two. As a result we are hopeful that we can obtain an effective hedge using the US Treasury bond futures contract.

A short position in the US Treasury bond futures contract represents the commitment to sell a $100 000 nominal 20-year 6% semi-annual coupon pay Treasury bond sometime during the expiry month of the futures contract. Since this bond does not actually exist, any number of US Treasury bonds may be delivered in satisfaction of the delivery requirements. In fact any Treasury bond not callable or not maturing within 15 years of the expiry date of the futures contract may be delivered. The choice for the bond that will actually be delivered rests with the party that sold the futures contract but the CBT insists that the amount of the bond that is actually delivered is suitably adjusted into the equivalent of the $100 000 face value

---

[1] By the way, this measure of hedge effectiveness can never be negative unless you do something strange like forget to include the constant in (7.7).

20-year 6% coupon nominal bond. However, this need not concern us unduly since the Treasury bond futures market is very liquid and we can easily terminate our hedge on any day by 'reversing out'. That is, we can offset our short obligations by buying the same Treasury bond futures contract. The CBT then allows us to net the long and short position in the same contract leaving us with no further obligation.

To determine the hedge ratio and to see whether we can expect an effective hedge, we collect daily prices for our cash bond and the Treasury futures contract from January 1, 2002 until September 6, 2002. This information and the subsequent analysis are contained in the workbook HEDB02.xls. We first compute the correlation coefficient between the changes in the price of the cash asset, the 5.25% Treasury bonds in this example, and the hedging instrument, the 20-year T-bond futures contract in this example. In the spreadsheet DATA, cell E189 we find a pleasing +0.965 correlation. This suggests that changes in the price of our cash and hedging instrument strongly move together and so our choice for the hedging instrument may prove to be a good one.

We now run an OLS regression choosing the changes in the price of the 5.25% cash bond as the dependent or y variable and changes in the price of the Treasury bond futures price as our independent or x variable. This can be easily done in Excel. Choose 'data analysis' under the 'tools' sub-menu.[2] Then select 'regression' and click OK. Following the instructions you will obtain an estimate of the regression and find that the value of the slope coefficients is $\beta = 0.948$ and the $R^2 = 0.931$. See the spreadsheet Regression in the workbook HEDB02.xls.

Our hedge ratio of 0.948 suggests that for every $100 000 face value amount we wish to hedge we need to short 0.948 futures contracts. Since we wish to hedge a $30 million face value investment in the cash bond or 300 $100 000 amounts, we need to short 284.4 (practically, 284) futures contracts. The R^2 suggests that we can expect to reduce the unexpected changes in the value of our cash position by 93.1% if we choose to use this 'optimal' hedge ratio.

However, as suggested earlier the R^2 is an optimistic estimate of hedge effectiveness. Note that the R^2 is estimated 'within sample'. That is, the regression routine 'knows' all the past price movements of the cash and hedging instruments and will be very diligent in estimating that slope coefficient β that maximizes R^2. The problem is of course that you are going to perform the hedge over the coming time period. This additional data was not taken into account in the

---

[2] It is possible that data analysis is not installed in your version of Excel. You need to select 'add ins' under the 'tools' sub-menu, and then tick off 'analysis tool pack'.

past estimate of the hedge ratio and R^2. Therefore the regression-based hedge ratio will not likely be able to reduce future unexpected losses and gains on the hedge portfolio by 93.1%.

7.7.2   Comments on the regression-based hedge ratio

The attractive feature of regression-based hedge ratios is that as long as you can find a hedging instrument that actively trades you can easily estimate the optimal hedge ratio and then implement your hedging strategy. Furthermore the technique is very flexible, as it does not require an economic model that describes the price movements of the cash and futures instruments. In many situations finance has not yet been able to develop the required model so it is useful to have a technique that does not require something that we do not have.

However, this flexibility comes at a cost. The regression model assumes that the relation between changes in the price of the cash and futures price is the same in the immediate future as it was in the past. It cannot anticipate shifts from past behaviour and when this happens the regression-based hedging strategy may perform poorly. More disturbingly, often this is precisely the set of circumstances that you need to hedge against. Consequently it is usually better to obtain hedge ratios from a pricing model as long as the model works to some degree. Such is the case in hedging Treasury bonds for we do have a traditional (crude) pricing model. This leads us to consider the traditional (modified) duration hedge ratio.

7.8   Duration-based hedge ratio

The advantage of the modified duration hedge ratio is that it is based on a pricing model. This means that we do not rely upon the past behaviour to model future behaviour and so the hedge can potentially respond well to a paradigm shift in interest rates. This is an important advantage for it is the unexpected that we wish to hedge against, not the expected from past behaviour.

However, as shown in (7.6) the pricing model that underlies the modified duration hedge ratio is the traditional bond valuation model based on the yield to maturity. This means that the modified duration hedge ratio suffers from the same set of restrictive assumptions that the traditional bond valuation model assumes. Specifically the pricing model and therefore the modified duration hedge ratio assumes a flat term structure that shifts in a parallel fashion. To appreciate what this means refer to Figure 7.3. The lower flat yield curve is assumed to be the current yield curve based on the bond's current yield to maturity, say 6%. Then if interest rates rise, say by 100 basis points, the traditional pricing model and the associated modified duration hedge ratio assumes that this flat yield curve shifts upward by 100 basis points to 7%. In contrast the initial yield curve is likely not flat and as depicted in Figure 7.3 the yield curve may shift upwards in a non-parallel fashion. In other words, the yield curve changes shape as it rises.

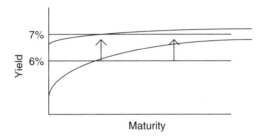

Figure 7.3 Duration assumes parallel shifts in a flat yield curve

Kolb and Chiang (1982) find that the practical effects of these restrictive assumptions are 'small'. This result should not be so surprising since Litterman and Scheinkman (1991) find that only three factors explain changes in the US Treasury term structure of interest rates and attribute approximately 80% of all changes in the term structure to parallel shifts. In other words, as crude as the assumption of a parallel shift in the yield curve is, it approximates reality reasonably well.

Equation 7.A(8), derived in the appendix section 7.10.2, is the modified duration hedge ratio. Notice that once again the hedge ratio is the price sensitivity of the asset to be hedged relative to the price sensitivity of the hedging asset. As explained in the appendix section 7.10.2 the term K is a measure of the responsiveness of the yield spread to changes in the cash bond and the hedge asset's yield. We assume K is 1 or we estimate it from past data using OLS regressions. Meanwhile D_B^* is the duration of the cash bond we wish to hedge, D_h^* is the duration of our hedging instrument and B and h are the price of the cash and hedging instrument respectively.

$$N = -\frac{D_B^* B}{D_h^* h} K \qquad (7.A(8))$$

To illustrate the workings of the hedge ratio we return to the two bonds we used to illustrate the workings of the modified duration calculation in section 7.3. Specifically we choose to hedge a 4% semi-annual coupon pay bond that matures in 20 years, yields 7.5%, is priced at $64.036 and has a modified duration of 11.78 with the 12% semi-annual coupon pay bond that matures in 20 years, yields 7.5%, is priced at $146.24 and has a modified duration of 9.43. Substituting appropriate values into 7.A(8) we obtain a hedge ratio of −0.547.

$$N = -\frac{11.78(64.036)}{9.43(146.24)}(1) = -0.547$$

This result suggests that for every 100 of the cheaper bonds that we buy for $64\,036$ we should short 54.7 or $79\,993.28$ of the more expensive bond. Therefore the value of our hedge portfolio will be a negative $15\,957$ as this position means that we will be short more than we are long in bonds. How well will this strategy work? Suppose yields rise unexpectedly by 100 basis points. Then according to (7.5a) the changes in the value of our cash bond will be precisely offset by changes in the value of our hedging asset. That is

$$\Delta V_B = (-11.78)(0.01)(64\,036) = -7543$$

$$\Delta V_h = (-9.43)(0.01)(-79\,993) = 7543$$

But as you may well guess the above illustration is highly simplified as it ignores some very serious practical problems. Among the most serious are delivery squeezes that invalidate the use of bonds as hedging instruments either when using the regression-based or the modified duration-based hedge ratio.

7.8.1 Delivery squeezes and the need for bond futures contracts

Imagine I actually shorted the 12% coupon bond in order to execute the hedging strategy in section 7.6.4. This means I have borrowed the 12% coupon bonds, sold them and hope to buy them back and return them to the lender at a cheaper price once yields rise. This also means I have taken on the commitment to buy them back since I do not own the bonds that I have sold.

Now suppose the yield of this bond increases to 8.5% so the bond is now priced at $133.385, a reduction of $12.855 per $100. Now I wish to repurchase the bond to cover my short position. Unfortunately, I cannot easily find anybody to sell the bond to me. This happens because the bond market is not very liquid. Furthermore bonds trade over the counter so there is no market maker that is committed to maintain liquidity as there is on the stock exchange. I have to keep phoning around trying to find someone willing to sell me enough bonds to cover my short position.

Eventually I will find someone willing to sell to me the bonds I require. However, from the tone of my voice, I betray my anxiety and the other trader realizes that I am desperate to buy. So the other trader asks for $135. What am I to do? The bonds should trade at $133.385, but now it looks like I have to pay a higher price. I will try to bargain the trader down but in the very process of doing so I am confirming that I really need to buy the bonds. If I refuse to trade then I will be unable to cover my short position. Then I suspect that something bad will happen to me because if the party that originally lent those bonds to me demands them back I will be in breach of contract. So I will have to swallow my pride and buy the bonds at a price that is too high given current market conditions. I will be squeezed. As a result, my hedge will not work as well as it should because I will experience a loss on my hedge portfolio not because of any failure of the hedge ratio, but because I have been squeezed.

To avoid delivery squeezes we use bond futures contracts as the hedging contract. Bond futures contracts are derivative securities where the underlying asset is a hypothetical bond. If we short a bond futures contract we are committed to sell the hypothetical bond at a priced agreed today (the futures price) at some future date, usually a few months but may be as long as a year or somewhat more. If yields were to rise we would gain since we agreed to sell at the fixed price and now the current market price is lower. Therefore the futures contract can act as a pseudo bond that can play the role of the short bond we need to execute the hedging strategy.

The advantage is that the bond futures contract is exchange traded. This means pricing is transparent because in contrast to the over-the-counter market, prices are published and are publicly available throughout the trading day. The futures contract is a much more liquid instrument than actual bonds that trade in the over-the-counter market. For one thing the supply or open interest of bond futures contracts are determined by the trading activity of bond traders rather than by an issuing authority as in the case of sovereign bonds. For another there is a centralized trading organization (the exchange) where buy and sell orders are executed quickly and effectively. Therefore it should be possible for those wishing to hedge to buy and sell futures contracts as needed.

There is little risk of a delivery squeeze because there are a wide variety of bonds that can be delivered in satisfaction of delivery requirements. The exchange establishes a formula that converts the value of the bonds that are deliverable into the hypothetical bond equivalent and publishes the cheapest (from the short futures contract perspective) deliverable bond that satisfies the delivery requirements.

Also there is little risk that the counterparty may fail to execute their side of the bargain. The exchange requires a deposit or margin based on the value of the futures contract bought or sold. This guarantees that both counterparties can perform according to the terms of the contract since the deposit will cover their losses in the event of adverse price movements. The exchange also marks to market, meaning that the exchange calculates the gains and losses on each open position daily so that if a series of adverse price movements occur, the adversely affected counterparty will receive a margin call. This means that the counterparty receiving the margin call must top up the margin or deposit to make sure that if the current adverse price trend continues the trader can continue to cover losses. If they do not, then the exchange terminates the position, losses are deducted from the margin accounts and the remainder is returned to the trader that failed to meet their margin call. Therefore the futures exchange ensures that there is little or no counterparty risk.

Finally, a hedger can choose when to terminate the hedge. They can terminate early by reversing out their positions. That is, since they are short the futures contract they can on any given day buy the same futures contract and then net their obligations to nil. Similarly they can extend the life of the hedge by 'rolling the contract over'. Here the hedger reverses out a short position in a futures contract approaching maturity but then shorts a longer date bond futures contract. In contrast hedging by shorting bonds means that the party that lends the bond and not the hedging party that shorted the bond may terminate the hedge.

In summary bond futures contracts are an attractive hedging instrument because

- Pricing is transparent.
- The bond futures contract tends to be very liquid where the risk of delivery squeezes is minimized.
- The contract is exchange traded with little or no counterparty risk.
- The hedger chooses when to terminate the hedge.

Finally, there are a wide variety of futures contracts available. As an example, Table 7.2 shows some of the bond futures contracts that are available in the US.

Notice in particular that there are a variety of Treasury security futures contracts that are available for trade all along the yield curve. Such is not the case for the Sterling and Euro sovereign

Table 7.2 Bond futures contracts that trade in the US*

Asset	Maturity	Coupon/Nominal value	Deliverable
T-bill (IMM)	90 days	Discount $FV=\$1\,000\,000$	Yes (90-, 91-, or 92- day T-bill)
2-year T-note (CBT)	2 years	6% $FV=\$200\,000$	Yes (1 year 9 months – 2 years)
5-year T-note (CBT)	5 years	6% $FV=\$100\,000$	Yes (4 years 3 months – 5 years 3 months)
10-year T-note (CBT)	10 years	6% $FV=\$100\,000$	Yes (6 years 6 months – 10 years)
20-year T-bond (CBT)	20 years	6% $FV=\$100\,000$	Yes (15 years or more)
Eurodollar (IMM)	3 months	Discount $FV=\$1\,000\,000$	Cash settlement
Bond buyer municipal bond index (40 bonds) (CBT)	Long term (all greater than 19 years)	6% $FV=\$100\,000$	Cash settlement

*IMM = International Money Market, CBT = Chicago Board of Trade

debt markets where typically there is only a short and long futures contract available for trade.[3]

7.8.2 An example of duration-based hedging

The hedge ratio, that is, the number of futures contracts you should short in order to hedge a long position in a bond portfolio, has already been presented. But how are we to calculate this ratio? The subtleties can best be explained through use of a numerical example.

On September 6, 2002 we wish to hedge a long position in the 5.25% semi-annual coupon pay US Treasury bond that matures on February 15, 2029. We choose to hedge this bond with the 20-year T-bond futures that trades on the CBT. One question that we must immediately confront is what is the duration of the futures contract? There are two aspects to this question. First, we do not know which bond will be delivered in satisfaction of the futures contract because the 'cheapest to deliver' bond may shift from one bond to another in response to a change in interest rates. To accurately predict which bond would be delivered would require a model that accurately predicts interest rates, a difficult task. Therefore we assume that the current cheapest to deliver bond will be the bond that is actually delivered in satisfaction of the delivery requirements. Second, one must keep in mind that as the futures contract moves through time

[3] Why are there not more futures contracts in Europe? This is a mystery to me too.

towards maturity, so does the cheapest to deliver bond. Therefore the duration of the futures contract is the same as the duration of the underlying cheapest to deliver bond, assuming of course that this current cheapest to deliver bond will actually be delivered. In other words the futures nature of the futures contract does not add any more or less interest rate sensitivity to the assumed cheapest to deliver bond. To put it another way, the seesaw of the futures contract and the cheapest to deliver bond is the same.

Bearing this in mind, the facts (points 1 and 2) and assumptions (points 3 and 4) of the example are as follows.

1. The bond to be hedged – the 5.25% semi-annual coupon pay US Treasury bond that matures on February 15, 2029. The bond trades for settlement on September 6, 2002 for a clean price of $102.75 and yields 5.06%. Therefore $B_{c0} = 102.75$.
2. The futures contract – a 20-year T-Bond futures contract will expire in six months. The cheapest to deliver (ctd) bond is the 5.25% US Treasury note that matures on February 15, 2019 currently yielding 5.12%. Therefore $B_{ctd0} = 101.430$. The futures price, the delivery price of the hypothetical 20-year 6% US T-Bond in six months from now is $110.625.[4] That is $B_F = 110.625$.
3. Yield spread assumption – in this example, we assume yield spreads remain constant such that six months from now, the yield spread between the bond to be hedged and the ctd is 6 bp. In practice you will have to make your own assumption. To the extent that your assumption does not hold, and yield spreads vary from your assumptions, net gains/losses will be realized. This is one source of *basis risk*, a concept that we will discuss in detail a little later.
4. Time horizon – we assume that the hedge is terminated on the date the futures contract matures. In practice this will rarely occur, more typically you will hedge using futures contracts that mature 'too early', so you plan to 'roll the contract over' (renew as the earlier one matures) until the date you wish to terminate the hedge occurs. Then you will reverse out your futures position (i.e. if you are short futures, you will buy to net the two out). The fact that your hedge time horizon and the maturity of the futures contract do not match is another source of *basis risk*.

All of the above information is available as of the beginning of the hedge. To solve for the hedge ratio, the following steps, integrated with the above information, must be followed.

---

[4] The equivalent long sterling and Euro futures contracts have a 7% gilt, 6% bund, all of no fixed maturity as the underlying asset respectively.

Step 1: Find the conversion factor for the ctd bond. This is the number of the cheapest to deliver bonds that are calculated to be the equivalent of the nominal bond that underlies the futures contract. This information is published by the exchange. On September 6, 2002 suppose this number is 0.923542.

Step 2: Calculate the *price* and *yield* of the ctd bond as of *maturity of the futures contract.* (Note that is why the relevant parameters are subscripted *m*.)

$$B_{ctdm} = B_F \times CF_m = (110.625)(0.923542) = \$102.167$$

Therefore yield can be found as

$$102.167 = 2.625 \left[\frac{1 - (1 + R_{ctdm}/2)^{-32}}{R_{ctdm}/2} \right] + \frac{100}{(1 + R_{ctdm}/2)^{32}}$$

Solving for the IRR (YTM) we have $R_{ctdm}/2 = 0.02525$ so $R_{ctdm} = 5.05\%$

Step 3: Calculate the *yield* and *price* of your cash bond as of *maturity of the futures contract.*
$R_{cm} = R_{ctdm} +$ assumed spread $= 5.05\% - 0.06\% = 4.99\%$ (note that now we calculate the yield first).

$$B_{cm} = \$2.625 \left[\frac{1 - (1 + 0.0499/2)^{-52}}{0.0499/2} \right] + \frac{100}{(1 + 0.0499/2)^{52}}$$

$$= \$103.764$$

Step 4: Calculate the $PVBP_{ctdm}$ and $PVBP_{cm}$ using the price and yield information as developed above. I prefer to use 'direct calculation' of the *PVBP*, that is to measure the price response of the bond to a 1 bp *annual* change in yield rather than calculate it from duration as this saves time and reduces mathematical errors.

$PVBP_{ctdm}$	Yield	Price (exact)
	5.05 (2.525 semi)	102.177255
	5.06 (2.53 semi)	102.066941
Difference (PVBP_{ctdm})		0.110314

$PVBP_{cm}$	Yield	Price (exact)
	4.99 (2.495 semi)	103.763871
	5.00 (2.50 semi)	103.615385
Difference (PVBP_{cm})		0.148486

Step 5: Calculate the hedge ratio.

$$N = -\frac{PVBP_{cm}}{PVBP_{ctdm}} \times CF_m = -\frac{0.148486}{0.110314} \times 0.923542 = -1.243$$

Notice that the hedge ratio is not simply the ratio of the price sensitivity of the cash to the hedging instrument, as we would normally expect. Instead this ratio is adjusted by the conversion factor *CF* because the ctd bond is not really the hedging instrument. Rather the hedging instrument is the hypothetical bond that underlies the futures contract so we need to convert the ctd into its hypothetical bond equivalent.

What does -1.243 mean? Recall that all futures have a standard contract size. For instance, the LIFFE sterling gilt is based on a £50 000 face value amount. The US T-bonds and notes are based on $100 000 face value amount. Therefore the above ratio says that for every $100 000 investment in the cash bond, you should short 1.243 futures contracts. For instance, if you want to hedge a $30 000 000 investment in US T-bonds, you have 30 000 000/100 000 or 300 $100 000 amounts. Therefore you need to short 300×1.243 or 372.9 (practically, 373) futures contracts.

How well can we expect this hedge to work? Suppose we experience an upward parallel shift in interest rates of 100 basis points. That is

	Was	Supposed to be	Turns out
R_{ctd}	5.12	5.05	6.12
R_c	5.06	4.99	6.06

The price of the cash bond B_{cm} and the cheapest to deliver bond B_{ctdm} at maturity of the futures contract are

$$B_{cm} = \$2.625 \left[\frac{1 - (1 + 0.0606/2)^{-52}}{0.0606/2} \right] + \frac{100}{(1 + 0.0606/2)^{522}}$$

$$= \$89.464$$

$$B_{ctdm} = \$2.625 \left[\frac{1 - (1 + 0.0612/2)^{-32}}{0.0612/2} \right] + \frac{100}{(1 + 0.0612/2)^{32}}$$

$$= \$91.203$$

Therefore the change in the value of the cash bond relative to what it was supposed to be at maturity of the futures contract is $-\$14.30(103.764 - 89.464)$ and the change in the value of the cheapest to deliver bond relative to what is was supposed to be at maturity of the futures contract is $-\$10.964(102.167 - 91.203)$.

Therefore the change in the value of our hedge portfolio is

$$\Delta V_H = \Delta B_{cm} - N \frac{\Delta B_{ctdm}}{CF}$$

$$= -14.30 - (1.243)\frac{-10.964}{0.923542} = +\$0.457$$

Notice that we need to convert the loss on the cheapest to deliver bond into the equivalent hypothetical 20-year 6% coupon bond that underlies the futures contract by dividing the loss by the conversion factor. In this example the value of the $30 million portfolio will unexpectedly rise by $137 100. This is due to positive convexity. A 100 basis point rise in yield is more than a small amount and as we know from Figure 7.2, modified duration will overestimate the loss in response to a rise in yield. This tells us that the modified duration hedge ratio was 'too large'. One could obtain a 'more accurate' hedge by adjusting the hedge ratio for convexity but this does not make sense. Why hedge away the beneficial effects of positive convexity?

However, the above example was highly artificial since we timed the termination of the hedge to coincide with the maturity of the futures contract. This will rarely happen in practice. In general we would need to terminate the hedge at some other date than the date of maturity of the futures contract and as briefly mentioned in our assumptions 3 and 4, we would have basis risk.

7.9 Basis risk

The *basis* is the price spread between the cash and futures price. Since the cash price refers to the asset's price that we wish to hedge as of today, and the futures price refers to the value of the asset that underlies the futures contract at some future point in time, there will be a difference between these prices in general. Unexpected changes in the basis, the price spread between the cash and futures price, is called *basis risk*. These unexpected changes in the basis will lead to unexpected changes in the value of the hedge portfolio and so lead to non-perfect hedging strategy results. The obvious questions to ask at this point are what are the sources of basis risk and how do we avoid them?

There are three sources of basis risk. The first is differences between the item to be hedged and the item that underlies the futures contract. In the above example we have basis risk because the bond we wanted to hedge was (roughly) a 27-year bond and the item that underlay the futures contract was (roughly) a 17-year bond. At the beginning of the hedge the yield spread (or the basis measured in terms of yield rather than price) was 6 basis points as the yield curve was very slightly downward sloping at the long end of the yield curve. Our artificial example assumed that the basis did not change; the yield spread was still 6 basis points upon termination of the hedge six months later. However, this is an unlikely scenario and we would expect that the yield spread between these two bonds would more or less randomly change through time. Given that our hedge ratio was established on the assumption that the yield spread between these two bonds would be 6 basis points as of maturity of the hedge (note that the hedge ratio was based on the *PVBP* at maturity of the futures contract) then unexpected changes in the yield spread would lead to unexpected gains and losses on our hedge portfolio.

A second source of basis risk is caused by the time distance between the date of termination of the hedge and the date of maturity of the futures contract. This source of basis risk will exist even in the case where the cash bond that we wish to hedge is the same as the hypothetical bond that underlies the futures contract. When one needs to terminate the hedge 'early' (prior to the maturity of the futures contract) one must repurchase the futures contract at the prevailing futures price. No doubt that when setting up the hedge we had a view as to what this futures price would be relative to the spot price at this future point in time but the unexpected may have happened based on the arrival of new information in the meantime. This would lead to unexpected changes in the basis and therefore unexpected gains and losses on our hedge portfolio even though the cash and futures bond are the same.

For example, imagine that we had to terminate the hedge in our example in four months, two months prior to maturity of the futures contract. Let's say we initially expect that the basis will be 6 basis points in four months' time. However, during the four months of our hedge new information is released that suggests that inflation will be higher in the future. Therefore the term structure of interest rates became upward rather than downward sloping. When we go to terminate the hedge, both the yields on our long bond that we wish to hedge and the same bond that underlies the futures contract rose, but our longer-term cash bond rose more as the term structure became more upward sloping. This happens because the futures price refers to the price of the cash bond two more months in the future and so the futures yield refers to a yield on the bond that is two months shorter than the cash bond's yield. Therefore we experience an unexpected loss because the yield on our cash bond rose more than the increase in yield implied by the futures price. In other words, the basis unexpectedly changed as the yield spread ended up at, say, a positive

3 basis points rather than a negative 6 basis points. Similarly when we need to terminate our hedge 'late' (after the first futures contract has expired) we need to sell the first futures contract prior to expiry and purchase another at the prevailing futures prices at this future point in time. Again the basis we expect to prevail at the date that we plan to execute these transactions may unexpectedly change leading to unexpected gains and losses.

The third source of basis risk is minor. Notice that in our example we need to short 372.9 futures contracts but we could only practically short 372 or 373. Therefore the size of our futures position was slightly different (we choose 373) than that suggested by our hedge ratio and as a result we were slightly overhedged. This of course could lead to additional unexpected gains and losses simply because we are not strictly acting in accordance with the duration-based hedge ratio.

To completely avoid basis risk we need to choose a futures contract where the item that underlies the contract is precisely the same as the asset we need to hedge, we need to terminate the hedge as of the expiry date of the futures contract and we need to sell the precise number of futures contracts as indicated by our hedge ratio. This will work because at the expiry date of the futures contract the futures contract and our cash asset *are precisely the same.* In the absence of arbitrage the short futures position and the long cash asset position must perfectly offset. The basis is zero and we have zero basis risk. The hedge will perform perfectly as there will be no unexpected gains and losses. However, as you can see this is a highly restrictive case and in general you can expect to take on basis risk whenever you hedge with futures contracts. In other words, whenever you hedge using futures contracts you trade price risk (unexpected changes in the value of your long cash position) for basis risk (unexpected changes in the price spread between the cash and futures price).

Therefore it makes sense to hedge only when you have some assurance that basis risk is less than price risk. This is the case as long as you can expect a positive correlation between changes in price between the asset you want to have hedged and the asset that underlies the futures contract. That way as yields rise, the yields on both the cash and futures asset rises so there is at least some offset between the losses on the cash asset that you hold long and gains on the futures asset that you hold short. This means that to set up your hedge you need to closely examine the correlation between the cash and futures asset.

Cheerfully we should expect a positive correlation among most assets, as it is quite unusual to find situations where assets move in opposite directions. However, there are exceptions. Imagine we decide to hedge our 27-year bond with the 90-day T-bill futures.

Suppose that during the hedge the yield curve experienced a violent twist where short-term yields fall and long-term yields rise and so the yield curve became steeply upward sloping. Then we would experience losses on our cash bond as long-term yields rise. The 90-day T-bill futures contract would experience gains as short-term interest rates fall but since we hold this futures contract short we experience losses. Therefore our 'hedge' would experience losses on the cash asset and losses on the short futures contract. Some hedge. In this situation it would be better if we had not hedged at all, for rather than reducing the range of outcomes the 'hedge' actually increased them. The moral of the story is that you have to be careful with hedging a cash asset with a futures contract whose underlying asset has maturity very different than your cash asset. This is usually not a problem in the US since as Table 7.2 shows the US futures market offers a wide variety of interest rate futures contracts spread out all along the yield curve. However, this is not the case in Europe where typically there is only a short- and a long-term interest rate futures contract on offer leaving wide maturity gaps for the unwary.

7.10 Appendix

Our task is to derive hedge ratios that we can use to form hedge portfolios. We will examine two standard hedge ratios that are used to hedge bond investments, the regression-based hedge ratio and the (modified) duration hedge ratio.

All hedge ratios attempt to minimize the change in value of a hedge portfolio V_H that consists of a long position in a cash asset that you wish to have hedged B_0 and a short position in a hedging instrument V_h. That is, you wish to minimize changes in the value of the following equation.

$$\Delta V_H = \Delta B_0 + N \Delta V_h$$

7.10.1 Derivation of the regression-based hedge ratio

We wish to minimize the variance of changes in the value of a hedge portfolio. Mathematically speaking

$$Var(\Delta V_H) = Var(\Delta B_0 + N \Delta V_h) = 0$$

That is, the variance var of the hedge portfolio consists of the variance of changes in our long bond and the variance of changes in the value of the hedging instruments the number N of which we hold short. From the properties of the variance operator, we have

$$\sigma_{HH} = \sigma_{BB} + N^2\sigma_{hh} + 2N\sigma_{Bh} \qquad (7.\text{A}(1))$$

Note that σ_{HH} represents the variance of the hedge portfolio, σ_{BB} represents the variance of the bond that you wish to hedge, σ_{hh} represents the variance of the hedging asset and σ_{Bh} represents the covariance between the bond B and the hedging instrument h. The above equation is just another application of portfolio theory. Recall that the variance of a two-asset portfolio X and Y with weights W_X and W_Y in asset X and Y respectively is

$$\sigma_{PP} = W_X^2\sigma_{XX} + W_Y^2\sigma_{YY} + 2W_XW_Y\sigma_{XY}$$

In other words, 7.A(1) is simply the variance of a two-asset portfolio where the weight N is defined as the number of hedging instruments per bond that we wish to hedge.

Assuming the above function is convex, we can find the minimum variance of the hedge portfolio by finding the first derivative with respect to N and set it equal to zero. The second order conditions require the second derivative with respect to N to be uniformly positive. To appreciate what these steps accomplish refer to Figure 7.A1.

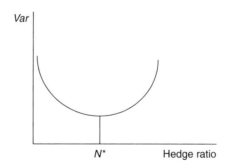

Figure 7.A1 Variance function

The graph in Figure 7.A1 shows how we expect the variance of the hedge portfolio to behave as we increase the size of the hedge ratio N. Notice that as N increases the hedge portfolio variance first decreases then increases. The graph in Figure 7.A1 is convex because any line drawn from one point on the graph to another point obtains a line segment where all intermediate points are above the graph. What we are interested in is that hedge ratio that reduces hedge portfolio variance to its minimum; just before portfolio variance begins to increase again. Graphically this is shown at point N^*. This point can be identified mathematically as that point where the slope (first derivative) is zero, and change in the slope (second derivative) is positive.

Therefore we find the first derivative of the hedge portfolio variance, set the result to zero and solve for N. This will be N^*, the minimum variance hedge ratio.

$$\frac{d\sigma_{HH}}{dN} = 0 + 2N\sigma_{hh} + 2\sigma_{Bh} = 0 \qquad (7.A(2))$$

Note that from 7.A(2) the second derivative is equal to $2\sigma_{hh}$ which is uniformly positive. Solving for N^* we find

$$N^* = \frac{-\sigma_{Bh}}{\sigma_{hh}}$$

Finally, note that since we can always write a covariance σ_{Bh} between two assets as the product of the standard deviations of the two assets σ_B and σ_h and the correlation coefficient between them ρ_{Bh} then we rewrite the above once more as

$$N^* = \frac{-\rho_{Bh}\sigma_B}{\sigma_h} \qquad (7.A(3))$$

Equation 7.A(3) clearly shows that the optimal regression-based hedge ratio is a ratio of the variability of the value of the cash asset relative to the variability of the value of the hedging instrument. This is in strict agreement with what we learned in section 2.1. In this case the relative variability is conditioned by the correlation coefficient. This hedge ratio is negative because when the hedging asset and the bond to be hedged are positively correlated the hedging instrument must be held short in order to hedge a long position in the bond.

The next step is to estimate the hedge ratio 7.A(3). It turns out that the slope coefficient of any one independent variable OLS regression has the interpretation of being a ratio of a covariance divided by a variance. This is the same as N in 7.A(3). This should not surprise you since the slope coefficient or beta in the capital asset pricing model, a one independent variable regression, has precisely that same interpretation. In general,

$$y_t = a + bx_t + \varepsilon_t \quad \text{and} \quad b = \frac{\sigma_{x,y}}{\sigma_{x,x}} = N$$

where y_t is a time series of observations of the dependent variable, changes in the price of the long bond that we wish to hedge in our application, x_t is a time series of observations of the independent variable, changes in the price of the hedging asset in our application and finally ε_t is the time series of errors produced by the regression.

In our application we run an OLS regression of

$$\Delta V_{Bt} = a + b\Delta V_{ht} + \varepsilon \quad \text{and} \quad b = \frac{\sigma_{Bh}}{\sigma_{hh}} = \frac{\rho_{Bh}\sigma_B}{\sigma_h}$$

7.10.2 The (modified) duration hedge ratio

This is very useful for straight bonds. Again our hedge portfolio is,

$$V_H = V_B + NV_h$$

where now our cash instrument is a bond portfolio and our hedging instrument is another fixed income instrument, typically a bond futures contract. We wish to minimize changes in the value of the following equation.

$$\Delta V_H = \Delta V_B + N\Delta V_h \tag{7.A(4)}$$

According to our duration model (7.5a), we believe that

$$\Delta V_B = -D_B^* B\Delta Y_B \quad \text{and} \quad \Delta V_h = -D_h^* h\Delta Y_h \tag{7.A(5)}$$

One complicating feature is that we have to assume some relationship between the change in yield on the cash asset ΔY_B and the change in yield on the hedging asset ΔY_h. Typically we assume the relationship is

$$\Delta Y_B = K\Delta Y_h + \varepsilon \tag{7.A(6)}$$

where K is a constant that determines the spread between the cash asset yield and the hedging asset yield. For example, if $K = 2$, then in response to a 100 basis point increase in hedging asset yield, the cash asset yield increases by 200 basis points. The parameter ε represents error in the above approximation where we assume the covariance between the error and changes in the hedging asset yield is zero. The latter assumption simplifies the derivation considerably.

Substituting 7.A(5) into 7.A(4) we have

$$\Delta V_H \cong -D_B^* B(\Delta Y_B) + (-ND_h^* h\Delta Y_h) \tag{7.A(7)}$$

Then substituting 7.A(6) into 7.A(7) above, we have a new expression for changes in the value of the hedge portfolio that we wish to equal zero.

$$\Delta V_H \cong -D_B^* B(K\Delta Y_h + \varepsilon) + (-ND_h^* h\Delta Y_h) = 0$$

Next we multiply through by -1 to get rid of the confusing minus signs. Then we collect the random terms (ΔY_h and ε) to find the desired equation, the variance of which we wish to minimize.

$$\Delta V_H \cong \left[D_B^* BK + ND_h^* h\right]\Delta Y_h + D_B^* B\varepsilon$$

Since $E(\varepsilon) = 0$, $E(\Delta Y_h) = 0$ and $E(\Delta Y_h, \varepsilon) = 0$, and using the properties of the expectations operator, the variance of changes in the value of the hedge portfolio is,

$$Var[\Delta V_H] = [D_B^*BK + ND_h^*h]^2 \, Var(\Delta Y_h) + (D_B^*B)^2 \, Var(\varepsilon)$$

This is yet another application of the variance of a two asset portfolio ΔY_h and ε where the weights are $[D_B^*BK + ND_h^*h]$ and (D_B^*B). The correlation between the two assets is zero so the covariance term is zero. Taking the first derivative with respect to N, setting the result equal to zero and solving for N we obtain,

$$N = -\frac{D_B^*B}{D_h^*h}K \qquad\qquad (7.A(8))$$

This is the modified duration-based hedge ratio. Sometimes it is more convenient to use the $PVBP$ rather than D^*. In that case our hedge ratio is

$$N = -\frac{PVBP_B}{PVBP_h}K \qquad\qquad (7.A(8))$$

One problem with 7.A(8) is how to estimate K. This is a problem because it represents the responsiveness of the cash asset yield to changes in the hedging asset yield. This requires a model of yield spreads. In general such models do not exist. Typically we assume that the factor $K = 1$, so that yield spreads are assumed constant. Alternatively we can estimate K through OLS as in the regression-based model.

7.11 Exercises

Question 1
You observe the following two bonds.

Bond	Maturity	Coupon rate	Yield to maturity (APR)
A	4 years	12%	7.5%
B	4 years	8%	7.0%

Answer the following two questions.

(a) Which bond would you expect to have a higher sensitivity to changes in interest rates? Explain why.

(b) Confirm your intuition by calculating the duration for bonds A and B.

(c) Would you expect the rankings by risk to be the same if you were using Macaulay's duration? Confirm your intuition by calculating Macaulay's duration for the above two bonds.

Question 2

Work out the 'optimal hedge ratio' based on the following information.

1. The portfolio to be hedged – A 19-year 10% coupon bond that is priced to yield 6.5%. Therefore $B_{co} =$?.
2. The futures contract – A 20-year T-bond futures contract will expire in six months. The cheapest to deliver (ctd) bond is a 16-year 7% coupon bond currently yielding 6.25%. Therefore $B_{ctd0} =$?. The futures price, the delivery price of the hypothetical 20-year 6% US (9% gilt, 6% bund, all of no fixed maturity) T-bond in six months from now is 105.519. The conversion factor CF is 1.100851.
3. *Yield spread assumption:* In this example, we assume yield spreads remain constant such that six months from now, the yield spread between the bond to be hedged and the ctd is 25 bp. $K =$?. In practice you will have to make your own assumption. To the extent that your assumption does not hold, and yield spreads vary from your assumptions, net gains/losses will be realized. This is one source of *basis risk*.
4. *Time horizon:* We assume the hedge is terminated upon the date the futures contract matures. In practice this will rarely occur, more typically you will hedge using futures contracts that mature 'too early', so you plan to 'roll the contract over' (renew as the earlier one matures) until the date you wish to terminate the hedge occurs. Then you will reverse out your futures position (i.e. if you are short futures, you will buy to net the two out). The fact that your hedge time horizon and the maturity of the futures contract does not match is another source of *basis risk*.

All of the above information is available as of the beginning of the hedge.

(a) Now work out the hedge ratio.
(b) Do you buy or short futures contracts?
(c) Based on a contract size of $100 000, how many futures contracts do you buy/short?

Question 3

You expect bond yields to rise. To avoid losses, you decide to hedge using futures contracts. Your current portfolio consists of a

$100 000 000 (face value) investment in a 7% coupon Ford Motor Corporation bond with 20 years to maturity that currently yields 6.25%. Therefore these bonds are currently priced at 108.496.

You plan to hedge using 20-year T-bond futures contracts that mature in six months time which is also the date you plan to unwind the hedge. The current cheapest to deliver bond is a 17.5-year, 6% coupon bond that yields 6%. The conversion factor is 0.815888. The futures price is 126.538. You expect that the current yield spread between the bond to be hedged and the current cheapest to deliver bond to remain at 25 basis points.

1. What is the hedge ratio?
2. Describe how the *above* hedge strategy can go wrong. Be careful to apply your answer to the above facts.

Question 4

Convexity can be used to refine the duration model to measure the anticipated price response of a bond for a given change in yield. Specifically

$$\Delta B = B_0 D_B^* \Delta Y + \tfrac{1}{2} B_0 C_B \Delta Y^2$$

where C_B is the convexity of the bond and other terms are as defined in the text. You anticipate that interest rates are likely to decline so you wish to switch into a bond that has higher duration and convexity. Below is a table that describes the bond that you wish to sell and the bond that you wish to purchase. Note that the bond you wish to sell has 22 coupon payments remaining and the bond that you wish to purchase has 44 coupons remaining.

Transaction	Name	Coupon	Price	Yield	Duration	Convexity
Sell	Govt. of Australia	9.625	111.651	7.997	6.978	65.485
Buy	Govt. of Australia	8.375	101.123	8.263	10.087	156.799

(a) If yields fall by 100 basis points, what would be the increase in price for both bonds according to the duration and convexity model of bond price changes?
(b) Find the actual price of these two bonds in response to a 100 basis point decrease in yield using the usual bond pricing model.
(c) Comment on the suitability of the convexity adjustment in modelling the price change of a bond in response to a change in yield.

Question 5

You wish to hedge the 5.25% Treasury bond maturing on February 15, 2029. You decide to hedge using the regression hedge ratio approach. The data you need is contained in the HEDB02 workbook, spreadsheet Exercise data.

(a) First, calculate the correlation between the daily change in the bond price with the daily change in the CBT T-bond futures contract price. Do you think the CBT T-bond futures contract is a good choice for a hedging instrument?

(b) Calculate the regression-based hedge ratio by regression daily price changes in the cash bond price (dependent or Y variable) against the daily price change in the T-bond futures contract (independent or X variable).

(c) How effective does this hedge ratio promise to be?

(d) Is it realistic to expect the hedge ratio to be as effective as promised?

Active and passive strategies

8.1 Introduction

In the last chapter we introduced Macaulay and modified duration measures and discussed traditional hedging strategies. These hedging strategies are useful for individual traders interested in controlling the risk of their positions in the bond market. In this chapter we intend to explore some more trading strategies that require the use of duration to control risk, often in a portfolio context. After detailing how one adjusts the duration of a portfolio we will look at some alternative uses for duration for those wishing to trade on the basis of forecasts of market conditions. Then we will explore passive strategies, specifically portfolio immunization and balance sheet immunization. These are techniques employed by the insurance and banking industries respectively.

8.2 Adjusting the duration of a portfolio

Imagine your interest rate model predicts that interest rates are likely to fall. To take advantage of this you would like to increase the duration of your bond portfolio. This raises two important questions: first, how do we measure the duration of a bond portfolio and second, how can we adjust the duration of a bond portfolio recognizing that bonds tend to be illiquid.

The duration of a zero coupon bond portfolio is a simple linear average of the duration of its component bonds. For example, suppose you want to form a portfolio with a modified duration of 10 years using two zero coupon bonds, one with a modified duration of 12 and another with a modified duration of nine. You need to know the percentage of the overall portfolio that should be placed in the high duration and low duration bonds to form a portfolio duration of 10. The simple way is to solve for X in the following equation:

$$X\%(12) + (1 - X\%)(9) = 10$$

Solving, we find that $X = 0.333$, so we place 33.3% of the portfolio value in the high duration zero coupon bond and 66.7% of the portfolio value in the low duration zero coupon bond.

This is the correct procedure for forming portfolios composed of zero coupon bonds but not for portfolios formed by combining coupon bonds. This happens because with zero coupon bonds there are no coupons that need to be reinvested during the life of the bond so there is no reinvestment income. Therefore there is no mixing of prior to maturity yields in the calculation of the zero coupon bond yield. The yield of a zero coupon bond is not a weighted average of the yields expected to hold throughout the life of the bond.

In contrast, the yield of a coupon bond is a coupon-weighted average of the yields expected to hold throughout the life of the bond. This happens because the bond pays coupons that must be reinvested at the prevailing yield at the date of coupon payment. In turn this means that bonds with different coupon payments have different weighting schemes of the yields that are expected to hold throughout the life of the different bonds. Therefore the combination of redemption yields implied by a portfolio of coupon bonds is *not* a simple average of the yields of bonds making up the portfolio. In turn, this means that portfolio duration, in part based on the portfolio yield, is not a simple average of the durations of bonds making up the portfolio. While the simply average approach to obtaining portfolio duration for coupon bonds is a good approximation, it is not exact.

In the case where you need to form a portfolio of a particular duration from coupon bonds, you have to iteratively solve for the weighting scheme to find the precise weights. You do this by performing the following steps.

1. Choose some arbitrary weighting scheme, say 50% in the high duration bond and 50% in the low duration bond.

2. Measure portfolio yield using this weighting scheme. That is the cash flow at any point in time is 50% from one bond and 50% from the other. Similarly, the price of the portfolio is 50% from the first bond and 50% from the second bond. Then you find the portfolio yield or IRR.
3. Use the above portfolio cash flows, price and yield to measure modified duration.
4. If the resulting portfolio duration is not equal to your target duration, adjust the weighting scheme to something other than 50/50.
5. Continue steps 2–4 until your portfolio duration is equal to your target time horizon.

As an example, consider forming a portfolio of two bonds, bond A is a 4% semi-annual coupon pay 20-year bond and bond B is a 12% semi-annual coupon pay 20-year bond. Both bonds yield 7.5%, so bond A is worth $64.036 and bond B is worth $146.24. Spreadsheet DurB02.xls shows that the correct weighting scheme to obtain a modified duration of 10 for a portfolio composed of these two bonds is 42.3% in bond A and 57.7% in bond B. Here we use the solver function found under the tools sub-menu. We set the modified duration of the portfolio cell K1 as the target cell, set the target value as −10 and the weighting scheme cell B1 as the change cell. When we click on solve we find the weighting values as mentioned above.

The second problem is that bonds tend to be infrequently traded and costly to trade. This means that bonds tend to be illiquid, so one would be reluctant to trade bonds frequently. If this proves to be the case, then interest rate futures may well represent the solution. A long position in a bond futures contract represents the obligation to purchase an underlying bond at some future point in time. Once a long futures position is formed, the investor gains and loses on the contract in the same way they would gain and lose on a long position in the underlying bond. In other words, a long bond futures contract has the same interest rate sensitivity as a long position in the underlying bond, so futures contracts can play the same role as bonds in implementing portfolio management strategies. As mentioned in Chapter 7, the advantages of the bond futures contract are liquidity and transparency. Bond futures contracts are exchange traded. This means pricing is transparent because in contrast to the over-the-counter market, prices are published and are publicly available throughout the trading day. The futures contract is a much more liquid instrument than actual bonds that trade in the over-the-counter market because there is a centralized trading organization (the exchange) where buy and sell orders are executed quickly and effectively. In section 8.4 we will illustrate the use of bond futures contracts in executing an active portfolio management strategy.

8.3 Active and passive strategies

We can obtain four stylized types of bond strategies according to our ability to forecast along two dimensions, our ability to make an interest rate forecast and then our ability to select mispriced bonds. In Figure 8.1 the horizontal axis depicts our ability to select mispriced bonds, the further along to the right the better is our ability to do so. The vertical axis depicts our ability to make an interest rate forecast and the further we move up on the vertical axis the better we are able to do so. As shown in Figure 8.1, this leads to four stylized types of strategies, pure timing, pure bond selection, truly active and truly passive strategies.

Interest rate forecast	**Truly active**
Pure timing	Pure yield pick-up
Rate anticipation swap	Intermarket spread
Truly passive	**Bond selection**
Portfolio immunization	
Balance sheet	**Pure bond selection**
immunization	
Indexing	Substitution swap

Figure 8.1 Active and passive strategies

When we can make an interest rate forecast but are unable to detect mispriced bonds we would follow a pure timing strategy. That is, we would move into and out of broad market segments according to our interest rate forecast but form a diversified portfolio of bonds to avoid disastrous selection mistakes. An example of a pure timing strategy is a rate anticipation swap. Say we forecast that interest rates will fall. Then we would sell our portfolio of low duration bonds and replace them with a portfolio of high duration bonds instead. If we forecast an increase in interest rates we would sell our bond portfolio and reinvest the proceeds in the money market.

When we cannot make an accurate interest rate forecast but we can detect mispriced bonds we would follow a pure bond selection strategy. Here we would include undervalued bonds in our portfolio that will also include fairly priced bonds to assure that our portfolio has a duration that is consistent with our level of risk tolerance. In contrast to a pure timing strategy, we would maintain the duration of our portfolio at this level throughout the business cycle and make no attempt to time our movements into and out of high duration bonds. An example of a pure bond selection strategy is the substitution swap. In a substitution swap we already hold a diversified portfolio of bonds with a duration that we feel comfortable with; however, we notice that a given bond is priced too low. We would add this bond to our portfolio but simultaneously we would adjust our portfolio to assure that the duration of the adjusted portfolio that includes the mispriced bond does not change.

If we can forecast interest rates and detect mispriced bonds we would follow a truly active strategy. That is, we would time movements into and out of broad market sectors, shorting bonds that we feel are overpriced and buying bonds that we feel are underpriced. An example of a truly active strategy is an intermarket spread swap. For example, suppose you believe that the BBB corporate yield spread is too wide because economic conditions are expected to improve. Here we would sell Treasury bonds and reinvest the money in what we believe are undervalued corporate bonds. As another example, consider the pure yield pick-up strategy. Here the investor forecasts that the upward sloping yield curve will not change its shape nor will the level of interest rates change. Then the investor would buy a medium-term bond where the positive slope of the yield curve is steepest. In a sense the investor believes that this bond is undervalued, for as the bond moves through time towards maturity, its yield will fall and its price will rise as the bond moves down the yield curve.

Finally, most investors would admit that they cannot forecast interest rates nor can they detect mispriced bonds. Then investors would follow a truly passive strategy where the objective is to buy and hold a portfolio of bonds with a duration level that is consistent with the investor's level of risk tolerance. In other words, they partially hedge their positions to take on an acceptable level of risk. Some examples of a truly passive strategy are portfolio immunization, balance sheet immunization and indexing. For example, indexing represents the attempt by investors to replicate the performance of a benchmark by forming a bond portfolio that mimics the composition of the benchmark. A common mistake is to suggest that a truly passive strategy is low risk. This is not necessarily the case. For example, a portfolio formed to mimic the composition of an emerging market bond index is a truly passive strategy, but is it low risk?

8.4 Implementing a rate anticipation swap

Imagine an investment bank predicts that interest rates will fall and therefore wishes to conduct a rate anticipation swap. Obviously the bank will wish to sell short-term low duration bonds and replace them with long-term high duration bonds. As you can imagine, these transactions will be costly because brokerage fees and the like must be paid both ways. Moreover it may take some time to offload a large position in short-term bonds and replace them with longer-term bonds. One would worry that the fleeting opportunity may be missed because interest rates may fall while still forming the longer duration portfolio.

As a result futures contracts are often used to execute active portfolio management strategies. They have two main advantages over trading in the underlying cash bonds. First, one can adjust the modified duration of the existing portfolio in just one trade by simply buying a large block of bond futures contracts. This will reduce the expense of trading and speed up the process of adjusting the modified duration of a portfolio considerably. A second advantage is that the portfolio manager gains flexibility. The manager can choose to make the duration adjustment temporary by reversing out the futures contract once the expected decrease in interest rates materializes. Alternatively the portfolio manager may choose to make the adjustment permanent by letting the futures contract mature and taking delivery on the underlying bond.

To see how one takes advantage of an interest rate forecast we conduct a numerical example. We represent the existing portfolio as a five-year 6% coupon bond that yields 5.5%. Therefore the portfolio is worth $102.16 per $100 of face value and has a modified duration of 4.28. We wish to adjust the duration of the portfolio to 7. We choose to purchase the 20-year Treasury bond futures contact. The cheapest to deliver bond is a 16-year 7% coupon bond that yields 6.25%. The cheapest to deliver bond is worth $107.519 and has a modified duration of 9.79. The conversion factor is 0.910632. Now we must determine the number of bonds we need to purchase in order to increase the duration of our portfolio from 4.28 to 7.

A simple formula that determines the number of futures contracts that needs to be purchased in order to achieve the target duration for the portfolio is as follows.

$$\#FC = \left[\frac{(D_T^* - D_I^*)B_I}{D_{ctd}^* \times B_{ctd}} \right] CF_{ctd}$$

This equation says that to achieve a target duration D_T^* one needs to purchase a number of futures contracts $\#FC$ according to the ratio of the price-weighted difference between the target and initial portfolio duration, $(D_T^* - D_I^*) \times B_I$, and the price-weighted duration of the cheapest to deliver bond $D_{ctd}^* \times B_{ctd}$ all adjusted by the conversion factor for the cheapest to deliver bond. Recall that the conversion factor represents the adjustment necessary to convert the non-standard cheapest to deliver bond that will be delivered on the futures contract at maturity into the standard hypothetical 6% coupon 20-year bond that underlies the T-bond futures contract.

Substituting the information from our example into the formula we find that the number of futures contracts that we need to purchase equals 0.2403.

$$\#FC = \left[\frac{(7 - 4.28)102.16}{9.79 \times 107.519} \right] 0.910632 = 0.2403$$

Since the contract size that underlies the T-bond futures contract is $100 000 the above result tells us that we need to purchase 0.2403 futures contracts per $100 000 of face value of our portfolio. Since our portfolio is $100 million, and there are 1000 $100 000 amounts in $100 million, we need to purchase 240.3 (practically, 240) T-bond futures contracts.

To confirm that the above result is correct we recalculate the duration of our new portfolio that consists of the long low duration bond and 240.3 futures contracts. Viewing the duration of the portfolio as a simple linear-weighted average of the duration of component securities we have the following result.

$$D_T^* = (B_I/V_N) \times D_I^* + (B_F/V_N) \times D_F^*$$

Since the value of the initial bond is $102.16, $100 million of face value of this bond B_I is worth $102.16 million. While the futures contract has a value of zero, it creates a nominal value in the hypothetical 6% 20-year T-bond equivalent to the following expression $\#FC \times FV \times B_F$. The price of the futures contract is found as the ratio of the price of the cheapest to deliver bond and the conversion factor, B_{ctd}/CF_{ctd}. Putting these facts together the purchase of 240.3

futures contracts creates a nominal investment of $28 372 400 B_F in the hypothetical 6% 20-year T-bond.

$$Nominal = 240.3 \times 100\,000 \times 1.07519/0.910632$$
$$= \$28\,372\,400$$

Since the initial value of the portfolio is not changed by the investment in the futures contract,[1] the post-futures trade value of the portfolio V_N remains at 102.16 million. Substituting these values into Fong and Vasicek (1991) we find that the post-futures trade duration is 7 as expected.

$$D_T^* = (102.16/102.16) \times 4.28 + (28.3724/102.16) \times 9.79 = 7$$

8.5   Implementing an asset substitution swap

In Figure 8.2 we highlight the sovereign yield curve at 2.5, 5 and 10 years and give the *PVBP* for each bond that underlies these key maturities. Notice that there appears to be a 'kink' in the yield curve as the five-year yield is lower than the shorter 2.5- and longer 10-year yields.

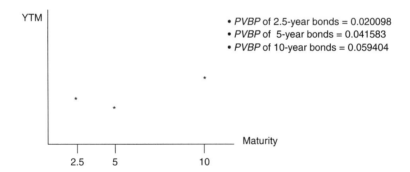

Figure 8.2   Motivation for a rate anticipation swap

We believe that the kink will soon straighten out and become a normal upward sloping yield curve as the yield on five-year bonds will rise by 10 basis points. The problem is that we hold $40 million of these bonds. If five-year yields were to rise by 10 basis points then

---

[1] Again you are reminded that the value of a futures contract is always zero at initiation.

according to its *PVBP* we would lose more than $160 000. Specifically

$$\Delta B = PVBP_{5yr} \ per \ \$100 \times \# \ of \ basis \ points \times Position \ size$$

$$= 0.041583 \times 10 \times \frac{\$40\,000\,000}{100} = \$166\,332$$

Obviously we must seek a safe haven. The likely candidates are the 2.5- and 10-year bonds. However, there is another problem. If we switch to 2.5-year bonds, we will reduce risk by switching from a position that has a *PVBP* of roughly $0.04 to one that has a *PVBP* of roughly $0.02. Remember, lower risk also implies lower potential returns. Similarly we may be reluctant to switch to 10-year bonds as that implies we will increase risk perhaps beyond our limits. What we would like to do is to find a safe haven that replicates the risk of our five-year bond.

It is possible to conduct an asset substitution swap, switching out of five-year bonds and into, say, 2.5-year bonds and yet (nearly) maintain the risk of our position as if we were still invested in five-year bonds provided that we are willing to change the size of our position. This requires us to reinvest in the target safe haven bond according to the ratio of the *PVBP* of the current position relative to the target safe haven. In this case

$$Reinvestment \ amount = \frac{PVBP_{Current}}{PVBP_{Safe \ haven}} = \frac{0.041583}{0.020098} = 2.069$$

Therefore if we sell $40 million five-year bonds we need to reinvest more than twice this amount, specifically 2.069 × $40 million or $82.76 million in 2.5-year bonds. If we do so then in response to, say, a 10 basis point parallel decrease in the yield curve we would gain just as much in the 2.5-year bond as if we were still invested in the five-year bond. This is demonstrated below.

$$\Delta B = PVBP_{2.5yr} \ per \ \$100 \times \# \ of \ basis \ points \times Position \ size$$

$$= 0.020098 \times 10 \times \frac{\$82\,760\,000}{100} = \$166\,331$$

Here we offset a halving of risk by doubling the size of the position. However, this version of the asset substitution swap still has two flaws. For one, it may not be possible for the investor to double the size of their investment. For another, we have not found a safe haven that truly mimics the risk of our five-year investment for if the yield curve was to change shape where, say, 2.5-year interest rates rise as five-year rates fall, we would experience losses on our safe haven when our original position would experience a gain. Therefore we see that the asset substitution swap finds a safe haven that only approximates the risk of our original position.

8.5.1 Butterfly/barbell swaps

There are two alternative methods for executing an asset substitution swap that seek to overcome the above disadvantages. The barbell/butterfly swap is a method for executing the asset substitution swap yet does not require a change in the size of the investor's position. However, the resulting safe haven only approximates the previous position where, like above, in response to a change in the shape of the yield curve the safe haven will respond differently than the previous position. The alternative is the barbell/butterfly arbitrage where the investor obtains a safe haven that responds very similarly to the previous position even in response to a change in the shape of the yield curve. Unfortunately the investor must change the size of their position to execute the barbell/butterfly arbitrage method.

To illustrate consider the three UK gilt securities in Table 8.1.

Table 8.1 Data for butterfly/barbell strategies

Bond maturity	25/09/09	7/12/15	7/06/21
PVBP	$0.0733	$0.1201	$0.1573
Clean price	$118.90562	129.71	138.14

For the butterfly/barbell swap we sell, say, $1 million of the gilt maturing on 7/12/15 and seek a safe haven by buying the short- and long-term gilts of 25/09/09 and 7/06/21 respectively. The question is how much do we invest in the short- and long-term bonds? The answer to this question is found by first solving for the percentage x in the following equation and second reinvesting the proceeds from the sale of the middle bond in the short and long bonds according to this percentage. That is

$$PVBP_m = (1 - x)PVBP_s + (x)PVBP_l$$

$$B_m = (1 - x)Bs + (x)B_l$$

The first equation says that the risk of investing an amount of $x\%$ in the long-term bond $PVBP_l$ and the risk of investing an amount of $(1 - x\%)$ in the short-term bond $PVBP_s$ must equal the risk of remaining in the medium-term bond $PVBP_m$. The second equation says that the total amount that we invest in the long B_l and short B_s

bond must equal the amount we receive from selling the medium-term bond B_m. Solving the first equation for x we find that we need to invest 56.17% of the proceeds from selling the medium-term bond in the long- and 43.83% in the short-term bond. Specifically

$$x\% = \frac{B_m - B_s}{B_l - B_s} = \frac{129.71 - 118.90562}{138.14 - 118.90562} = 56.17\%$$

So when we sell $1 million of the medium-term bond we reinvest $438 300 in the short-term bond and $561 700 in the long-term bond. For a 10 basis point decrease in yield, the value of our safe haven will rise by $12 048.28 ($3212.74 + $8835.54).

$$\Delta B_s = PVBP_s \text{ per } \$100 \times \# \text{ of basis points} \times \text{Position size}$$

$$= 0.0733 \times 10 \times \frac{\$438\,300}{100} = \$3212.74$$

$$\Delta B_l = PVBP_l \text{ per } \$100 \times \# \text{ of basis points} \times \text{Position size}$$

$$= 0.1573 \times 10 \times \frac{\$561\,700}{100} = \$8835.54$$

Which is nearly equal to the gain we would have obtained had we stayed in the medium-term bond, $12 010. The trivial difference of $38.28 is attributable to convexity.

$$\Delta B_m = PVBP_m \text{ per } \$100 \times \# \text{ of basis points} \times \text{Position size}$$

$$= 0.1201 \times 10 \times \frac{\$1\,000\,000}{100} = \$12\,010$$

8.5.2 Butterfly/barbell arbitrage

As explained earlier, the safe haven provided by the butterfly/barbell swap does not fully replicate the original position for if the yield curve was to change shape, gains or losses would be experienced in the safe haven that would not have been experienced in the original position. Therefore our safe haven does not fully replicate the original position, as we must change our risk profile. If this is of concern the alternative method of executing the asset substitution swap is to use the butterfly/barbell arbitrage strategy. In this case we sell our medium-term bond and construct the safe haven where the risk of the safe haven is equal to the risk of our original position *and* the risk of the long- and short-term bonds used to construct the safe haven are also set to be equal. Then even in response to a change in the shape of the yield curve the safe haven will replicate the same sort of gains and losses that would have been experienced had the investor stayed in the original bond. The cost of doing this, however, is that the investor must be willing and able to change the size of their position as the cost of forming the safe haven is different than the proceeds from selling the original bond.

The procedure for forming the safe haven in the butterfly/barbell arbitrage strategy starts with measuring the total risk of the original position where the total risk is the product of the price of the medium-term bond and its *PVBP*. In this case this value is $B_m \times PVBP_m = 129.71 \times 0.1201 = 15.57817$. According to the first condition, the safe haven must have the same total risk. Additionally each bond used to construct the safe haven must have the same total risk. Therefore the short- and long-term bonds must have a total risk of one half of the total risk of the original bond or $15.578171/2 = 7.789085$. Therefore for each medium-term bond that we sell for $129.71 the amount to be reinvested in the short-term bond and long-term bond respectively is $106.2631 and $49.5174.

$$B_s \times PVBP_s = 7.789085 \Rightarrow B_s = 7.789085/PVBP_s$$

$$= 7.789085/0.0733 = 106.2631$$

$$B_l \times PVBP_l = 7.789085 \Rightarrow B_l = 7.789085/PVBP_l$$

$$= 7.789085/0.1573 = 49.5174$$

In other words, we must invest 20% more than we had invested in the medium-term bond. That is, the total investment in the safe haven per medium-term bond sold at $129.71 is $106.2631 + $49.5174 = $155.7805, or $155.7805/129.71 = 1.2$. Therefore for a $1 million investment in the medium-term bond we must reinvest $1.2 million. The portion that we must invest in the short-term bond is $106.2631/155.7805 = 68.21\%$ or $818 520 and the portion that we must invest in the long-term bond is $49.5174/155.7805 = 31.79\%$ or $381 480.

The total risk of the short- and long-term bond position is equal. For a 10 basis point decrease in yield the short- and long-term bond experiences equal gains of approximately $6000 which together nearly equals the gains that would have been experienced in the original bond when we had invested $1 million.

$$\Delta B_s = PVBP_s \ per \ \$100 \times \# \ of \ basis \ points \times Position \ size$$

$$= 0.0733 \times 10 \times \frac{\$818\,520}{100} = \$5999.75$$

$$\Delta B_l = PVBP_l \ per \ \$100 \times \# \ of \ basis \ points \times Position \ size$$

$$= 0.1573 \times 10 \times \frac{\$381\,480}{100} = \$6000.68$$

Moreover we experience the same sort of gains and losses in our safe haven as we would have experienced in our original investment even if the yield curve was to change shape. For example, imagine that the yield curve was to become more upward sloping as it fell where, say, the yield on the short-term bond fell 50 basis points, the yield on the medium-term bond fell 25 basis points and the yield on the long-term bond remained unchanged.

$$\Delta B_s = PVBP_s \ per \ \$100 \times \# \ of \ basis \ points \times Position \ size$$

$$= 0.0733 \times 50 \times \frac{\$818\,520}{100} = \$29\,998.76$$

$$\Delta B_m = PVBP_m \ per \ \$100 \times \# \ of \ basis \ points \times Position \ size$$

$$= 0.1201 \times 25 \times \frac{\$1\,000\,000}{100} = \$30\,025$$

The difference is only $26.24. In contrast for the butterfly/barbell swap this difference would be a loss of $13\,961.30(30\,025 − 16\,063.70) relative to what would have been gained if we had remained invested in the original bond.

$$\Delta B_s = PVBP_s \ per \ \$100 \times \# \ of \ basis \ points \times Position \ size$$

$$= 0.0733 \times 50 \times \frac{\$438\,300}{100} = \$16\,063.70$$

Table 8.2 gives the gains and losses on our butterfly/barbell arbitrage example less the gains and losses on our original investment in the medium-term bond. This table highlights the extent to which the safe haven does not perfectly replicate the position in the original investment. Notice that these deviations are very small in all cases.

Table 8.2 Deviations of the butterfly/barbell arbitrage safe haven from the original investment*

S	M	L	S	M	L	S	M	L
+50	+25	0	+25	+25	+25	0	+25	+50
	$26.24			$23.92			$21.60	
+25	0	−25	0	0	0	−25	0	+25
	$2.32			$0.00			−$2.32	
0	−25	−50	−25	−25	−25	−50	−25	0
	−$21.60			−$23.92			−$26.24	

*S = short-term bond, M = original bond, L = long-term bond. All changes in yields are in basis points.

8.6 Portfolio immunization

Portfolio immunization promises to lock in a realized yield over an investment time horizon even though interest rates may be decreasing or increasing throughout this time. To understand why this happens, we need to consider the *reinvestment effect*. Consider a $1000 investment in an 8% coupon (paid semi-annually) 20-year gilt. We know that we will receive $40 every six months for 20 years, 40 payments in all, plus the return of principal at the end of 20 years. What will be the total cash return in 20 years?

$$FV = PV(1 + r/M)^{NM} = 1000(1 + 0.08/2)^{40} = \$4801.02$$

What is this cash return composed of? We know that $1000 is the return of principal and $1600 represents the payment of the coupons (40 × $40). The remaining $2201.02 represents the interest earned on reinvestment of coupons received each six-month period throughout the life of the gilt issue. Note that the importance of interest earned on reinvestment of coupons (interest on interest) increases with the interest rate, coupon rate and maturity of the gilt.

If interest rates rise, the *capital effect* is the fact that the *immediate* market value of the gilt will decline. But the *reinvestment effect* is the fact that if interest rates rise, then more interest on interest will be earned *through time*. This suggests that there may be some optimal time to sell the bond such that if interest rates rise, losses on the capital effect will be balanced with gains on the reinvestment effect thus locking in total cash returns. It turns out that *Macaulay duration* indicates this ideal time horizon where it is appropriate to sell the bond. If executed correctly, then the total cash return (and its corresponding interest rate called total return, or alternatively, the realized compound yield RCY) is locked in.

Notice, however, we are using Macaulay duration rather than modified duration. This is because we are concerned with balancing a timing effect, the immediate losses on the capital effect with a deferred increase in value from the reinvestment effect as coupons are reinvested at higher rates that build up value over time. It turns out that Macaulay duration, being a measure of the time-weighted average of the present value of a bond, indicates this ideal time horizon to liquidate the bond to lock in total return.

Therefore the objective of portfolio immunization is to guarantee a total rate of return on an investment over some length of time. If an investor's planning horizon is equal to the duration of their bond portfolio, the rate of return from the portfolio will not decrease in response to an unexpected change in interest rates. As a result, you are sure that a certain amount will be available at the planning horizon to fund your liability due at that time.

Another way to look at immunization is to recognize that immunization is an application of the preferred habitat theory of Chapter 3. Life insurance companies can predict with some degree of accuracy the incidence (to put it delicately) of life insurance payments in large groups of clients. Consequently they can predict that they need, say, $100 million in 10 years' time. This means that they will have a flow of premiums that can be invested for 10 years. The only requirement is that they will need to pay $100 million at the end of the investment time horizon. Therefore they have the opportunity to fix a rate of return over a 10-year time horizon. If they invest for 10 years they need to be concerned with preservation of capital and the preservation of income. The correct balance point between these two risks is indicated by Macaulay duration. In other words, if the life insurance company invests their income in a portfolio of bonds that have Macaulay duration equal to their planning horizon, 10 years in our example, then the capital and reinvestment effects will balance out. As interest rates rise, enough time remains for the positive reinvestment effect to offset the immediate negative capital effect. Similarly as interest rates fall, losses on the negative reinvestment effect are offset by the positive capital effect.

To show how portfolio immunization works and how the exact measure of duration of a portfolio is preferable to the approximation weighting scheme method when dealing in coupon bonds let us first look at what happens when we use the *approximate weights* to obtain a portfolio's Macaulay duration to lock in a yield over a 10-year planning horizon. Then we look at what happens when we use the correct weighting scheme. Again we consider forming a portfolio of two bonds, bond A is a 4% semi-annual coupon pay 20-year bond and bond B is a 12% semi-annual coupon pay 20-year bond. Both bonds yield 7.5%, so bond A is worth $64.036 and bond B is worth $146.24. As shown in spreadsheet DurB02.xls the Macaulay duration of bond A is 12.22 and of bond B 9.78. Using the simple linear average approach we find the approximate weights below.

$$X\%(12.22) + (1 - X\%)(9.79) = 10$$

Solving, we find that $X = 0.0905$, so we place 9.095% of the portfolio value in the high duration coupon bond and 90.95% of the portfolio value in the low duration coupon bond. Spreadsheet DurB02.xls shows that the correct weighing scheme is 18.3% in bond A and 81.7% in bond B. Here we use the solver function found under the tools sub-menu. We set the Macaulay duration of the portfolio cell K2 as the target cell, set the target value as -10 and the weighting scheme cell B1 as the change cell. When we click on solve we find the weighting values as mentioned above.

First, we use the approximation weighting scheme and find that the promised total return is the same as the yield of the portfolio 7.5%. As reported in Table 8.3, we find this promised return by performing a horizon analysis. That is, we calculate the total future value expected from the portfolio as of 10 years in the future, one half way through the life of the bonds in the portfolio. Here we find the future value *FV* of the flow of coupon payments for the first 20 semi-annual periods and then the present value *PV* of the remaining 20 semi-annual coupon payments and final redemption amount in 10 years' time for each bond assuming that yields remain constant at 7.5%. Adding these values up for each bond obtains the total cash return we can expect from each bond in 10 years' time, $133.714 for bond A and $305.370 for bond B. The corresponding portfolio total cash return is found as 9.02% of the total cash return of bond A and 90.98% of the total cash return of bond B. We then find the total return *TR* of the portfolio in the last left-hand row in Table 8.3.

This scenario is not terribly interesting, as we have assumed yields remain constant at 7.5%. But what happens if interest rates were to change from current levels? In Tables 8.4 and 8.5 we work through the results from Table 8.3, only now we use two alternative interest rate scenarios, an optimistic scenario where yields decline by 200 basis points to 5.5% and a pessimistic scenario where interest rates rise by 200 basis points to 9.5%.

Notice that the lower interest rate scenario of Table 8.4 obtains a portfolio yield of 7.566% and the higher interest rate scenario of Table 8.5 obtains a portfolio yield of 7.608% and that both scenarios obtain a portfolio yield that is higher than the promised 7.5%. To see why this is the case, Table 8.6 examines the incremental changes from the base case of Table 8.3 as yields fall and rise. In the case that interest rates fall, the positive capital effect *PV* dominates the negative reinvestment effect *FV* resulting in an increase in total return at the end of 10 years. In the case that interest rates rise, the positive reinvestment effect *FV* dominates the negative capital effect *PV* so again the total return at the end of 10 years increases.

Now, what if we use exact weights of 18.3% invested in bond A and 81.7% invested in bond B? In exercise one at the end of the chapter we make exactly the same calculations as above, only now we use the exact weighting scheme. The results show that in both cases, when interest rates rise or fall by 200 basis points, the total return increases from 7.5% to 7.62%.

Both the approximation and exact weighting methods managed to achieve immunization in that whether yields rise or fall we obtain

Table 8.3 Portfolio immunization using approximate weights: base case

Bond A: coupon 4%, yield 7.5%, maturity 20 years, modified duration 11.78, Macaulay duration 12.22, portfolio weight 9.02%

Bond B: coupon 12%, yield 7.5%, maturity 20 years, modified duration 9.43, Macaulay duration 9.78, portfolio weight 90.98%

Promised total return

	Bond A			Bond B	
Cash flow	Calculation	Amt	Cash flow	Calculation	Amt
$FV(t = 1 - 20)$	$2*[(1.0375)^{20} - 1]/0.0375$	58.035	$FV(t = 1 - 20)$	$6*[(1.0375)^{20} - 1]/0.0375$	174.104
$PV(t = 21 - 40)$	$2*[1 - (1.0375)^{-20}]/0.0375$	27.790	$PV(t = 21 - 40)$	$6*[1 - (1.0375)^{-20}]/0.0375$	83.377
PV of prin.	$100*(1.0375)^{-20}$	47.889	PV of prin.	$100*(1.0375)^{-20}$	47.889
Total		133.714	Total		305.370
TR	$[(133.714/64.036)^{1/20} - 1]*2$	7.5%	TR	$[(305.370/146.24)^{1/20} - 1]*2$	7.5%

Portfolio

Cost	$0.0902*64.036 + 0.9098*146.24$	138.825	FV	$0.0902*133.714 + 0.9098*305.370$	289.887
TR	$[(289.887/138.825)^{1/20} - 1]*2$	7.5%			

Table 8.4 Yields fall by 200 basis points to 5.5%

Promised total return

Cash flow	Bond A Calculation	Amt	Cash flow	Bond B Calculation	Amt
$FV(t = 1 - 20)$	$2*[(1.0275)^{20} - 1]/0.0275$	52.395	$FV(t = 1 - 20)$	$6*[(1.0275)^{20} - 1]/0.0275$	157.184
$PV(t = 21 - 40)$	$2*[1 - (1.0275)^{-20}]/0.0275$	30.455	$PV(t = 21 - 40)$	$6*[1 - (1.0275)^{-20}]/0.0275$	91.364
PV of prin.	$100*(1.0275)^{-20}$	58.125	PV of prin.	$100*(1.0275)^{-20}$	58.125
Total		140.975	Total		306.673
TR	$[(140.975/64.036)^{1/20} - 1]*2$	8.049%	TR	$[(306.673/146.24)^{1/20} - 1]*2$	7.544%

Portfolio

	Calculation	Amt		Calculation	Amt
Cost	$0.0902*64.036 + 0.9098*146.24$	138.825	FV	$0.0902*140.975 + 0.9098*306.673$	291.727
TR	$[(291.727/138.825)^{1/20} - 1]*2$	7.566%			

Table 8.5 Yields rise by 200 basis points to 9.5%

Promised total return

	Bond A			Bond B	
Cash flow	Calculation	Amt	Cash flow	Calculation	Amt
$FV(t = 1 - 20)$	$2*[(1.0475)^{20} - 1]/0.0475$	64.411	$FV(t = 1 - 20)$	$6*[(1.0475)^{20} - 1]/0.0475$	193.234
$PV(t = 21 - 40)$	$2*[1 - (1.0475)^{-20}]/0.0475$	25.461	$PV(t = 21 - 40)$	$6*[1 - (1.0475)^{-20}]/0.0475$	76.384
PV of prin.	$100*(1.0475)^{-20}$	39.529	PV of prin.	$100*(1.0475)^{-20}$	39.529
Total		129.401	Total		309.147
TR	$[(129.401/64.036)^{1/20} - 1]*2$	7.160%	TR	$[(309.147/146.24)^{1/20} - 1]*2$	7.628%

Portfolio

Cost	$0.0902*64.036 + 0.9098*146.24$	138.825
	FV	$0.0902*129.401 + 0.9098*309.147$	292.934
TR	$[(292.934/138.825)^{1/20} - 1]*2$	7.608%

Table 8.6 The capital and reinvestment effects

Cash flow	Yields fall to 5.5%			Yields rise to 9.5	
	Yield = 7.5%	Yield = 5.5%	Difference	Yield = 9.5%	Difference
Bond A					
$FV(t = 1 - 20)$	58.035	52.395	−5.64	64.411	+6.376
$PV(t = 21 - 40)$	27.790	30.455	+2.665	25.461	−2.329
PV of prin.	47.889	58.125	+10.236	39.529	−8.36
Total	133.714	140.975	+7.261	129.401	−4.313
TR	7.5%	8.049%		7.160%	
Bond B					
$FV(t = 1 - 20)$	174.104	157.184	−16.92	193.234	+19.13
$PV(t = 21 - 40)$	83.377	91.364	+7.987	76.384	−6.993
PV of prin.	47.889	58.125	+10.236	39.529	−8.36
Total	305.370	306.673	+1.303	309.147	+3.777
Portfolio	289.887	291.727	+1.84	292.934	+3.047
TR	7.5%	7.544%		7.628%	

a total return that is the same as promised or higher. That is why we suggest the simple average is a 'good' approximation for coupon bonds. However, this example is somewhat artificial since our portfolio is composed of same maturity and yield bonds where the importance of using the exact method is much reduced. Even in this case notice that actual yields varied by 8 basis points for the approximation, and by 0 basis points for the exact method as we vary yields by a range of 400 basis points. This is evidence that the exact method is still better and should be used, particularly when forming portfolios of bonds of different maturity and yields.

To truly appreciate why immunization works, we examine the reason why immunization obtains the promised yield or a *higher* amount. The reason is that when we set the portfolio Macaulay duration equal to our planning horizon we are actually locking in a minimum yield that occurs when yields do not change. In this scenario, the planning horizon (*PH*) as measured in time units equals Macaulay duration. As Figure 8.3 illustrates, the total cash return (*TCR*) at some planning time horizon is a convex function of yield and the saddle point that returns the minimum total cash return occurs at the current or promised yield.

Notice that *TCR* will be higher if actual yield *I* turns out to be larger or smaller than the current yield *I**, 7.5% in our earlier example. This happens because as yields rise, Macaulay duration decreases, but our planning horizon is not affected by a change in yield. Then Macaulay duration will be smaller than the planning horizon. The longer planning horizon allows the reinvestment effect to dominate.

Since the reinvestment effect is positive as yields rise, a larger than promised total cash return results. Similarly as yields fall, Macaulay duration increases, but our planning horizon is not affected by a change in yield. Then Macaulay duration will be larger than the planning horizon. The larger duration allows the capital effect to dominate. Since the capital effect is positive as yields fall, a larger than promised total cash return results.

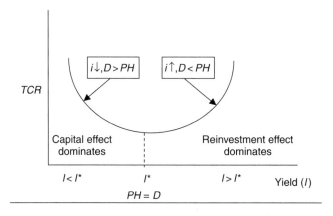

Figure 8.3 Immunization

A failure of immunization occurs when the portfolio's realized yield falls below the initial promised yield. This can happen when the planning horizon is far different than the portfolio duration. For example, imagine we invest 70% in the low coupon bond A and 30% in the high coupon bond B. The duration of this portfolio will be greater than 11 years, more than one year longer than our planning horizon. The capital effect dominates so if interest rates increase the portfolio may have a realized return less than the initial promised 7.5%. For example, using the 70/30 weighting scheme the portfolio realized yield will be 7.39% if yields were to average 9.5% for 10 years.

8.7   Balance sheet immunization

This is a classic bank risk management strategy, but any firm that has 'assets' and 'liabilities' that respond to changes in interest rates can use this strategy.

This strategy is a variation of the classic duration-based hedging strategy as discussed in Chapter 7. Assets are our 'long cash instrument' and our liabilities are our 'short hedging instrument'. To make this more concrete, a bank's loans to consumers represent the bank's assets and the consumers' deposits represent the bank's liabilities. The bank would like to be in a situation where in response to an increase in interest rates decreases in the value of the assets (representing a loss) will be offset with decreases in the value of liabilities (representing a gain). If these two effects balance out, then the value of the firm's capital (the third item on the balance sheet that absorbs net decreases and increases in the difference between assets and liabilities) will be protected. On the other hand, if losses on assets exceed gains on liabilities by a large enough amount, then capital will be negative and the bank will be bankrupt.

We use *modified duration* to indicate the correct balance between the interest rate sensitivity of assets and liabilities to achieve this ideal result. This occurs since we are concerned with price volatility. Specifically how does the value of assets and liabilities respond to a change in interest rates?

It is best to illustrate balance sheet immunization through use of an example. Consider the following hypothetical bank in Table 8.7. All figures are in millions.

Table 8.7 Illustrative balance sheet for immunization example

Assets		Liabilities	
Market value	1050	Market value	1000
Face value	1000	Face value	975
Coupon rate	8%	Coupon rate	6%
Maturity	5 years	Maturity	1 year
Yield	6.787%	Yield	3.35%
		Capital	50

Note that payments on assets and liabilities are monthly and we are concerned with market values. The first step is to calculate the modified duration of the assets and liabilities. One problem is that our closed form solution for modified duration must be scaled in terms of a face value FV of 100. To solve this problem we find the market value MV of $1 of face value and then multiply it by 100. For assets this is $MV/FV \times 100 = 1050/1000 \times 100 = 105$. Then applying our modified duration formula we find that the duration of assets is

$$D^* = \cfrac{\cfrac{£0.667}{(0.0056558)^2}\left[1 - \cfrac{1}{(1+0.0056558)^{60}}\right] + \cfrac{60\left(100 - \cfrac{£0.667}{0.0056558}\right)}{(1+0.0056558)^{60+1}}}{105}$$

= 49.7468 on a monthly basis, so dividing by 12 we find that the correct answer is 4.1456.

Similarly the market value of liabilities in terms of a face value of 100 is $1000/975 \times 100 = 102.564$. Then applying our modified duration formula we find that the duration of liabilities is

$$D^* = \cfrac{\cfrac{£0.50}{(0.0027917)^2}\left[1 - \cfrac{1}{(1+0.0027917)^{12}}\right] + \cfrac{12\left(100 - \cfrac{£0.50}{0.0027917}\right)}{(1+0.0027917)^{12+1}}}{102.564}$$

= 10.983 on a monthly basis, so dividing by 12 we find that the correct answer is 0.9153.

We now need to develop a model of how we can expect the value of the bank's capital to respond to a change in interest rates. Therefore the next step is to measure the interest rate sensitivity of assets relative to the interest rate sensitivity of liabilities so that we can determine the change in value of the bank's capital in response to a shift in interest rates. This is done below using the duration gap model.

8.7.1 The duration gap model

The objective is to set the duration of assets relative to the duration of liabilities such that in response to an increase in interest rates losses on assets due to a reduction in the value of assets are offset by gains in liabilities due to a reduction in the value of liabilities. That is, we want the change in the value of assets to equal the change in the value of liabilities.

$$dP_A = dP_L$$

Modified duration assumes that the price response of *any* interest rate sensitive item is linearly related to the change in the interest rate in the following way $dP = D^*PdY$. Therefore we can rewrite the above equality as follows.

$$D_A^* P_A dY_A = D_L^* P_L dY_L$$

Now we solve the above expression for the modified duration of assets D_A^*.

$$D_A^* = D_L^* \frac{P_L dY_L}{P_A dY_A} \tag{8.1}$$

Finally, we move the right-hand side of (8.1) to the left to show the conditions necessary to obtain a duration gap of zero.

$$D_A^* - D_L^* \frac{P_L dY_L}{P_A dY_A} = 0 \tag{8.2}$$

In other words, the duration of assets must be set relative to the duration of liabilities according to the ratio of prices of liabilities to assets P_L/P_A and to the ratio of the change in yields of liabilities to assets dY_L/dY_A. A problem with (8.2) is that we need to anticipate changes in the yield spread between the yield of liabilities and assets. This is a difficult task. Consequently we typically assume that the yield spread is constant so that the ratio dY_L/dY_A is one. In other words, if asset yields increase by 100 basis points so too does the yield on liabilities such that the yield spread between assets and liabilities is constant. Substituting the above balance sheet information into (8.2) and assuming that the yield spread is constant we find that our hypothetical bank has a duration gap of 3.2739.

$$4.1456 - 0.9153 \frac{1000}{1050} = 3.2739$$

This result tells us that our bank has a positive duration gap of 3.2739. This means that as interest rates rise, the value of the bank's capital will decrease. It is also a measure of the duration of the bank's capital, 3.2739 in this case. For example, in response to a 100 basis point increase in yields the value of the bank's capital will decrease by 34.37595 million.

$$\Delta P_c = D_g^* P_A \Delta Y = -3.2739(1050)(0.01) = -34.376$$

Note that the base upon which we calculate the change in the value of capital is the market value of the bank's assets. We use the asset values as the base because the asset figure is the measure of the size of the bank's balance sheet. To confirm that this is in fact the case, we can measure the change in the value of the bank's assets and liabilities separately and then recognizing that excess losses on assets are absorbed by capital we can recalculate the value of the bank's capital. Given an increase of 100 basis points in the yield of assets and liabilities the change in the value of assets and liabilities are respectively,

$$D_A^* P_A dY_A = -4.1456(1050)(0.01) = -43.529$$
$$D_L^* P_L dY_L = -0.9153(1000)(0.01) = -9.153$$

Since a reduction in the value of a liability is a gain the overall loss to the firm is reduced by 9.153 million to 34.376 million. Therefore the value of the bank's capital shrinks by 34.376 million from 50 million to 15.624.

Obviously a bank with a large positive duration gap is exposed to the risk that interest rates may increase. This is a natural tendency for retail banks because the style of loans, home mortgages, auto loans and personal loans tends to be multi-year whereas most deposits, current accounts, 30-, 60- and 90-day deposits are very typical, tend to be of much shorter terms. We know that maturity is directly related to duration so with longer-term assets and shorter-term liabilities it is not surprising that the duration gap of a given bank is positive since the duration of assets is much greater than the duration of liabilities.

8.7.2 *How can we eliminate the duration gap?*

It is tempting to think that a zero duration gap is 'right' and non-zero duration gap is 'wrong'. For instance, the above example shows that the hypothetical bank is terribly exposed to interest rate risk. A 100 basis point increase in interest rates is unusual but it has happened in the past. Then with a follow-on modest increase in interest rates the excess losses on assets that capital must absorb will be so great that the value of the bank's capital will be negative. Then the bank will be bankrupt.

We should avoid such simplistic thinking and instead think of the duration gap as an indicator of the bank's strategy. For instance, the bank may have experts that are forecasting that interest rates are expected to decrease, so the bank is positioning itself to benefit from the expected decrease in interest rates. For example, if interest rates were to decrease by 100 basis points, the value of the bank's capital will increase rather than decrease by 34.376 million. Similarly a negative duration gap can be interpreted as a strategic bet that interest rates are to increase. That is, if the bank has a negative duration gap the interest rate sensitivity of liabilities is greater than the interest rate sensitivity of assets. In this case, as interest rates rise, losses on assets are more than offset by gains from the reduction in the value of liabilities. Consequently an intelligent view of the duration gap is to view the size and sign of the duration gap as an indicator of the bank's view on the direction of future interest rates. A positive gap suggests the bank is betting that interest rates will fall and the larger the positive gap the bigger the bet. Similarly a negative gap suggests the bank is betting that interest rates will rise and the larger the negative gap the bigger the bet. A zero duration gap suggests that the bank is playing it safe not wishing to bet on changes in interest rates. In this case the bank is immunized from interest rate changes. With a zero duration gap, as interest rates rise, losses on assets are offset by gains in liabilities and the value of capital does not change.

Viewing the duration gap as a strategic decision leads us to consider how a bank may change the duration gap. In our example the bank has a huge positive duration gap so perhaps the bank should reduce the size of this positive gap. It is tempting to suggest that the bank should increase the duration of liabilities and decrease the duration of assets. This implies that the bank should raise more long-term debt and invest in short-term assets thereby increasing the interest rate sensitivity of liabilities and decreasing the interest rate sensitivity of assets.

But does this make sense? Remember that a bank's assets are loans it has made to consumers and liabilities are deposits made by consumers and the bank cannot dictate terms to consumers. To take a hypothetical example, imagine someone was to win the lottery and then wishes to deposit the money short term with the bank. They cannot be convinced to place the money in a long-term deposit. If the bank accepts the short-term deposit the positive duration gap will increase, but if the bank refuses the deposit the consumer will simply go next door and make a deposit with another bank. Similarly a triple A credit consumer wishes to borrow money long term and cannot be convinced to borrow short term. If the bank accepts the long-term loan the positive duration gap will increase, but if the bank refuses the loan the consumer will simply go next door and borrow from another bank. Clearly the bank's core business is making loans and collecting deposits and it is ridiculous to suggest that the bank's duration gap strategy should interfere with the core business activities of the bank. In our example the bank would refuse the lottery winner's short-term deposit and reject the triple A credit's long-term loan in order to reduce the bank's positive duration gap. Clearly this does not make sense.

Instead the bank arranges its affairs such that duration gap management does not interfere with the core banking business. There are a variety of tools available. For example, in recent decades banks have passed title on groups of long-term mortgages and sold them in the debt markets as mortgage-backed securities. The bank continues to manage the mortgage, collecting the payments and dealing with early repayments and defaults, but payments on the mortgage are passed on to investors that own the mortgage-backed security. For providing the mortgage management service, the bank collects a fee. The great point here, however, is that these long-term mortgages sold via the mortgage-backed security are no longer assets of the bank and so are removed from the bank's balance sheet. This reduces the duration of the bank's asset portfolio thereby reducing the positive duration gap.

Another way the bank can manage the duration gap is to manipulate the bank's liquidity portfolio. By regulation the bank is required to maintain substantial amounts of cash and near cash to ensure they can always meet the cash needs of the consumer even in trying circumstances. Banks economize on holding non-interest bearing currency by investing a substantial amount of their liquid assets in a bond investment portfolio. This investment portfolio usually consists of long-term domestic sovereign bonds and short-term T-bills because these securities are considered default free and are relatively liquid being easily converted into cash. The investment portfolio forms a 'degree of freedom' that allows the bank to adjust its duration gap. Since the investment portfolio is a part of the asset portfolio that is under the discretionary control of the bank, the bank is free to adjust this portfolio at will. If they wish to narrow a positive duration gap they could sell some of the long-term (high duration) Treasury bonds and reinvest in short-term (low duration) T-bills thereby shortening the duration of the investment portfolio by a large amount. In turn this will nudge the duration of the bank's assets downward thereby narrowing the positive duration gap.

8.8 Bond portfolio management

The portfolio immunization and balance sheet strategies of sections 8.6 and 8.7 above were introduced in a static context. In this section we explain how you can maintain these strategies through time. We will first look at portfolio immunization explaining that you actually lock in the current yield only approximately. Then we examine how you can maintain the duration gap through time.

There are two sobering facts that you have to appreciate to understand the limitations of portfolio immunization. First, you can only lock in the prevailing yield at the time you form the immunization strategy. As a result when yields are low, many portfolio managers forgo portfolio immunization strategies. Second, as time continues adjustments need to be made to match the declining time horizon to the declining portfolio duration. This happens as a consequence of convexity, as time continues the duration of a portfolio decreases at a decreasing rate where as calendar time decreases at a constant rate. This means that over time the duration of a portfolio will wander away from the remaining time until the planning date. To the extent that a mismatch between the remaining Macaulay duration of your portfolio and the planning horizon evolves then there will be a risk that the portfolio immunization strategy may fail. Therefore occasionally there is a need to rebalance the portfolio to reset the remaining Macaulay duration of the portfolio equal to the planning horizon. Together, this means that the final yield will be close to the immunized yield. Slight differences will occur since bonds have to be sold and bought at later time periods where the prevailing yields may be different, in order to maintain your immunization strategy.

Of course, this leads to a trade-off between the risks of immunization failure and the transactions costs of maintaining the duration of the portfolio equal to the declining planning horizon. The items to consider are as follows. First, the risk of immunization failure is very slight if the duration of the portfolio is only modestly different than the remaining planning horizon. Second, the costs of trading in sovereign bonds are higher the more frequently the portfolio is adjusted. Together these facts suggest that one would not bother to adjust the duration of the bond portfolio as long as the portfolio duration is not very different than the remaining planning horizon. Only when the time distance between the portfolio's duration and the planning horizon is significant is it worthwhile to make adjustments and incur transactions costs. Therefore one needs to examine the risks of immunization failure and the costs of transactions needed to readjust the portfolio duration to determine the trigger point where portfolio adjustments need to be made.

The portfolio immunization strategy will enable you to ensure that an approximate cash amount will be available in the future, no matter what the prevailing interest rates do in the meantime. In other words, we are locking in a one time spread. Another problem is how to maintain duration at a particular level for a length of time either to maintain the value of the bank's capital or to 'fix' a profit spread on a 'flow' of obligations. The problem here is that all bonds are fixed term investments so the duration of bonds will decrease as time continues.

The key to understanding how to maintain duration at a particular value given that the duration of all bonds decreases as time continues is to realize that financial institutions need to worry about liquidity as well as duration, as all financial institutions still need cash or near cash to meet unexpected contingencies. As mentioned earlier, to provide liquidity the bank holds a portion of their assets in an investment portfolio consisting of short- and long-term sovereign bonds. This type of portfolio is called a barbell portfolio and is ideally suited to maintaining duration of the investment portfolio at a particular level indefinitely. To illustrate how this is done refer to Figure 8.4.

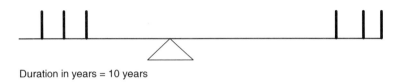

Duration in years = 10 years

Figure 8.4   Barbell portfolio

Figure 8.4 illustrates that the barbell portfolio holds only two types of bonds, long term and short term, such that the average duration of both portfolios equals the desired duration. In other words, like the weightlifting equipment namesake, 'weights' are placed at each end of the maturity spectrum representing investment in short- and long-term bonds. As short-term bonds mature, the bank reinvests in other short-term bonds at the end of the allowed maturity for the short-term bond portfolio. Similarly, as long-term bonds approach the short end of the allowed long-term bond range, the bank sells them and reinvests in other long-term bonds at the end of the long-term range. In this way duration can be maintained through relatively minor adjustments to lock in the value of the bank's capital.

The barbell strategy is ideally suited for institutions such as banks that are intent on balance sheet immunization as it not only allows the bank to maintain duration at a particular level through time, but also allows the bank to make radical adjustments in the duration of the investment barbell portfolio should the bank need to adjust the size of the bank's duration gap. For other investors intent on portfolio immunization by matching the duration of their portfolio to their remaining planning horizon the barbell has a serious disadvantage. There is a risk that the yield curve may twist. For example, imagine short-term interest rates fall but long-term interest rates rise. Given that long-term bonds have higher duration than short-term bonds, it is obvious that immediate capital losses on long-term bonds will be greater than capital gains on short-term bonds. The real problem, however, is that long-term bonds will be sold prior to maturity in order to maintain the duration of the barbell at a particular level. This means that the positive reinvestment effect on long-term bonds will not have enough time to offset the negative capital effect. In turn this means that a barbell is exposed to portfolio immunization failure in that the realized yield may turn out to be less than the initial promised yield because in the face of a yield curve twist it is possible that the positive reinvestment effect is not given enough time to offset the negative capital effect.

To avoid this sort of problem bond managers intent on portfolio immunization tend to form 'barbell' type portfolios where the 'long' and 'short' bonds closely bracket the target duration level. Since only a small segment of the yield curve is involved there is a greatly reduced likelihood that a twist in the yield curve will cause portfolio immunization failure. Investing in zero coupon bonds is even better as the Macaulay duration of a zero is the same as its maturity. If the manager buys zeros with a maturity that is the same as the planning horizon then there is absolutely no chance of portfolio immunization failure. Moreover as the Macaulay duration of a zero decreases in step with calendar time there is no need to make adjustments in the portfolio to maintain the match between the remaining time horizon and the duration of the portfolio as time continues.

This of course implies that strips, zero coupon bonds formed from coupon bonds in the manner explained in Chapter 3, section 3.3.3, are unsuitable for estimating zero coupon yield curves. Portfolio managers concerned with portfolio immunization failure will buy and then hold strips until maturity thereby ensuring strips do not trade very often. This means strip prices are inaccurate and subject to severe stale pricing problems.

However, this still leaves the manager with the problem of how to maintain the duration of the overall portfolio at a particular level when attempting to fix a profit spread on a flow of obligations. To overcome this problem the manager may consider the ladder portfolio as depicted in Figure 8.5.

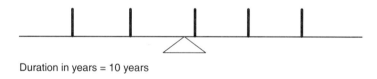

Duration in years = 10 years

Figure 8.5 Ladder portfolio

In the ladder portfolio the investors hold bonds of different maturity (duration), each of which is matched with a planning horizon and so locks in a yield on a given obligation. Overall the ladder provides an average duration at the desired range. As near-term bonds mature, the manager reinvests proceeds in a longer-term bond at the end of the ladder, to maintain duration at, say, 10 years. Additionally the manager can 'lock in' a series of yields, as essentially the manager has a series of portfolios each of which has a duration that is matched to fund a specific group of liabilities.

The ladder strategy is ideally suited for insurance companies. As the insurance company signs up more clients, a new portfolio is set up at the end of the ladder such that it has duration equal to the time horizon when the clients are expected to receive insurance payouts. This allows the insurance company to lock in a flow of profit spreads on a series of obligations and yet the insurance company is also able to maintain the duration of the overall investment portfolio at a particular level through time. Of course, the amount of liquidity provided by the ladder is much less than the liquidity provided by the barbell. Additionally it would be difficult for the insurance company to make radical alterations in the duration of the overall investment portfolio. However, these are not serious issues for many insurance companies as liquidity requirements are not as severe and, in general, insurance companies have no particularly strong expertise in forecasting interest rates.

8.9 Exercises

Question 1
Work out the realized compound yield for a planning horizon of 10 years for a portfolio composed of 18.3% invested in bond A and 81.7% invested in bond B in response to a 200 basis point fall in yields to 5.5% and once again in response to a 200 basis point rise in yields to 9.5%. Bond A is a 4% semi-annual coupon pay 20-year bond and bond B is a 12% semi-annual coupon pay 20-year bond. Both bonds yield 7.5%, so bond A is worth $64.036 and bond B is worth $146.24. The Macaulay duration of bond A is 12.22 and of bond B 9.78.

Question 2
Consider the following semi-annual coupon pay bonds.

Bond A: 6-year 6% coupon bond that yields 8%.
Bond B: 20-year, 10% coupon bond that yields 8%.

(a) *For a planned time horizon of nine years,* what are the approximate percentages you need to invest in bond A, and in bond B in order to form an immunized portfolio? Use the linear interpolation method for working out the percentages.
(b) Approximately what yield will you be locking in?
(c) What are the flaws of this strategy?

Question 3
An S&L (an American building society) has the following asset and liability structure.

	Assets	Liabilities
Portfolio market value	$120 000 000	$110 000 000
Portfolio yield	11%	7%
Portfolio duration	7.64	2.81

(a) What is the S&L's duration gap?
(b) What will happen to the firm's capital if interest rates rise by 200 basis points.
(c) The S&L currently holds $10 million 90-day T-bills that yield 5% (quoted on a semi-annual basis) and $10 million 8% coupon (paid semi-annually) 20-year T-bonds priced at 110.668 per $100 face value. The rest is held in 12% coupon 30-year mortgages. These mortgages are priced at par (face value = market value) and payments are made monthly. Find the *approximate* weights the S&L should have to close the duration gap to zero. (Hint: Consider all long-term assets as one asset and all short-term assets as the other. That way your problem is reduced to deciding the allocation among just two assets.)
(d) Is this strategy feasible?

Question 4
You have a €50 million long position in the $6\frac{3}{4}$% German 10-year bund currently priced at €101.39. Amid market talk of a further cut in the Lombard rate you expect the yield curve to shift down significantly in the 3–5 year area and you decide to do an ordinary asset substitution swap and switch out of the $6\frac{3}{4}$ 10-year bund and into the $5\frac{1}{2}$% five-year bund which is currently trading at 94.50. Note that bunds are annual coupon pay.

(a) How much of the $5\frac{1}{2}$% bund should you buy so as to maintain the same outright risk as you currently have with your present holding?
    Suppose that instead of switching out of one bund and into the other you decided to short Dm50 million of the $6\frac{3}{4}$% bund and long the calculated amount of the $5\frac{1}{2}$% bund.
(b) What would be your expected profit/loss if there were parallel shift down (or up) in the yield curve?
(c) What would be your position if the yield curve also became 'more positive' as it fell? (Long-term yields decrease less than short-term yields.)

Question 5

Today is April 8, 2003. We currently hold £30 million of the 5.75%, December 7, 2009 gilt priced at $105.05. We anticipate that yields in the 5–7 year area will rise so we wish to seek a safe haven. Two candidate bonds attract our interest, the 8% gilt due on December 7, 2015 priced at 126.8 and the 7.5% gilt due on December 7, 2006 priced at 109.21. Note that gilts are semi-annual coupon pay and use the actual/actual day count convention. Use the price and yield worksheet functions in Excel to find the *PVBP* for these bonds. The syntax of these worksheet functions is

$$= \text{PRICE(settlement,maturity,rate,yld,redemption,frequency,}$$
$$\text{basis)}$$

$$= \text{YIELD(settlement,maturity,rate,pr,redemption,frequency,}$$
$$\text{basis)}$$

(a) Ignoring accrued interest, form a safe haven from the 2006 and 2015 gilts using the barbell/butterfly swap.

(b) Relative to the gains and losses that would have occurred had you stayed in the 2009 bond, what would be the change in the value of your position should all interest rates increase by 25 basis points.

Alternative hedge ratios

9.1 Improvements in modified duration hedge ratios

In Chapter 7 we introduced modified duration and its associated hedge ratio. We noted that modified duration makes severely restrictive assumptions concerning movements in the sovereign term structure. Specifically modified duration assumes parallel shifts in a flat term structure. However, we note that Litterman and Scheinkman (1991) find that approximately 80% of US Treasury yield curve changes can be attributed to changes in the level of the yield curve, so as primitive as the assumptions are, modified duration provides an adequate description of reality. That is not to say that there is no room for improvement, particularly when we note that Litterman and Scheinkman (1991) also find that approximately 10% of additional changes in the US Treasury yield curve can be attributed to changes in the slope and a further 3 to 5% can be attributed to changes in the shape of the yield curve.

These additional factors provide the justification for additional measures of duration. Specifically Fisher Weil (1971) duration allows for non-parallel shifts in the yield curve and thus attempts to incorporate a second influence, namely change in the slope of the yield curve. Key rate duration carries the process one step further and allows for changes in the level, slope and shape of the yield curve. None of this work considers the influence of credit risk, so Fooladi, Roberts and Skinner (1997) and Skinner (1998) adjust the Macaulay and modified duration hedge ratios respectively for credit risk.

Finally, we consider how we can use the binomial stochastic interest rate and credit risk models to form hedge positions.

Therefore in this chapter we will review alternative measures of interest rate and credit risk sensitivity. Always bear in mind that the corresponding hedge ratio is simply the price sensitivity of the long bond, as measured by the alternative measure of price sensitivity, divided by the corresponding measure of price sensitivity for the short hedging asset. We will review these measures in order of simplicity, Fisher Weil (1971), key rate duration, Fooladi, Roberts and Skinner (1997), Skinner (1998) and binomial hedge ratios, showing how each model seeks to improve the previous measure by relaxing restrictive assumptions.

9.2 Fisher Weil (1971)

Fisher and Weil (1971) extend modified duration by allowing for a non-flat term structure. There are two variations of Fisher Weil duration. The first variation assumes that the term structure is non-flat but experiences parallel shifts. That is, zero coupon spot rates are not equal $_0r_1 \neq {_0r_2}$ but changes in the spot rates are $\Delta_0 r_1 = \Delta_0 r_2$. The second assumes that the term structure is non-flat and may experience non-parallel shifts but the term structure shifts are proportional. That is, zero coupon spot rates are not equal $_0r_1 \neq {_0r_2}$ and changes in the spot rates are not equal $\Delta_0 r_1 \neq \Delta_0 r_2$ but changes in longer spot rates are proportional to changes in the short rate $\Delta_0 r_2 = \Delta_0 r_1[(1 + {_0r_2})/(1 + {_0r_1})]$ where the short rate $_0r_1$ is used as the common denominator throughout the yield curve.

The unfortunate consequence of the second variation is that while it allows for non-parallel shifts in the term structure it does so in a very restrictive way. If we have an upward sloping yield curve, then $_0r_2 > {_0r_1}$. Then restricting non-parallel shifts to proportional shifts implies that changes in longer rates are greater than changes in the short rate. That is

$$\Delta_0 r_2 = \Delta_0 r_1 \left[\frac{1 + {_0r_2}}{1 + {_0r_1}} \right] \quad \text{and} \quad {_0r_2} > {_0r_1} \Rightarrow \Delta_0 r_2 > \Delta_0 r_1$$

This implies that longer rates are expected to have greater volatility than short rates. This contradicts stylized facts concerning the term structure of interest rate volatility where in general we expect precisely the opposite. On the other hand if we have a downward sloping yield curve, then $_0r_2 < {}_0r_1$. Then restricting non-parallel shifts to proportional shifts implies that changes in shorter rates are greater than changes in the long rate. That is

$$\Delta_0 r_2 = \Delta_0 r_1 \left[\frac{1 + {}_0r_2}{1 + {}_0r_1} \right] \quad \text{and} \quad {}_0r_2 < {}_0r_1 \Rightarrow \Delta_0 r_2 < \Delta_0 r_1$$

This implies that the short rate is expected to have greater volatility than longer rates. This is in agreement with stylized facts concerning the term structure of interest rate volatility but notice that this happens only when we have a downward sloping yield curve. Consequently the second variation of Fisher Weil duration contains a flaw that restricts its usefulness as a model of how bond prices respond to changes in interest rates.

To appreciate how Fisher Weil duration works we look at how it is derived. You will recall from Chapter 7 that modified duration includes the first partial derivative of changes in the bond's price with respect to a change in yield. This partial derivative, prior to the application of annuity formulas to obtain a closed form solution, is as follows.

$$\frac{-dB}{dY} = \frac{1}{(1+Y)} \left[\frac{1C}{(1+Y)^1} + \frac{2C}{(1+Y)^2} + \cdots + \frac{n(FV+C)}{(1+Y)^n} \right]$$

Only now we have a non-flat term structure so we replace the yield Y with the zero coupon term structure of interest rates.

$$\frac{-dB}{dY} = \left[\frac{1C}{(1+{}_0r_1)^2} + \frac{2C}{(1+{}_0r_2)^3} + \cdots + \frac{n(M+C)}{(1+{}_0r_n)^{n+1}} \right]$$

Recall that a coupon bond can be considered to be a portfolio of zero coupon bonds where each zero corresponds to a coupon or principal payment. Furthermore we note that the Macaulay duration of a zero is the time until payment. Combining these facts we can rewrite the above as

$$\frac{-dB}{dY} = \left[\frac{C(D_1)}{(1+{}_0r_1)^2} + \frac{C(D_2)}{(1+{}_0r_2)^3} + \cdots + \frac{(FV+C)(D_n)}{(1+{}_0r_n)^{n+1}} \right]$$

Notice that we replace the time unit measures 1 through n with the Macaulay duration D. Now we note that the coupon payment made in year n discounted back at the zero coupon yield for n periods $_0r_n$ is the present value of the coupon zero Z_n. If we divide through the above first partial derivative by the coupon bond's price B_0 we can interpret the ratio of any zero coupon price, say Z_n, divided by the price of the bond Z_n/B_0 as the weight W_n that this zero contributes towards the value of the bond seen as a portfolio of zeros. This means we can replace each term $C/(1 + {}_0r_t)^t$ with W_t.

Finally, this leaves one additional discount factor for each coupon payment. If we note that Macaulay duration divided through by one plus one period's yield is modified duration we can simplify the expression further by replacing the Macaulay duration divided by the corresponding $(1 + {}_0r_t)$ with modified duration D_t^*. Combining these facts together we find that the first variation of Fisher Weil duration is a weighted average of the modified duration of each of the bond's component zeros.

$$D_{FW}^* = [D_1^* W_1 + D_2^* W_2 + \cdots + D_n^* W_n] = \sum_{t=1}^{n} D_t^* W_t \qquad (9.1)$$

This variation of Fisher Weil duration (9.1) allows for a non-flat term structure but still assumes parallel shifts in the term structure. As already mentioned, to allow for non-parallel shifts Fisher Weil assumes that these shifts are proportional to the slope of the yield curve using the short rate as the common denominator throughout. This means all we need to do is to adjust the weights W_t in (9.1) by the slope of the term structure at each coupon date to obtain the second variation of Fisher Weil duration that allows for a (restrictive) non-parallel shift in the yield curve. That is, we multiply each weight W_t in (9.1) by the slope measured as one plus the corresponding zero yield as of the coupon date divided by one plus the short rate of interest or $(1 + {}_0r_t)/(1 + {}_0r_1)$. Therefore the measure of Fisher Weil duration for non-parallel shifts in the yield curve is as follows.

$$D_{FW2}^* = \sum_{t=1}^{n} \left[\frac{(1 + {}_0r_t)}{(1 + {}_0r_1)} \right] W_t D_t^* \qquad (9.2)$$

9.2.1   Examples of Fisher Weil duration

Consider a 1.5-year bond with a 12% coupon rate. The zero coupon term structure is ${}_0r_1 = 0.03992$, ${}_0r_2 = 0.04442$, ${}_0r_3 = 0.04752$ at annual rates. The \$1 face value coupon zero prices are:

$$d_1 = 1/(1 + 0.03992/2) = 0.98043$$

$$d_2 = 1/(1 + 0.04442/2)^2 = 0.95702$$

$$d_3 = 1/(1 + 0.04752/2)^3 = 0.93198$$

Employing the zero coupon portfolio approach to pricing the bond we have:

$$B_0 = \$6.00 \times 0.98043 + \$6.00 \times 0.95702 + \$106 \times 0.93198$$

$$= 5.88258 + 5.74212 + 98.78988$$

$$= 110.415$$

So the weights are:

$$W_1 = d_1 Q_1/B_0, W_2 = d_2 Q_2/B_0, W_3 = d_3 Q_3/B_0$$

or $5.88258/110.415 = 0.053$, $5.74212/110.415 = 0.052$, and $98.78988/110.415 = 0.895$ respectively.

Then Fisher Weil duration is calculated:

$$D_{FW}^* = (0.053) * 1/(1 + 0.03992/2) + (0.052)$$

$$* 2/(1 + 0.04442/2) + (0.895) * 3/(1 + 0.04752/2)$$

$$= 0.052 + 0.102 + 2.623$$

$$= 2.777 \text{ in semi-annual units or } 1.388 \text{ in annual units}$$

To obtain a hedge ratio using Fisher Weil duration, measure the Fisher Weil duration of the cash and the cheapest to deliver bond. Take the ratio of price sensitivities (cash to cheapest to deliver) and adjust the hedge ratio for the conversion factor and possibly for the yield spread sensitivity K as well. In this case we assume $K = 1$ so

$$N = -\frac{D_{cm,FW}^* B_{cm}}{D_{ctdm,FW}^* B_{ctdm}} (CF_m)$$

For Fisher Weil with proportional shifts in the yield curve we need to adjust the weights by the slope of the term structure at each coupon date. Using the above example,

$$D_{FW2}^* = [(1 + 0.03992/2)/(1 + 0.03992/2)](0.052)$$

$$+ [(1 + 0.04442/2)/(1 + 0.03992/2)](0.102)$$

$$+ [(1 + 0.04752/2)/(1 + 0.03992/2)](2.623)$$

$$= 2.787 \text{ in semi-annual units or } 1.393 \text{ in annual units}$$

Notice that this measure of duration is slightly higher than the first variation of Fisher Weil duration for this bond. This happens because we have an upward sloping yield curve, so the weights are higher for the longer-term and more interest rate sensitive zero coupon bonds. For downward sloping yield curves we obtain precisely the opposite.

9.3 Key rate duration

Fisher Weil duration makes unreasonable assumptions regarding the behaviour of interest rate shifts because it is still a one factor model. Ho (1992) extends Fisher Weil by allowing for more than one factor. While adding more factors increases complexity, it also increases flexibility to the point where we can capture any type of shift in the term structure, parallel, non-parallel or even violent twists in the shape of the term structure.

The major premise of Ho's key rate duration is that there are a few key influential interest rates that determine the shape of the yield curve. That is, if the yield curve were to change shape, the yield curve would pivot at one or more of these key rates and the intervening yields will follow suit. Some obvious candidates for key rates would be the yields of 'on the run' bonds in the US. In other markets the benchmark bonds may provide good 'key rates'.

Ho assumes that these key rates influence non-key rates in proportion to the time distance the non-key rates are from the key rate. He further assumes that non-key rates are influenced by adjacent key rates only. To appreciate what these assumptions imply refer to Table 9.1.

Table 9.1 The influence of key rates in key rate duration

First key rate	Second key rate	Term structure (flat at 5% initially)
$\Delta_0 r_1 = \frac{3}{3}\Delta_0 r_1 = \frac{3}{3}(120) = 120$ bp	$\Delta_0 r_1 = \frac{0}{3}\Delta_0 r_4 = \frac{0}{3}(90) = 0$ bp	6.20%
$\Delta_0 r_2 = \frac{2}{3}\Delta_0 r_1 = \frac{2}{3}(120) = 80$ bp	$\Delta_0 r_2 = \frac{1}{3}\Delta_0 r_4 = \frac{1}{3}(90) = 30$ bp	6.10%
$\Delta_0 r_3 = \frac{1}{3}\Delta_0 r_1 = \frac{1}{3}(120) = 40$ bp	$\Delta_0 r_3 = \frac{2}{3}\Delta_0 r_4 = \frac{2}{3}(90) = 60$ bp	6.00%
$\Delta_0 r_4 = \frac{0}{3}\Delta_0 r_1 = \frac{0}{3}(120) = 0$ bp	$\Delta_0 r_4 = \frac{3}{3}\Delta_0 r_4 = \frac{3}{3}(90) = 90$ bp	5.90%

For illustrative purposes we look at a four period yield curve where the first $_0 r_1$ and fourth $_0 r_4$ zero yields are key rates. There are three six-month periods between our two key rates so the time distance between each key rate is divided into thirds. Similarly if non-key rates were at three-month intervals there would be six three-month intervals between the key rates and time distance between key rates would be measured in sixths. In our illustration the remaining yields

$_0r_2$ and $_0r_3$ are non-key rates observed at six-month intervals. In the first column, the first key rate changes by 120 basis points. Since $_0r_2$ is two thirds of the time distance from the next adjacent key rate at $_0r_4$ to the current key rate $_0r_1$, it changes by two thirds of the current key rate or 80 basis points. Similarly the non-key rate $_0r_3$ changes by 40 basis points because it is one third of the time distance from the next adjacent key rate at $_0r_4$ to the current key rate $_0r_1$. Notice that the first key rate $_0r_1$ has no influence on the second key rate $_0r_4$. Similarly the second key rate $_0r_4$ changes by 90 basis points so the non-key rates change in proportion to the time distance from the next adjacent key rate $_0r_1$ and the currently changing key rate $_0r_4$. Together these changes in the key rates show how a non-parallel shift in the term structure is generated. In this case an initial flat yield curve at 5% is transformed into a much higher, gently downward sloping yield curve.

Key rate duration is a direct extension of the parallel shift version of Fisher Weil duration, itself being a direct extension of modified duration. All key rate duration does is to adjust the weights in Fisher Weil duration for the time distance between the key rates. That is, key rate duration is the time-weighted sum of modified durations of component zeros of the corresponding coupon bond. The difference is that now we have many duration measures, one each for each key rate. In our example we have two.

To see this recall that the parallel shift version of Fisher Weil duration is

$$D_{FW}^* = -[D_1^* W_1 + D_2^* W_2 + \cdots + D_n^* W_n]$$

Adjusting for key rates, we have, for the first key rate:

$$D_{KR1}^* = -[D_1^* W_1 + D_2^*(2/3)W_2 + D_3^*(1/3)W_3]$$

Notice that we ignore the time weight for the duration of the key rate as the weight (3/3) is one, and that we ignore the duration term for the fourth interest rate, as it is a key rate, so the first key rate has a zero weight (0/3) in influencing this duration. For the second key rate,

$$D_{KR4}^* = -[D_2^*(1/3)W_2 + D_3^*(2/3)W_3 + D_4^* W_4]$$

No doubt an example will help.

9.3.1 Example of key rate duration

Assume key rates are the six-month rate $_0r_1$ and the two-year rate $_0r_4$. This leads to two key rate durations one each for the six-month $_0r_1$ and the two-year $_0r_4$ key rates that describe how changes in interest rates affect a bond's price. So changes in the six-month rate affect all rates up to (but not including) the two-year rate, and the two-year rate will affect all yields down to (but not including) the six-month rate in a linear fashion.

Suppose we wish to measure the interest rate sensitivity of a $4\frac{5}{8}$ semi-annual coupon pay bond that matures in two years and is priced at $100\,375$ of $100\,000$ face value. The total coupon is $2312.50 for each semi-annual coupon. The initial zero curve measured at six-month intervals is $_0r_n = 0.0356$, $_0r_2 = 0.039$, $_0r_3 = 0.0418$ and $_0r_4 = 0.0444$ where $_0r_1$ and $_0r_4$ are our key rates. The Fisher Weil weights are as follows.

$$w_1 = \left[\frac{2312.5}{(1.0178)^1}\right]\frac{1}{100\,375} = 0.0226$$

$$w_2 = \left[\frac{2312.5}{(1.0195)^2}\right]\frac{1}{100\,375} = 0.0222$$

$$w_3 = \left[\frac{2312.5}{(1.0209)^3}\right]\frac{1}{100\,375} = 0.0217$$

$$w_4 = \left[\frac{102\,312.5}{(1.0222)^4}\right]\frac{1}{100\,375} = 0.9336$$

The modified duration of each $1 face value zero coupon bond that underlies our initial sovereign term structure is

$$D_1^* = 1/(1.0178) = 0.9825, \quad D_2^* = 2/(1.0195) = 1.9618,$$

$$D_3^* = 3/(1.0209) = 2.9386, \quad D_4^* = 4/(1.0222) = 3.9131$$

Therefore the first key rate has duration of

$$D_{KR1}^* = (0.0226)(0.9825)(3/3) + (0.0222)(1.9618)(2/3)$$

$$+ (0.0217)(2.9386)(1/3)$$

$$= 0.0724(0.0362 \text{ annual})$$

We leave it to you to work out that the second key rate D_{KR4}^* has duration of 3.71 semi-annual and 1.855 annual.

Suppose the six-month rate increases by 10 bp, and the two-year rate by 50 bp, what would be the change in the bond's price?

$$\Delta B = \sum_{i=1}^{2} D_{KRi}^* B\Delta y_i$$

$$\Delta B = D_{KR1}^* B\Delta y_1 + D_{KR2}^* B\Delta y_2$$

$$= [-(0.0362)(100\,375)(0.001)] + [-(1.855)(100\,375)(0.005)]$$

$$= -934.61$$

In other words, the price of the bond would decline from $100 375 to $99 440.39. To see that indeed key rate duration is a direct extension of Fisher Weil duration, imagine we have a parallel shift in the term structure. Then the first and second key rates would change by the same amount, say 90 basis points, and so will all intermediate non-key rates. This happens because the two key rate adjustments together add 90 basis points to all non-key rates. This means that for parallel shifts key rate duration is the sum of the Fisher Weil durations.

$$D_{FW}^* = D_{KR1}^* + D_{KR2}^* = 0.0362 + 1.855 = 1.8912$$

To obtain a hedge ratio using key rate duration, measure the key rate durations of the cash and the cheapest to deliver bond. Take the ratio of price sensitivities (cash to cheapest to deliver) for each key rate and adjust the hedge ratio for the conversion factor. In this case

$$N = \frac{D_{cm,KR1}^* B_{cm}}{D_{ctdm,KR1}^* B_{ctdm}}(CF_m) + \frac{D_{cm,KR2}^* B_{cm}}{D_{ctdm,KR2}^* B_{ctdm}}(CF_m)$$

9.3.2 Measuring the volatility of a portfolio

Duration can be used to measure the risk of a portfolio. This is of interest in risk management particularly when needing to measure the value at risk (*VAR*) for a fixed income position. If you are willing to assume parallel shifts in a flat sovereign yield curve then (7.5) can be used. Specifically

$$\frac{\Delta B}{B} = D^* \Delta Y \tag{7.5}$$

So taking the variance of (7.5) we have an expression for the variance of unexpected percentage changes in the value of a portfolio.

$$Var\left(\frac{\Delta B}{B}\right) = (D^*)^2 \sigma_{yy} \tag{9.3}$$

Then taking the square root of (9.3) and placing the bond (or portfolio price) *B* on the right-hand side we have an expression for the volatility of unexpected changes in the value of the portfolio.

$$\Delta B = D^* B \sigma_y \tag{9.4}$$

For *VAR* applications σ_y is the daily yield volatility measured as a standard deviation. Typically daily earnings at risk (*DEAR*) attempts to measure the maximum loss that can occur within a 20 trading day (approximately one calendar month) time frame. If we assume that daily yield volatility is normally distributed, we would multiply the right-hand side of (9.4) by a factor of 1.645 to measure the loss we can expect in one day in 20. The result is called *DEAR*.

$$DEAR = D^* B \sigma_y (1.645) \tag{9.5}$$

If we assume that it takes, say, three days to liquidate our portfolio then the corresponding value at risk *VAR* is

$$VAR = D^* B \sigma_y (1.645) \sqrt{3} \tag{9.6}$$

Notice that since the *VAR* is measured in standard deviation units then the time it takes to sell the portfolio is measured in standard deviation units as well.

For example, suppose we have a \$30 000 000 portfolio with a modified duration of 14.45. We measure the bond's daily yield volatility as 5 basis points. If we assume that unexpected bond price changes are normally distributed we can anticipate that we could lose \$356 554 one day in 20. This is the *DEAR* of our portfolio and it is calculated using (9.5).

$$DEAR = 14.45(30\,000\,000)(0.0005)(1.645) = 356\,554$$

If it takes three days to liquidate our portfolio then the price concession we may need to make in order sell our position may compound our losses. To account for this we measure the *VAR* as the *DEAR* multiplied by the square root of three.

$$VAR = 14.45(30\,000\,000)(0.0005)(1.645)\sqrt{3} = 617\,569$$

However, if one believes that the term structure is not flat and that interest rates do not necessarily move in a parallel fashion and that only a few key rates are important in describing term structure movements then key rate duration can be helpful. For example, if we believe that there are two key rates, say, at six months and another at five years then using a six-month time step we obtain the key rate duration analogue of (7.5).

$$\frac{\Delta B}{B} = D^*_{KR1} \Delta Y_{or_1} + D^*_{KR10} \Delta Y_{or_{10}} \tag{9.7}$$

Taking the variance of (9.7) we develop a two factor model for the variance of our fixed income position.

$$Var\left(\frac{\Delta B}{B}\right) = (D^*_{KR1})^2 \sigma_{or_1,or_1} + (D^*_{KR10})^2 \sigma_{or_{10},or_{10}} \tag{9.8}$$

In (9.8) $\sigma_0 r_{1,0} r_1$ is the variance of the first key rate, $\sigma_0 r_{10,0} r_{10}$ is the variance of the second key rate and the correlation between the first and second key rates is assumed to be zero. If we were to use N key rates (9.8) would be expanded to include N variances just as we do in portfolio theory.

Taking the square root of the above expression, placing the bond price on the right-hand side and multiplying the result by a factor of 1.645 we obtain an alternative measure of *DEAR*. If we multiply this measure of *DEAR* by the square root of the number of days it takes to sell the portfolio we have the corresponding measure of *VAR*. The resulting expressions for *DEAR* and *VAR* are as follows.

$$DEAR = \left[\left(D^*_{KR1}\sigma_0 r_1\right)^2 + \left(D^*_{KR10}\sigma_0 r_{10}\right)^2\right]^{1/2} B(1.645)$$

$$VAR = \left[\left(D^*_{KR1}\sigma_0 r_1\right)^2 + \left(D^*_{KR10}\sigma_0 r_{10}\right)^2\right]^{1/2} B(1.645)\sqrt{t}$$

9.4 Duration for corporate bonds

So far we have only examined how to hedge sovereign bonds. We now turn to corporate bonds that are subject to both interest rate and credit risk.

It is tempting to suggest that we should simply apply the usual duration measures to corporate bonds without making any explicit adjustment for credit risk. In other words, we would apply (7.2) to measure *corporate Macaulay duration* and (7.6a) to measure *corporate modified duration* by measuring the price sensitivity of the bond to a change in its yield rather than its price sensitivity to a change in interest rates. The latter distinction is important because in contrast to sovereign bonds, corporate bonds are subject not only to interest rate risk but to credit risk as well. The yield of a sovereign bond is set considering interest risk only whereas the yield of a corporate bond summarizes the impact of interest rate and credit risk on promised return.

The result we obtain from using corporate duration is surprising. Note that a corporate bond has a higher yield and on average a higher coupon than the corresponding maturity sovereign bond. From our seesaw analogy we realize that the duration of the corporate bond is less than the duration of the corresponding maturity sovereign bond. This leads to the uncomfortable conclusion that the corporate bond is less risky than the corresponding maturity sovereign bond.

We obtain this perplexing result because corporate bonds are subject to two sources of risk, interest rate and credit risk, whereas sovereign bonds have interest rate risk only. There is no assurance that interest and credit risk have zero correlation, so these sources of risk may not be simply additive. Some kind of diversification effect may be possible so that the actual price volatility of corporate bonds would be less than the sum of the price volatility due to interest rate and credit risk added separately. In fact the consensuses of recent research (Duffie 1998, Kiesel, Perraudin and Taylor 2002 and Papageorgiou and Skinner 2003) find that these sources of risk are mildly negatively correlated. Specifically they find that as the level of the sovereign term structure increases the credit spread for investment grade bonds decreases. This suggests that the sum of volatility due to credit and interest risk for corporate bonds may be less than the volatility due to interest rate risk only for sovereign bonds.

It is not difficult to see why there may be a mild negative correlation between interest and credit risk. Interest rates rise when inflation increases. This means the real burden of servicing outstanding higher coupon corporate debt may be less and so corporate debt may be less credit risky. Conversely when interest rates decrease, inflation is expected to be lower so the real burden of servicing existing higher coupon corporate debt may increase thereby increasing credit risk. This is just one possible reason why we observe a negative correlation between changes in the level of the sovereign term structure and the size of the credit spread.

Nevertheless it is doubtful that corporate modified duration should be lower than the modified duration of the corresponding maturity sovereign bond since this implies a strong rather than a mild negative correlation between interest and credit risks. Moreover, if we were to use corporate modified duration we will include both interest and credit risk in our hedge ratio but this would be done only implicitly through use of the corporate bond's yield. We would rather have a hedge ratio that explicitly models the relation between interest and credit risk so that the hedge can respond to a paradigm shift in the relation between interest rate and credit risk.

9.4.1   Credit risk adjusted duration

Standard methods can be applied to the Jonkhart bond valuation equation (6.21) to obtain the corporate bond analogue of Macaulay and modified duration measures. We call these measures of duration *pure interest duration* because they measure the interest sensitivity of a corporate bond's price holding credit risk, as summarized by the probability of default and the recovery rate in the event of default, constant. These measures have potential as they help us to compare the interest rate risk of corporate and sovereign bonds in a consistent manner.

The general form of pure interest Macaulay duration is as follows.

$$D_{PI} = \left[\sum_{t=1}^{n} \frac{E(CF_t)t}{(1 + {}_0r_t)^t} \bigg/ B_c \right] \tag{9.9}$$

Equation (9.9) tells us that we measure the Macaulay pure interest rate duration D_{PI} in the same way that we measure ordinary Macaulay duration except that we apply time weights to the *expected E* (or credit risk adjusted) cash flows rather than the promised cash flows. These expected time-weighted cash flows are discounted to the present using the sovereign zero coupon term structure of interest rates. There will be a tendency for Macaulay pure interest duration to be less than the corresponding corporate Macaulay duration because there will be an earlier redistribution of the timing of cash flows as we move from the promised to the expected. This happens because part of the 'coupon' payments in earlier cash flows will include the possibility of receiving a recovery amount.

Once we measure pure interest Macaulay duration D_{PI} it is a simple step to convert it into the equivalent modified pure interest rate duration D_{PI}^* by dividing the pure interest rate duration (9.9) by one plus one period's sovereign yield. This will give us a measure of the price response of a corporate bond to a change in the underlying sovereign rate of interest.

To illustrate the calculations of pure interest duration, we use a three-year corporate bond that pays an *annual* coupon of 7.65 and is priced at 102.346. The probabilities of survival are, $P_1 = 0.995$, $P_2 = 0.99$, $P_3 = 0.98$. The recovery fraction δ is constant at 40% and the term structure ${}_0r_n$ is flat at 6%. To illustrate the calculation of pure interest Macaulay duration we construct Table 9.2.

Table 9.2   Pure interest Macaulay duration

	$t = 1$	$t = 2$	$t = 3$
Cash flows	7.65	7.65	107.65
Expected cash flows (*ECF*)	7.812	7.934	104.708
$t \times (ECF)$	7.812	15.868	314.124
$PV[t \times (ECF)]$	7.37	14.122	263.745

We write in the promised cash flows in the first row and then calculate the expected cash flows (ECF) according to Jonkhart (1979)
in the second row. The details of the calculation of the ECF are as
follows.

$$T = 1 : [(0.995)(7.65) + (1 - 0.995)(40)](1) = 7.812$$
$$T = 2 : [(0.99)(7.65) + (1 - 0.99)(40)](1)(0.995) = 7.934$$
$$T = 3 : [(0.98)(107.65) + (1 - 0.98)(40)](1)(0.995)(0.99)$$
$$= 104.708$$

As instructed by (9.9) we multiply these ECF by the time they occur
in row 3 and finally we find the present value of this result in row
4 using the sovereign zero coupon term structure of interest rates
as the discount rates. Finding the sum of the present value of the
time-weighted expected cash flows in row 4 and dividing this result by the bond's price obtains the pure interest Macaulay duration
for this bond. Note that if the bond was semi-annual coupon pay,
t, $_0r_n$ and the coupon payment would be semi-annual measures
and the final result should be divided by two just as we do for
ordinary Macaulay duration. When we divide the pure interest rate
Macaulay duration by one plus one period's sovereign yield we obtain
the corresponding pure interest modified duration. If the bond was
semi-annual coupon pay, the Macaulay duration measure should be
divided by one plus one half year's sovereign yield just as we do
for ordinary modified duration. These calculations are illustrated
below.

$$D_{PI} = \sum \frac{PV[T \times (ECF)]}{B} = \frac{285.237}{102.346} = 2.787$$
$$D_{PI}^* = \frac{2.787}{1.06} = 2.629$$

It is interesting to compare these measures of pure interest rate
sensitivity with the corresponding corporate modified and Macaulay
duration. These are ordinary duration measures that use the corporate bond yield thereby only implicitly adjusting for the combination
of interest and credit risk embedded in the bond's corporate yield.
Using the closed form solution for modified duration (7.6a) we find
that the bond's pure interest modified duration (2.629) is higher than
the corresponding corporate modified duration (2.617). However, we
find that pure interest Macaulay duration (2.787) is slightly lower
than the corresponding corporate Macaulay duration (2.794). The

corporate duration measures are calculated below.

$$D^* = \frac{\dfrac{7.65}{(0.0676)^2}\left[1 - \dfrac{1}{(1+0.0676)^3}\right] + \dfrac{3\left(100 - \dfrac{7.65}{0.0676}\right)}{(1+0.0676)^{3+1}}}{102.346}$$

$$= \frac{(1674.05)[0.178185] - 30.40397}{102.346} = 2.617$$

$$D = 2.617(1.0676) = 2.794$$

Pure interest Macaulay duration is slightly less than corporate Macaulay duration as potential recoveries in the event of default add additional weight to expected cash flows received earlier. In terms of our seesaw analogy, the size of the 'coupon' containers is larger because part of the expected value of these containers includes the possibility of early principal repayments. In this example the effect of this time redistribution is not fully offset by discounting at lower sovereign yields.

On the other hand pure interest modified duration (2.629) is greater than corporate modified duration (2.617) since only one factor (changes in interest rates) is examined when we use pure interest duration. Corporate credit risk is held constant. For corporate modified duration, there is no explicit accounting for credit risk, as summarized by the probability of survival P and the recovery fraction δ in the pure interest duration measure. Instead this is *implicitly* included in D^* through use of the corporate bonds yield, Y. This suggests that if we were worried about the interest rate sensitivity of the corporate bond, we should use pure interest rate sensitivity rather than corporate modified duration. Pure interest duration adjusts for the effect of credit explicitly, so we are sure that we study the sensitivity of the bond's price to a change in interest rates, holding credit risk constant.

Fooladi, Roberts and Skinner (1997) first derived pure interest Macaulay duration and demonstrated analytically and numerically that this measure of duration would enable more effective portfolio immunization strategies for corporate bonds than corporate Macaulay duration. Skinner (1998) derived the pure interest modified duration as well as two other measures of duration based on the survival probability and the interaction between the survival probability and the rate of pure interest included in the Jonkhart (1979) model. He found that the improvements in hedging effectiveness thereby obtained were not significantly better either economically or statistically than using corporate duration. Moreover he found that all hedges performed very poorly in times of economic stress.

Ioannides and Skinner (1999) examined alternative hedging instruments to see if using a hedging instrument subject to credit risk rather than finding a more effective hedge ratio could find an effective hedging strategy for corporate bonds. They find that only a hypothetical corporate hedging instrument could potentially form an effective hedging strategy for corporate bonds. Clare, Ioannides and Skinner (2000) demonstrate that a combination of stock index futures and Treasury interest rate futures do not form an effective hedge for corporate bonds.

In summary there does not appear to be an effective hedging strategy for corporate bonds, a highly unsatisfactory state of affairs. However, there appear to be two possible solutions to the problem. Perhaps the emerging credit derivatives market may prove effective in controlling the credit risk for corporate bond portfolios. Alternatively delta hedging using the binomial trees from credit risk models such as Jarrow and Turnbull (1995) may yet provide an effective hedge ratio.

9.5   Delta hedging

So far we have not exploited the binomial interest and credit risk models that we have explored in Chapter 5. In contrast with the traditional hedge ratios and indeed Fisher Weil, key rate and pure interest duration-based hedge ratios, delta hedging uses these models thereby explicitly recognizing the stochastic nature of interest rates and credit risk. There are two variations of delta hedging, however. The first is a variation of the *PVBP* but uses the calibrated term structure of interest rates that we input into the binomial interest rate model. Alternatively we can delta hedge in the same way that we can delta hedge equities using the binomial option pricing model. Both variations are numerical techniques that do not use any closed form solution. Therefore it is best to illustrate these techniques using numerical examples.

9.5.1   PVBP delta hedge

Suppose we wish to hedge a 2.5-year 10% semi-annual coupon pay sovereign bond. We choose to use the Ho and Lee model presented in section 5.2.3. We go to HLb02.xls and change the coupon in cell b35 to 10% and find that the current price of this bond is $109.3823. Now we choose some yield curve shift that we think is likely. For example, suppose we think that the yield curve may experience a 10 basis point upward parallel shift. We input this new yield curve in row 30 and then calibrate the Ho and Lee model to this year curve making sure that the zero coupon yields implied by replicating portfolios of state securities (row 27) equal the new input yield curve (row 30).

Notice that the 10% 2.5-year bond is now worth $109.1399. We can work out the *PVBP* for this bond as follows.

$$PVBP_B = \frac{dB/dY}{10\,000} = \frac{(109.3823 - 109.1399) \div 0.001}{10\,000} = 0.02424$$

That is since the *PVBP* is simply the change in the value of the bond due to a 1 basis point change in yield we divide the price response (109.3823 − 109.1399) to a 10 basis point change by 10 basis points (0.001). We divide the result by 10 000 to convert a 1 basis point change back into a change in price per quoted $100. We do the same for a hedging instrument to find its *PVBP* and so construct our usual hedge ratio.

The attractive feature of this approach is that we can use any term structure shift that we desire. Moreover we can apply this to corporate bonds by adjusting the input corporate yield curve and then finding the implied *PVBP* for a corporate bond.

9.5.2 Binomial delta hedging

To illustrate binomial delta hedging we again use the Ho and Lee spreadsheet found in HL02.xls. The calibrated bond price tree reported in block A33 to E38 contains information concerning the sensitivity of the bond's price to the binomial stochastic interest rate process. From this tree we can calculate the bond's price response to an up- or downtick in interest rates thereby obtaining a numerical estimate of a delta. We could use the first branch to obtain this numerical estimate of the delta but generally this will result in a measure of the delta that is too crude as the step size is too large. It is recommended that we use the second branch instead. Furthermore the step size of six months used in the example is far too large. One should use a binomial model that has been calibrated to the zero yield curve using a much smaller time step, at least one month or less.

We start by calculating the average price response of the bond in the second time step in the 'up' node's cells C36 and C37 (UU + UD)/2 and the 'down' node's cells C37 and C38 (UD + DD)/2. The respective values are

$$\text{Up} = \frac{97.2187 + 99.9935}{2} = 98.6061$$

$$\text{Down} = \frac{99.9935 + 102.8772}{2} = 101.4354$$

The difference between these two numbers $(101.4354 - 98.6061)$ is 2.8293 and forms an estimate of the delta (price sensitivity) of the bond to movement towards an uptick or downtick in interest rates according to the binomial process. We calculate the delta of the hedging instrument in the same way. As always the ratio of the cash delta to the hedging asset delta forms the hedge ratio.

The advantage of this approach is that it specifically takes into account the binomial stochastic nature of interest rates. Binomial delta hedging can be applied to interest and credit risk models such as Jarrow and Turnbull and so this method is easily extended to credit risk models as well.

9.6 Exercises

Question 1
The zero coupon spot curve is $r_1 = 0.025$, $r_2 = 0.03$ and $r_3 = 0.035$. Consider a $4\frac{3}{8}$ coupon bond (coupons paid annually) with maturity in three years (three periods) from now and a face value of £100 000. r_1 and r_3 are your *key* rates.

1. Calculate the two key rate durations of the bond.
2. Use these key rate durations to evaluate the effect on the bond price of a *simultaneous* 100 basis point *increase* in r_1 and of a 100 basis point *decrease* in r_3.

Question 2
If a company were to default on its bonds, 40% of its face value would be recovered. The probability of the firm defaulting in the next two years is $P_1 = 0.90$, $P_2 = 0.85$. The zero coupon risk-free spot curve is flat at 5%. The firm has a two-year 7% coupon bond (paid annually) with a face value of 100.

1. What is the value of this bond?
2. What is its yield to maturity?
3. What is the default spread?
4. What is its modified duration?
5. What is the 'pure interest' duration?
6. In general, what does modified duration and pure interest duration indicate about the interest rate sensitivity of a corporate bond?

Question 3

A five-year corporate bond is priced at 102.035 and pays a 6% annual coupon. The spot sovereign yield curve is $r_1 = 0.05$, $r_2 = 0.055$, $r_3 = 0.0575$, $r_4 = 0.06$ and $r_5 = 0.055$. We assume the one-year r_1 and five-year r_5 interest rates are key rates.

(a) Calculate the bond's modified, Fisher Weil (parallel shift version) and key rate durations. Round to four decimal places.
(b) How reasonable are each of these sensitivity measures? Discuss.

Question 4

For parallel shifts in the yield curve, the sum of the key rate durations is the same as Fisher Weil duration. Is this statement true? Explain why or why not.

Pricing and hedging non-fixed income securities

10.1 Introduction

So far we have learned how to price and hedge traditional fixed income securities, both sovereign and corporate. We now turn our attention to pricing and hedging non-fixed income securities. In this chapter we will examine *structured securities* such as floaters, inverse floaters and interest rate swaps and *interest rate derivatives* such as caps, floors and collars. The methodologies we establish to price these securities will enable us to price more complex structured securities that include embedded options such as callable, putable and sinking fund bonds in Chapter 12.

10.2 Floaters

A floater is the simplest form of structured security. A floater is an ordinary fixed income security except that its income is not fixed. I realize this sounds a bit silly but actually there is a lot of truth to that statement. Just like ordinary bonds floaters pay coupons

periodically; annually, semi-annually or quarterly are common payment structures. A floater is priced in terms of $100 and at maturity
it returns the last coupon payment and the final redemption amount.
In other words, the basic structure of the financial contract is precisely the same as an ordinary bond, except that the coupon rate will
be adjusted or reset periodically.

The coupon rate of a floater varies directly with some 'reference'
rate, say the six-month libor rate or the 90-day T-bill rate. That is, as,
say, the libor rate increases the floating rate coupon increases. The
coupon is reset, say annually, semi-annually or quarterly, according to some defined relationship with the reference rate. Typically
the reset date is the beginning of the coupon period. For example, a
floater may pay the six-month libor rate flat every six months (semi-
annual coupon pay) and the floating coupon is reset every six months
at the beginning of each six-month period. If today is the reset date
and the six-month libor rate is 4%, then in six months the floater will
pay a coupon of $2 (4%/2 × 100). The great point is that we know
what the first coupon will be, but we do not know what the second
coupon will be because that will depend upon the six-month libor
rate that evolves in six months' time, at the beginning of the second
coupon payment period.

The challenge is to determine a way to price, say, a 10-year floater
where we know the first coupon payment and the final redemption
amount but we do not know what the other 19 (assuming semi-
annual coupon pay) coupon payments will be. However, we can
see how to price a floater once we break the problem down into a
sequence of one period problems beginning with the last period.

For the sake of illustration, we examine the pricing of a 10-year
semi-annual coupon pay floater. The coupon resets at the beginning
of each six-month coupon period to equal the six-month libor rate
flat. We start by looking at the pricing problem at the beginning of
the last coupon period, 9.5 years from now. In the last period we
know the final coupon payment, as today, at the beginning of the last
period, is the reset date. Since libor rates are, say, 6% then we know
we will receive $3 at maturity plus the final redemption amount of
$100. Therefore viewed from 9.5 years from now the pricing problem
is simply how to discount these cash flows back one semi-annual
period. Mathematically speaking the problem is expressed as follows.

$$B_{F(1)} = \frac{FV + FV(r_L/2)}{(1 + r_?/2)}$$

$B_{F(1)}$ is the price of the floater one period prior to maturity, FV is the
final redemption amount of $100, r_L is the six-month libor rate and
$r_?$ is the six-month interest rate that we use to discount future values

to find the price of the floater, the identity of which we have to determine. We note that $r_?$ must be r_L because the floater is as interest rate sensitive as the six-month libor rate. This will become more evident as we continue. Then it is easy to find that the value of the floater six months prior to maturity is $100 by application of discounting.

$$B_{F(1)} = \frac{100 + 100\,(0.06/2)}{(1 + 0.06/2)} = 100$$

Now we view the pricing problem at the beginning of the second to last coupon period, two periods prior to maturity, nine years from today. Again we know the coupon payment expected in six-months' time because today is the reset date. If the six-month libor rate is 5%, we know we will be paid $2.5 at the end of the period. Moreover we know that we can sell the floater for $100 after the second to last coupon payment is paid because from the previous step we know that the floater will be priced at par six months prior to maturity. Finally, we know that we should use the six-month libor rate as the discount rate because the floater is as interest rate risky as the six-month libor rate. Therefore we find that the value of the floater one year prior to maturity is $100 as shown below.

$$B_{F(2)} = \frac{B_{F(1)} + FV\,(r_L/2)}{(1 + r_L/2)} = \frac{100 + 100\,(0.05/2)}{(1 + 0.05/2)} = 100$$

We can continue backwards step by step finding that the value of the floater at the reset date is par. Specifically we note that since the beginning of the coupon period is the reset date we know the coupon payment that will be made at the end of the coupon period. We know that at the end of the period we can sell the floater at par. Therefore the valuation problem degenerates into a one period valuation problem. Since the discount rate and the coupon rate are the same, the value of the floater must be par. This is true even when the coupon rate is specified as libor plus or minus some premium because the appropriate discount rate is libor plus or minus the same premium. In other words, the floater is reset to par at the beginning of each period because the floater is designed to do just that. Whenever we set the coupon rate equal to the discount rate the value of the bond must be par.

   In between reset dates the floater behaves as if it were a bond with only one more coupon remaining. For example, supposing today is the reset date and the next coupon is libor at 6%. The price of the floater is par on this day. In say two months, four months prior to the next reset date the bond may be above or below par since the next coupon is still fixed (for the next four months only) at 6%, but current libor rates may be higher or lower than 6%. Now the discount rate may be different than the coupon rate so the floater may have some other value than par. However, as the reset date approaches, the floater will be 'pulled to par' because on the next reset date the coupon rate will be adjusted to agree with the libor rate whatever the libor rate turns out to be. Table 10.1 illustrates the 'pull to par' for a floater reset in January and July of the year.

Table 10.1 Floater values between reset dates

Month	Libor rate/Coupon rate	Dirty price	Clean price
January	6%/6%	$100	$100
February	6.25%/6%	$100.3923	$99.8923
March	6.5%/6%	$100.8271	$99.8271
April	6.75%/6%	$101.3047	$99.8047
May	7%/6%	$101.8256	$99.8256
June	7.25%/6%	$102.3905	$99.8905
July	7.5%/7.5%	$103.0000	$100.0000

For example, in March, four months prior to the next coupon date the dirty price is $100.8271.

$$B_{F(2)} = \frac{100 + 100\,(0.06/2)}{(1 + 0.065/2)^{4/6}} = 100.8271$$

The dirty price is above par as two months of interest $1 ($2/6 \times 3) is earned. The clean price is $99.8271. However, as we continue to roll through the months towards the reset date the clean price begins to pull towards par even though libor rates continue to rise because on the next reset date the floater will once again have a coupon rate that equals the discount rate. So we see that a floater behaves like a bond with only one period remaining until maturity because on every reset date the bond price will be par, just as would any maturing bond. Pricing a floater is easy, all we need to do to calculate the price is to discount the current coupon plus the principal payment by the current libor rate (plus any premium above libor if that is specified in the floater contract) for the remaining time to the next reset date.

So far we have assumed that the floater is not subject to credit risk. If the floater is subject to credit risk, then the floater's credit rating may change. If that happens then the coupon rate will be set according to the original credit rating when the bond was, say, AA. Now, after the credit rating change, say to A+, the discount rate will reflect its A+ status but its coupon rate will be set according to its historical AA status. These credit quality changes will create a wedge between the floating reference rate used for discounting and the coupon rate set at the reset date and so the floater would not reset to par. Essentially the coupon will be set according to one yield curve, but the floater will be priced using discount rates from another yield curve and so the price at reset will reflect differences in the credit spread between the two yield curves. The above pricing methodology will break down because credit spreads are not constant. In fact credit spreads are constantly changing. To price floaters in such circumstances requires an analysis of the different credit spreads and an assessment of the likelihood of changes and the size of these changes in the credit spread. This is a difficult task. Perhaps this explains why most floaters are originally rated very high at issue.

A similar problem occurs when the reference rate is set according to a term that is different than the periodicity of the coupon payments. For example, the coupon could be paid every six months according to the three-month libor rate. There is no guarantee that the floater will reset to par at the beginning of each coupon period because that will depend upon the slope of the underlying yield curve. It could be that in a given period the libor yield curve is flat such that the three-month libor rate used to set the coupon is the same as the six-month libor rate that is used as the discount rate. Then the bond will be set at par on that particular reset date. However, on the next reset date the libor yield curve could become upward sloping such that the coupon rate (based on the lower three-month libor rate) is below the six-month libor rate that is used for discounting. Then the floater will not reset to par on the reset date.

In general this may happen at anytime so there is no guarantee that the floater will reset to par. Like changes in credit risk, these yield curve shifts will create a wedge between the floating reference rate used for discounting and the floating reference rate used to determine the coupon so the floater will not reset to par. Essentially the coupon will be set according to one maturity but the floater will be priced using a discount rate from another maturity and so the price at reset will reflect these differences in the yield spread between the two maturities. The above pricing methodology will again break down, as the maturity spread is not constant. To price a floater in these circumstances requires an analysis of the yield spread and an assessment of the likelihood of changes and the size of these changes in the yield spread. Again this is a difficult task. Perhaps this explains why the coupons for most floaters are set according to a reference rate whose maturity matches the periodicity of the coupon payments.

Once we realize that floaters, where the periodicy of coupon payments and the floating rates match, and to the extent we can ignore the possibility of credit quality changes, are essentially pseudo one period bonds, then measuring the bond's interest rate sensitivity is trivial. The bond's clean price must be par at the reset date so it behaves just like a zero coupon bond, for what is a zero coupon bond but an ordinary bond with only one more payment remaining? Since the Macaulay duration of a zero is the time until maturity, so too the

Macaulay duration of a floater is the time until reset. Since modified duration is Macaulay duration divided by one plus one period's yield so the modified duration of a floater is the time to reset (Macaulay duration) divided by one plus one period's yield as determined by the reference rate.

In summary pricing and measuring the duration of a floater where the periodicity of coupon payments and the floating rates match, and when we can safely ignore credit risk, is easy. Since the floater is essentially a periodic zero, resetting to par by contract, the price is found by discounting par plus next period's known coupon back one period using the reference rate as the discount rate. Its Macaulay duration is the time until reset and its modified duration is the time until reset divided by one plus the current reference rate.

10.3   Inverse floaters

An inverse floater is an ordinary floater except that the coupon rate that is reset periodically varies inversely with the reference rate. Specifically the inverse floater pays a coupon equivalent to the difference between a stated coupon rate less the floating rate at the reset date. For example, if the stated rate is 14% and, say, the six-month libor rate is 6%, then the coupon rate would be 8%. As the libor rate increases, the inverse floater's coupon rate decreases. For example, if the libor rate is 6.5% at the next reset date then the new coupon rate is 7.5%. Like floaters the coupon is determined at the beginning but paid at the end of the coupon period so investors in inverse floaters always know the next coupon amount. Otherwise inverse floaters, like floaters, are just like ordinary bonds that pay coupons periodically; annually, semi-annually or quarterly are common payment structures. It is priced in terms of $100 and at maturity the inverse floater returns the last coupon payment and the final redemption amount. In other words, the basic structure of the financial contract is precisely the same as an ordinary bond, except that the coupon rate will be adjusted or reset periodically.

Since the inverse floater is so similar to the floater it is tempting to price and measure the duration of an inverse floater in the same way that we did for floaters. However, this will not be appropriate because in contrast to the floater, the inverse floater does not reset to par on the reset date. To appreciate why we look at a simple numerical example.

We examine a 10-year inverse floater. The floater's coupon is reset, say, every six months at the beginning of the coupon period as the difference between the stated coupon rate S of 14% and the six-month libor rate r_L. Today is the reset date 9.5 years after the inverse floater was originally sold, so there is only one more coupon remaining. The six-month libor rate stands at 6%, so the last coupon is 8%. We know that we will receive the original principal in six months' time. Arguing that since the inverse floater is as risky as investing in any six-month libor instrument we should use the six-month libor rate as the discount rate to find that the value of the inverse floater on the last reset rate prior to maturity is $100.971.[1] That is

$$B_{IF(1)} = \frac{FV + FV\left(\dfrac{S - r_L}{2}\right)}{(1 + r_L/2)} = \frac{100 + 100\left(\dfrac{0.14 - 0.06}{2}\right)}{(1 + 0.06/2)}$$

$$= 100.971$$

In other words, the inverse floater does not reset to par even though in the last period of the inverse floater's life we know that the inverse floater will repay the final redemption amount next period. Therefore in general inverse floaters do not reset to par at the reset date, so we cannot easily price or measure the duration of an inverse floater. However, by using the principle of value additivity we can.

10.3.1   Pricing inverse floaters via value additivity

Suppose we purchase an 8% semi-annual coupon pay sovereign bond priced at $105 with a face value FV of $100. We then sell two new securities, a floater that pays the six-month libor rate and an inverse floater that pays 16% less the six-month libor rate. Both of these new securities have a face value of 50 and a maturity date that is precisely the same as the maturity date of the fixed coupon bond. Payments made on the floater and inverse floater are legally backed by the payments from the 8% sovereign bond. In other words, we have *securitized* the 8% sovereign bond by using it as backing for two new securities, the floater and inverse floater, sold to investors. To see precisely what we are doing, refer to Figure 10.1.

From section 10.2 we know that the floater will be worth $50 (100% of par) at the reset date. Then the inverse floater must be worth $55, the difference between the value of the fixed coupon bond $105 and the value of the floater $50. This must be true because values must add up. Notice that the total coupon paid to the floater and inverse floater equals the coupon received from the fixed coupon bond. For example, if the libor rate were 6% on the reset date we would pay $1.5

---

[1] Actually using the six-month libor rate as the discount rate is wrong. As we shall see later the inverse floater has a great deal more risk than the corresponding reference rate so the above is only for illustrative purposes.

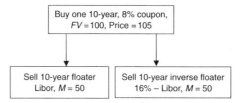

Figure 10.1   Securitizing floaters and inverse floaters

to the floater $(50 \times 0.06/2)$ and \$2.5 to the inverse floater $(50 \times [16\% - 6\%]/2)$ that just equals the \$4 we receive from the underlying fixed coupon bond $(100 \times 8\%/2)$. Furthermore the risk of payments to the floater and inverse floater is the same as the risk of receipts from the fixed coupon bond as the 'variableness' of the floating and inverse floating payments wash out. In other words, the combination of the floater and the corresponding inverse floater *is* the fixed coupon bond as both the risk and payments on the portfolio (the floater and inverse floater) equal the risk and receipts on the package (the fixed coupon bond). It follows that the value of the portfolio must equal the value of the package. This is just another application of value additivity that we discussed in section 3.3.2.

To show that in fact the value of the inverse floater must be \$55, consider the contrary case. Suppose we can sell the inverse floater for \$60 and the floater for \$50. Then we would eagerly buy the underlying fixed coupon bond for \$105, split it up into the floater and the corresponding inverse floater and sell this portfolio for \$110 making a tidy profit of \$5 for doing nothing. If libor rates rise to 7%, we still receive \$4 from the fixed coupon bond but we still pay out \$4, \$1.75 to the floater and \$2.25 to the inverse floater. We do not make any net payments; we have assumed no risk, yet we are paid \$5 for doing this. This is a pure arbitrage opportunity. Therefore the price of the inverse floater must drop to \$55, as we, with no help from anybody else, will satiate the demand for inverse floaters.

Of course, we can see the flaw in the above example. Suppose libor rates rise above 16%, say to 18%. This is an unlikely event but it is possible. Then we would pay \$4.5 to the floater and 'pay' a negative \$0.50 (that is, they must pay us) to the inverse floater. Investors in inverse floaters will not be happy, as they will in effect be paying you to borrow money from them. Potential investors will notice this possible scenario, so they will demand a 'floor', a minimum payment regardless of the actual libor rate. To protect ourselves, we will place a 'cap', a maximum amount we will pay to the floater regardless of the actual libor rate. To prevent arbitrage, the cap and floor must add up to the stated rate on the inverse floater. For example, if we place a floor of 4% on the inverse floater, we must place a cap of 12% on the floater. That way if indeed libor rates turn out to be 18% on the reset date, then the floater will receive the maximum of $3 (50 × 12%/2) and the inverse floater will receive the minimum of $1 (50 × 4%/2), both payments adding to the $4 we receive fixed from the underlying bond.

It is unconventional to quote a floater or an inverse floater in terms of a hypothetical $50 face value amount. What actually happens is that the issuer of floaters and inverse floaters purchases two fixed coupon bonds for each matched pair of a floater and an inverse floater. As another example, consider a 10-year 6% semi-annual coupon pay sovereign bond priced at $107.795 yielding 5%. At the reset date the value of the floater is par, either $50 for each face value of $50 or more conventionally $100 per $100 of face value. The price of the inverse floater is found as $(B_c - F) \times 2 = (107.795 - 50) \times 2 = \$115.59$. Alternatively we can find the value of the inverse floater based on the price of two fixed coupon bonds as $(2B_c - F) = (2 \times 107.795 - 100) = \$115.59$.

In between reset dates we can find the value of the floater using the current libor rate. Knowing the fixed coupon bond price, we find the value of the inverse floater as two times the difference between the values of the fixed coupon bond less the value of the floater based on a hypothetical face value of $50. As above we can alternatively find the value of the inverse floater as the difference between the values of two fixed coupon bonds less the value of the floater, conventionally priced in terms of $100 of face value.

For example, imagine one month into the semi-annual coupon period the yield on the 10-year 6% semi-annual coupon bond has increased by 25 basis points to 5.25%. The clean price of the fixed coupon bond is

$$B_C = \frac{C}{2}\left[\frac{1-\left(1+\frac{y}{2}\right)^{-2n}}{\frac{y}{2}}\right] + \frac{FV}{\left(1+\frac{y}{2}\right)^{2n}}$$

$$= \frac{6}{2}\left[\frac{1-\left(1+\frac{0.0525}{2}\right)^{-2\times10}}{\frac{0.0525}{2}}\right] + \frac{100}{\left(1+\frac{0.0525}{2}\right)^{2\times10}}$$

$$= \$46.22 + \$59.557 = \$105.777$$

Actually this is just an approximation of the clean price since the formula is assuming that there is a full six month period remaining in the life of the bond. To correct for this one must future value the bond one month and then deduct one-month interest. That is $105.777×(1+0.0525/2)^{1/6}−(\$6/2×1/6) = \$105.735$. However for illustrative purposes, we will continue to use this approximation throughout this chapter.

The floater pays the six-month libor rate plus 50 basis points every six months. Since libor rates were 4.75% one month ago, the next coupon will be 5.25%. Since the coupon rate is libor plus 50 basis points so too the discount rate will be libor plus 50 basis points. Now, one month into the next coupon period libor rates have increased by 25 basis points and so the current libor rate is 5.00% and the discount rate is 5.50%. Therefore the clean price of the floater is $99.878 as shown below.

$$B_{F(20)} = \frac{B_{F(19)} + FV\left(\frac{r_{L(t-1)} + 0.50}{2}\right)}{(1 + (r_{Lt} + 0.005)/2)}$$

$$= \frac{100 + 100\left(\frac{0.0475 + 0.0005}{2}\right)}{(1 + (0.05 + 0.005)/2)} = 99.878$$

Finally the clean price of the corresponding inverse floater is $111.676. That is $[2 \times B_C - B_F] = [2 \times \$105.777 - 99.878] = 111.676$.

10.3.2 Duration of an inverse floater

Just as we were able to price an inverse floater by viewing the floater and inverse floater as component securities of the corresponding fixed coupon bond so we are able to measure the duration of an inverse floater. In other words, because we can view an ordinary sovereign bond as a portfolio composed of the floater and inverse floater, value additivity says that the *value* of the floater and inverse floater must add up to the *value* of the corresponding sovereign bond. Therefore not only the price, but also the risk of the floater and inverse floater must equal the price and risk of the corresponding fixed coupon bond.

From this point of view we can see that the duration of a fixed coupon bond is a weighted average of the duration of the floater and inverse floater. That is

$$D_C^* = \frac{B_F}{B_C}D_F^* + \frac{B_{IF}}{B_C}D_{IF}^* \tag{10.1}$$

It is important to note that the weights or the percentage that the floater (B_F/B_C) and inverse floater (B_{IF}/B_C) contribute towards the duration of the fixed coupon bond must add up to 100%. Since the fixed coupon bond is priced using a face value of $100, the floater and inverse floater are priced in (10.1) using a face value of 50. Otherwise the weights would be more than 100% and (10.1) will not give you sensible results.

Notice that in (10.1) we have one equation and one unknown for we know how to measure the duration D_C^* and the price of the coupon bond B_C and in this chapter we have already learned how to measure the price of the floater B_F and inverse floater B_{IF} and the duration of the floater D_F^*. All that remains to be done is to solve (10.1) for the one unknown, the duration of the inverse floater D_{IF}^*. This is done below.

$$D_{IF}^* = \left[D_C^* - \frac{B_F}{B_C} D_F^* \right] \frac{B_C}{B_{IF}}$$

To illustrate we do an example. The 6% semi-annual coupon pay 10-year sovereign bond that yields 5% has duration of 7.527 and a price of $107.795. Libor rates are currently at 4.75%. The floater pays 50 basis points above libor rates. Today is the reset date and the coupon is reset every six months, so the value of the floater is $100 and the duration is $0.5/(1 + [0.0475 + 0.005]/2) = 0.4872$. We use the portfolio approach to find that the value of the inverse floater is $115.59 $(2B_c - F) = (2 \times 107.795 - 100) = \$115.59$. Therefore the duration of the inverse floater is 13.701.

$$D_{IF}^* = \left[7.572 - \frac{50}{107.795} 0.4872 \right] \frac{107.795}{57.795} = 13.701$$

At first glance this result may seem surprising, as the duration of the inverse floater is extremely high, higher even than the duration of the underlying fixed coupon bond. However, a little thought reveals that this is a sensible result. If the duration of the floater and inverse floater must add up 7.572, the duration of the fixed coupon bond, and almost 50% of that average, the duration of the floater, is only 0.4872 then that last 50% must be extremely high to achieve an overall average of 7.572. But more profoundly think about what happens to an inverse floater as the reference rate, the six-month libor rate in the above illustration, rises. First, like all 'fixed income' bonds, the value of an inverse floater will fall as yields rise because the discount rate will be higher. But additionally the *coupon* will fall as yields rise depressing the value of the inverse floater still further. This 'double whammy' effect will severely depress the value of the inverse floater as yields rise, so it is entirely sensible that the inverse floater should have a high duration.

The latter point reveals the purpose of inverse floaters. Suppose you anticipate a fall in yields. Then the inverse floater would look very attractive because in response to a fall in yields its price will rise by more than even the underlying bond. For instance in our example, the inverse floater has a higher duration than even a long-term 10-year bond. This happens because not only does a fall in yield result in a higher price due to the lower discount rate that will be applied, but also because the coupon will increase. Of course, always bear in mind that an increase in yields will have a devastating effect on the value of the inverse floater; there is no free lunch here.

To reinforce these points we do a numerical example based on the above illustration. Suppose the six-month libor rate and the yield on the above 6% sovereign bond increase by 25 basis points. The duration of the fixed coupon bond D_c^* is 7.572, the floater D_F^* 0.4872 and the inverse floater D_{IF}^* is 13.701. Then according to our modified duration model we can anticipate the following price response for the coupon bond, floater and inverse floater respectively.

$$\Delta B_C = -D_C^* B_C(\Delta Y) = -(7.5272)107.795(0.0025) = -\$2.041$$

$$\Delta B_F = -D_F^* B_F(\Delta Y) = -(0.4872)100(0.0025) = -\$0.122$$

$$\Delta B_{IF} = -D_{IF}^* B_{IF}(\Delta Y) = -(13.701)115.59(0.0025) = -\$3.959$$

To appreciate how accurate these results are we recompute the values of these instruments given the 25 basis point increase in yield. The new prices for the straight bond B_{CN}, the floater B_{FN} and the inverse floater B_{IFN} given by modified duration are compared to the actual prices (found by discounting, in brackets).

$$B_{CN} = B_{CO} - \Delta B_C = 107.795 - 2.041 = \$105.754(\$105.777)$$

$$B_{FN} = B_{FO} - \Delta B_F = 100 - 0.122 = \$99.878(\$99.878)$$

$$B_{IFN} = B_{IFO} - \Delta B_{IF} = 115.59 - 3.959 = \$111.631(\$111.676)^2$$

This example reinforces two important points. First, notice that modified duration overestimates the actual price response of the security in response to an increase in yield. This illustrates that, like the fixed coupon bond, the floater and inverse floater are subject to positive convexity. Second, notice that for investors in inverse floaters, the price response of the inverse floater is far larger than the corresponding price response of the underlying bond.

The seller of the floater and inverse floater may wish to take comfort in the fact that to hedge the short position in the floater and inverse floater priced in terms of a face value of $100 they buy two

---

[2] Using the methods of this chapter, the new value of the inverse floater is found as follows. $B_{IFN} = 2 \times B_{CN} - B_{FN} = 2 \times 105.777 - 99.878 = \$111.676$.

sovereign bonds. Then in our example the long and short positions offset. That is, an actual loss of $2.018 is experienced on each of the two long sovereign bonds for a total loss of $4.036 which is offset by the gains in the reduction of the value of the short floater $0.122 and the inverse floater $3.914.

However, this hedge is often subject to basis risk. Basis risk occurs when the underlying floater and inverse floater are created from a Treasury bond but the reference rate used to determine the coupon payments on the floater and inverse floater is libor. This can lead to unanticipated gains and losses on the hedge as the Treasury interest rate used to price the long coupon bond experiences a change not fully shared by the libor rate used to determine the coupon on the floater and inverse floater held short. Another source of basis risk is that the floating reference rate is short term, say six months, yet the underlying bond has a much greater maturity, say 10 years. Combined these two sources of basis risk can lead to disappointing results.

For example, imagine both the libor and Treasury yield curves become more upward sloping as short-term rates fall but long-term rates rise. Say six-month libor rates decrease by 75 basis points but yields on the underlying 10-year Treasury bond increase by 25 basis points. Then losses on the sovereign bonds held long are compounded by losses on the floater and inverse floater held short. Moreover the method we have used here to price an inverse floater breaks down, for with an increase in the 10-year bond yield by 25 basis points the 10-year bond's price will *decrease* to $105.777 and a decrease in the six-month libor yield by 75 basis points the floater's price will *increase* to $100.367. Then according to our value additivity method the value of the inverse floater will *decrease* (!) to $111.187($2 \times 105.777 - 100.367$) in response to a decrease in yield when in fact it will increase strongly as the discount rate falls and the coupon rate increases. This exposes an important assumption behind the value additivity approach we have used here to price inverse floaters. The yield curves used to determine the coupon for the floater and inverse floater and the value of the fixed coupon bond must experience only parallel shifts for value additivity to hold.

10.4   Caps, floors and collars

Variable rate bonds and loans are very common in today's debt markets. Some examples include floating rate notes in the bond market, floaters in the asset-backed security market and even variable rate home mortgages in the UK retail home loan market. To broaden the appeal of these securities sellers of such securities had to address concerns about interest rate risk. For example, some homeowners were reluctant to agree to high ratio fully variable rate home loans because if the reference lending rate rose substantially, the homeowner may default resulting in the loss of the family home. Borrowers and lenders in the capital market share similar concerns. To address these problems, caps, floors and collars were developed.

As the name suggests an interest rate cap is a guarantee that the variable rate on a loan will not exceed the 'capped' rate. Conversely, a floor is the guarantee that the interest rate paid on a loan will never fall below the 'floored' rate. From the borrower's perspective, a cap is a long position in a call option written on the reference interest rate and pays off when the reference rate exceeds the cap rate. The floor on the other hand is a short position in a put option written on the reference rate that pays off when the reference rate falls below the floor. In either case the strike price is an interest rate, the cap rate in the case of the call option and the floor rate in the case of the put option. The borrower may find that the long cap is too expensive, so often they will agree to sell a floor to the lender. A combination of a cap and a floor is called a collar. In effect a collared loan is a partly variable rate loan where the interest rate charged may vary within a restrictive range as defined by the cap and floor rates.

As an illustration of how to value caps and floors we examine the use of caps and floors when selling floater and inverse floaters. As we mentioned earlier it makes sense to sell a floor to an investor in inverse floaters because they wish to avoid the possibility that they may have to pay to lend money if the reference rate rises enough. Once the inverse floater includes a floor the sellers of floaters and inverse floaters need to protect themselves from paying more than received from the underlying coupon bond by attaching a cap to the corresponding floater.

As mentioned earlier, caps are interest rate call options and floors are interest rate put options where the payoff is conditional upon the reference rate, the six-month libor rate in our illustration, from moving above (in the case of a cap) or below (in the case of the floor) the reference rate strike price. The payoff function for a cap is therefore

$$Cap = \text{If}(R_L - Cap > 0, \text{Then}, R_L - Cap, \text{Otherwise}, 0) \qquad (10.2)$$

Equation (10.2) says that we use the logic operators 'If', 'Then' and 'Otherwise'. The above equation says quite literally that if the reference rate R_L is above the capped rate *Cap* then the payoff is the difference between the two rates, otherwise the libor rate is the same as or below the capped rate so the payoff is zero. We can easily convert the above interest rate payoff into the equivalent cash payoff amounts by multiplying the interest payoff by the nomial amount of the floater the above cap applies to.

Similarly the payoff function for a floor is

$$Floor = \text{If}(R_L - Floor < 0, \text{Then}, Floor - R_L, \text{Otherwise}, 0)$$

$$(10.3)$$

The above equation says quite literally that if the reference rate R_L is below the floored rate *Floor* then the payoff is the difference between the two rates, otherwise the libor rate is the same as or above the floored rate so the payoff is zero. As with the cap we can easily convert the above interest rate payoff into the equivalent cash payoff amounts by multiplying the interest payoff by the nominal amount of the inverse floater the above floor applies to. The only additional 'wrinkle' that applies to a floor on an inverse floater rather than most other instruments is that the reference rate is not just the libor rates R_L, rather the reference rate is the difference between the stated rate S and the libor rate R_L.

$$Floor = \text{If}((S - R_L) - Floor < 0, \text{Then}, Floor - (S - R_L),$$

$$\text{Otherwise}, 0) \qquad (10.4)$$

10.4.1 Cap example

It is best to illustrate the valuation of caps and floors via a numerical example. We choose to use the Ho and Lee model contained in HLb02.xls. Note that we could employ any term structure consistent model to price caps and floors in precisely the same way that we illustrate in this chapter. We are going to price the cap and in the next section a floor that is attached to a floater and an inverse floater respectively. The floater and inverse floater are based on the 2.5-year 6% sovereign bond priced in block A33 to E38 and reported in Table 5.4. The cap is based on a $50 000 notional amount. The cap rate is 7% and is binding for 2.5 years. The interest rate tree generated by Ho and Lee represents all possible interest rate levels that may evolve in the next 2.5 years. In Table 10.2 we report this interest rate tree.

Table 10.2   Ho and Lee interest rate tree

	A	B	C	D	E
6	0	1	2	3	4
7					10.26276955
8	I.R. Tree			8.913156615	8.262769546
9			7.868582704	6.913156615	6.262769546
10		6.587114257	5.868582704	4.913156615	4.262769546
11	6.036	4.587114257	3.868582704	2.913156615	2.262769546

We first determine the interest rate payoffs from the cap using the logic operator 'IF'. For example, in cell C44 we write IF (C9 − $B$40 > 0,C9 − $B$40,0), where C9 is the $r(2,2)$ and B40 is the cap rate. This statement says that if $r(2,2)$ is greater than the cap rate of 7%, then the interest rate payoff on the cap is the difference between the two, otherwise the payoff is zero. The interest rate payoffs are reported in Table 10.3.

Table 10.3   Cap interest rate payoffs

	A	B	C	D	E
40	Cap Rate	7			
41	Cap Interest Payoffs				
42					3.262769546
43				1.913156615	1.262769546
44			0.868582704	0	0
45		0	0	0	0
46	0	0	0	0	0

The next step is to convert these interest rate payoffs into the cash equivalent payoff using the notional principal amount of $50 000. Note that as we discussed in Chapter 3 interest rates are revealed at the beginning of the period but cash payoffs on the interest rate cap, in common with all securities, occur at the end of the period. Therefore we have to discount the cash payoff one period using the corresponding time and state interest rate as the discount rate. For example, the cash payoff for interest rate state $r(4,4)$ is found as follows.

$$Cap_S(4,4) = \frac{Notional\left(\dfrac{Cap_r(4,4)}{2}\right)}{1 + \dfrac{r(4,4)}{2}} = \frac{50\,000\left(\dfrac{0.032627}{2}\right)}{1 + \dfrac{0.102627}{2}}$$

$$= \$775.86$$

Continuing in this manner for all other interest rate states we find the present value of the cash payoffs on the interest rate cap as of the beginning of each period. The results are reported in Table 10.4.

Table 10.4 Cap cash payoffs

	A	B	C	D	E
48	Notional Principal	50 000			
49	Cash Payoffs				
50					775.88
51				457.88	303.17
52			208.93	0.00	0.00
53		0.00	0.00	0.00	0.00
54	0.00	0.00	0.00	0.00	0.00

At this point we have a choice of how to find the present value of the cap. We could use the familiar backward induction method, discounting backwards through the tree using the state contingent discount factors and the 50/50 rule. Alternatively we could simply multiply the interest rate state contingent cap payoff by the corresponding state security price. The latter method is possible because the state price tree is calibrated to the sovereign yield curve just as the interest rate tree is, so either method is equally valid. You will get precisely the same answer using either method. We choose to use the forward induction method, as it is easier. For example, all we have to do to find the present value of the cash payment in interest rate state $r(4,4)$ is to multiply the cash payout $Cap_S(4,4)$ by the state security price $S(4,4)$ to obtain a present value of \$41.98. That is $S(4,4) \times Cap_S(4,4) = 0.0541002 \times \$775.88 = \$41.98$. Performing this operation for all other cap cash payoffs and adding them up we find the price of the cap is \$209.38 as reported in Table 10.5.

Table 10.5 The value of the cap

	A	B	C	D	E	F
57	Value of Cap					41.98
58	209.38				51.75	66.57
59				49.08	0.00	0.00
60			0.00	0.00	0.00	0.00
61		0.00	0.00	0.00	0.00	0.00
62		Sum	0.00	0.00	49.08	51.75	108.54

Since there are 500 $100 amounts in the nominal $50 000 underlying amount, the cost per 100 is $0.419 (209.38/500). In this example, which uses the above Ho and Lee binomial stochastic interest rate tree, a floater capped at 7% would be worth $99.581 $(100 - 0.419)$ on the reset date.

10.4.2 Floor example

We again use the Ho and Lee interest rate tree reported in Table 10.2 to price a floor at 5%. This floor is attached to a $50 000 nominal inverse floater where the stated rate is 12%. The underlying bond used to price the inverse floater is the 2.5-year 6% coupon bond reported in Table 5.4 and contained in HLB02.xls. The interest rate payoff function (10.4) is used to generate the floor interest payoff tree for the floor attached to the inverse floater as shown in Table 10.6.

Table 10.6 Floor interest rate payoffs

	G	H	I	J	K
40	Floor Rate	5			
41	Stated Rate	12			
42	Floor Interest Payoffs				3.262769546
43				1.913156615	1.262769546
44			0.868582704	0	0
45		0	0	0	0
46	0	0	0	0	0

For example, for interest rate state $r(4,4)$ the interest rate payoff is 3.26277. For the inverse floater the payoff in interest rate state $r(4,4)$ is IF (($H$41 - E7) - $H$40 < 0, $H$40 - ($H$41 - E7), 0) which is the sum of the floor rate H40 less the difference between the stated rate H41 and the actual interest rate that evolves E7.

As with the cap, the next step is to convert these interest rate payoffs into the cash equivalent payoff using the notional principal amount of $50 000. As explained in section 10.4.1 we have to discount the cash payoff one period using the corresponding time and state interest rate as the discount rate. For example, the cash payoff for interest rate state $r(4,4)$ is found as follows.

$$Floor_\$(4,4) = \frac{Notional \left(\dfrac{Floor_r(4,4)}{2} \right)}{1 + \dfrac{r(4,4)}{2}} = \frac{50\,000 \left(\dfrac{0.032627}{2} \right)}{1 + \dfrac{0.102627}{2}}$$

$$= \$775.86$$

Continuing in this manner for all other interest rate states we find the present value of the cash payoffs on the interest rate floor as of the beginning of each period. The results are reported in Table 10.7.

Table 10.7 Floor cash payoffs

	A	B	C	D	E
48	Notional Principal	50 000			
49	Cash Payoffs				
50					775.88
51				457.88	303.17
52			208.93	0.00	0.00
53		0.00	0.00	0.00	0.00
54	0.00	0.00	0.00	0.00	0.00

As with the cap we can use the familiar backward induction method, discounting backwards through the tree using the state contingent discount factors and the 50/50 rule, or we could use the forward induction method by multiplying the interest rate state contingent floor payoff by the corresponding state security price. We choose to use the forward induction method, as it is easier. For example, all we have to do to find the present value of the cash payment in interest rate state $r(4,4)$ is to multiply the cash payout $Floor_\$(4,4)$ by the state security price $S(4,4)$ to obtain a present value of $-\$41.98$. That is, $S(4,4) \times Floor_\$(4,4) = 0.0541002 \times \$775.88 = -\$41.98$. Performing this operation for all other floor cash payoffs and adding them up we find the price of the floor is $209.38 as reported in Table 10.8.

Since there are 500 $100 amounts in the nominal $50 000 underlying amount, the cost per 100 is $0.419 (209.38/500). In this example, which uses the above Ho and Lee binomial stochastic interest rate tree, an inverse floater floored at 5% would be worth $100.831. This is composed of the price of the unfloored inverse floater $100.412, found as two times the price of the underlying 6% 2.5-year sovereign bond $100.206 less the value of the uncapped floater on the reset date $100, plus the value of the interest rate floor per 100 $0.419 (100.412 + 0.419).

At first glance the fact that the cap and the floater have precisely the same price might appear surprising. However, a little thought reveals that this is simply another consequence of value additivity. Recall that all we are doing with the floater and inverse floater is reallocating the cash flows and risk of the underlying semi-annual

Table 10.8 The value of the floor

	G	H	I	J	K
56	Floor Price				
57					41.98
58				51.75	66.57
59			49.08	0.00	0.00
60		0.00	0.00	0.00	0.00
61		0.00	0.00	0.00	0.00
62	Sum				
63		0.00	0.00	49.08	51.75	108.54
64	Value of Floor				
65		209.38				

coupon pay 6% 2.5-year sovereign bond into the corresponding float-ing rate instruments. Therefore values must add up. If we subtract a value of $0.419 from the value of the floater by imposing a cap on future floating interest rate payments we are adding the same amount to the inverse floater by flooring future inverse floating interest rate payments. Therefore the value of the capped floater and the floored inverse floater still add up to the value of the underlying bond, which is $100.206.

$$B_c = 0.5(B_F + B_{IF}) = 0.5(99.581 + 100.831) = 100.206$$

10.4.3 Collar example

Of course, the collar implied by the cap and floor attached to the floater and inverse floater respectively implies that the value of the collar is zero. This is a degenerate case because the terms of the cap and floor are designed to insure that the value of the capped floater and floored inverse floater adds to zero as otherwise there will be an unsustainable arbitrage opportunity. More generally collars are used to dampen the cost of interest rate protection when agreeing to borrow at variable rates.

For instance, suppose one agrees to a cap of 7% on variable rates of interest as described by the interest rate tree in HLb02.xls. From section 10.4.1 we know this costs $0.419 per $100 of notional prin-cipal. For, say, a $250 000 variable rate mortgage this means we would have to pay $1047.50. Some may find this too expensive and so are willing to sell a floor to the bank (euphemistically called a 'cash back' in the UK) thereby agreeing that they will continue to make a mortgage payment based on the floor rate when the unrestricted variable rate is lower.

To illustrate we use the regular floor payoff function (10.3) to generate the floor interest payoff tree in block A70 to E74 in HLb02.xls. We change the notional amount to $250 000. We change the floor rate in cell B68. If the mortgage holder agrees to pay a floor of, say, 4%, then the value of this floor is $317.19. This lowers the overall cost of interest rate protection to $730.31 but of course the homeowner will have to pay the higher floor rate of 4% should interest rate state $r(2,0)$, $r(3,0)$ or $r(4,0)$ evolve.

10.5   Interest rate swaps

An interest rate swap is a contract that allows users to convert a fixed rate loan into a synthetic variable rate loan or vice versa. To understand the contract, refer to Figure 10.2.

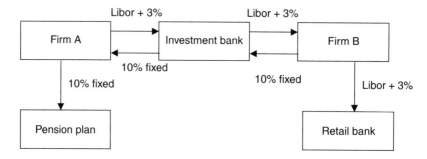

Figure 10.2   Interest rate swap

In Figure 10.2 firm A is short a swap and firm B is long a swap. Being short a swap allows firm A to convert a fixed rate bond into a synthetic variable rate loan. Firm A borrowed, say, $100 million from the pension plan by selling them a 10% bond even though the structure of the firm's assets is such that $50 million of the loan should be borrowed at a variable rate. Therefore firm A sells a swap by agreeing to pay libor plus 3% to an investment bank and in return receiving 10% fixed from the investment bank based on a notional principal of $50 million. In effect firm A converts $50 million of its fixed rate obligations into a libor-based variable rate loan.

Meanwhile firm B is long a swap allowing the firm to convert a variable rate loan into a fixed rate loan. Firm B has borrowed $20 million from a retail bank at a variable rate and would like to borrow fixed. However, it is expensive to issue a fixed rate bond based on such a small amount so instead they buy a swap from the investment bank agreeing to pay 10% fixed in return for a variable payment of libor plus 3% based on a notional principal of $20 million. Notice that firm A has still borrowed $100 fixed from the pension plan and firm B has still borrowed $20 million variable from a bank, so these swap transactions do not affect the underlying capital market. Swaps themselves do not involve capital flows nor affect aggregate lending or borrowing and so are a true derivative security.

This of course means that the investment bank is net exposed by $30 million, so they must hedge this net exposure. The investment bank agrees to act as the counterparty to these transactions, buying a swap from firm A and selling a swap to firm B, because the actual payments are slightly different, in the investment bank's favour, from the ones illustrated above. For example, firm A may actually pay libor plus 3.02% to the investment bank and in turn the investment bank may actually pay libor plus 2.98% to firm B thereby collecting 2 basis points each from its counterparties. This compensates the investment bank for the cost of the transactions and the net exposure they must either accept or attempt to hedge. In the meantime firm A and B are involved in the swap market because swaps allow them to respond to the needs of investors thereby lowering the costs of borrowing but still allowing the firms to change the characteristics of their debt to be more suitable to their own needs.

10.5.1 Valuation of swaps

As seen in Figure 10.2, a long swap position (firm B) means that we agree to pay fixed and receive floating thereby converting an underlying variable rate loan into a fixed rate loan. Shorting a swap (firm A) is the opposite where we convert a fixed rate loan into a variable rate loan by agreeing to pay floating and receive fixed. It is extremely easy to value an interest rate swap once we view the payments in terms of their underlying debt instruments. A long swap position is like a long position in a floater (firm B receives libor plus 3%) and a short position in a fixed rate bond (firm B pays 10% fixed). Therefore the value of this long swap position must be the value of the floater less the value of the 10% fixed rate bond.

To illustrate we start with the simplest of cases and assume we are dealing with a long swap where we agree to receive libor flat and pay 10% fixed for 2.5 years. The Ho and Lee interest rate tree in HLB02.xls is assumed to describe all possible six-month libor rates that may evolve over the next 2.5 years. If today is the reset date the value of the floater must be par. Then all we have to do is to value a 2.5-year-10% semi annual coupon pay fixed rate bond. We change the coupon rate in cell B34 to 10% and find that the price of this bond is $109.382. Therefore the value of the long swap is

$$S = B_F - B_C = 100 - 109.382 = -9.382$$

Obviously this swap must have been agreed to some time ago, as the value of the long swap is strongly negative. It is hard to believe that the benefits of this swap are so large that someone would be willing to take on the initial obligation to pay fixed on such disadvantageous terms.

To entice someone to take on the long position we have to price the swap on more equal terms. We can easily find the terms that would price the swap at zero by adjusting the fixed coupon rate such that the value of the fixed coupon bond is par at the reset date. Then we could either agree to pay the lower fixed rate or to receive a higher floating rate or some combination of both. We can use solver to find the appropriate adjustment. Click on solver found under the tools menu. Set the price of the bond cell A38 as the target cell. Choose to make this cell 100 and make the change cell the coupon rate cell B34. Click on solve and you will find that in order to reset the value of the swap to zero, the fixed rate should be 5.91%. Alternatively we could agree to receive libor as described by the Ho and Lee interest rate tree less 4.09% (10 − 5.91 = 4.09%) or any combination of the two possibilities.

The situation illustrated in Figure 10.2 is slightly more complicated because firm B agrees to receive libor plus 300 basis points. This means that in effect firm B is not only long the floater at libor and short the fixed coupon bond at 10%, but is also long a hypothetical fixed coupon bond where the coupon is equal to the amount by which the long swap position receives above libor, 3% in this case. Since the swap only involves the interest payments the long swap position is also short one more instrument, a hypothetical zero coupon bond with a maturity equal to the maturity of the hypothetical 3% coupon bond. This short zero coupon bond must be added to the long swap position to delete the principal payment on the low coupon 3% bond. In summary a long swap position is long a floater B_F and a hypothetical low coupon bond, the coupon of which is equal to the amount received above the libor rate B_{+libor} and short the fixed high coupon bond B_C and a hypothetical zero coupon bond B_Z.

$$S = B_F + B_{+libor} - B_C - B_Z$$

To illustrate we value the long swap of firm B in Figure 10.2. We assume a flat spot curve at 6% for convenience, but otherwise data is from the original Ho and Lee example in HLB02.xls. The notional principal amount FV is, say, $100 000, the yield curve Y is flat at

6%, the fixed coupon is 10%, the variable rate is libor $+3\%$ and the swap agreement is for 2.5 years ($n \times M = 5$). We break the problem down into the net payments to be received and the net payments to be made. At the reset date the net payments to be received P_r are the payments on the floater B_F, low coupon bond B_{+libor} less the zero coupon bond B_Z.

$$B_F = 100\,000$$

$$B_{+libor} - B_z = \frac{\dfrac{C}{2} \times FV}{\dfrac{Y}{2}} \left[1 - \frac{1}{\left(1 + \dfrac{Y}{2}\right)^{n \times M}} \right] + \frac{FV}{\left(1 + \dfrac{Y}{2}\right)^{n \times M}}$$

$$- \frac{FV}{\left(1 + \dfrac{Y}{2}\right)^{n \times M}}$$

$$= \frac{0.015 \times 100\,000}{0.03} \left[1 - \frac{1}{(1 + 0.03)^5} \right] = 6869.56$$

$$\therefore P_r = F + B_{+libor} - B_z = 100\,000 + 6869.56$$

$$= 106\,869.56$$

The payments to be made P_m are simply the coupon payments on the 10% fixed semi-annual coupon pay bond.

$$P_m = \frac{\dfrac{C}{2} \times FV}{\dfrac{Y}{2}} \left[1 - \frac{1}{\left(1 + \dfrac{Y}{2}\right)^{n \times M}} \right] + \frac{FV}{\left(1 + \dfrac{Y}{2}\right)^{n \times M}}$$

$$= \frac{0.05 \times 100\,000}{0.03} \left[1 - \frac{1}{(1.03)^5} \right] + \frac{100\,000}{(1.03)^5}$$

$$= 22\,898.54 + 86\,260.88 = 109\,159.42$$

Therefore the value of the long swap is a negative $2289.86.

$$V_s = P_r - P_m = 106\,869.56 - 109\,159.42 = -2289.86$$

To reset the value of the swap to zero the fixed rate should be adjusted until the payments received P_r equal the payments to be made P_m. As above it is easiest to adjust the payments to be made by adjusting the fixed coupon on the high coupon bond.

$$V_s = P_r - P_m = 0, \text{so } P_m = 106\,869.56 = P_r$$

Therefore we must find that coupon that sets the value of the payments to be made to equal the value of payments to be received,

$106\,869.56$ in this case.

$$P_m = \frac{C \times 100\,000}{0.03}\left[1 - \frac{1}{(1.03)^5}\right] + \frac{100\,000}{(1.03)^5} = 106\,869.56$$

In the above equation there is only one unknown, so you can solve algebraically, or by trial and error (or by spreadsheet) to find $C = 9\%$ (annual).

10.5.2 Hedging a long swap

As we saw in Figure 10.2 the investment bank may find that they have a net exposure in the swap market. In our illustration the investment bank was net long the swap by $30 million notional. To hedge this net position the investment bank could use the hedging concepts we have developed in Chapters 7 and 9. To illustrate we use the modified duration hedge ratio approach of Chapter 7 and the same data as section 10.5.1 bearing in mind that we could just as easily use the more advanced techniques of Chapter 9 as well. At the reset date:

$$D_F^* = 1/(1.03) = 0.9709\ (0.485\ \text{years})$$

$$D_Z^* = 5/(1.03) = 4.854\ (2.427\ \text{years})$$

As always, the duration of a fixed income security is found from the closed form modified duration equation (7.6a).

$$D_{+libor}^* = \frac{\frac{1.5}{(0.03)^2}\left[1 - \frac{1}{(1+0.03)^5}\right] + \frac{5\left(100 - \frac{1.5}{0.03}\right)}{(1+0.03)^6}}{93.13}$$

$$= 4.707\ (2.353\ \text{years})$$

$$D_C^* = \frac{\frac{5}{(0.03)^2}\left[1 - \frac{1}{(1+0.03)^5}\right] + \frac{5\left(100 - \frac{5}{0.03}\right)}{(1+0.03)^6}}{109.159}$$

$$= 4.435\ (2.217\ \text{years})$$

Now we can find the price sensitivity of the net long $30 million position in the interest rate swap by converting these measures of duration into the corresponding $PVBP$ measures.[3] Since the long swap position is long the libor-based floater B_F and a low fixed coupon bond B_{+libor} but short the high coupon B_C and zero coupon bonds B_Z then the

---

[3] If you need a reminder of how this is done see section 7.4.

PVBP of the swap is a sum of these price sensitivities as shown below. From section 10.5.1 we know that per $100 000 notional, the price of the floater B_F is $100 000, the low coupon bond B_{+libor} is $93 130, the zero coupon bond B_Z is $86 260.88 and the fixed high coupon bond B_C (or P_m) is $109 159.42. Therefore the $PVBP_S$ is

$$PVBP_S \cong [D_F^* F + D_{+libor}^* B_{+libor} - D_Z^* B_Z - D_C^* B_C] \times (1/10\,000)$$

$$PVBP_S \cong [(0.485)(100\,000) + (2.353)(93\,130)$$

$$- (2.427)(86\,260.88)$$

$$- (2.217)(109\,159.42)] \times (1/10\,000)$$

$$= -18.37$$

The above $PVBP_S$ is based on a notional amount of $100 000. Since the net exposure of the investment bank is $30 million, and there are 300 $100 000 amounts in $30 million, we multiply the above $PVBP_S$ by 300 to find the total exposure of the investment bank is $5511. Note the price sensitivity is *negative* even though we have neglected the minus signs for our measures of duration. This means that the buyer (the investment bank) *gains* $5511 for each one basis point *increase* in interest rates. This is opposite of the usual result.

This makes sense because the buyer *receives* floating, so as interest rates increase, the value of the swap from the buyer's perspective increases. Of course, the seller of the swap loses $5511 for each basis point increase in interest rates.

From here, you calculate your hedge ratio as always and go *long* (from the buyer's point of view) in the appropriate number of hedging securities. That is

$$HR = -\frac{PVBP_S}{PVBP_{ctdm}} \times CF_{ctd}$$

The usual negative sign of the hedge ratio *HR* is reversed in the case of a long swap because the value of the $PVBP_S$ is negative even though we continue the usual convention and ignore the negative sign for duration.

10.6 Exercises

Question 1
Consider the following swap with notional principal of £100 000, and maturity $n = 10$. The buyer makes fixed payments of

$$P_m = C \times 100\,000$$

where P_m is the value of payments to be made and C is the fixed coupon rate. The seller makes variable payments of

$$P_m = (Libor + 1\%) \times 100\,000$$

Let *libor* and the term structure be flat at 5%.

Required:
1. What should the fixed coupon rate be to reset the value of the swap to zero?
2. What is the price value of a basis point (*PVBP*) for the buyer if the fixed coupon rate was set to price the swap as zero?
3. If interest rates rise by 100 basis points, what would be the gain/loss by the buyer?
4. Explain how the buyer can hedge this position.

Question 2
Consider the following swap with notional principal of £100 000, and maturity $n = 10$. The buyer makes fixed payments of

$$Fixed\ payment = Coupon\ rate \times 100\,000$$

The seller makes a variable payment of

$$Variable\ payment = (Libor + p) \times 100\,000$$

where the premium above libor p is 0.5% and *libor* is currently 4.5%. The spot curve is flat at 4.5%. Assume all payments, including coupons, are made annually.

Required:
(a) What is the fixed rate the buyer should pay in order for this contract to have a value of zero?
(b) What is the price value of a basis point (*PVBP*) for the buyer?
(c) Describe how the seller can hedge this swap exposure.

Question 3
Consider the following interest rate tree that has been calibrated to the existing sovereign yield curve.

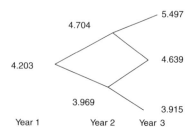

(a) What is the value of a 5% annual coupon three-year sovereign bond?
(b) You wish to sell a three-year floater based on the purchase of the above 5% coupon bond that will pay the above floating rates. What will be its value and modified duration today?
(c) You wish to sell a three-year inverse floater again based on the purchase of the above 5% coupon bond that will pay 5% less the above floating rates. What will be its value and modified duration today?
(d) Do you foresee any problems with selling the above floater and an inverse floater? Be specific. If there is a problem, suggest a specific numerical solution.

Question 4

Consider the following interest rate tree that has been calibrated to the sovereign yield curve. A one-year time step is used.

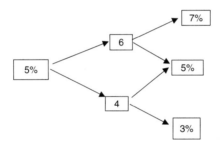

Required:
(a) What are caps, floors and collars? Define or explain in enough detail to convey your understanding of them and why some borrowers desire them.
(b) What is the cost of a three-year cap based on a notional value of £50 000 where the interest rate is capped at 5%?
(c) What is the value of a floor based on a notional value of £50 000 where the floored rate is floored at 4%?
(d) From the point of view of a borrower, what is the value of a collar based on a notional principal of £50 000 where the interest rate is capped at 5% and floored at 4%?

Credit derivatives

11.1 Introduction

The International Swaps and Derivatives Association (ISDA) first publicly introduced credit derivatives in 1992. These innovative instruments allow investment banks to isolate and trade pure credit risk. Typically investment banks are active buyers and sellers of credit derivatives and run a credit derivatives desk. Buyers of credit derivatives free up credit lines by reducing counterparty exposure and sellers enhance returns by assuming more credit risk. Typical sellers of credit protection are insurance companies who presumably use their expertise in evaluating credit to seek additional exposure to credit risk thereby enhancing returns.

Like the interest rate swap market of the early 1980s, the credit swap market is enjoying explosive growth. The British Bankers Association (BBA) estimates that from 1996 to June 1998 the notional principal amount of credit derivatives outstanding grew from $20 billion to $170 billion. By June 2002 the BBA estimates that there were $2 trillion in notional principal amounts of credit derivatives outstanding.[1] Yet there exists considerable uncertainty with respect to a pricing methodology.[2]

---

[1] See the BBA Credit Derivatives Report (1996), the BBA 1997/1998 Credit Derivatives Survey (July 1998) and the BBA 2001/2002 Credit Derivatives Survey (July 2002), all published by the British Bankers Association.

[2] The following represent but a few of the recently proposed credit derivative pricing models. Das, R. S. and R. Sundaram, 'A Direct Approach to Arbitrage-free Pricing of Credit Derivatives', working paper 6635, NBER (1998). Duffie, D. and K. J. Singleton, 'Modeling Term Structures of Defaultable Bonds', *Review of Financial Studies*, 12 (1999), 687–720. Jarrow, R., D. Lando and S. Turnbull, 'A Markov Model for the Term Structure of Credit Spreads', *The Review of Financial Studies*, 10 (1997), 481–523. There are many others.

We will first discuss the main types and uses of credit derivatives and then deal with pricing methodology. We intend to price two types of credit derivatives, vulnerable derivatives and credit default swaps. Last, we will also discuss some documentation issues that have an impact on the pricing of credit derivatives.

11.2   Types of credit derivatives

All types of credit derivatives can be classified as either single name or multi-name credit derivatives. A single name credit derivative is one in which the credit risk of just one entity is traded whereas a multi-name credit derivative is one in which the credit risk of a group of entities is traded. The most common single name credit derivatives are credit default swaps, asset swaps, credit spread options and the total return swap. Multi-name credit derivatives include basket swaps, portfolio credit default swaps and credit linked notes.

11.2.1   Single name credit derivatives

The BBA (2002) estimates that in terms of the notional principal amounts outstanding around 45% of all credit derivatives are credit default swaps. As we argue later, credit default swaps can be viewed as a put option, payments from which are triggered by a defined credit event. The buyer of credit protection is long the put option where in the event of default the buyer typically receives the difference between par value and the value of the bond post-default. In return the buyer of credit protection pays a credit default premium, usually quarterly, to the seller of credit protection. The flow of premiums ceases once the credit event occurs. Consequently we see that the credit default swap is a vehicle that, for the cost of the premium, transfers the risk of a defined credit event to the seller of credit protection.

Strictly speaking an asset swap is not a credit derivative as credit risk is not transferred in the transaction, but it is often classified as one since being long an asset swap is a way of forming pure credit risk exposure. To go long an asset swap one buys a fixed rate corporate bond and then buys an interest rate swap agreeing to pay the fixed rate and receive a floating rate. In effect the long asset swap transfers interest rate risk leaving only the credit risk exposure. Consequently the asset swap is a vehicle for those wishing exposure to the credit risk of a given corporate bond.

Credit spread options are options that pay off based on the size of a given credit spread defined as the yield on a given target corporate bond and a benchmark sovereign instrument. Payments are made to the long position in the event that the credit spread is above (call option) or below (put option) the strike prior to maturity (American) or only at maturity (European). Obviously this structure allows for the possibility of Asian style, lookbacks, knock-in and knock-out barrier options and so on.

A total return swap represents the purchase of a given bond in all but name in return for making a floating rate payment typically defined as a spread over a short-term libor rate. The party that is long the total return swap receives the fixed coupon payment from the underlying bond and receives the difference in value of the bond from the date of inception to the maturity date of the total return swap if the bond appreciates, otherwise they pay this difference. Should default occur the total return swap terminates and the long counterparty pays the difference between the inception value of the reference bond and its value post-default.

11.2.2 Multi-name credit derivatives

As mentioned previously, multi-name credit derivatives involve trading credit risk of portfolios of instruments subject to credit risk. The basket swap is essentially a credit default swap based on a portfolio of corporate bonds. In a first to default basket swap payoffs are triggered and the basket swap terminates when the first bond included in the portfolio defaults. Correspondingly, the second to default basket swap terminates when a second bond in the portfolio defaults and so on. Effectively the long position pays a credit default swap premium for protection on a portion of the default risk involved in a portfolio of corporate bonds. Basket swaps are particularly attractive for those holding portfolios of corporate bonds where the incidence of default is thought to be idiosyncratic rather than systematic. For instance, if one held a portfolio of single B bonds and a recession was to occur then one can reasonably anticipate that there would be multiple defaults, so a basket default swap would not be very effective in transferring credit risk. On the other hand, insuring a portfolio of single A bonds via a basket default swap would make more sense as even in a recessionary environment the incidence of default would likely be random.

A flaw in the basket swap structure is that default payments are not triggered based on the severity of the default event. This can be a problem when a mild default event terminates credit protection just before a more severe default event occurs. To overcome this problem payment on portfolio credit default swaps are triggered by the loss rate on a portfolio of corporate bonds. If the loss rate was defined as, say, 15%, then default payments will occur only when 15% of the portfolio was lost due to some credit event and this threshold may occur after more than one bond defaulted. The loss rate is sometimes used to divide credit protection into tranches. The first loss tranche would make credit default swap payments once, say 10% of the portfolio was lost due to some credit event. The second loss tranche would make credit default swap payments once, say 20% of the portfolio was lost due to some credit event and so on.

A credit-linked note is a vehicle for investors to avoid regulations, either internal or external, that prevent them from participating in the credit derivatives market. Going long in a credit-linked note is a way of obtaining credit risk exposure on a loan that does not trade without resorting to a credit derivative, say a credit default swap. The long counterparty invests a principal amount in a credit-linked note and receives a coupon payment as long as a reference loan does not default. Should default occur the long position must pay the difference between par and the value of the reference loan post-default. Otherwise they continue to receive the coupon payment and final principal amount at maturity of the credit-linked note. In other words, a long position in a credit-linked note is the same as a long position in the loan that does not trade. Credit-linked notes can also be referenced to a portfolio of loans.

To hedge the credit risk exposure the seller of a credit-linked note would invest the principal amount in a high quality bond and sell a credit default swap on the reference loan. From then on the seller passes through the coupon payment from the high credit quality bond and the credit default swap premium less a fee. Should the reference loan default the seller of the credit-linked note ceases coupon payments to the buyer. The seller then sells the high credit quality bond, pays the default swap payment and remits the difference to the buyer of the credit-linked note.

11.3 Vulnerable derivatives

Vulnerable derivatives are derivatives written by a counterparty that is subject to credit risk, but the underlying asset is not. Therefore in the money promised payments may not materialize should the obligating counterparty default. For example, we may buy an interest rate cap at, say, 7% only to find that when interest rates rise above 7%, the promised payment does not materialize because the writer of the option defaults. Here the underlying asset, say the six-month Treasury interest rate, is not subject to credit risk, but the writer is. Therefore we need to apply some credit risk model to determine the credit risk adjusted value of the interest rate cap. The general method is to value the underlying asset using an interest rate model that does not adjust for credit risk, but then value the vulnerable nature of the writer by applying an interest rate model that is adjusted for credit risk on the expected but only promised in the money values. It is important to realize that the credit risk model must match the credit risk of the writer. For example, if the writer is, say, an investment bank rated AA and we are using Jarrow and Turnbull to adjust for the writer's credit risk, Jarrow and Turnbull should be calibrated to an AA financial yield curve.

To illustrate we price a 2.5-year cap on the six-month Treasury interest rate as generated by Black Derman and Toy. Although the underlying asset, the binomial stochastic Treasury interest rate is not subject to credit risk, the writer of the option is. Therefore we price the vulnerable cap using Jarrow and Turnbull. The Treasury interest rate tree we use is found in JTB02.xls, worksheet 'cap', cell block C2 to G8. This interest rate tree is reported in Table 5.8. The cap is set at the current six-month rate of interest 6.036%, and the notional principal amount is $50 000. From here we proceed to value the cap in precisely the same way as we did in Chapter 10 except that we include one additional step. Specifically we first value the cap as if it were not subject to credit risk and then multiply the present value of each interest rate state contingent payoff by the credit risk adjusted or 'expected value' as calculated in spreadsheet JT, row 11. It is appropriate to do this since Jarrow and Turnbull assume that there is a zero correlation between credit risk and interest rate risk. Specifically the present value of promised payments at a particular date, say $t = 5$, are all equally likely to default no matter which interest rate state arrives (i.e. payoffs in cells G29 to G33 are equally credit risky), so the same credit risk adjustment is applied to all these payoffs (i.e. 0.980584). The results of this exercise are reported in Table 11.1.

As expected the vulnerable cap is less valuable than the credit risk-free cap. Since there are 500 $100 dollar amounts in the notional principal of $50 000, the vulnerable cap is worth $0.075 per 100 whereas the credit risk-free cap is worth $0.077. In this case counterparty risk is minor, costing only $0.002.

As another example of vulnerable options, consider a European call option on a 6.75% three-year sovereign bond. The bond is callable at 100 at $t = 4$. While the underlying bond is not subject to credit risk, the writer of the option is. We apply Black Derman and Toy to value the bond. The value of the bond, reported below in

Table 11.1 Vulnerable cap

	C	D	E	F	G
27	Cap Price-Credit Risk Free				
28	0	1	2	3	4
29					2.55
30				0.00	9.90
31			0.00	0.00	14.39
32		0.00	0.00	0.00	9.29
33	0.00	0.00	0.00	0.00	2.24
34	Sum				
35	0.00	0.00	0.00	0.00	38.39
36	Value of Cap			38.39	
37	Cap Price-vulnerable				
38					2.50
39				0.00	9.71
40			0.00	0.00	14.11
41		0.00	0.00	0.00	9.11
42	0.00	0.00	0.00	0.00	2.20
43	Sum				
44	0.00	0.00	0.00	0.00	37.64
45	Value of Vulnerable Cap			37.64	

Table 11.2, is calculated in workbook JTB02.xls, spreadsheet 'Call' in cell block B2 to H10.

Notice that the call option is in the money in all interest rate states at $t = 4$ where promised payoffs range from $0.3357 to $0.3557. Unlike our earlier cap example, the above payoffs are already priced as of the beginning of the period, so the above amounts are already aligned with the state security prices. Therefore all we need to do to find the value of a vulnerable call option is to multiply the promised payoff by the corresponding credit risky state security price. The results of this example are reported below in Table 11.3.

As expected, the value of the vulnerable option is less than the value of the corresponding option that is not subject to credit risk. In this case counterparty risk has reduced the value of the call option from $0.3076 to $0.3017.

Table 11.2   Value of a 6.75% sovereign bond

	B	C	D	E	F	G	H
2	Sovereign Price Tree 6 Period Bond						
3	Coupon	6.75					
4	Period	0	1	2	3	4	5
5							100.1319
6						100.3357	100.1341
7					100.7006	100.3407	100.1363
8				101.0702	100.7093	100.3457	100.1385
9			101.5681	101.0862	100.7181	100.3507	100.1406
10		101.8406	101.6038	101.1021	100.7268	100.3557	100.1428

Table 11.3   Vulnerable call option on a sovereign bond

	B	C	D
13	4 period European Call on 6% Sovereign Bond		
14	Payoff (1)	Credit Risk Free	Vulnerable
15	MAX{B(4, i) − 100; 0)}	(1) × S(4, i)	(1) × C(4, i)
16	0.3357	0.0187	0.0183
17	0.3407	0.0758	0.0743
18	0.3457	0.1153	0.1132
19	0.3507	0.0780	0.0765
20	0.3557	0.0198	0.0194
21	Value	0.3076	0.3017

11.4   Credit default swaps

Credit default swaps are not swaps. Instead they are put options that are designed to compensate the long position for losses on a bond should the bond default. Therefore they are actually default insurance. The long position is a buyer of credit protection and the short position is a seller of credit protection. The credit default swap ticket defines important details of the premium, credit event parameters and the payout structure in the event of default of the bond insured by the credit default swap (hereafter, the reference bond). The premium is specified as the total number of basis points to be paid each year. Payments are made in instalments, typically quarterly, and are based on the specified notional principal amount. Applicable credit events are specified, which include 'failure to pay', 'bankruptcy', 'repudiation', 'downgrade', 'sovereign event', 'moratorium' and 'restructuring'.[3] Payoffs in the event of default are typically defined as par value less the value of the defaulted security, where the value of the defaulted bond is established as the average of (typically) five independent dealer quotes.

An additional complication with credit default swaps is that premium payments and default amounts are conditional. Premium payments are made at the beginning of the period covered by the premium only if the bond has not yet defaulted. If the bond defaults, the credit default swap contract is terminated. The default amount is paid out and no further premium payments are made. In other words, premium payments are made conditional upon survival and default amounts are paid conditional upon default. Therefore the payoff function for credit default swap premium payments is as follows.

$$Payments = C_S(n,i)S_W M \qquad\qquad (11.1)$$

The term $C_S(n,i)$ is the corporate (that is to say, credit risky) state security price *conditional upon survival* at time n and interest rate state i. It is found by multiplying the state security price that is not subject to credit risk at time n and interest rate state i by the cumulative probability of survival. For example, assuming that interest and credit risk are not correlated (as does Jarrow and Turnbull), $C_S(3,2)$ is found as $S(3,2) \times P_1 \times P_2 \times P_3$ where $S(3,2)$ is the state security price that is not subject to credit risk three time steps into the future and two interest rate levels above the lowest possible interest rate that may arrive in three time periods multiplied by the likelihood P that no default has occurred in the first, second or third periods. Meanwhile S_W is the, say, semi-annual credit default swap premium that is expressed in basis points and M is the notional principal amount.

Equation (11.1) finds the present value of a premium payment made at interest rate state $r(n,i)$ so we apply this formula to all possible states and then add them up to find the present, credit risk adjusted (for the default risk of the reference bond) value of the premium payments. This is the value of the credit default swap from the point of view of the seller of the credit default swap. If the buyer is subject to credit risk, then the seller may wish to adjust this

---

[3] A bond may 'fail to pay' and yet not cause bankruptcy because a bond may miss a coupon payment and pay later without any bankruptcy event. In the event of a missed coupon payment on the underlying bond, the credit default swap will pay off.

amount for the credit risk of the buyer because the buyer may default on their promised premium payments independent of the default on the reference (insured) bond. In other words, the seller may wish to account for the vulnerable nature of the swap premium. To adjust for the vulnerable nature of the credit default swap, all the seller needs to do is to multiply the value of the state contingent swap premiums in (11.1) by the credit risk adjusted or 'expected value' as we did when valuing a vulnerable cap. Of course, this credit risk adjustment should be in line with the credit rating of the buyer of credit protection.

The value of the credit default swap from the point of view of the buyer of credit protection is the expected value of default payments in the event of default. The payoff function for credit default swap default payments is as follows.

$$Receipts = C_d(n,i)\{100 - B_C(n,i)\delta(n,i)\} \tag{11.2}$$

The term $C_d(n,i)$ is the corporate (that is to say, credit risky) state security price *conditional upon default* at time n and interest rate state i. It is found by multiplying the state security price that is not subject to credit risk at time n and interest rate state i by the cumulative probability of *prior period* survival and by the probability of default at time n and interest rate state i. For example, assuming that interest and credit risk is not correlated (as does Jarrow and Turnbull), $C_d(3,2)$ is found as $S(3,2) \times P_1 \times P_2 \times (1 - P_3)$ where $S(3,2)$ is the state security price that is not subject to credit risk three time steps into the future and two interest rate levels above the lowest possible interest rate that may arrive in three time periods multiplied by the likelihood P that no default has occurred in the first or second periods multiplied by the probability of default in the third period. Meanwhile the term in curly brackets is the payoff amount. As mentioned earlier the payoff in the event of default is typically defined as par value 100 less the value of the defaulted security. The value of the defaulted security is found as the expected value (as of today) of the bond $B_C(n,i)$ multiplied by the fraction we expect to recover at the time n and state i if default occurs $\delta(n,i)$.

Equation (11.2) finds the present value of the default amount (receipt) at interest rate state $r(n,i)$ so we apply this formula to all possible states and then add them up to find the present, credit risk adjusted (for the default risk of the reference bond) value of the default amounts. This is the value of the credit default swap from the point of view of the buyer of the credit default swap. If the seller is subject to credit risk, then the buyer may wish to adjust this amount for the credit risk of the seller because the seller may default on their promised default payments independent of the default on the reference (insured) bond. In other words, the seller may wish to account for the vulnerable nature of the promised default payments. To adjust for the vulnerable nature of the credit default swap, all the buyer needs to do is to multiply the value of the state contingent receipts in (11.2) by the credit risk adjusted or 'expected value' as we did when valuing a vulnerable credit default swap. Of course, this credit risk adjustment should be in line with the credit rating of the seller of credit protection. Also one may wish to consider the correlation between the likelihood that the seller and the reference bond may default simultaneously.

11.4.1 An example of a credit default swap

Suppose we wish to buy credit protection on our 6% semi-annual coupon pay 2.5-year corporate bond. If the bond defaults we expect to recover δ 60% of what it would have been worth had it not defaulted. The first question is how much credit protection would be offered to us if we buy a standard credit default swap? In order to use (11.2) we need to measure the corporate state prices conditional upon default $C_d(n,i)$ and survival $C_S(n,i)$. We again employ the Jarrow and Turnbull model as reported in workbook JTB02.xls and calibrate the Black Derman and Toy interest rate process to the sovereign zero coupon and interest rate volatility term structures and the Jarrow and Turnbull credit risk process to the corporate zero coupon term structure using a constant recovery rate δ of 60%. The results of these two steps are reported in workbook JTB02.xls, spreadsheets BDT and JT respectively. These steps have been previously discussed in Chapter 6. We then calculate the conditional corporate state prices $C_S(n,i)$ and $C_d(n,i)$ using the calibrated pure interest state securities prices $S(n,i)$ from Black Derman and Toy and the structure of one period probabilities of survival P from Jarrow and Turnbull as building blocks. The results we obtain are reported in JTB02.xls spreadsheet CDS in block A2 to F23 and are repeated in Table 11.4.

The values of the 6% coupon corporate bond at all possible interest rate states are reported in Table 11.5. This corporate price tree gives us the price of what the corporate bond would have been if the bond had not defaulted. Multiplying these amounts by the recovery fraction δ of 60% gives us the recovery amount. This recovery amount is then subtracted from par value to obtain the payoff we, as buyers of credit protection, would receive in the event of default.

The next step is to value these receipts. We multiply these recovery amounts by the corporate state security prices conditional upon default $C_d(n,i)$ and then add them up. We find that the expected

Table 11.4   Conditional corporate state prices

	A	B	C	D	E	F
2		BDT	JT	Probability	$Cs(n,i)$	$Cd(n,i)$
3	State	$S(n,i)$	$C(n,i)$	of Survival	ie: $P \times P \times P \times S(n,i)$	$P \times P \times (1-P) \times S(n,i)$
4	$r(1,1)$	0.4851354	0.4811990	0.9797149	0.4752944	0.0098410
5	$r(1,0)$	0.4851354	0.4811990	0.9797149	0.4752944	0.0098410
6	$r(2,2)$	0.2358679	0.2326794	0.9862100	0.2278967	0.0031866
7	$r(2,1)$	0.4717826	0.4654049	0.9862100	0.4558385	0.0063739
8	$r(2,0)$	0.2359147	0.2327256	0.9862100	0.2279419	0.0031873
9	$r(3,3)$	0.1145236	0.1126349	0.9923066	0.1098019	0.0008513
10	$r(3,2)$	0.3436103	0.3379437	0.9923066	0.3294437	0.0025542
11	$r(3,1)$	0.3436500	0.3379827	0.9923066	0.3294818	0.0025545
12	$r(3,0)$	0.1145632	0.1126739	0.9923066	0.1098399	0.0008516
13	$r(4,4)$	0.0555985	0.0545432	0.9935094	0.0529602	0.0003460
14	$r(4,3)$	0.2224196	0.2181979	0.9935094	0.2118654	0.0013841
15	$r(4,2)$	0.3336679	0.3273347	0.9935094	0.3178348	0.0020764
16	$r(4,1)$	0.2224710	0.2182483	0.9935094	0.2119143	0.0013844
17	$r(4,0)$	0.0556242	0.0545684	0.9935094	0.0529847	0.0003461
18	$r(5,5)$	0.0269472	0.0264240	0.9988580	0.0256392	0.0000293
19	$r(5,4)$	0.1347518	0.1321355	0.9988580	0.1282110	0.0001466
20	$r(5,3)$	0.2695347	0.2643014	0.9988580	0.2564516	0.0002932
21	$r(5,2)$	0.2695657	0.2643319	0.9988580	0.2564812	0.0002932
22	$r(5,1)$	0.1347984	0.1321812	0.9988580	0.1282554	0.0001466
23	$r(5,0)$	0.0269628	0.0264393	0.9988580	0.0256540	0.0000293

Table 11.5   6% corporate bond price tree

	C	D	E	F	G	H
27	Corporate Price Tree (6% 5 Period Bond)					
28	Coupon		6			
29	0	1	2	3	4	5
30						103
31					97.9047124	103
32				97.9197731	97.9075298	103
33			97.9565152	97.9262868	97.9103446	103
34		98.1352162	97.9700879	97.9327935	97.9131569	103
35	98.1207780	98.1678716	97.9836369	97.9392932	97.9159667	103

present value of the receipts from the credit default swap is worth $1.88 per $100 notional of the reference 6% corporate bond. This result is reported in Table 11.6.

A question that immediately comes to mind is how much should we pay for credit protection? If the cost to the buyer of the credit default swap is set equal to the expected value of receipts as given by (11.2) then as shown in Table 11.6 the semi-annual swap premium

Table 11.6 Value of a credit default swap

	A	B	C	D
37			$\delta =$	0.60
38			$M =$	100
39		Default	$Sw =$	0.00426
40		Amounts	Receipts	Payments
41	State	$(100 - \delta B)$	$(100 - \delta B) \times Cd(n,i)$	$Cs(n,i) \times Sw$
42	$r(1,1)$	41.119	0.405	0.2026339
43	$r(1,0)$	41.099	0.404	0.2026339
44	$r(2,2)$	41.226	0.131	0.0971600
45	$r(2,1)$	41.218	0.263	0.1943392
46	$r(2,0)$	41.210	0.131	0.0971793
47	$r(3,3)$	41.248	0.035	0.0468122
48	$r(3,2)$	41.244	0.105	0.1404529
49	$r(3,1)$	41.240	0.105	0.1404691
50	$r(3,0)$	41.236	0.035	0.0468284
51	$r(4,4)$	41.257	0.014	0.0225787
52	$r(4,3)$	41.255	0.057	0.0903253
53	$r(4,2)$	41.254	0.086	0.1355036
54	$r(4,1)$	41.252	0.057	0.0903462
55	$r(4,0)$	41.250	0.014	0.0225892
56	$r(5,5)$	38.200	0.001	0.0109309
57	$r(5,4)$	38.200	0.006	0.0546606
58	$r(5,3)$	38.200	0.011	0.1093339
59	$r(5,2)$	38.200	0.011	0.1093465
60	$r(5,1)$	38.200	0.006	0.0546796
61	$r(5,0)$	38.200	0.001	0.0109372
62		Value	1.8797407	1.8797407

is 42.6 basis points or 85.2 basis points per year. This value is found by using the solver utility found under the tools menu in Excel.[4] We set the value of payments cell D62 as the target cell and the value of receipts $1.8797407 as the target value. The change cell is D39. When we click on solve the basis point price S_w changes until the sum of expected values of payments adds up to the value of the receipts. Multiplying this semi-annual swap premium by 2 obtains the quoted annual premium the buyer of credit protection pays for credit protection on the 6% semi-annual coupon pay 2.5-year corporate bond.

We can determine how reasonable this price is by comparing the swap premium of 85.2 basis points to the credit spread. As shown in workbook JTB02.xls, spreadsheet JT, cell block F25 to J32, the yield spread between the 2.5-year 6% corporate bond and the corresponding 6% sovereign bond is 83.2 basis points. The swap premium is only 2 basis points higher than the credit spread. This happens only because the corporate bond is projected to be below par in most future interest rate states, so the credit default swap payoffs are somewhat larger than 40%. In other words, the credit default swap pays off 'too much' as it compensates the buyer for some small amount of interest rate risk as well as credit risk. If the payoff was strictly 40%, then the swap premium that sets the value of payments (11.2) equal to the value of receipts (11.1) would be 83 basis points, only two tenths of a basis point less than the credit spread.

This result should not be surprising. Recall that Jarrow and Turnbull is a term structure consistent model so the probabilities of survival, given a constant recovery fraction, replicate the credit spread. Therefore if credit default swap payoffs replicate the loss given default, 40% in our example, then the conditional (upon survival) swap premiums paid to compensate these losses should replicate the credit spread too.

11.5   Issues in default swap pricing

To obtain a 'fair' value for the swap premium is not as clear-cut as our example in section 11.3 may suggest. To appreciate the issues involved we first take a hard look at theoretically ideal circumstances

---

[4] It is possible that solver is not installed in your version of Excel. You need to select 'add ins' under the 'tools' sub-menu, and then tick off 'solver'.

and then relax restrictive conditions. We first look at two theoretical cases, when the reference bond is a floating rate bond and then when the reference bond is a fixed coupon bond. We then relax theoretically ideal circumstances by looking at the effects of liquidity and then we look at the effects of information asymmetries.

11.5.1 Theory: floating rate reference bond

If the reference bond is a floater that defaults only on the reset dates, Duffie (1999) shows that the swap premium should equal the expected value of swap receipts so (11.1) should equal (11.2). The basis point value of the credit default swap premium is equal to the fixed credit spread between the floater that is subject to credit risk and the floater than is not subject to credit risk. For example, an A+ rated corporate floater may pay libor plus 75 basis points whereas a sovereign floater would pay libor flat then the credit default swap premium should be 75 basis points.[5]

Arbitrage forces this to hold true. A seller of credit protection could hedge this position by going long a sovereign floater and shorting the reference corporate floater where both floaters have the same maturity and periodicity of coupon payments. If the corporate floater does not default then the sovereign and corporate floater mature at par, so proceeds from the sale of the sovereign floater will cover the short corporate floater. Meanwhile the credit default swap matures with no obligation on behalf of the seller. Therefore in the case that the bond does not default the receipts from the hedge offset the obligations on the credit default swap. If the corporate floater should default at the reset date then losses on the credit default swap would be offset by the residual value obtained by selling the sovereign floater at par and buying the defaulted floater at $B_F \delta$. This residual, $100 - B_F \delta$ is precisely the amount required by the seller to pay on the credit default swap.

Since the cost of maintaining the hedge portfolio, the long sovereign and short corporate floater, is equal to the fixed credit spread of, say, 75 basis points and offers precisely the same cash flow structure as the credit default swap, we know from the law of one price that the credit default swap and the hedge portfolio must have the same price. Therefore the credit default swap premium must be 75 basis

---

[5] Duffie (1999) notes that libor itself is subject to some small degree of credit risk, so the 'sovereign' floater is also subject to some small degree of credit risk. This means that the default swap premium may be slightly higher than the fixed credit spread, say by 5 basis points. Also Duffie notes that this analysis abstracts from several market frictions such as accrued interest, transactions costs and the like.

points. Moreover the cash value of the premium payments (11.1) must equal receipts (11.2) to the buyer of credit protection since buying credit protection on the corporate floater and holding the corporate floater long is equivalent to buying the sovereign floater. In other words, the swap premium (11.1) represents the cost of credit risk and therefore the expected value of payments in the event of default (11.2).

11.5.2   Theory: fixed rate reference bond

However, if the reference bond is a fixed coupon bond then the situation is not so clear. Essentially the problem is that there is no guarantee that the long sovereign bond is worth par in the event of default. To appreciate why this is important we examine the pricing problem from the point of view of the seller of credit protection.

The seller of credit protection sells a credit default swap S obligating themselves to pay par less the value of the reference bond B_C post-default and in return receive the swap premium S_w. The obligation in the event of default that underlies the credit default swap is given by the payoff function, which is par less the value of the reference bond post-default.

$$Payoff = [100 - B_C\delta] \qquad (11.3)$$

The seller can (nearly) hedge this conditional obligation by buying a sovereign bond and a shorting the reference bond where both have the same maturity. In other words, the hedge portfolio is

$$Hedge\ portfolio \approx B_S - B_C \qquad (11.4)$$

Since the reference bond has a higher yield than the sovereign bond the seller of credit protection pays the credit spread on the hedge portfolio. However, the seller of credit protection receives the credit default swap premium. The issue is whether the credit default swap premium fully offsets the payment of the credit spread on the hedge portfolio. The answer depends upon how good a hedge (11.4) forms in offsetting the obligations on the credit default swap (11.3).

The hedge portfolio approximately offsets the obligations on the credit default swap. If default does not occur the sovereign and reference bonds mature at par so the seller uses the proceeds from the maturing sovereign bond to cover the short position in the reference bond. The hedge portfolio expires worthless just as the credit default swap expires worthless, so obligations of the hedge portfolio and the credit default swap offset. If default should occur during the life of the swap, the seller must pay (11.3). The seller will attempt to recover this loss by selling the sovereign bond B_S and repurchasing the now defaulted corporate bond at price $B_C\delta$. The question is, will the pay-off on (11.4), $B_S - B_C\delta$, equal the cost of the obligation of (11.3), $100 - B_C\delta$?

Clearly this will depend upon whether the sovereign bond is priced at par. If the sovereign bond is priced above par then the seller will actually gain from the hedge, as the hedge portfolio will be worth more than the obligations from the credit default swap. On the other hand, if the sovereign bond is worth less than par then the seller loses from the hedge, as the hedge portfolio will be worth less than the obligations from the credit default swap. Therefore the answer as to whether (11.4) forms a good hedge depends upon the correlation between sovereign interest rates and the credit spread. Recall from section 6.7.1 that as the credit spread increases the probability of default increases.

If correlation is zero then there should be no reason to expect that systematically the sovereign bond will be below, or above, par when the corporate bond defaults. We would expect that the above hedge portfolio would be a good approximate hedge, so the swap premium would be close to the credit spread. On the other hand if there is a positive correlation between the sovereign interest rate and the credit spread then defaults tend to occur when sovereign interest rates are high. This means that (11.4) will not form such a good hedge for a seller of credit protection. When the corporate bond defaults the long sovereign bond in (11.4) is below par so that the payoff from the hedge will be less than the obligations on the credit default swap. This means that the seller of credit protection needs to charge a credit default swap premium that is more than the credit spread because the payment of the credit spread implied by the hedge portfolio still does not obtain a portfolio that covers losses on the credit default swap in the event of default.

If there is a negative correlation between the sovereign interest rate and credit spread then defaults tend to occur when sovereign interest rates are low. This means that (11.4) will tend to pay more than the obligations on the credit default swap because when default occurs the sovereign bond in the hedge portfolio is above par. If there is competition for selling credit protection, credit default swaps premiums will decrease below that of the credit spread because the cost of hedging is less than the credit spread as implied by paying the credit spread by forming the hedge portfolio.

To date the weight of empirical evidence from Duffie (1998), Collin-Dufresne, Goldstein and Martin (2001) and Papageorgiou and Skinner (2003) is that there exists a weak negative correlation between the level of US Treasury interest rates and the investment grade credit spread. This suggests that from the point of view of a buyer of credit protection the credit default swap should have a positive economic value. That is, the expected value of payments in the event of default (11.2) should be greater than the expected value of premium payments (11.1) because the credit default swap premium should tend to be below the credit spread.

11.5.3 Market imperfections: liquidity

From the above theory we understand that credit default swaps may have a slightly positive economic value from the point of view of buyers of credit protection. That is, receipts paid in the event of default (11.2) may be slightly larger than payments made (11.1) to the seller of credit protection because empirical evidence suggests that there may be a slight negative correlation between sovereign interest rates and the credit spread. However, this analysis ignores the impact of liquidity.

It is likely that the bonds that underlie estimates of the corporate yield curve are less liquid than the corresponding maturity sovereign bond. As we noted in Chapter 3, the issue size of corporate bonds tends to be much smaller than the corresponding maturity sovereign issues and so we can expect much more trading activity in sovereign bonds than in corporate bonds. If corporate bonds trade less frequently we can expect fewer dealers willing to offer firm two-way quotes. This means that when one buys a corporate bond it may be more difficult to sell (liquidate) the bond quickly at a reasonable price. Bondholders value liquidity as it enables them to respond to changing market conditions by adjusting their positions quickly and cheaply. Bondholders take this into account when buying less liquid bonds and so demand a higher yield for the less liquid bond. This suggests that the credit spread between the more valuable (more liquid) sovereign bond and the less valuable (less liquid) corporate bond would in part be determined by the difference in liquidity as well as the difference in credit risk.

Looking at the behaviour of term structure consistent models we realize that these models uncritically accept that the credit spread is solely due to credit risk. For example, the Jarrow and Turnbull credit risk model, being a fundamental extension of Bierman and Hass (1975), assumes that the sole determinate of the credit spread is the probability of default P and the recovery in the event of default δ. We have implemented the Jarrow and Turnbull model by assuming a constant recovery rate δ and then by calibrating the probability of survival P such that the model obtained portfolios of corporate state security prices the yield of which agrees with the corporate yield curve. Since this was done by adjusting the corresponding sovereign state security prices, replicating portfolios of which agree with the sovereign term structure, then we see that the probability of survival is actually calibrated to the credit spread. But we know that the credit spread is in part determined by the difference in liquidity between the more liquid sovereign and the corresponding maturity but less liquid corporate bond. Therefore our probability of survival (that Jarrow and Turnbull is careful to call a pseudoprobability) is 'too low' as it is forced to agree with a credit spread that is wider than that justified by credit risk alone.

This means that our measure of the probability of survival is too low. In turn this means that we overestimate the likelihood of default, so our estimate of receipts (11.2) is too high. Meanwhile our estimate of premium payments (11.1) is too low, as we have underestimated the likelihood that the buyer of credit protection will make payment as we have underestimated the probability of survival. Therefore we can expect that term structure consistent models will estimate a positive economic value for credit default swaps from the buyer of credit protection point of view.

11.5.4 Market imperfections: moral hazard

Documentation issues are an additional source of market imperfection that have an impact as to whether a credit default swap would have a positive or negative economic value from the point of view of the buyer of credit protection. For one thing many clauses in credit default swaps have never been tested in the courts so the enforceability of many clauses is uncertain. For another there is uncertainty regarding the definition of what constitutes a credit event and indeed there is uncertainty regarding the conditions upon which counterparties can agree that a credit event has actually occurred. A prime example of this sort of documentation issue concerns the 'restructuring clause' which defines restructuring as an event that triggers the default payment to the buyer of credit protection.

Realizing that bankruptcy is imminent, lenders and borrowers may choose to face up to their problems and restructure loans on concessionary terms prior to formal default. Therefore there is no doubt that restructuring, properly defined, is a credit event that results in losses on behalf of lenders. It is entirely reasonable that restructuring be defined as a credit event that triggers payments on a credit default swap and lenders seeking insurance against credit risk would wish to have such a clause. The problem is that the lenders have an influence on the likelihood of restructuring and the size of the credit losses thereby experienced. If these lenders are also buyers of credit protection, then we have a *moral hazard* problem because the insured party, the buyer of credit protection, has an influence on the conditions and of the size of default payments upon which insurance is paid out. The worry is that the buyer of credit protection would be more likely to encourage restructuring or would be believed to be more generous in the terms of restructuring when they are insured via the credit default swap. The additional costs of this moral hazard problem will at least in the first instance be borne by the seller of credit protection.

To make matters worse, the seller of credit protection also faces an *information asymmetry*. That is, the buyer of credit protection, being the lender of the reference bond, would know more about the likelihood of restructuring than the seller of credit protection. Sellers of credit protection would worry that they would be picked off if they were to ask for a relatively low credit default swap premium because they did not realize that restructuring was imminent. In other words, sellers realize that if they make a mistake and underprice the credit default swap because they underestimate the likelihood of restructuring then buyers would take advantage and eagerly buy up these underpriced credit default swap agreements.

The moral hazard and information asymmetry problems would motivate the seller of credit default swaps to ask for higher premiums thereby raising the value of payments as estimated by (11.1). It is entirely possible that in their attempts to protect themselves from these problems they end up asking for a credit default swap premium greater than that justified by the default probability as derived from credit risk models such as Jarrow and Turnbull. In other words, receipts (11.2), based on the Jarrow and Turnbull estimated probability of default, would be lower than the payments (11.1) because the swap premium is too high. To put it another way, the credit default swap may have a negative economic value from the point of view of buyers of credit protection since payments (11.1) are higher than receipts (11.2).[6] In fact Skinner and Diaz (2003) find evidence of this problem.

11.5.5 Conclusions

Evidently we should expect that the credit default swap would appear to have a slight positive economic value from the point of view of the

---

[6] Some credit default swap dealers responded to this problem by offering two sets of quotes, one for swaps with and another for swaps without restructuring as a credit event.

buyer of credit protection when we abstract from market imperfections. However, when we apply term structure consistent credit risk models that do not adjust for liquidity we may apparently obtain positive economic values due to liquidity bias in overestimating the hazard probabilities. For credit default swaps where 'restructuring' is a defined credit event we may have a moral hazard problem that if disruptive enough may result in an apparent negative economic value for the credit default swap.

11.6 Exercises

Question 1

You wish to buy a one-year credit default swap written on a 7% semi-annual coupon pay bond that matures in 2.5 years. The bond's binomial price tree is shown below along with the sovereign state security prices and one period probabilities of survival. For the one-year credit protection you must pay 50 basis points at the time of each coupon payment. If default occurs, swap premium payments cease. In return you receive the difference between par value and the value of the bond in default if the bond defaults at the end of the first or second semi-annual period. You anticipate that should the bond default the bond would be worth 60% of face value.

Coupon		7			
0	1	2	3	4	
				97.51868	
			98.00837	97.52148	
		98.52372	98.01488	97.52429	
	99.17985	98.53733	98.02138	97.52709	
99.63366	99.21275	98.55092	98.02787	97.52989	
Probabilities of survival					
0.99296	0.98301	0.98500	0.98092	0.98610	
State price tree					
				0.05560	
			0.11452	0.22242	
		0.23587	0.34361	0.33367	
	0.48514	0.47178	0.34365	0.22247	
1.00000	0.48514	0.23591	0.11456	0.05562	

(a) According to the Jarrow and Turnbull (1995) model, what is the value of the payments?

(b) According to the Jarrow and Turnbull (1995) model, what is the value of the receipts from insurance?

(c) The corporate bond's yield is 98 basis points above the corresponding maturity sovereign bond. If we were to calculate the value of the swap premium using a quote of 98 basis points (paid semi-annually) would the value of the swap premium be equal (nearly) to the value of receipts? Why or why not would they be nearly the same?

Question 2

If the reference bond is a floater that defaults only on the reset dates, the credit default swap premium (cost of default insurance) equals the expected value of credit default swap receipts (amount of insurance). Is this statement true? Discuss.

Question 3

Describe and explain the replicating portfolio that underlies the Jarrow and Turnbull (1995) calibrated model. In your answer, be careful to define or explain in enough detail to convey your understanding of what is meant by 'replicating portfolio'.

Question 4

Consider the following calibrated corporate discount factor tree and the sovereign state security price tree. The corporate discount factor tree is obtained from Duffie and Singleton and the sovereign state security price tree is from Black Derman and Toy (1990). You are offered credit protection on a 5% semi-annual coupon pay 2.5-year double A rated bond for one year. If the bond defaults, 45% of the value of the bond is likely to be recovered. In all states, the likelihood that the bond would survive is 0.99638. You are required to pay 100 basis points, 50 in six months' time and 50 basis points at the end of the year. In return you will receive par value less the bond post-default should the bond default. If the bond does default you do not have to make any further premium payments. Round all intermediate steps to five decimal places.

(a) What is the cost of default insurance?

(b) What is the amount of insurance?

(c) Is this offer of default insurance reasonable? Explain why or why not.

	0	1	2	3	4
					0.964009
dc(n,i)				0.975455	0.964572
			0.979991	0.975849	0.965126
		0.980044	0.980446	0.976238	0.965672
	0.98167	0.981333	0.980891	0.976619	0.966209
					0.027845
				0.057711	0.139385
			0.118208	0.231043	0.279091
S(n,i)		0.241002	0.354889	0.346863	0.27941
	0.491326	0.48232	0.355153	0.231439	0.139863
	0.491326	0.241319	0.118472	0.057909	0.028004

Embedded options

12.1 Introduction

A large fraction of corporate bonds are structured securities that contain complex structures of options. This creates problems for those wishing to trade in these securities, as it is difficult to assess the value of these contracts. Normally we assess relative value by comparing the yield of a bond with the par coupon yield curve but this is not possible when dealing with bonds that have options embedded in the bond contract. Recall from Chapter 3 that the par coupon yield curve is derived from straight bonds so when assessing the relative value of structured securities by comparing their promised yield with a par coupon yield curve we are not comparing like with like.

To get around this problem we intend to value options that are often embedded in corporate bond contracts. We will concentrate on the American call option that is included in callable bonds and the European call option that is included in many types of sinking fund bonds. We view structured securities as packages of a hypothetical straight bond and the embedded option. We can value, say, a callable bond because we can value the underlying hypothetical straight bond and the American call option. This is possible because we can generate the binomial stochastic structure of interest rates with which *all* securities must agree. The yield on the hypothetical straight bond is the *option adjusted yield* of the structured security. It is a clear indicator of the value of the structured security as the option adjusted yield is the equivalent straight bond yield of the structured security. We can compare the option adjusted yield to the par coupon yield curve to assess relative value of the structured security as then we would be comparing like with like.

12.2 An introduction to callable/putable bonds

As suggested above, a callable bond is a structured security that consists of two securities, a long position in a hypothetical straight bond and a short position in a call option. To put it mathematically,

$$B_{CA} = B_{ST} - C_O \qquad (12.1)$$

The straight bond B_{ST} has the same coupon and maturity as the structured security. In the meantime the call option C_O has an exercise price and an expiry date as specified by the call feature included in the structured security's bond covenants.

So why would a corporation want a call feature included in what is otherwise an ordinary straight bond? There are two reasons, interest rate risk and credit risk. First, let's talk about interest rate risk. Sometimes a corporation needs to fund a long-term project so it needs to issue a 10-year bond for, say, £100 million. However, the yield curve is downward sloping. In other words, everybody expects that current interest rates are high and that interest rates will be lower in, say, two years' time. This creates a serious problem for the corporation. Imagine they issue a 10-year straight bond sold at par with a 10% coupon. If the expected interest rate scenario develops, and two years later interest rates decline such that a new eight-year bond can be issued at par with a coupon of 8%, the corporation will find that its interest cost is too high. Meanwhile their competitor's interest cost is only 8%, so they are not competitive in their market. They would look back at the decision to issue straight debt two years ago with regret.

To avoid this sort of problem, they issue callable bonds today. The call feature would essentially say that the corporation could repurchase the bond at, say, £105 at any time. If indeed interest rates decline in two years' time, the corporation can refund the old high coupon debt by issuing a new lower coupon bond. That is, the corporation will first issue a new bond (for a total issue size of £105 million) at par with, say, a coupon of 8%. With the money thereby obtained, they will call (pay back) the old debt at £105. Then all they have is a new bond that costs only 8%.

As you can immediately see, the call feature works to the advantage of the corporation but to the disadvantage of the bond investor. While the corporation gains by reducing their interest cost, investors lose as their income is cut from 10% to 8%. So why would investors agree to buy a callable bond? The answer is that the investor is paid to accept the call feature. First, the bond is usually callable at a premium above par. More importantly, however, is that in order to be sold at par, a callable bond will have to offer a coupon rate that is higher than a corresponding straight bond.

The second reason why callable bonds are issued is because of changing credit risk. This can be most clearly seen in the single B (junk, or high yield, take your pick) bond market. Here corporations are not very creditworthy, but they have their hopes. For example, think of some 'dot com' company that needs long-term funding. Since they are a new company, they do not have much in the way of credit history. Their product is new and untested. The best they could hope for is a single B rating and pay a high coupon, say 14%, in order for the bond to be sold at par. However, they truly believe they have a great product and that the company will do extremely well in the future. If this comes to pass, then the rating of the company, and of the 14% coupon bond, will improve, say, to triple B. The price of the 14% coupon bond will now be above par, not due to a decrease in interest rates, but because credit quality has improved. Now the corporation could issue new triple B debt at par for only 10%. They would regret that they did not make the old 14% coupon bond callable.

To avoid this problem the 'dot com' company would make the single B bond callable and may be pay a little more, say 14.5% rather than 14%. But if things work out as they hope, they will be able to call the bond when the bond is re-rated into a higher category. Hence it is no surprise that the vast majority of single B bonds are callable.[1]

Similarly putable bonds are a combination of a hypothetical straight bond plus a long position in a put option. To put it mathematically,

$$B_{PU} = S_{ST} + P_O \tag{12.2}$$

In this case the put option P_O is added to the value of the putable bond B_{PU} because it is held long by the investor in the putable bond. It is the investor's choice when to sell (put) the putable bond, typically at par, back to the issuing corporation. Sometimes investors desire putable bonds because they are concerned that interest rates may rise. If they buy a long-term, say 10-year 6%, bond they receive a coupon rate of 6% for 10 years. If, say, two years later interest rates

---

[1] Besides if the single B bond is *not* callable the issuing corporation may be inadvertently signalling that there is no hope that the credit quality of the bond will improve. Hence the fact that a bond is callable is not a reliable signal that the bond may be upgraded in the future.

rise so that new eight-year bonds are sold at par with a coupon rate of 8%, their 6% coupon bond will fall in value. They would wish that they had the opportunity to sell this 6% coupon bond at par and reinvest in the new 8% coupon bond.

Corporations would issue putable bonds when they need long-term financing in spite of the general expectation that interest rates may rise soon. In order to convince investors to buy their long-term debt they include a put provision that allows the investor to sell the bond back to the issuing corporation at par at a date, or a series of dates in the future. Of course, the corporation is paid for giving this option to the investor. As with the call option embedded in the callable bond, the price of the put option is implicitly included in the bond covenants of the putable bond. For example, the coupon rate on a putable bond is typically lower than otherwise identical but straight bonds.

In recent years the interest rate environment has been characterized by falling rather than increasing interest rates. As a result putable bonds have been rarely issued and most of the old putable bonds sold in the 1980s have matured. Consequently there are very few putable bonds outstanding in today's bond markets. Therefore we intend to concentrate on valuing callable bonds but we will point out how putable bonds can be valued using techniques similar to those we use to price callable bonds.

12.2.1 Valuing callable bonds

Our method will be to value the straight bond B_{ST} and then the call option C_O and then back out the value of the callable bond B_{CA}. For example, suppose we find that the value of the call option is $2.50 and the straight bond B_{ST} is $103.50. Therefore according to (11.1) the callable bond B_{CA} is worth $101. We can do this because we know that once we have obtained a binomial interest rate tree, the value of *all* interest sensitive securities must be consistent with it. Otherwise this would lead to pure arbitrage opportunities. Therefore we follow five steps to value the callable bond.

1. We develop an interest rate tree as found by running a binomial stochastic interest rate and credit risk model.
2. We price the otherwise identical but straight bond by solving backwards through the interest rate tree using the coupon and scheduled maturity of the callable bond and ignoring the call feature.
3. We then find the in the money (intrinsic) value of the call option at every node of the above straight bond price tree by subtracting

the call exercise price from the value of the straight bond at each node.

4. We then apply our backward solving valuation routine to the above intrinsic call option value tree with one important modification. At each step in our backward solving routine we take the higher of the intrinsic (European) or time (American) value of the choice to exercise at that node or delay exercise by one more time period. This step finds the value of the implied American call option as specified by the call feature.

5. Finally we deduct the value of the call feature (from step 4) from the underlying straight bond (from step 2) to find the value of the callable bond.

To implement the above five-step procedure it is more convenient to employ backward induction using credit risk adjusted one period discount factors rather than employing forward induction using credit risk adjusted state security prices. However, it is awkward to obtain the credit risk adjusted discount factor tree using Jarrow and Turnbull (1995). This is true because the Jarrow and Turnbull (1995) model requires that this period's discount factor depends in part upon earlier periods' survival and default probabilities and the terms that include earlier periods' survival and default probabilities must be added together. That is the reason why until now we have employed forward induction, using the credit risk adjusted state security prices rather than backward induction, using a credit risk adjusted discount factor tree, to value credit risky instruments.

In contrast Duffie and Singleton allows us to conveniently employ forward induction since recoveries are modelled as a fraction of next periods' survival contingent value. The advantage of this formulation is that if recoveries are fractions of survival contingent values then values associated with prior period defaults are included in the state contingent discount factor as a *multiplicative* term. This allows us to apply default free interest rate modelling techniques directly to a corporate rate of interest without the extra computational complexity of adding values associated with prior period default to each corporate state price. Therefore we value a callable bond using Duffie and Singleton (1999).

12.2.2   An example of valuing a callable bond

We choose to value an 8% semi-annual coupon pay 2.5-year callable bond. The option to call is American where the issuer can call the bond on any coupon date. The call (exercise) price is based on the clean bond price. The call feature includes a stepdown clause where the call price decreases with time. Specifically the bond can be called at any time in the first six-month period at 103, during the second period at 102, the third at 101 and 100 thereafter. The calculations we perform are reported in workbook DSB02.xls, spreadsheet DS.

We must first estimate the binomial stochastic interest rate tree. We use Black Derman and Toy as our pure interest rate process and add credit risk by implementing a binomial version of Duffie and Singleton assuming zero correlation between interest and credit risk. We use the return of market value recovery assumption as discussed in Chapter 6, section 6.9, otherwise Duffie and Singleton is the more familiar Jarrow and Turnbull. As always, the pure interest rate process is calibrated to the sovereign yield curve and the credit risk process is calibrated to the corporate yield curve. The corporate yield curve is estimated via Nelson and Siegel from non-callable corporate bonds of the same rating class and industry as the target callable bond. The resulting corporate interest rate tree as well as the corresponding discount factor tree are reported in Table 12.1.

Table 12.1 Corporate interest and discount factor trees

	B	C	D	E	F
5	$R(n,i)$				0.063142
6				0.064024	0.063085
7			0.064726	0.063946	0.063027
8		0.066945	0.064578	0.063869	0.06297
9	0.076654	0.066548	0.06443	0.063792	0.062913
10	0	1	2	3	4
11					0.968922
12	$dc(n,i)$			0.968495	0.96895
13			0.968155	0.968533	0.968978
14		0.967082	0.968227	0.96857	0.969006
15	0.962398	0.967274	0.968298	0.968607	0.969033

We use the discount factor tree to price the hypothetical 8% semi-annual coupon 2.5-year straight corporate bond by backward induction. Mechanically, this procedure is precisely the same as valuing a straight sovereign coupon bond as reported in Table 5.5, the only difference is that we use the Duffie and Singleton *corporate* discount factor tree rather than a pure interest discount factor tree that is not subject to credit risk. The result is reported in Table 12.2.

Table 12.2   The price of an 8% 2.5-year straight bond

	B	C	D	E	F	G
56	Coupon	8				
57		0	1	2	3	4
58						100.7679
59					101.4686	100.7708
60				102.1132	101.4753	100.7737
61			102.627	102.1273	101.482	100.7766
62		102.6339	102.6609	102.1413	101.4887	100.7795

The value of this bond is $102.6339. This price must be correct even though this bond does not exist. Remember that the price of this hypothetical straight corporate bond is priced according to the corporate zero coupon yield curve and therefore is fully consistent with the implied structure of zero coupon bond prices. If this bond did exist and for some reason was valued at some other price one could arbitrage by replicating the cash flows of the coupon bond by buying or selling the coupons separately and then taking the opposite position in the coupon bond and make pure arbitrage profits.[2]

Once the hypothetical straight bond price is calculated then one can calculate the implied straight bond yield of the callable bond using the scheduled maturity and coupon rate of the callable bond but the straight bond price. This implied yield is called the option adjusted yield and is directly comparable to the par coupon yield curve that is composed of straight bonds to assess relative value. This is possible because the option adjusted yield strips the effects of callability from the callable bond's yield so that when one compares this option adjusted yield to the par coupon yield curve constructed from straight bonds one is comparing like with like. The decision rules are exactly what one would expect. If the option adjusted yield is higher than the corresponding maturity yield on the par coupon yield curve then in the absence of liquidity and tax effects, the callable

---

[2] The coupon stripping argument for corporate bonds is weaker than for sovereign bonds. For example, suppose the corporate bond is priced lower than implied by the structure of zero coupon yields. Then one is supposed to buy the coupon bond, strip the bond into coupon and principal zeros, and sell them at the higher zero coupon prices. For sovereign bonds the difference between the higher coupon strip prices and the lower coupon bond price is locked in as the long coupon and short strip positions always offset in all future states of nature. Corporate bonds may default, however, leaving the party attempting to arbitrage exposed to fulfilling their strip obligations without the backing of the coupon bond. Therefore the coupon stripping argument does not strictly hold for corporate bonds and only holds to the extent that we can ignore default. This implies that the approximation deteroriates with credit rating. See section 3.3.2.1 for further details.

bond is attractive as its implied straight bond yield is too high. Similarly if the option adjusted yield is lower than the corresponding maturity yield on the par coupon yield curve then again in the absence of liquidity and tax effects, the callable bond is not attractive as its implied straight bond yield is too low.

The next step is to find the intrinsic value of the call feature at all possible time steps. We use the conditional IF statement to test whether the value of the underlying straight bond is above the call price. If so then the call option implied by the call feature is 'in the money' as then the corporation can call the bond and buy it back at a cheaper than market price. Therefore the intrinsic value is the difference between the straight bond's price and the current call price. If the difference is zero or negative then the option is 'out of the money' and the intrinsic value is zero, otherwise the intrinsic value is the straight bond price less the call price. The intrinsic value of the callable bond at all possible nodes is reported in Table 12.3.

Table 12.3 Intrinsic value of the call feature

	B	C	D	E	F	G
63	Intrinsic value of the call option					
64	Call Price	103	102	101	100	100
65						0.767885
66					1.468597	0.770784
67				1.113234	1.475321	0.773681
68			0.626972	1.127298	1.482037	0.776576
69		0	0.660922	1.141338	1.488746	0.779468

The next step is to determine whether it is worth the issuer's while to take the 'European' or intrinsic value and call immediately or to take the 'American' or time value and delay exercise one more period. At first glance one would think that the issuer should always exercise as soon as the option is in the money. If the issuer delays then the corporation would continue to pay coupons at a rate that is too high given current market conditions thereby conferring a needless gain on behalf of the bondholders at the expense of the shareholders. However, there are at least three reasons why it might make sense for the issuer to delay call.

First, calling the bond is a costly process. The issuer must first issue a new bond at par with a lower prevailing coupon. With the money thereby obtained the old high coupon callable bond would be repurchased through exercising the call feature. Therefore to call the bond the issuer must pay issue fees for the new bond, pay double interest by paying interest on the new issue while for a time the old issue is still outstanding and pay the administrative costs of the call procedure. Therefore it is unlikely that the issuer will call the bond as soon as the call feature is in the money. Rather the corporation will wait until the call feature is in the money enough to pay for these additional costs. Second, the call feature, as illustrated in our example, often contains a stepdown feature. This creates an incentive for the issuer to delay call, for by delaying one more period the issuer can reduce the costs of financing still further. Finally, it is well known that interest rates are mean reverting to some central tendency. The corporation has to ask itself whether interest rates are trending towards its central tendency at a lower rate than prevails presently. Therefore they ask if by delaying call one more period would interest rates be even lower so that an even lower coupon bond can replace the callable bond.

Therefore it is not obvious when the issuer will call the bond. We handle the problem by evaluating the decision to call or delay one more period at all possible nodes of the call price tree. At each node of the call price tree we compare the intrinsic value of the call feature with the present value of next period's expected value of the call feature and then take the higher of the two. We start at the last possible date of call, when there is no choice to delay any further so we know that the value of the call feature is its intrinsic value. Then we work backwards taking the higher of the second to last period's intrinsic value and the expected present value obtained by delaying until the last period and taking the intrinsic value at that last period. Then we move to the third to last period and again repeat this process. We continue to move backwards, period by period, until we obtain the present value of the American call option implied by the call feature.

To illustrate, look at Table 12.3. The value of the call option one period prior to maturity at, say, interest rate states $r_c(4,0)$ and $r_c(4,1)$ is its intrinsic value of \$0.779468 and \$0.776576 respectively. There is no choice to delay one more period as the bond matures at $t=5$, so the value of the call feature at the last possible date of call is its intrinsic value. Now we move backwards one more period to $t=3$ and evaluate the choice to delay call or take the intrinsic value. The value of delay, say for interest rate state $r_c(3,0)$, is found by our usual backward induction procedure where $d_c(3,0)$ is the corporate discount factor at interest rate state $r_c(3,0)$ and $c(4,1)$ and $c(4,0)$ are the values of the call option at $t=4$, interest rate states 1 and 0 respectively.

$$c(3,0) = 0.5[c(4,1) + c(4,0)]d_c(3,0)$$
$$= 0.5[0.776576 + 0.779468]0.968607 = 0.753598$$

The time value of delay by one more period if interest rate state $r_c(3,0)$ was to arrive is \$0.753598, which is less than the intrinsic value of \$1.488746 as seen in Table 12.3. Obviously we are better off in interest rate state $r_c(3,0)$ by exercising the call option and refunding the high coupon issue thereby extracting the higher intrinsic value. Similarly we find that we are better off exercising the call option at all interest rate states at date $t = 3$ since the intrinsic value is higher than the value of delay. We now move to the third to last time period at $t = 2$. At interest rate state $r_c(2,0)$ the time value is as follows.

$$c(2,0) = 0.5[c(3,1) + c(3,0)]d_c(2,0)$$

$$= 0.5[1.482037 + 1.488746]0.968298 = 1.438302$$

The time value of \$1.438302 is higher than the intrinsic value of \$1.141338 as indicated in Table 12.3, so we prefer to take the time value rather than the intrinsic value if we were to reach interest rate state $r_c(2,0)$. In other words, we choose not to exercise the call option even though evidently it is profitable to do so because the expected present value of calling next period is even higher. We continue to work our way backwards in this manner to find that the value of the call feature as reported in Table 12.4 is \$1.33264.

Table 12.4 Value of the call feature

	B	C	D	E	F	G
71	Call Option Value					0.76788
72					1.46860	0.77078
73				1.42508	1.47532	0.77368
74			1.38137	1.43170	1.48204	0.77658
75		1.33264	1.38804	1.43830	1.48875	0.77947

The final step is to find the value of the callable bond. As mentioned previously this is the value of the hypothetical straight bond, \$102.6339 less the value of the call feature \$1.33264 or \$101.30126.

12.2.3 Valuing putable bonds

As mentioned earlier, not many putable bonds are available in today's market so we confine ourselves with just outlining how one could value a putable bond. To value a putable bond one would first value the straight bond B_{ST} and then the put option P_O and then back out the value of the putable bond B_{PU}. We can do this because we know that once we have obtained a binomial interest rate tree, the value of *all* interest sensitive securities must be consistent with it.

Otherwise this would lead to pure arbitrage opportunities. According to (12.2) the put option embedded in a putable bond is held by the investor so the value of a putable bond is equivalent to a long position in the hypothetical straight bond and a long position in the put option. For example, suppose we find that the value of the put option P_O is $1.50 and the straight bond B_{ST} is $103.50 then the putable bond B_{PU} is worth $105.

To value a putable bond we follow the same five steps we followed when valuing the callable bond provided that the embedded option is American. If the embedded option is European then we will modify our steps slightly. Specifically:

1. We develop an interest rate tree as found by running a binomial stochastic interest rate and credit risk model.
2. We price the otherwise identical but straight bond by solving backwards through the interest rate tree using the coupon and scheduled maturity of the putable bond and ignoring the put feature.
3. Sometimes the put option is European rather than American since the investor may have a single date when they can sell the bond back to the corporation at par. Therefore we need to modify our valuation procedure depending whether the put option is European or American.
    (a) If the put option is European we find the in the money (intrinsic) value of the put option for every interest rate level on the date of put by subtracting the straight bond price from the put exercise price at each node available on that exercise date. We then multiply these intrinsic values by the corresponding state security price. The sum of the value of these products is the value of the European put option. We then proceed to step 5.
    (b) If the put option is American because the investor can put the bond back to the corporation on any date, then we continue as we did for callable bonds. That is, we find the in the money (intrinsic) value of the put option at every node of the above straight bond price tree by subtracting the straight bond price from the put exercise price at each node. We then proceed to step 4.
4. We then apply our backward solving valuation routine to the above intrinsic put option value tree with one important modification. At each step in our backward solving routine we take the higher of the intrinsic (European) or time (American) value of the choice to exercise at that node or delay exercise by one more time period. This step finds the value of the implied American put option as specified by the put feature.

5. Finally, we add the value of the put feature (from step 3 for European and step 4 for American puts) to the underlying straight bond (from step 2) to find the value of the putable bond.

We can also calculate the corresponding option adjusted yield for a putable bond. Once the hypothetical straight bond price is calculated in step 2 above we can calculate the implied straight bond yield of the putable bond using the scheduled maturity and coupon rate of the putable bond but the straight bond price. This implied yield is called the option adjusted yield and is directly comparable to the par coupon yield curve that is composed of straight bonds to assess relative value. This is possible because the option adjusted yield strips the effects of the put option from the putable bond's yield so that when one compares this option adjusted yield to the par coupon yield curve constructed from straight bonds one is comparing like with like. The decision rules are exactly what one would expect. If the option adjusted yield is higher than the corresponding maturity yield on the par coupon yield curve then in the absence of liquidity and tax effects, the putable bond is attractive as its implied straight bond yield is too high. Similarly if the option adjusted yield is lower than the corresponding maturity yield on the par coupon yield curve then again in the absence of liquidity and tax effects, the putable bond is not attractive as its implied straight bond yield is too low.

12.3   Measures of interest rate sensitivity for callable bonds

To measure the duration of a callable bond we recognize that the callable bond is composed of positions in two underlying securities, a long position in the hypothetical straight bond and a short position in the underlying American call option implied by the call feature. Therefore the interest rate sensitivity of the callable bond is reduced by the interest rate sensitivity of the call option. To appreciate the effect a call option has on reducing the interest rate sensitivity of the callable bond, we look at modified duration.

We know how to measure the duration of a straight bond but we do not know how to measure the duration of the call option implied by the call feature. However, with a bit of standard calculus we can figure out how to measure the duration of the embedded call feature. We start with basic principles and recognize that the interest rate sensitivity of any security is the first partial derivative of its price with respect to a change in its yield all scaled by its price. Therefore the modified duration of the call feature D_C^* is the first partial derivative of the call price with respect to a change in its yield dC/dY scaled by the call price C_o.

$$D_C^* = \frac{dC_o}{dY} \times \frac{1}{C_o} \qquad (12.3)$$

The next step is to recognize that the call price itself is *not* a direct function of its yield. Instead the value of a call is first determined as a function of the underlying straight bond price, and *then* the straight bond itself is a function of the yield. This indicates that we need to use the chain rule of calculus. We now apply this rule to the partial derivative contained in (12.3).

$$\frac{dC_o}{dY} = \frac{dC_o}{dB_{ST}} \frac{dB_{ST}}{dY}$$

In other words, a change in the call price dC_o ultimately results from a change in yield dY through a chain of effects. Working backwards, a change in the yield dY first causes the straight bond price to change dB_{ST} and then the change in the bond price causes the price of the call to change dC_o. We now substitute the chain rule into (12.3).

$$D_C^* = \left[\frac{dC_o}{dB_{ST}} \frac{dB_{ST}}{dY} \right] \times \frac{1}{C_o}$$

We now multiply both sides by B_{ST}/B_{ST} to obtain an expression that allows us to break down the interest rate sensitivity of a call feature into its components.

$$D_C^* = \frac{dC_o}{dB_{ST}} \times \frac{dB_{ST}}{dY} \frac{1}{B_{ST}} \times \frac{B_{ST}}{C_o}$$

Notice that the first term on the right-hand side of the above expression is the call feature's delta, being the first partial derivative of the call price with respect to a change in the value of the underlying instrument, the value of the straight bond dC_o/dB_{ST}. The next term is the modified duration of the underlying straight bond. The final term is the ratio of the underlying straight bond price to the call option price. In other words, the modified duration of the call feature is its delta Δ_C multiplied by the underlying straight bond's modified duration D_{ST}^* all multiplied by the ratio of the straight bond to call feature price B_{ST}/C_o.

$$D_C^* = \Delta_C \times D_{ST}^* \times \frac{B_{ST}}{C_o} \qquad (12.4)$$

Therefore recognizing that the duration of a callable bond is a weighted average duration of its component securities, the callable bond and the embedded call feature, we obtain our expression for the duration of a callable bond.

$$D_{CB}^* = \frac{B_{ST}}{B_{CB}} D_{ST}^* - \frac{C_o}{B_{CB}} D_C^* \qquad (12.5)$$

We illustrate how to calculate the duration of a callable bond through use of a numerical example. We will use the same 8% coupon 5 period callable bond that we used in section 12.3.3. Its price is \$101.30126. The otherwise equivalent straight bond is worth \$102.6339 and the call is worth \$1.33264. The yield on the straight bond is 6.836%.[3] Using this information the modified duration of the underlying straight bond D_{ST}^* is,

$$D_{ST}^* = \frac{\dfrac{4}{(0.03418)^2}\left[1 - \dfrac{1}{(1+0.03418)^5}\right] + \dfrac{5\left(100 - \dfrac{4}{0.03418}\right)}{(1+0.03418)^{5+1}}}{102.6339}$$

$$= 4.4822 \ (2.241 \ \text{annual})$$

The delta of the call Δ_C (see the call price tree in Table 12.4) is

$$\Delta_C = \frac{C_d - C_u}{B_{STd} - B_{STu}} = \frac{1.38804 - 1.38137}{102.6609 - 102.627} = 0.19676$$

The parameters C_d and C_u refer to the price of the call option next period should interest rates fall and rise respectively and the parameters B_{STd} and B_{STu} refer to the price of the underlying straight bond next period should interest rates fall and rise respectively. Therefore the duration of the call feature according to (12.4) is 33.959.

$$D_C^* = \Delta_C \times D_{ST}^* \times \frac{B_{ST}}{C_o} = (0.19676)(2.241)\left(\frac{102.6339}{1.33264}\right) = 33.959$$

The duration of a callable bond according to (12.5) is a price-weighted average of the duration of its component securities. That is,

$$D_{CB}^* = \frac{B_{ST}}{B_{CB}} D_{ST}^* - \frac{C_o}{B_{CB}} D_C^* = \frac{102.6339}{101.30126}(2.241)$$

$$- \frac{1.33264}{101.30126}(33.959)$$

$$= 2.2705 - 0.4467 = 1.824$$

---

[3] Using a *BEY* may appear to be inconsistent with the prices we have obtained under a stochastic, non-flat term structure. However, remember that the yield on a bond is purely a descriptive number and it is derived from a price found using the actual term structure and a stochastic interest and credit risk model.

As interest rates decrease, the duration of the callable bond will get smaller because the value of the call feature will rise. Eventually the duration will fall to the earliest date the bond may be called. As interest rates increase, the call will be priced out of the money, so its price will decline. The weight placed on the call duration will also decline, so the duration of the callable bond will rise. As interest rates continue to increase eventually the duration of the callable bond will resemble a non-callable bond.

12.3.1 Negative convexity

The problem with hedging callable bonds is that callable bonds have negative convexity. This means that in response to a decrease in interest rates the callable bond may increase by *less* than what we would expect using a linear approximation to the price/yield relationship. To put it another way, modified duration may overestimate the price response of the callable bond to a decrease in yield. In contrast, straight bonds have positive convexity so modified duration will underestimate the price response of the bond to a decrease in yield. To see why callable bonds have negative convexity consider Figure 12.1.

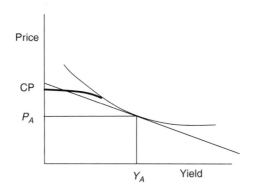

Figure 12.1   Negative convexity of callable bonds

In Figure 12.1 the non-linear thin line represents the actual price response of a straight bond for a given change in yield. The callable bond follows the usual price response to the right of the current price yield combination as indicated by the intersection of points Y_A, P_A. However, as the current yield decreases below Y_A the callable bond at first follows the usual price response curve but eventually moves away from this line and follows the flatter thick line instead. Meanwhile the straight line represents modified duration's linear approximation of the price response of any bond, straight or callable, to a given change in yield. The distance between the straight line and the non-linear lines indicates the error made by using modified duration to approximate the actual price response of a bond to a given change in yield. For yield changes above point Y_A modified duration will always overestimate the fall in price in response to an increase in yield. This is the same result we expect from positive convexity. As yields fall below point Y_A modified duration will underestimate the increase in price for straight bonds that continue to follow the thin non-linear curve. Therefore we say that straight bonds have positive convexity because investors in straight bonds gain more in price than expected (by using the linear approximation as provided by modified duration) in response to a decrease in yield and lose less than expected (by using the linear approximation provided by modified duration) in response to an increase in yield. The more positively convex the thin line in Figure 12.1 is, the more curvature it has, and the more of the upside is available in response to a decrease in yield and the less of the downside is available in response to an increase in yield.

However, for callable bonds the situation is different. As yields fall below yield Y_A, at some point the callable bond moves along the thick non-linear curve and modified duration will overestimate the actual increase in price. This is what is meant by negative convexity. In contrast to straight bonds, holders of callable bonds may gain less than what they expect (by using the linear approximation as provided by modified duration) in response to a decrease in yield. This happens because as yields decrease the price of the bond rises making it more likely that the bond may be called to the disadvantage of the holder of the callable bond. Potential callable bond investors can anticipate that this may happen and so are reluctant to pay as high a price for a callable bond that may be called than for an otherwise equivalent straight bond that will not be called. Therefore at first the thick non-liner curve continues to rise as yields continue to fall but at a slower rate than the price/yield curve followed by straight bonds. The weaker price response is called price compression, a weaker form of negative convexity because it still is the case that investors gain more than expected when approximating the price/yield relation using modified duration, but less than what would have been available had they held a straight bond. Finally, yields have decreased so much that investors are certain that the bond will be called. At that point the value of the bond hits a ceiling beyond which the price of the callable bond will not rise even as interest rates continue to fall. This ceiling is the call price, for investors will not pay more than the call price for a bond if there is a strong likelihood that the bond may soon be called at the call price.

The challenge presented to us is how are we to model the price response of a callable bond in the presence of negative convexity. To illustrate we use the 2.5-year 8% semi-annual coupon bond of section 12.3.3. We follow the portfolio approach to measure the convexity of the callable bond. That is, we first measure the convexity of the underlying straight bond, and then the convexity of the call feature. Then the convexity of the callable bond will be the weighted average of the convexity of the straight bond less the weighted average of the convexity of the call feature, the weights being determined by the value of the straight bond and the call feature relative to the value of the callable bond.

Convexity of a straight bond is the second partial derivative of the bond's price with respect to a change in its yield all scaled by its price. This second derivative of the straight bond SD_S is,

$$SD_{ST} = \frac{d^2 B_{ST}}{dY^2} = \left[\frac{2C}{(Y)^3} \left[1 - \frac{1}{(1+Y)^N} \right] - \frac{2CN}{Y^2(1+Y)^{N+1}} \right.$$
$$\left. + \frac{N(N+1)\left(100 - \frac{C}{Y}\right)}{(1+Y)^{N+2}} \right]$$

The parameters have the same interpretation as with the formula for modified duration, namely C is the cash value of the coupon payment, N is the number of promised coupon payments, Y is the yield where for semi-annual coupon pay bonds the yield is semi-annual. For the underlying straight bond, the convexity can be found as follows.

$$\left[\frac{2(4)}{(0.03418)^3} \left[1 - \frac{1}{(1.03418)^5} \right] - \frac{2(4)(5)}{(0.03418)^2(1.03418)^6} \right.$$
$$\left. + \frac{5(6)\left(100 - \frac{4}{0.03418}\right)}{(1+0.03418)^7} \right]$$

$$= 30\,989.7384 - 27\,985.8864 - 403.7376$$
$$= 2600.1144 \text{ (semi-annual) } 650.0286 \text{ (annual)}$$

Notice that we divide by 2^2 or 4 to obtain the annual measure of the second derivative. If the bond were monthly coupon pay we would have to divide by 12^2 or 144 to obtain the annual measure of the second derivative. Now we divide by price $102.6339 to obtain the annual measure of convexity as 6.3335.

Now we need to measure the gamma Γ_C of the embedded call option included in the callable bond contract. Recall that the gamma represents the change in delta Δ_C with respect to a change in the underlying asset's (straight bond's) price B_{ST}. In other words, the gamma is the second derivative of the call price with respect to a change in the value of the straight bond. That is,

$$\Gamma_C = \frac{d^2 C_o}{dB_{ST}^2}$$

An estimate of this gamma is found from the second time period of the binomial tree.

$$\Gamma_C = \frac{\Delta_{CL} - \Delta_{CU}}{M_B} \quad \text{where } \Delta_{CL} = \frac{C_L - C_M}{B_{STL} - B_{STM}},$$

$$\Delta_{CU} = \frac{C_M - C_U}{B_{STM} - B_{STU}}, \quad \text{and } M_B = \frac{1}{2}\left[B_{STL} - B_{STU}\right]$$

Note that Δ_{CL} and Δ_{CU} represent the delta of the call option calculated from the lower and middle and the upper and middle nodes of the call price tree at $t = 2$. Meanwhile C_L, C_M and C_U are the values of the call option in the lower, medium and higher nodes of the call price tree at $t = 2$ and the parameters B_{STL}, B_{STM} and B_{STU} are the corresponding values of the straight bond price. Numerically,

$$\Gamma_C = \left(\frac{1.43830 - 1.43170}{102.1413 - 102.1273} - \frac{1.43170 - 1.42508}{102.1273 - 102.1132}\right) \Big/$$

$$\left(\frac{1}{2}\left[102.1413 - 102.1132\right]\right)$$

$$= \frac{0.471429 - 0.469504}{0.01405} = \frac{0.001925}{0.01405} = 0.137011$$

From the measure of gamma we can calculate the second derivative of the call feature SD_C.

$$SD_C = \left[\Gamma_C D_{ST}^* + \Delta_C SD_{ST}^*\right]\frac{B_{ST}}{C}$$

$$= \left[(0.137011)(2.241) + (0.19676)(650.0286)\right]\frac{102.6339}{1.33264}$$

$$= 9850.5573$$

As you can see, the embedded call option is *much* more convex than the underlying straight bond as its second derivative is much higher. This is typical, options are *much* more convex than straight bonds. That is why most conventional hedge ratios that are applied to straight bonds ignore convexity. It simply is not important enough to warrant much attention in a price hedging context.

Now we can work out the second derivative of the callable bond SD_{CB} from which we can calculate its convexity. The second derivative of the callable bond SD_{CB} is a price-weighted average of its component securities' second derivatives.

$$
\begin{aligned}
SD_{CB} &= \frac{B_{ST}}{B_{CB}}SD_{ST} - \frac{C}{B_{CB}}SD_C \\
&= \frac{102.6339}{101.30126}(650.0286) - \frac{1.33264}{101.30126}(9850.5573) \\
&= 658.580 - 129.586 \\
&= 528.994
\end{aligned}
$$

Note that since our measures of the second derivative of the straight bond SD_{ST} and the call feature SD_C are annual measures then the above measure of the second derivative of the callable bond SD_{CB} is an annual measure. We divide the above by the callable bond price to obtain the convexity of the callable bond as 5.222.

Note that at lower interest rates, the convexity of the callable bond can turn negative, as the value of the call will rise giving more 'weight' to the negative component of the callable bond's convexity.

12.4 Sinking fund bonds

It is a common misconception that a sinking fund is some corporate bank account where money accumulates.[4] This is not the case. Instead, a sinking fund is the commitment to repurchase a portion of the bond issue periodically during the life of the bond. This means that at maturity, only a portion, say 50% of the original issue size, remains to be repaid.

This helps reduce the crisis at maturity problem. To see this consider a 10-year triple B bond issue of £100 million. How easy will it be to roll over this bond issue in 10 years' time? It is impossible to tell. So the bond includes a clause that 5% of the bond's principal (£5 million) will be repaid each year. This means that at the end of 10 years, only £55 million will be outstanding. It would be easier

[4] Actually this used to be the case but during the 1930s several corporations could not resist the temptation to use the sinking fund account for corporate purposes. Ever since bondholders demanded repayment thereby ensuring that the sinking fund is indeed used to retire some portion of the sinking fund bond. See Dunn and Spatt (1984).

to reissue £55 million rather than £100 million of triple B bonds in 10 years' time, no matter what the economic conditions turn out to be. Therefore this clause helps alleviate the crisis at maturity problem. In addition, by requiring weaker corporations to repay part of the debt periodically, the sinking fund serves as a test of the financial condition of the corporation thereby serving as an early warning mechanism of potential financial distress.

There are two ways to sink a bond. The sinking fund clause may say that the bond can be sunk by lottery only at a price of par, or by a choice of lottery or open market purchase. Since all registered bonds have unique serial numbers, it is a simple matter to sink a bond by lottery. Take the £100 million triple B sinking fund bond introduced above. All serial numbers representing all the remaining bonds of the issue are placed in a pool and 5000 numbers, each one corresponding to a particular bond of £1000 principal, are randomly drawn. All selected bonds are now 'sunk'. The registered owners will receive a check for £1000 plus accrued interest along with a notification that the bond is sunk and will receive no further interest or principal payments.

To sink by open market purchase is even simpler; the corporation simply enters the market to buy up £5 million face value of its bonds paying whatever price is available in the secondary market. The bonds are then cancelled.

The lottery only system seems fairer to bondholders than the lottery or open market purchase system. In the lottery only system, if yields were low so the bond is priced above par, bonds would be sunk at par. Bondholders would lose in this instance. However, if yields were high so the bond is priced below par, bonds would still be sunk at par. Bondholders would gain in this instance. Given that we really cannot expect to know whether yields will be higher or lower than the coupon rate in the future, it seems fair that bondholders have more or less an equal chance to gain or lose from the sinking fund provision.

Contrast this now with the choice of sink by lottery or open market purchase. Put yourself in the position of a treasury officer of the corporation that sold the bond. If yields are high, the bond is priced below par, so would you sink by lottery and pay par or sink by open market purchase and pay less than par for the firm's debt? Similarly, if yields are low, and the bond is priced above par, would you sink by lottery and pay par or sink by open market purchase and pay more than par for the firm's debt? Obviously you would take advantage of the situation by taking the least costly option. Of course, this means that bondholders will never gain anything from the sinking fund. When interest rates are low and the bond is priced above par they lose because the bonds would be bought at par through lottery. When interest rates are high they will not gain, as the bond will be bought at fair market value that is below par because the bonds would be sunk by open market purchase. So why do bondholders agree to the sink by lottery or open market purchase sinking fund, particularly when both types of sinking funds have the advantage of reducing the crisis at maturity problem?

The key to this puzzle is to realize that sinking fund bonds are subject to credit risk, and the credit risk of a bond may change. When a triple B bond downgrades to double B the obvious question in bond investors' minds is whether the bond will continue to downgrade and eventually default. Different bond investors would have different beliefs. By allowing for open market purchase, the most pessimistic bond investors have the ability to sell their bond investment. That is, after downgrade the bond is likely to be priced below par, so the corporation will be in the market to satisfy the sinking fund requirement. This creates an artificial demand for the bonds enabling the more pessimistic bondholders to voluntarily sell their holdings of the downgraded bonds.

But the artificial demand created by the sink by lottery or open market purchase sinking fund has another consequence, the accumulation game. Suppose a sinking fund bond is priced below par because yields are high rather than bond downgrade. Remember that lower rated corporate bonds are not very liquid, many investors hold these bonds to maturity rather than actively trade them. This means only a portion, sometimes only a small portion, of the total bond issue is held by investors willing to trade their bonds. Therefore it is possible for an accumulator to 'corner the market' in this bond by buying up all the actively traded sinking fund bonds of this issue, say at a price of £90. Then they sit by the phone. The corporation enters the market seeking to buy the bond below par to satisfy the sinking fund requirement at £90. At first, they cannot find anybody to sell the bonds to them. Eventually they find the accumulator that earlier bought all the actively traded bonds. Knowing that they must buy, the accumulator suggests a price of £96. The corporation now really has no choice, for if they refuse to buy at £96, they must sink by lottery and pay £100.[5] As you can see, this kind of activity, although not illegal, will make you unpopular with the victim corporation, so do not plan to apply for a job or underwrite an issue from this corporation in the future if you plan on playing the accumulation game.

---

[5] Some of you may notice that this is actually a variation of the 'delivery squeeze' that is a concern in the bond futures market.

12.4.1 Valuing a sinking fund bond: the sink by lottery only case

When the sinking fund operates by sink by lottery only the corporation retains no option to choose how to sink the bond. The total value of the sinking fund issue is the same as the total value of a serial bond issue where the corporation issues tranches of bonds that mature sequentially at future dates in time. The value of a bond that is sunk by lottery only can be valued as unit investment in a portfolio of serial bonds where a portion of each $100 face value bond is sunk at each sinking fund date. This happens because the lottery system is completely random and so no one single bond is more or less likely to be sunk than another.

For example, imagine our 8% semi-annual coupon pay 2.5-year corporate bond is a sink by lottery only sinking fund bond where 20% of the bond is repaid at the end of each year. Therefore only 60% of the bond issue remains to be repaid at maturity in 2.5 years' time. Since the lottery is fair each bond is equally likely to be sunk, so we can model the value of an individual bond as a 'representative' bond. That is, we value a $100 face value bond where the structure of future principal payments is assumed to be $20 at the end of the first year at $t = 2$, $20 at the end of the second year at $t = 4$ and $60 at maturity at the end of 2.5 years at $t = 5$. The coupon payments are correspondingly reduced. We then apply our usual backward solution procedure to value the sinking fund bond. As shown in DSB02.xls, spreadsheet 'Sink' and reported in Table 12.5 the value of this bond is $102.103.

Table 12.5 Sink by lottery only 8% coupon 2.5-year sinking fund bond

	C	D	E	F	G	H
19	Coupon	8				
20	Time	0	1	2	3	4
21	S. F. %	0	0	0.2	0	0.4
22						60.4607
23					81.0259	60.4625
24				81.546	81.0307	60.4642
25			102.077	81.5567	81.0355	60.4659
26		102.10284	102.107	81.5674	81.0403	60.4677

We find that the value of the sinking fund bond, priced at $102.103, is lower than the corresponding straight bond of Table 12.2 that is priced at $102.6339. This happens because principal repayments made through the sinking fund are repaid at par on dates when the corresponding straight bond is priced above par. Therefore in this instance the sinking fund bond investor suffers a loss when the bond is sunk so the sinking fund bond is less valuable than the corresponding straight bond.

Although the backward solution procedure does obtain the correct price for the lottery only sinking fund bond, the results in later time steps after a sinking fund payment has been made can be somewhat misleading. We are used to pricing bonds in terms of a hypothetical $100 par value so we can interpret the market value as a percentage relative to its face value, so a price of $81.0403 in interest rate state $r_c(3,0)$ might be misinterpreted as a value of 81.0403% of par. This is incorrect since at this point only 80% of the bond remains outstanding, as 20% of the bond has been repaid at par. To correct this misleading interpretation, we divide the values at all nodes of the bond price tree by the percentage of par of the amount actually outstanding at that date to convert all the prices in terms of $100 face value. The results are reported in DSB02.xls, spreadsheet 'Sink' in cell block C28 to H35 and are repeated in Table 12.6.

Table 12.6   Price of representative sinking fund bond in terms of $100 par value

	C	D	E	F	G	H
28	Coupon	8				
29	Time	0	1	2	3	4
30	S. F. %	0	0	0.2	0	0.4
31						100.768
32					101.282	100.771
33				101.933	101.288	100.774
34			102.077	101.946	101.294	100.777
35		102.10284	102.107	101.959	101.300	100.779

The above analysis is correct because there are no opportunities for accumulators to squeeze extra value from the corporation. For example, if the bond is priced below par at the date of a sinking fund payment, say 80, and the bond could be sunk at market value then it is possible that an individual investor may be able to extract a higher price by playing the accumulation game as described in section 12.4. Then the sinking fund bond of the accumulator would have a value greater than the corresponding 'representative bond'. This is not the case here because the bond is sink by lottery only so there are no opportunities for accumulators to squeeze extra value from the bond. Hence it is correct to value a sink by lottery only bond by using the representative bond approach as we have done here.

12.4.2 Sink by lottery or sink by open market purchase

In contrast with the sink by lottery only sinking fund bond, the issuer obtains a valuable option when given the choice to sink by lottery or sink by open market purchase. This choice of how to call is a European call option. Specifically the exercise price is par. When the bond is above par on the sinking fund date the option is in the money and the issuer will sink by lottery at par. When the bond is priced below par the option is out of the money and the issuer pays (in the absence of accumulation) fair market value for the bonds sunk. The option is European since the issuer can only exercise the option on the date of the sinking fund payment. Finally, since there is typically a sequence of sinking fund payments to be made throughout the life of the bond the sink by lottery or sink by open market purchase sinking fund option is a sequence of European call options where each particular call expires on the date of a particular sinking fund payment.

Since we have no reason to expect that any particular bond is more likely to be sunk by lottery than any other we can value the sequence of European call options implied by the sink by lottery or sink by open market purchase using the representative bond approach employed earlier to value the sink by lottery only sink fund bond. For example, imagine that 20% of the 8% semi-annual coupon pay 2.5-year bond of section 11.5.1 can be sunk by a choice of sink by lottery or sink by open market purchase at the end of the first year and another 20% is sunk at the end of the second year leaving only 60% of the issue to be repaid at maturity. Therefore there is a 20% chance that a particular bond may be sunk at the end of the first year and a 20% chance that the bond may be sunk at the end of the second year. In effect this means that the issuer holds one fifth of an option to call (sink) the bond at par at each of these two dates. The value of the sinking fund bond is found as the value of a hypothetical straight bond less the value of one fifth of the value of two call options, one maturing in two periods' and another maturing in four periods' time. Mathematically this statement is as follows.

$$B_{SF} = B_{ST} - (1/5)C_2 - (1/5)C_4 \qquad (12.6)$$

We need to value the two period European call C_2 and the four period European call C_4 separately. We follow the same steps in valuing the European call embedded in the terms of the sinking fund as we followed in valuing caps and floors in Chapter 10. That is, we first find the in the money or intrinsic values at the date of maturity of the European option. Then we present value the intrinsic values. We have two methods to present value the intrinsic values, either use backward induction by solving backwards, discounting period by period using the 50/50 rule, or use forward induction by multiplying the intrinsic values by the corresponding corporate state security price. We use the corporate discount factor tree in the backward induction methods and the corporate state security tree in the forward induction methods. We have this choice because we employ Duffie and Singleton rather than Jarrow and Turnbull to model the credit risky interest rate process. Recall that Duffie and Singleton provides a convenient method to generate a corporate interest rate (and the corresponding discount factor) tree, so we can, if we choose, employ backward induction methods. While it is possible to generate the same information from Jarrow and Turnbull, it is awkward to do so.

To illustrate these points we first value the four period call option using backward induction and then value the two period and four period European call options using forward induction. Common to both methods, we need to generate the intrinsic values for both options at their respective maturity dates. This information is contained in DSB02.xls spreadsheet 'Sink' cell block C37 to H45 and is reported in Table 12.7.

Note that these intrinsic values are the difference between the value of the underlying straight bond as reported in Table 12.2 and the exercise price of $100. We multiply this difference by 20% because we have no reason to suspect that one bond is more likely to be sunk than another.

Table 12.7 European intrinsic values for two and four period sinking fund payments

	C	D	E	F	G	H
37	Lottery and Purchase Sinking Fund Bond-Intrinsic Values					
38	Coupon	8	Exercise	100		
39	Time	0	1	2	3	4
40	S. F. %	0	0	0.2	0	0.2
41						0.15358
42					0	0.15416
43				0.42265	0	0.15474
44			0	0.42546	0	0.15532
45		0	0	0.42827	0	0.15589

We now apply the backward induction procedure to the intrinsic values reported in column H of Table 12.7 to find the value of the European call option implied by the choice to sink by lottery or open market purchase at the end of the fourth time period. We use the Duffie and Singleton discount factors as reported in Table 12.1 along with the 50/50 rule according to the backward solution procedure first explained in section 4.2. The results are contained in workbook DSB02.xls spreadsheet 'Sink' in cell block D47 to H52 and reported in Table 12.8.

Table 12.8 Value of the four period European call using backward induction

	D	E	F	G	H
47	Four Period Sinking fund call option				
48					0.153577
49				0.149019	0.154157
50			0.144548	0.149587	0.154736
51		0.140061	0.145108	0.150153	0.155315
52	0.13506797	0.14063	0.145667	0.15072	0.155894

We now find the value of the four and two period European call option using forward induction. We multiply the European payoffs by their corresponding corporate state security prices. Recall that these state security prices adjust promised payments for credit risk, interest rate risk and the time value of money to find the present value of each promised payment. Adding the products for each European option we find the value of the option. The results of this exercise are reported in Table 12.9.

Table 12.9 Value of the four and two period European call using forward induction

	C	D	E	F	G	H	I
54		Two Period Call			Four Period Call		
55	State	State Price	Payoff	Product	State Price	Payoff	Product
56	S(2,2)	0.2326794	0.422647	0.098341			
57	S(2,1)	0.46540495	0.42546	0.198011			
58	S(2,0)	0.23272555	0.428268	0.099669			
59	S(4,4)				0.054543	0.153577	0.00837657
60	S(4,3)				0.218198	0.154157	0.0336367
61	S(4,2)				0.327335	0.154736	0.05065055
62	S(4,1)				0.218248	0.155315	0.03389728
63	S(4,0)				0.054568	0.155894	0.00850686
64	Value			0.396021			0.13506797

Notice that the value of the four period European call found by backward induction is precisely the same as the value obtained by forward induction. The values are the same because as we calibrate any term structure consistent model, Duffie and Singleton in this case, the structure of pure interest rates and corporate interest rates is calibrated to ensure that replicating portfolios of state security and corporate state security prices agree with an input sovereign and corporate term structure. Therefore the structure of interest rates and their corresponding discount factor trees are forced to agree with their respective state security trees as they are all forced to agree with their respective input yield curves. Therefore these European call option prices are as accurate as our estimate of the sovereign and corporate yield curves as well as the validity of the term structure consistent model.

The final step is to value the sink by lottery or sink by open market purchase sinking fund bond. We use (12.6) to find that the value of the sinking fund bond is $102.1028. Specifically,

$$B_{SF} = B_S - (1/5)C_2 = (1/5)C_4 = 102.6339 - (0.3960)$$
$$- (0.1351) = \$102.1028$$

12.5 Exercises

Question 1
Consider the following interest rate tree.

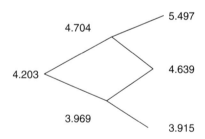

Consider a coupon bond with maturity $n = 3$, coupon rate $c = 0.05$, and maturity value $M = 100$. Assume the bond is callable, beginning today $(T = 0)$ at $X = 101$, falling to 100.5 at $T = 1$, and to 100 at $T = 2$, remaining at 100 from then on.
Required:

(a) Calculate the market value of the implied option.
(b) Calculate today's price of the callable bond.
(c) Calculate the option adjusted yield.
(d) You observe two bonds, one callable, the other straight, both having the same maturity and credit rating and both are priced

at par. The callable bond has a higher yield since it has a higher coupon. How can you determine if the callable bond is correctly priced relative to the straight bond?

Question 2
How do accumulators make money?

Question 3
Some market practitioners believe that calculating the 'yield to call' and the 'yield to maturity' brackets the true yield of a callable bond. Is this true? Explain why or why not.

Question 4
Consider the following interest rate tree that has been calibrated to the sovereign yield curve. A one-year time step is used.

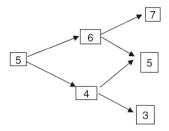

Required

(a) What is the value today of a 5% annual coupon pay three-year *non-callable* sovereign bond?
(b) What is the value of a two-year European call option on this coupon bond, where the exercise price is 100?
(c) What is the value of a 5% annual coupon pay three-year *callable* sovereign bond that can be called at 100 at any time after one year.
(d) The above interest rate tree was generated by Ho and Lee (1986) where volatility was constant at 1% and there is no mean reversion in interest rates. Compared to your answer in (c) above, *briefly* discuss what may happen to the callable bond price if:
    (i) Interest rate volatility was decreasing from 1%.
    (ii) Interest rates were revering to the mean of 6%.

Answers to selected problems

Chapter 1

Question 1

(a) Last coupon was on August 15. Therefore August has 15 days of interest, September 30, October 30, November 30 and 16 days of interest in December for a total of 121 days' interest. Therefore $121/180 \times €4 = €2.689$.

(b) Last coupon was on August 15. Therefore August has 16 days of interest, September 30, October 31, November 30 and 16 days of interest in December for a total of 123 days' interest. There are 184 calendar days in the coupon period August 15, 2002 to February 15, 2003. Therefore $123/184 \times €4 = €2.674$.

Question 3

Minimum current ratio: refers to the accounting ratio of current assets divided by current liabilities. Current assets are cash and near-cash items such as accounts receivable (sales sold on credit, to be collected within, say, 30 days) and inventory. Current liabilities are short-term borrowing to be paid within one year, and accounts payable (items that you have bought on credit and must pay within, say, 30 days). Therefore a current ratio of two has the interpretation of being a measure of liquidity representing the amount of cash and near-cash on hand available to pay short-term liabilities as they come due. A current ratio of two means that for every £1 a firm owes short term, £2 of cash and near-cash are available to pay it.

You would desire a high current ratio since firms with high current ratios are more liquid and are less likely to fall into financial distress because they cannot pay liabilities (like coupon payments) as they come due.

Seniority clause: a bond covenant that specifies that the senior bond stands in line ahead of junior and subordinated debt in the event of bankruptcy. If the absolute priority rule holds true, then if bankruptcy were to occur, the senior claims would receive 100% of what they are owed before the junior, subordinated and unsecured debt claims receive anything.

Obviously bondholders like seniority clauses as it enhances recoveries in the event of default. Even if the absolute priority rule is not applied in the case of reorganization rather than bankruptcy, it still remains true that senior bonds have a stronger claim and will usually recover more than junior claims.

Event risk covenant: this is a relatively new covenant term included to protect the debt claims in the case of a catastrophic event, such as the destruction of a major asset of the corporation, or a takeover bid. Sometimes the covenant requires immediate repayment of the claim if a takeover bid is successful (sometimes called a poison pill), other times it requires that the coupon rate on the bond must be adjusted to reset the value of the bond to par. In the first case, the event risk covenant allows the investor to get out of the bond if the event radically alters the credit risk of the existing claim. In the second, the bondholder still stays with the now more credit risky claim, but at least they receive compensation for the additional risk.

Obviously bondholders desire these covenants since they can protect them from unforeseen circumstances that alter the credit risk of their claim.

Chapter 2

Question 1
(a) The forward rates are:

Maturity	Rate (%)
$_0f_{0.5} = {_0}R_{0.5}$	3.00
$_{0.5}f_1$	3.30
$_1f_{1.5}$	3.45
$_{1.5}f_2$	3.85
$_2f_{2.5}$	4.40
$_{2.5}f_3$	6.02

Notice that the six-month forward rate today is the six-month spot rate. To obtain the six-month forward rate that will evolve in six months' time we use the following formula.

$$
\begin{aligned}
{}_Sf_L &= \left[\left(\frac{(1+{}_0R_n)^L}{(1+{}_0R_S)^S}\right)^{1/(L-S)} - 1\right] \\[2mm]
&= \left[\left(\frac{(1+{}_0R_1)^1}{(1+{}_0R_{0.5})^{0.5}}\right)^{1/(1-0.5)} - 1\right] \\[2mm]
&= \left[\left(\frac{(1+0.0315)^1}{(1+0.03)^{0.5}}\right)^{1/(1-0.5)} - 1\right] = 3.30\%
\end{aligned}
$$

As another example, consider the six-month forward rate due in two years, ${}_2f_{2.5}$.

$$
\begin{aligned}
{}_Sf_L &= \left[\left(\frac{(1+{}_0R_{2.5})^{2.5}}{(1+{}_0R_2)^2}\right)^{1/(2.5-2)} - 1\right] \\[2mm]
&= \left[\left(\frac{(1+0.036)^{2.5}}{(1+0.034)^2}\right)^{1/(2.5-2)} - 1\right] = 4.40\%
\end{aligned}
$$

Continuing in this manner for the remaining observations we obtain the data in the above table.

(b) Only when the risk of holding a long-term bond is the same as the risk of holding a sequence of short-term bonds that add up to the same maturity as the long-term bond. If that is the case then the total expected return from holding a long-term bond must equal the total expected return from investing in the sequence of short-term bonds. To put it in terms of maths, the above sentences are equivalent to saying

$$(1+{}_0R_L)^L = (1+{}_0R_S)^S(1+{}_Sf_L)^L$$

For example, look at the second example illustrated in (a). The six-month forward rate projected in two years' time ${}_2f_{2.5}$ was 4.4%. Given that the two-year and 2.5-year spot rates were 3.4% and 3.6% respectively, the total return of investing in a 2.5-year bond was the same as investing in a two-year bond, letting it mature and then reinvesting in a six-month bond in two years' time. That is

$$(1+0.036)^{2.5} = (1+0.034)^2(1+0.044)^{0.5}$$

$$1.0924 = 1.0924$$

If the risk of investing in long-term bonds was more than the risk of investing in a sequence of short-term bonds, then investors would demand a risk premium for investing in long-term bonds. For example, investors may be worried about preservation of capital since for a given increase in interest rates long-term bonds fall more in price. This means that on average the left-hand side (LHS) of the above equation should be larger. This implies that the forward rate derived from the above expression would be too high, on average the future rates of interest that actually evolve will be smaller than that suggested by the forward rate. Essentially this is the liquidity premium hypothesis.

Similarly, short-term bonds may be considered more risky than long-term bonds and so investors would demand a risk premium for investing in short-term bonds. For example, investors may be worried about preservation of income because upon renewal, the entire proceeds of short-term bonds are reinvested at the prevailing rate that might be lower than expected. In contrast longer-term bonds will continue to earn the fixed coupon rate which is likely to be higher than prevailing coupon rates if interest rates have decreased. If this is the case then investing in short-term bonds is more risky and so on average the right-hand side (RHS) of the above equation should be larger. This implies that the forward rate derived from the above expression would be too low; on average the future rates of interest that actually evolve will be larger than that suggested by the forward rate. The problem is that what is 'short term' and what is 'long term' depends upon the investor's investment horizon or 'preferred habitat'. Since different investors have different investment horizons (e.g. pension plans tend to prefer to invest long term, commercial banks prefer to invest short term) it is impossible to determine if a particular spot rate, long or short, has a risk premium. Consequently the forward rate would be a biased forecast of future rates of interest but it would be impossible to work out what the degree or direction of this bias may be. Essentially this is the preferred habitat hypothesis.

Question 3

(a) The Fisher effect suggests that nominal rates $_0R_N$ are related to real rates r and the rate of inflation I in the following way.

$$(1 + {_0R_N}) = (1 + r)(1 + I)$$

If inflation is 10%, then the real rate of return on one-year bonds is

$$I = (1 + {_0R_N})/(1 + r) - 1 = (1 + 0.18)/(1 + 0.10) - 1 = 7.27\%$$

(b) You have every right to suspect large promised returns. In this case even if we ignore inflation risk and term premiums (preferred habitat, liquidity) we must consider another source of risk premiums, default risk. Only if we feel the likelihood and consequence of default is compensated by 7.27% would an investment in these bonds be justified.

(c) As in question 1, we use the forward rate formula. According to the term structure, the one-year interest rate one year from now is 21.02% and the four-year rate one year from now is 21.76%.

$$
{}_S f_L = \left[\left(\frac{(1 + {}_0 R_n)^L}{(1 + {}_0 R_S)^S} \right)^{1/(L-S)} - 1 \right] = \left[\left(\frac{(1 + {}_0 R_2)^2}{(1 + {}_0 R_1)^1} \right)^{1/(2-1)} - 1 \right]
$$

$$
= \left[\left(\frac{(1 + 0.195)^2}{(1 + 0.18)^1} \right)^1 - 1 \right] = 21.02\%
$$

$$
\left[\left(\frac{(1 + {}_0 R_5)^5}{(1 + {}_0 R_1)^1} \right)^{1/(5-1)} - 1 \right] = \left[\left(\frac{(1 + 0.21)^5}{(1 + 0.18)^1} \right)^{1/4} - 1 \right] = 21.76\%
$$

Question 5

1(a) All of class A (1500 million) and 47% of class B (1250 million) will be accepted.

1(b) The non-competitive bidders will receive the weighted average of the accepted bidders yield. Specifically,

$$
\frac{1.5}{2.75}(4.67\%) + \frac{1.25}{2.75}(4.68\%) = 4.675\%
$$

1(c) The stop yield is the highest yield necessary to sell the entire issue. In this case the stop yield is 4.68%.

1(d) The tail is the difference between the stop and average yield. It is a measure of the dispersion of the yields received and is considered to be a measure of winner's curse. In this case the tail is tiny, only one half of a basis point ($4.68 - 4.675 = 0.005$).

2(a) The same bids will be accepted.

2(b) The non-competitive bidders will receive, along with all accepted competitive bids, the stop yield of 4.68%.

3. It is tempting to say that the Dutch auction is more expensive than the American auction since in the above example the sovereign must pay 4.68% if the auction was Dutch, but pay on average one

half of a basis point less if the auction was American. This can be incorrect since the behaviour of the competitive bidders will change depending if the auction is American or Dutch. If the auction is American, bidders have to worry about making a bid that is too aggressive, for if they bid for a very high price (low yield) they surely will 'win' the bid. Unfortunately some of their competitors who 'lost' bid at lower but still accepted prices and received higher yields. This problem is called winner's curse and creates caution on behalf of competitive bidders. They will be reluctant to bid aggressively and so may bid at lower prices (and ask for higher yields) than they would otherwise make.

In a Dutch auction, all accepted bids (including all non-competitive bids) receive the stop yield. This reduces winner's curse for if a bidder made a bid that in retrospect was too high they will still receive the higher stop yield. Therefore it is possible that in a Dutch auction the stop yield will be lower than the average yield in the corresponding American auction if the Dutch auction encouraged much more aggressive bidding. Therefore we cannot say that a Dutch auction is in general more expensive than an American auction from the point of view of the sovereign.

Chapter 3

Question 1
When attempting to estimate a sovereign zero coupon yield curve typically we must face three problems.

1. A lack of liquidity. Often prices are 'stale', reflecting a trade that occurred some time ago and therefore not reflective of current market conditions. Alternatively the price is not a firm quote but only an indicator price based on a matrix pricing approach. We question the accuracy of the matrix price (and empirical evidence of Warga (1991) backs this up) not because the matrix algorithm is inaccurate but because the matrix price is only an indicator quote where the firm issuing the matrix price is not punished for inaccurate prices. In any event, inaccurate prices, either because they are stale or only indicator prices, will spoil the accuracy of the resulting estimated sovereign yield curve.

2. The sovereign has no zero coupon bonds outstanding. Even for those sovereigns that do have zeros, typically they are not accurately priced and so are not appropriate for estimating zero coupon yield curves.

3. We need a continuous yield curve so some sort of interpolation scheme is needed. This means we have to choose among spline and parsimonious methods and the various interpolation models included within each category.

The first step in overcoming these problems is to carefully select the data. We need bond prices that reflect interest rate risk only and are as accurate as possible. We reject bonds that contain optionality and other special features (e.g. inflation protection) as the prices of these bonds reflect the special feature as well as interest rate risk. To obtain accurate prices we would like to select bonds that trade frequently. In the US, 'on the run' bonds or the most recently issued bonds at maturities regularly used to issue new bonds are frequently traded but for most sovereigns 'on the run' bonds do not exist as the sovereign does not follow a regular auction cycle in issuing new bonds. Besides even in the US there are only a handful of 'on the run' bonds and typically more bond prices are needed to estimate a sovereign yield curve accurately.

Therefore we apply additional filter rules besides 'eliminate all bonds with optionality and special features'. We would select all bonds that have a minimum amount outstanding, say £1 billion in the hope that with a larger issue size, traders will be active in these issues and more recent prices may result. We may decide to reject all bonds that have been issued more than, say, five years ago because even if they are of a large issue size the issue is so old that most of the bonds have leaked into passive investors' portfolios and so do not trade very often. We may decide to eliminate all bonds outside a price range of, say, £95 to £105 because we may be concerned with tax effects and the reluctance of some investors to incur capital losses (for premium bonds) and capital gains (low or tax exempt investors who do not benefit from the potential low tax rate associated with discount bonds). Of course, applying all these filters may result in a sample size that is too small. In that case one must relax the filter, taking bonds with an issue size of at least, say, £750 million rather than £1 billion.

Once the data is selected we can overcome the second and third problems simultaneously by selecting an appropriate interpolation scheme. Both spline and parsimonious methods view a coupon bond as a portfolio of zeros, each zero being composed of a coupon and/or principal payment, and build the zero coupon yield curve on this basis. This technique, at least for sovereigns not subject to credit risk, is firmly grounded in financial theory being based on the principle of pure arbitrage. The choice between spline and parsimonious methods is difficult to resolve, as empirical work has not been able to declare one method superior to the other. We can say, however, that if the sample size is small, parsimonious methods seem to produce a more accurate zero yield curve. Additionally the natural spline technique is very simple and useful as an illustration of the spline technique but it is too restrictive as it forces the same discount function to apply for the whole yield curve. If spline methods are preferred then one is better off selecting a more flexible spline model such as McCulloch (1975).

Question 3

(a) The yield to maturity is 3%, 3.15%, 3.25%, 3.4%, 3.6% and 4%. If you do not have a financial calculator you can use the Excel yield worksheet function. The syntax is YIELD(settlement,maturity,rate,pr, redemption,frequency,basis). So for the 1.5-year bond we write in Excel = YIELD("30/08/2003", "28/02/2005", 0.04, 101.089, 100, 2,1) = 0.032515.

(b) To find the value of the last three bonds we can use the following closed form solution for the price of a bond. For example, to find the value of 2.5-year bond,

$$B_S = \frac{C}{M}\left[\frac{1 - \left(1 + \frac{y}{M}\right)^{-nM}}{\frac{y}{M}}\right] + \frac{FV}{\left(1 + \frac{y}{M}\right)^{nM}}$$

$$= \frac{10}{2}\left[\frac{1 - \left(1 + \frac{0.036}{2}\right)^{-2.5(2)}}{\frac{0.036}{2}}\right] + \frac{100}{\left(1 + \frac{0.036}{2}\right)^{(2.5)2}}$$

$$= 115.171$$

Alternatively you can use a financial calculator or the Excel price worksheet function. The syntax of this function is PRICE (settlement,maturity,rate,yld,redemption,frequency,basis) so for the 2.5-year bond we write in Excel = PRICE("30/08/2003", "28/02/2006", 0.1,0.036,100,2,1) = 115.1865. Notice the very slight difference in price when using Excel as the price function. Excel gives the clean price using the precisely correct day count convention.

The prices of the last three bonds are €103.068, €115.171 and €105.601.

(c) To find the zero coupon yields we view a bond as if it were a portfolio of zero coupon bonds, each one representing the payment of a coupon or the principal. For the six-month bond, there is only one payment remaining so the YTM is the zero coupon yield. Therefore we first look at the one-year bond. The value of the one-year bond is then represented as

$$B_1 = C_1 d_1 + (C_2 + FV)d_2$$

Recall from the text that d_1 represents today's value of a €1 payment received in six months' time. Since we know d_1 is one-hundredth of the six-month bond's price, it is 0.98522. We also know that C_1 and C_2 are €4 and that FV is €100, so there is only one unknown d_2. Since we have one equation and one unknown, we can solve for the unknown.

$$d_2 = \frac{B_S - C_1 d_1}{C_2 + FV} = \frac{104.738 - (4)0.98522}{4 + 100} = 0.96920$$

Now we apply the bond equivalent yield formula where d_2 is our PV, and €1 is the FV since in one year's time the €1 face value discount factor will pay off €1 in one year's time.

$$BEY = \left(\left[\frac{FV}{PV} \right]^{1/(n \times m)} - 1 \right) \times m$$

$$= \left(\left[\frac{1}{0.9692} \right]^{1/(1 \times 2)} - 1 \right) \times 2 = 3.15\%$$

Now that we know the value of d_2 we can find the value of d_3 (and the 1.5-year zero coupon yield) by continuing to bootstrap. Specifically

$$B_3 = C_1 d_1 + C_2 d_2 + (C_3 + FV)d_3$$

So

$$d_3 = \frac{B_S - C_1 d_1 - C_2 d_2}{C_3 + FV}$$

$$= \frac{101.089 - (2)0.98522 - (2)0.96920}{2 + 100} = 0.95275$$

And finally,

$$BEY = \left(\left[\frac{FV}{PV} \right]^{1/(n \times m)} - 1 \right) \times m$$

$$= \left(\left[\frac{1}{0.95275} \right]^{1/(1.5 \times 2)} - 1 \right) \times 2 = 3.25\%$$

We can continue in this numerical two-step procedure (bootstrap) because at the end of the previous round we find the value of an additional discount factor, so that in the next round there is only one more discount factor we need to know. Then viewing the bond as the sum of the value of the individual zero coupon payments, there is only one unknown, the longest maturity discount factor that we can solve for.

(d) The bootstrap method must be correct as otherwise you will be able to pure arbitrage. That is, you will be able to make money yet take on no risk or invest any of your own wealth. In other words, you will make money for free. As an illustration, consider the one-year 8% semi-annual coupon bond priced at €104.738 in (c). This price is consistent with a yield to maturity of 3.25% and is consistent with pricing the bond as a portfolio of zeros with discount factors $d_1 = €0.98522$ and $d_2 = €0.9692$. Specifically,

$$B_1 = C_1 d_1 + (C_2 + FV)d_2$$
$$= 4(0.98522) + (104)(0.9692) = 104.738$$

$$B_S = \frac{8}{2} \left[\frac{1 - \left(1 + \frac{0.0315}{2}\right)^{-1(2)}}{\frac{0.0315}{2}} \right] + \frac{100}{\left(1 + \frac{0.0315}{2}\right)^{1(2)}}$$

$$= 104.738 \tag{1}$$

Now supposing somebody made a mistake and offers the bond for sale at £104. This is too cheap so you buy it. You then finance the purchase by coupon stripping, selling the coupons separately to other investors at the per Euro price of €0.98522 for the first coupon (€3.94 in total for the first €4 coupon) and €0.9692 for the final coupon and principal repayment (€100.797 in total for the last coupon and principal repayment). This means you buy at €104 and sell the bond at €104.738, netting €0.738 in the process. Rather than costing you money, this strategy pays you.

What have you done to deserve this money? Nothing! You would expect that if a position pays you money, you should be earning it by taking on risk. In this case, however, you have no risk. Whenever you have to pay off one of the zeros, the underlying coupon bond that you hold long will pay the necessary amount, the €4 coupon payment will be paid in six months just when you need to pay off the first zero coupon bond that you have sold, and the €104 final coupon and principal repayment in one year's time just when the final zero coupon payment comes due. As there is no risk, and you invest none of your own wealth in the process and yet you are paid money, you will recognize that this opportunity offers you free money. No matter how risk adverse you are you will eagerly buy up the coupon bond and sell the coupons by coupon stripping. As you do so the price of the coupon bond will be bid up and you will saturate the market with zeros driving their prices down. You will continue to arbitrage until the price of the coupon bond equals the value of the bond as if it were a portfolio of zeros as priced by discount factors found through the bootstrap method. Through your own actions (and not depending on any one else) the price of the coupon bond and the price of the coupon bond as if it were a portfolio of zeros must agree.

By the way, in several bond markets, the US, the UK and Spain come immediately to mind, at least some market participants are permitted to coupon strip, so the above arbitrage strategy is not hypothetical. Also, if the coupon bond price was above the zero coupon bond portfolio price, say €106 in our example, then you do the reverse and reverse coupon strip. That is, buy up the zeros, form the coupon bond and sell the reformed coupon bond at the higher price.

Question 5
We reject the natural spline as the forward curve plunges at the long end thereby revealing that the spot curve has a problem. Meanwhile the Nelson and Siegel estimated spot and forward curves are believable.

Chapter 4

Question 1
Using backward induction the value of the bond is

Bond price tree (6% 5 period bond)

Coupon = 6					98.56459
				98.11611	99.51691
			98.60792	100.00229	100.48780
		100.02190	101.43718	101.94394	101.47783
	102.36724	103.83094	104.37793	103.94326	102.48756

Mechanically we start at maturity and solve backwards.

$$B(4,4) = \frac{0.5B(5,5) + 0.5B(5,4) + C}{1 + r(4,4)/2}$$

$$= \frac{0.5(100) + 0.5(100) + 3}{1 + 0.09/2} = 98.56459$$

Similarly we find the values of $B(4,3), B(4,2) \ldots B(4,0)$.

For $B(3,3)$

$$B(3,3) = \frac{0.5B(4,4) + 0.5B(4,3) + C}{1 + r(3,3)/2}$$

$$= \frac{0.5(98.56459) + 0.5(99.51691) + 3}{1 + 0.08/2} = 98.11611$$

Similarly we find $B(3,2)$, $B(3,1)$ and $B(3,0)$. We use these results to find $B(2,2)$, $B(2,1)$ and $B(2,0)$ and so on. Finally the value of the bond today at $B(0,0)$ is

$$B(0,0) = \frac{0.5B(1,1) + 0.5B(1,0) + C}{1 + r(0,0)/2}$$

$$= \frac{0.5(100.02190) + 0.5(103.83094) + 3}{1 + 0.05/2} = 102.36724$$

Question 3

(a) The interest rate tree is simply

$T = 0$	$T = 1$
	6%
4%	2%

The corresponding discount factors are

$T = 0$	$T = 1$
	0.943396
0.961538	0.980392

Therefore the state security price tree is

$T = 0$	$T = 1$	$T = 2$
		0.226778
	0.480769	0.462449
1	0.480769	0.235671

The replicating portfolios are the sum of the columns of state security prices, the yield of which are the zero coupon yields.

Date	$T = 1$	$T = 2$
Zero coupon bond price	0.961538	0.924898
Yield	$_0r_2 = \left[\dfrac{1}{0.924898}\right]^{1/2} - 1$	3.9808%

Alternatively

$$\left(\frac{1}{1+_0r_1}\times 0.5\left[\left(\frac{1}{1+_0r_2}\right)^u+\left(\frac{1}{1+_0r_2}\right)^d\right]\right)^{-1/2}-1$$

$$=\left(0.961538\times 0.5[0.943396+0.980393]\right)^{-0.5}-1$$

(b) The option payoff structure is

$T=0$	$T=1$
	0
0	0.020392

Therefore the value of the portfolio in one period's time is

Portfolio replicating $T=1$(up):   Portfolio replicating $T=1$ (down):
$F_{0.5}+0.943396F_1=0$ $F_{0.5}+0.980392F_1=0.020392$

Therefore $F_{0.5}=-0.519995$ and $F_1=0.551195$.

(c) Therefore the value of the portfolio today is

$$B_{0.5}F_{0.5}+B_1F_1=-0.961538(0.519995)+0.924898(0.551195)$$

$$=0.009804$$

(d) Yes. Since the replicating portfolio is composed of assets priced in the market by risk adverse investors, the replicating portfolio price contains a risk premium. Since the price of the replicating portfolio must be the price of the derivative, the derivative price also includes a risk premium. The replicating portfolio price must be the price of the derivative security as otherwise the risk adverse investor can conduct pure arbitrage and make money using none of their own wealth and taking no risk. For example, let's say the above call option was trading for $0.01. The investor would short the derivative, gaining $100\,000\times 0.01=\$1000$. Then they would buy the replicating portfolio costing them $\$100\,000(-0.9615381\times 0.519995+0.924898\times 0.551195)=980.4$. This leaves net cash inflow of $\$19.60(1000-980.4)$. If interest rates were to rise to 6% next period, the short call is zero, and the replicating portfolio is also worth zero $\{\$100\,000\times(-\$1\times 0.519995+0.943396\times 0.551195)\}$. If interest rates fall to 2% next period, the short call costs $\$100\,000\times 0.020302=\$2039.2$ but the replicating portfolio held long is worth $\$2039.2\{100\,000\times(-1\times 0.519995+0.980392\times 0.551195)\}$. Hence in all future states of nature the investor suffers no gain or loss, so they keep the initial cash inflow of $19.60.

In other words, they invest none of their own money and take no risk yet receive payment of $19.60 for doing so. Given this opportunity, investors would eagerly short the call option, thereby driving the price down, and buy the replicating portfolio, driving its price up until the pure arbitrage opportunity disappears. Notice that the investor does not depend upon anyone else to do this; they will do it on their own. Therefore the price we receive from the replicating portfolio must be correct, as otherwise investors would exploit the discrepancy and force it to hold true.

Chapter 5

Question 1

All three models are one factor term structure consistent models. They are one factor models in the sense that they attempt to model the term structure of interest rates through the evolution of the short rate only (the single factor). They are term structure consistent models because all are adjusted or fine tuned to agree with an input estimate of the current sovereign term structure of interest rates.

The ideal one factor term structure consistent model would have four characteristics. They would incorporate information from the term structure of interest rates, would not generate negative interest rates, would incorporate mean reversion (central tendency) and incorporate a volatility term structure. Moreover the ideal model would incorporate mean reversion and a volatility term structure independently. All three-candidate term structure consistent models incorporate information from the existing term structure of interest rates via calibration. This means that to the extent that the term structure of interest rates is driven by risk aversion then so too are the interest rate trees, and the resulting prices of interest rate derivatives derived from using these trees.

Ho and Lee, however, fails the last three characteristics as it allows for negative interest rates and does not incorporate mean reversion and includes constant volatility rather than a term structure of volatility. Negative interest rates are particularly worrying since this would imply that future value is greater than present value, a reversal of all that we have learned in finance and obviously a ridiculous result. Without mean reversion, the model assigns too much probability mass for extremes in the interest rate trees. All else equal this would lead to derivative prices that are too high. However, all is not equal since the model also assumes constant volatility when we know volatility is not constant. To the extent that volatility is too low (high) derivative prices will be too low (high). With so many flaws it is difficult to make any judgement concerning the direction of the biases in Ho and Lee and the user is well advised to avoid this model.

Black Derman and Toy is somewhat better as it does prevent negative interest rates and it does incorporate a term structure of volatility. Specifically the model is double calibrated, to the existing term structure of interest rates and the existing term structure of volatility. Moreover some unknown amount of mean reversion is incorporated as well because when we input a non-flat volatility curve we are implicitly incorporating a degree of mean reversion. The major flaw, however, is that the model does not allow for control of the degree of mean reversion as this is implied by the input volatility curve. We know that there is a relationship that to the extent that we underestimate mean reversion via our selection of the input volatility curve (or errors in measurement of the volatility curve) we overestimate future volatility and future derivative prices. One may argue, however, that if one can detect the direction of this bias in derivative prices obtained by the model then one can still use the model by obtaining an approximate price, the basis of which will be used to obtain the trade price as the trader negotiates with counterparties.

Technically Black and Karasinski satisfies all four criteria. In particular it allows for control in incorporating mean reversion. It does this by varying the size of the time step in the interest rate trees thereby adding an extra degree of freedom. However, this model is awkward to use as it results in a non-recombining tree. In other words, instead of $N+1$ possible interest rates at time $T = N$, there are 2^N possible interest rates. When valuing American options this can be a serious computational disadvantage since in order to value American options one needs to evaluate the payoff at all interest rate nodes of the tree. To all intents and purposes one will have to retreat to Monte Carlo type methods to value American options where one hopes that the optimal stopping rule used to evaluate each path of the simulation is in fact optimal.

Question 3
The bond is worth $112.547624. The detailed answer to this question is contained in BDTB02 exercise.

Question 5
(a) To find the two period volatility we must first find the value of a three period (three-year) zero and then calculate the yield on this zero next period should interest rates rise Y_u or fall Y_d. Then apply (5.10) using Y_u and Y_d in place of $r(n,1)$ and $r(n,0)$ in (5.10). This

obtains the two-year volatility since one year later, the three-year zero is a two-year zero and the volatility implied by the (now) two-year up and down yield is the two-year volatility.

The price of the three period zero is $0.87877.

			1
		0.94789	1
	0.90902	0.95567	1
0.87877	0.92239	0.96232	1

That is

$d(2,2) = 1/(1 + r(2,2)) = 1/(1.05497) = 0.94789$ and similarly for $d(2,1)$ and $d(2,0)$. $d(1,1) = 0.5\{d(2,2) + d(2,1)\}/(1 + r(1,1)) = d(1,1) = 0.5\{0.94789 + 0.95567\}/(1.04704) = 0.90902$ and similarly for $d(1,0)$, so $d(0,0) = 0.5\{d(1,1)+d(1,0)\}/(1+r(0,0)) = d(0,0) = 0.5\{0.90902 + 0.92239\}/(1.04203) = 0.87877$

The *BEY* yield implied by $d(1,1)$ and $d(1,0)$ (see Chapter 3, section 3.3.2) is

$$TR^d = \left[\frac{FV}{PV}\right] = \left[\frac{1}{0.92239}\right] = 1.08414$$

$$TR^U = \left[\frac{FV}{PV}\right] = \left[\frac{1}{0.90902}\right] = 1.10009$$

$$BEY^U = \left([TR]^{1/(NM)} - 1\right)M = \left([1.10009]^{1/(2\times1)} - 1\right)1 = 4.885\%$$

$$BEY^d = \left([TR]^{1/(NM)} - 1\right)M = \left([1.08414]^{1/(2\times1)} - 1\right)1 = 4.122\%$$

Now we apply (5.10).

$$Local\ vol(t) = d(t)\left[Ln\left(\frac{r(n,1)}{r(n,0)}\right)\Big/\sqrt{d(t)}\right]$$

$$= 1 \times \left[Ln\left(\frac{0.04885}{0.04122}\right)\Big/\sqrt{1}\right] = 16.98\%$$

(b) BDT (constant volatility) assumes that the term structure of volatiles is flat. We do not believe that is true. Generally speaking we expect that the term structure of volatility would sharply increase at the very short end and then decline at a decreasing rate.

(c) We cannot definitely say whether the volatility of BDT (constant volatility) is too high or too low for a given option, but we suspect it is wrong. To the extent that the BDT (constant volatility) volatility is too high, then interest rate option prices obtained from the model will be too high, and vice versa.

(d) Not much. A floater is a cash instrument. Unlike a derivative, the price of a cash instrument is much less sensitive to errors in the value of volatility. This happens because as the volatility, say, increases, the distribution of the interest rate tree widens symmetrically. Payoffs on a cash security are also symmetrical, so gains from a possible payoff on a low interest rate are more or less offset from the possibility of losses from a payoff on the corresponding high interest rate. This is especially true in this case even though the payoff on a floater, just like an option, is dependent upon the actual interest rate that evolves. This happens because as interest rates change so too does the coupon on the floater at the reset date, so the value of the floater does not move much from par. Therefore the value of the floater will be relatively insensitive to biases in incorporating volatility in the interest rate model.

Chapter 6

Question 1

First, we should be careful to recognize that 'term structure consistent' and 'evolutionary' models are not distinct classes of models. Rather they represent the extreme ends of a continuum and that there are models, Hull and White (1990) for example, that combine elements of both. Term structure consistent models are 'fine tuned' to empirical estimates of the zero coupon yield curve and so are forced to agree with it. Evolutionary models attempt to model the term structure of interest rates. An output of the evolutionary model is an estimate of the sovereign yield curve that typically does not agree with an empirical estimate of the sovereign yield curve.

Typically term structure consistent models are more popular with practitioners than evolutionary models because they feel more comfortable with a model that replicates known market prices such as the price of coupon bonds that underlie the zero coupon term structure of interest rates. Therefore they are willing to trust the term structure consistent model to give reasonable prices for securities such as interest rate caps for which there are no market prices. In contrast evolutionary models are unable to replicate the price of coupon bonds since the model cannot agree with an empirical estimate of the existing term structure. What is worse is that practitioners need the model to price interest rate derivatives. Derivatives are highly levered positions in a portion of the payoff on the underlying asset, so small errors in pricing the underlying asset result in much larger errors in pricing the derivative.

However, that is not to say the evolutionary models are wrong and term structure consistent models are right. One factor term structure consistent models may also have a serious flaw. Since the term structure consistent model does not attempt to model the term structure of interest rates it must be recalibrated each day. While this is inconvenient, this does not in itself create any serious problem. However, what is the problem is the extent to which the model ties mean reversion and volatility together then underestimates of mean reversion results in overestimates of volatility, and therefore overestimates of interest rate derivative prices and vice versa. This means that when pricing the derivative today, the model will look correct and the derivative price looks reasonable as the model is precisely calibrated to an empirical estimate of today's term structure. Next day the model must be recalibrated. Since the model, say, underestimated mean reversion, the recalibrated model will reveal that the derivative sold yesterday is now overpriced.

Once we accept that neither approach is the 'correct' one, then we are left to determining the advantages and disadvantages of each approach in an attempt to discover which approach is best under a given set of circumstances. There are four points to consider.

1. Obtaining the inputs: for well-developed debt markets it is easy to obtain the inputs for term structure consistent models since the data is readily available in the market. This is not the case for many less well-developed markets, however. Evolutionary models depend more on historical data, for example estimates of the speed of mean reversion must be estimated from the past behaviour of interest rates. This sort of information is always subject to some degree of measurement error and we would worry if older data were relevant to current market conditions.

2. Errors in the data: term structure consistent models depend upon market data and therefore the results of this model are sensitive to market imperfections such as liquidity. In applying the model one must pay careful attention to the data selection procedures as outlined in Chapter 3. Evolutionary models are less sensitive to errors in market data but of course there is always the worry concerning measurement error as previously discussed.

3. Bond trading strategies: term structure consistent models are useless for trading in bonds since the model is forced to agree with the price of relatively liquid bonds. These are precisely the bonds that one would be interested in trading, so the model will be unable to detect which bonds are not priced correctly. Meanwhile the evolutionary model should be able to detect bonds that

are not priced correctly as the output yield curve is not dependent upon market prices.

4. Derivative trading strategies: evolutionary models often fail to replicate bond prices, so the model will tend to signal that the corresponding derivative is not priced correctly too. For this reason it is difficult to justify this model for trading in derivatives. On the one hand one would say the model is correct in signalling the derivative is not priced correctly and yet on the other one would say that the model is wrong in signalling the bond is not priced correctly so it is permissible to use the bond to hedge the derivative position. In other words, when using the evolutionary model to trade in derivatives one is internally inconsistent and it would take some fast talking on the part of the trader to his/her boss if the trading strategy goes wrong. Meanwhile the term structure consistent model is consistent in claiming that the underlying bond is priced correctly so it can be used in hedging the corresponding incorrectly priced derivative position.

Question 3

First, we need to work out the expected values.

$$\text{At } t = 1: EV_1 = P_1 + (1 - P_1)\delta = 0.9787 + (1 - 0.9787)(0.6)$$

$$= 0.9915$$

$$\text{At } t = 2: EV_2 = P_1 P_2 + (1 - P_1)\delta + (1 - P_2)P_1\delta$$

$$= 0.9787(0.9878) + (1 - 0.9787)(0.6)$$

$$+ (1 - 0.9878)(0.9787)(0.6)$$

$$= 0.9867$$

$$\text{At } t = 3: EV_3$$

$$= P_1 P_2 P_3 + (1 - P_1)\delta + (1 - P_2)P_1\delta + (1 - P_3)P_1 P_2\delta$$

$$= 0.9787(0.9878)0.9845 + (1 - 0.9787)(0.6)$$

$$+ (1 - 0.9878)(0.9787)(0.6) + (1 - 0.9845)$$

$$\times (0.9878)0.9787(0.6)$$

$$= 0.9807$$

Now we find the value of the bond using a slightly modified backward solving procedure.

$$B(2,2) = \{0.5(B(3,3) + B(3,2)) + C\}\,d(2,2) \times EV_3$$

$$= \{0.5(100 + 100) + 5\}0.941 \times 0.9807 = 96.8981$$

$$B(2,1) = \{0.5(B(3,2) + B(3,1)) + C\}d(2,1) \times EV_3$$
$$= \{0.5(100 + 100) + 5\}0.9432 \times 0.9807 = 97.1246$$
$$B(2,0) = \{0.5(B(3,1) + B(3,0)) + C\}d(2,0) \times EV_3$$
$$= \{0.5(100 + 100) + 5\}0.9454 \times 0.9807 = 97.3511$$
$$B(1,1) = \{0.5(B(2,2) + B(2,1)) + C \times EV_2\}d(1,1)$$
$$= \{0.5(96.8981 + 97.1246) + 5(0.9867)\}0.9388$$
$$= 95.7058$$
$$B(1,0) = \{0.5(B(2,1) + B(2,0)) + C \times EV_2\}d(1,0)$$
$$= \{0.5(97.1246 + 97.3511) + 5(0.9867)\}0.9411$$
$$= 96.1535$$
$$B(0,0) = \{0.5(B(1,1) + B(1,0)) + C \times EV_1\}d(0,0)$$
$$= \{0.5(95.7058 + 96.1535) + 5(0.9915)\}0.9342$$
$$= 94.2488$$

Notice that in this step, the expected value factor is multiplied by the promised coupon payment only as the values expected next period have already been adjusted for cumulative credit risk.

Chapter 7

Question 1
(a) Bond B will be more risky than bond A. Bond B has both a lower coupon rate and a lower yield, therefore it will have a higher duration.

(b) First step is to calculate the price of both bonds:

$$Price = CF\left[\frac{1}{(k/2)} - \frac{1}{(k/2)(1 + k/2)^{2*n}}\right] + \frac{Redemption}{(1 + k/2)^{2*n}}$$

$$P(A) = 6\left[\frac{1}{(0.075/2)} - \frac{1}{(0.075/2)(1 + 0.075/2)^{2*10}}\right]$$
$$+ \frac{100}{(1 + 0.075/2)^{2*10}}$$

$$P(A) = 131.2665$$
$$P(B) = 107.1062$$

Second step is to calculate the modified duration of both bonds:

$$D^* = \frac{\dfrac{C}{Y^2}\left[1 - \dfrac{1}{(1+Y)^N}\right] + \dfrac{N\left(100 - \dfrac{C}{Y}\right)}{(1+Y)^{N+1}}}{P}$$

$$D_A^* = \frac{\dfrac{6}{0.0375^2}\left[1 - \dfrac{1}{(1+0.0375)^{20}}\right] + \dfrac{20\left(100 - \dfrac{6}{0.0375}\right)}{(1+0.0375)^{20+1}}}{131.2665}$$

$D_A^* = 12.7183$ *semi-annually*

$D_A^* = 6.3592$ *annually*

$D_B^* = 6.9349$ *annually*

(c)   Macaulay's duration = Modified duration$*(1 + Y/2)$

Macaulay's duration $(A) = 6.3592*(1 + 0.075/2)$

Macaulay's duration $(A) = 6.5976$

Macaulay's duration $(B) = 7.1776$

Question 3

1. *Step 1:* The conversion factor at maturity of the futures contract is given as 0.815888.

Step 2: Calculate the price and yield of the ctd bond as of maturity of the futures contract.

$$B_{ctdm} = B_F \times CF_m = (126.538)(0.815888) = 103.241$$

Therefore yield can be found as

$$103.241 = \$3\left[\frac{1 - (1 + R_{ctdm}/2)^{-34}}{R_{ctdm}/2}\right] + \frac{100}{(1 + R_{ctdm}/2)^{34}}$$

$$R_{ctdm} = 5.70\%$$

Step 3: Calculate the yield and price of your cash bond as of maturity of the futures contract.

$$R_{cm} = R_{ctdm} + Assumed\ spread = 5.70\% + 0.25\%$$

$$= 5.95\% \text{ (Note that now we calculate the yield first)}$$

$$B_{cm} = \$3.5\left[\frac{1 - (1 + 0.0595/2)^{-39}}{0.0595/2}\right] + \frac{100}{(1 + 0.0595/2)^{39}}$$

$$= \$112.021935$$

Steps 4 and 5: Calculate the interest rate sensitivity of the ctd bond and the cash bond. We choose to use the *PVBP* hedge in this instance.

Cash bond	Yield $(R/2)$	Price
	2.975	112.021935
	2.98	111.897984
$PVBP_c$		−0.123951
Cash bond	Yield	Price
	2.85	103.238739
	2.855	103.128525
$PVBP_{CTD}$		−0.110214

Step 5: Calculate the hedge ratio.

$$N = -\frac{PVBP_c}{PVBP_{CTD}} \times K \times CF_m$$

$$N = -\frac{0.123951}{0.110214} \times 1 \times 0.815888 = -0.91758$$

This means that for every $100 000 we need to hedge we need to short 0.91758 futures contracts. Since we need to hedge $100 million and there are 1000 $100 000 amounts in $100 million, we need to short 918 futures contracts.

2. In general whenever we hedge we are trading price risk in favour of basis risk. Therefore any factor that causes a non-perfect correlation between the cash (Ford bond) and the hedging instrument (futures contract) is a source of basis risk that may lead to problems. In general basis risk is less than price risk as long as the correlation between the cash and hedging instrument is positive. In this case there is no time distance between the date that we wish to terminate the hedge and the date of maturity of the futures contract. As is usual there is a small discrepancy between the precise number of futures contracts that we should short and the actual number that is practical to do so, but this source of basis risk is trivial. The real problem is that we are attempting to hedge a corporate bond with a futures contract whose underlying is a sovereign bond. To the extent that the credit spread changes we will in effect have a negative correlation that can lead to a serious failure to hedge where rather than reduce the range of possible outcomes we will actually increase them. For example, imagine that Ford's credit rating deteriorates as Treasury interest rates decrease. Then we would lose on our long cash position, as the value of Ford bonds decreases and the value of our short position would decrease as the Treasury bond futures increase.

Also notice that the hedge ratio is based on duration style concepts that assume a linear relation between prices and yield. To the extent that this is not true due to convexity then we may also obtain unexpected gains and losses.

Question 5

(a) The correlation is very high, 0.966. Therefore we expect that since the positive relation between change in the cash and hedging instruments is very strong, a short position in the hedging instrument should eliminate a large portion of the price movements in the long cash position. In other words the CBT T-bond futures contract should form a good hedge for our investment in the 5.25% bond.

(b) The hedge ratio is 0.9506 meaning that for every $1000 nominal of the cash bond we wish to hedge we need to short $950.60 nominal of the futures contract.

(c) The r^2 is a measure of hedge effectiveness. In this case the r^2 is 0.9325. This suggests that 93.25% of the variability of our unhedged cash position will be eliminated by shorting $950.60 nominal of the CBT futures contract for every $1000 of the 5.25% bond that we wish to hedge.

(d) We should realize that the r^2 in a regression is an optimistic measure of hedge effectiveness. This is true because the regression had all the data available and so was permitted to find that regression hedge ratio that maximized hedge effectiveness. However, when we actually go to apply the hedge the critical data point is next period's results, which was not included in the calculation of the hedge ratio. Therefore the actual effectiveness of the hedge is likely to be less than expected, on average. An extreme example of this is when something happens during the hedging period that broke the normal relation between the cash and hedging instrument during the past that was used to estimate the hedge. In the later case the results of the hedge may be quite disappointing.

Chapter 8

Question 1

Promised total return

Portfolio: $Cost = 0.183{*}64.036 + 0.817{*}146.24 = 131.197$

$FV = 0.183{*}133.714 + 0.817{*}305.370 = 273.957$

$TR : [(273.957/131.197)^{1/20} - 1]{*}2 = 7.5\%$

Scenarios

	If IR decline by 200 bp per year	If IR increase by 200 bp per year
Bond A	Value at $T = 10$ years	Value at $T = 10$ years
FV of int. $(t = 1 - 20)$	$52.395	$64.411
PV of int. $(t = 21 - 40)$	30.455	25.461
PV of prin.	58.125	39.529
Total	140.975 * 0.183 = 25.798	129.401 * 0.183 = 23.68
Bond B	Value at $T = 10$ years	Value at $T = 10$ years
FV of int. $(t = 1 - 20)$	$157.184	$193.234
PV of int. $(t = 21 - 40)$	91.364	76.384
PV of prin.	58.125	39.529
Total	306.673 * 0.817 = 250.552	309.147 * 0.817 = 252.573
Portfolio total FV	276.35	276.253
Realized yield	7.62%	7.62%

Question 3
(a) The duration gap model is defined in the text as:

$$D_A^* - D_L^* * \frac{P_L}{P_A} = 0$$

where D_A^* is the modified duration of the assets and D_L^* is the modified duration of the liabilities. Applying this equation, the duration gap is $7.64 - (2.81 * 110/120) = 5.0642$.

(b) A 200 basis point rise in interest rates would result in a decline in the firm's capital. This is $\Delta P_c = -D_{gap}^* P_A \Delta Y = 5.0642 * (\$120 \text{ m}) * (0.02) = -\$12.154 \text{ m}$.

(c) This was a 'challenge question'. The most important element is the calculation of duration for a variety of instruments, so if you got this right then you are all right. The first few critical steps in solving this exercise are to calculate yield and duration of each of the instruments.

(i)   Modified duration for 90-day T-bills

$$D^* = (90/360)/(1 + 0.05/2) = 0.2439$$

Notice that even though the T-bill does not pay coupons annually (in fact it does not pay any coupons at all!) we still find its modified duration as if it did. This is because the market calculates and quotes the yield on T-bills using the bond equivalent yield method (which assumes semi-annual compounding) and so the market also measures the modified duration as if the T-bill paid coupons semi-annually.

(ii) 8% 20-year T-bond: this is a direct application of the closed form solution for the modified duration of a bond.

The yield of 8% coupon bond is 7% (use the calculator). Applying the closed form solution to find the modified duration of the 20-year T-bond we find that its duration is 10.3966 years.

$$D^* = \frac{\dfrac{C}{Y^2}\left[1 - \dfrac{1}{(1+Y)^N}\right] + \dfrac{N\left(100 - \dfrac{C}{Y}\right)}{(1+Y)^{N+1}}}{P}$$

$$= \frac{\dfrac{4}{0.035^2}\left[1 - \dfrac{1}{(1+0.035)^{40}}\right] + \dfrac{40\left(100 - \dfrac{4}{0.035}\right)}{(1+0.035)^{40+1}}}{110.668}$$

$$= 20.7931 \text{ (semi-annually)}$$

$$= 20.7931/2 = 10.3966 \text{ in years}$$

(iii) 12% 30-year mortgages: the question does not give you enough information about the mortgages to calculate the duration of the mortgages directly. However, we know that the duration of assets is 7.64, and we know the duration of the T-bills and T-bond. We also know the total value of assets and the value of the short-term assets.

$$D^*_A = \frac{110}{120}D^*_{LA} + \frac{10}{120}D^*_{SA} = 7.64$$

Now we take the hint and split the long-term asset into its two components.

$$= \frac{110}{120}\left[\frac{100}{110}D^*_M + \frac{10}{110}D^*_{LB}\right] + \frac{10}{120}D^*_{SA} = 7.64$$

$$= 0.916667 * (0.9091D^*_M + 0.0909 * 10.3966)$$

$$+ 0.0833 * 0.2439 = 7.64$$

We now have one equation and one unknown, the duration of the mortgage D_M^*

$$\Rightarrow 7.64 = 0.8333D_M^* + 0.8664 + 0.0203$$

$$\Rightarrow D_M^* = 8.1043$$

Now we can work out the duration of the long-term assets and the duration of short-term assets.

$$D_{LA}^* = \left[\frac{100}{110}8.1043 + \frac{10}{110}10.3966\right] = 8.31269$$

$$D_{SA}^* = \frac{0.25}{1.025} = 0.2439$$

If we would like to close the duration gap, we should adjust the weights of long-term assets and short-term assets so that
$$D_A^* = D_L^* * \frac{P_L}{P_A}$$

$$W_1 * D_{LA}^* + W_2 * D_{SA}^* = 2.81 * \frac{110}{120}$$

$$W_1 * 8.31269 + W_2 * 0.2439 = 2.81 * \frac{110}{120}$$

Subject: $W_1 + W_2 = 1$

$$\Rightarrow W_1 = 28.9\% \quad W_2 = 71.1\%$$

Solving the latter reveals that:
90-day T-bill = 71.1%
8% Treasury bond = 28.9% * 10/110 = 2.62727%
12% mortgage bonds = 28.9% * 100/110 = 26.2727%
 We can see that these weights are correct because we can substitute them back into the original condition. That is

$$D_A^* = D_L^* * \frac{P_L}{P_A} = 2.81 * \frac{110}{120} = 2.5758$$

So: $W_{T\text{-}bill} \times D_{T\text{-}bill}^* + W_{T\text{-}bond} \times D_{T\text{-}bond}^*$

$$+ W_{mortgages} \times D_{mortgages}^* = 2.5758$$

$$0.711(0.2439) + 0.0262727(10.3966) + 0.262727(8.1043)$$

$$= 2.5758$$

(d) Notice that the bank is required to reduce its mortgage portfolio from \$100 million to \$31.53 million. This may appear to be impossible as then the bank would be much less profitable since it is on the mortgages that the bank actually makes its money. It may surprise you to learn that banks actually do this by 'securitizing' their mortgage portfolio. That is, they create a new security called a mortgage-backed security that passes title on their portfolio of mortgages and then they sell this security in the capital market. The bank still administers the loan on behalf of the investors in the mortgage-backed security and for this the bank collects a fee. This fee is taken from the monthly mortgage payments paid to the bank by the homeowners. The bank then passes on these payments, less their fee, to the investors in the mortgage-backed security. So, yes, this strategy is feasible. Commercial banks are becoming service-rather than asset- (loan) based institutions.

Question 5

(a) We wish to avoid the anticipated increase in yields in the 6–7 year area, but we wish to maintain the level of risk we would have had had we stayed in the 2009 gilt. To do this we have to satisfy the constraint.

$$PVBP_m = (1 - x)PVBP_s + (x)PVBP_l$$

The *PVBP* of the instruments are

Bond	Current price	Price with $+1$ bp	*PVBP*
December 7, 2006	109.21	109.17487	-0.03513
December 7, 2009	105.05	104.99195	-0.05805
December 7, 2015	126.80	126.69211	-0.10789

Solving this equation we have $x = 31.5\%$. Therefore we invest 31.5% (£9 450 000) of the proceeds from the sale of the 2009 bond in the 2015 bond and 68.5% (£20 550 000) in the 2006 bond.

(b) In response to a 25 basis point increase in yield the value of our safe haven decreases by £435 370.50.

$$\Delta B_s = PVBP_s \text{ per } £100 \times \#of \text{ basis points} \times Position \text{ size}$$

$$= 0.03513 \times 25 \times \frac{£20\,550.000}{100}$$

$$= -£180\,480.38$$

$$\Delta B_l = PVBP_l \text{ per } \$100 \times \#of \text{ basis points} \times Position \text{ size}$$

$$= 0.10789 \times 25 \times \frac{£9\,450\,000}{100}$$

$$= -£254\,890.12$$

However, had we stayed in the medium bond we would have lost $435 375.

$$\Delta B_m = PVBP_m \text{ per } \$100 \times \# \text{ of basis points} \times \text{Position size}$$

$$= 0.05805 \times 25 \times \frac{\$30\,000\,000}{100}$$

$$= \$435\,375$$

Therefore we have found a safe haven that approximates the risk of our previous position.

Chapter 9

Question 1

1. A coupon bond is a portfolio of zeros. Its modified duration is maturity discounted back one period at the corresponding rate of interest. Priced as a portfolio the value of the bond is

$$B = \$4375 \times 0.97561 + \$4375 \times 0.942596 + \$104\,375$$
$$\times\, 0.901943 = \$102\,532$$

The modified duration of each coupon payment and the formula for key rate duration are

$$D_1^* = \frac{1}{1.025} = 0.97561 \quad D_2^* = \frac{2}{1.03} = 1.941748$$

$$D_2^* = \frac{2}{1.03} = 1.941748 \quad D_{KRi}^* = \sum_{i=1}^{2} T_i W_i D_i$$

$$D_{KR1}^* = \left(\frac{2}{2}\right)\left[\frac{4375 \times 0.97561}{102\,532}\right](0.97561)$$

$$+ \left(\frac{1}{2}\right)\left[\frac{4375 \times 0.942596}{102\,532}\right](1.941748)$$

$$= 0.040614 + 0.039049 = 0.079663$$

$$D_{KR2}^* = \left(\frac{1}{2}\right)\left[\frac{4375 \times 0.942594}{102\,532}\right](1.941748)$$

$$+ \left(\frac{2}{2}\right)\left[\frac{4375 \times 0.0901943}{102\,532}\right](2.89855)$$

$$= 0.039049 + 2.661319 = 2.700368$$

2. $\Delta B = D_{KR1}^* B \Delta Y + D_{KR1}^* B \Delta Y$

$$= -0.079663(102\,532)(0.01) + 2.700368(102\,572)(0.01)$$

$$= -81.68 + 2768.74$$

$$= +2687.06$$

Question 3

(a) The yield for the corporate bond is 5.523%. Therefore the modified duration for the bond is 4.237.

$$D^* = \frac{\left(\dfrac{6}{(0.05523)^2}\left[1 - \dfrac{1}{(1.05523)^5}\right] + \dfrac{5\left(100 - \dfrac{6}{0.05523}\right)}{(1+0.05523)^{5+1}} \right)}{102.035} = 4.237$$

The bond's Fisher Weil duration is 4.238.

$$FW = \sum_{T=1}^{5} D_T^* W_T = \frac{1}{(1.05)}(0.056) + \frac{2}{(1.055)}(0.0528)$$

$$+ \frac{3}{(1.0575)}(0.0497) + \frac{4}{(1.06)}(0.0466) + \frac{5}{(1.055)}(0.7949)$$

$$= 0.0533 + 0.1 + 0.141 + 0.1758 + 3.7673$$

$$= 4.238$$

The bond's first and second key rate durations are 0.2428 and 3.995 respectively.

$$D_{KR1}^* = (4/4)D_1^* W_1 + (3/4)D_2^* W_2 + (2/4)D_3^* W_3 + (1/4)D_4^* W_4$$

$$D_{KR1}^* = (4/4)(0.0533) + (3/4)(0.1) + (2/4)(0.141)$$

$$+ (1/4)(0.1758) = 0.2428$$

$$D_{KR2}^* = (1/4)D_2^* W_2 + (2/4)D_3^* W_3 + (3/4)D_4^* W_4 + (4/4)D_5^* W_5$$

$$D_{KR2}^* = (1/4)(0.1) + (2/4)(0.141) + (3/4)(0.1758)$$

$$+ (4/4)(3.7673) = 3.995$$

(b) As the yield curve is nearly flat and the bond is only five years to maturity, the three interest sensitivity measures are similar in magnitude. Nevertheless the results from the use of these three models will differ depending upon how interest rates may shift in the future.

Modified duration assumes that if interest rates change, they will result from a parallel shift in the yield curve. While this may appear restrictive, component analysis studies of interest rates changes suggest that the vast amount of variation in interest rates is associated with a parallel shift in the yield curve. Therefore even the simplest duration measure has much to recommend it. Nevertheless some variation in interest rates is associated with non-parallel shifts in the yield curve, so some improvement in modelling interest rate changes can be obtained by relaxing the assumption of parallel only shifts in the yield curve.

Fisher Weil (1971) begins the process of relaxing the parallel only shift in the yield curve. Although they are able to relax the flat yield curve assumption that also underlies modified duration, the only robust model they obtain still has to assume parallel shifts in the yield. Therefore the performance of Fisher Weil tends to resemble that of modified duration. However, their derivation of duration pointed the way to further extensions and was later exploited by Ho in his key rate duration model.

The key rate duration model is completely flexible as one is able to model any yield curve shape and any change in shape of the yield curve. It is able to do this, as key rate duration is a multifactor model with as many factors as key rates. If fact some may find key rate duration too flexible as the choice of the number and location of the key rates may be uncertain.

Another issue raised by the question is that all of these measures model interest rate changes only and do not specifically allow for changes in yield due to changes in credit risk. Another way to look at this is to realize that we are actually modelling yield changes where yield changes are a result from two sources of risk, interest and credit risk. The problem with the above duration measures is that they attempt to model yield changes as if they were a result of one source of risk. To the extent that interest rate and credit risks are not perfectly correlated, then these models will fail to capture the full variation in yield.

Chapter 10

Question 1

1. A buyer of a swap is long a floating rate bond and short a fixed coupon bond. Therefore the total package is $V_s = F - B_c$. In this case the floater pays a fixed rate of interest above the floating rate so the value of the swap is now

$$V_s = F + B_{+libor} - B_z - B_c$$

Note that $B_{+libor} - B_z$ is the value of the fixed interest rate stream that is paid above the libor rate.

The payments to be received at the reset date.

$F = £100\,000$

$$B_{+libor} - B_Z = \frac{C \times M}{Y}\left[1 - \frac{1}{(1+Y)^N}\right] + \frac{M}{(1+Y)^N} - \frac{M}{(1+Y)^N}$$

Therefore total payment to be received is £107 721.73.

Payments to be made at the reset date should be set equal to the payments to be received. We set the coupon rate on the fixed rate bond to achieve this.

$$B_C = \frac{C \times M}{Y}\left[1 - \frac{1}{(1+Y)^N}\right] + \frac{M}{(1+Y)^N} = £107\,721.73$$

We know all the values of the above expression except for the coupon rate C. Solving this expression for C we find that the coupon rate should be 6%.

2. *PVBP* when the swap is priced at zero.

$$PVBP_S = BVBP_F + PVBP_{+libor} - PVBP_Z - PVBP_B$$

$$= [D_F^* F + D_{+libor}^* B_{+libor} - D_Z^* B_Z - D_C^* B_C] \times 1/10\,000$$

$$D_F^* = 1/1.05 = 0.95238$$

$$D_{+libor}^* = \frac{\frac{1}{0.05^2}\left[1 - \frac{1}{(1+0.05)^{10}}\right] + \frac{10\left(100 - \frac{1}{0.05}\right)}{(1+0.05)^{10+1}}}{69.112} = 9$$

$$D_Z^* = 10/1.05 = 9.5238$$

$$D_C^* = \frac{\frac{6}{0.05^2}\left[1 - \frac{1}{(1+0.05)^{10}}\right] + \frac{10\left(100 - \frac{6}{0.05}\right)}{(1+0.05)^{10+1}}}{107.721} = 7.516$$

$$PVBP_S = [0.95238(100\,000) + 9(69\,112) - 9.5238(61\,391)$$

$$- 7.518(107\,721)] \times 1/10\,000$$

$$= -67.73$$

3. If interest rates were to rise by 100 bp the buyer will gain 67.73 per basis point or $67.73 \times 100 = £6773$.

4. Form a hedge ratio of $PVBP_S/PVBP_{ctd} \times CF_{ctd}$ and go long the futures contract. Since we gain on our long swap as interest rates rise, to offset we need a long position in the futures contract such that as interest rates rise, the cheapest to deliver will fall in value leading to a loss on our long futures position.

Question 3

1. The value of the 5% annual coupon pay sovereign bond is

$T = 0$	$T = 1$	$T = 2$
		99.529
	100.223	100.345
101.668	101.660	101.044

The details of the calculations are as follows.

$$B(2,2) = 105/1.05497 = 99.529$$

$$B(2,1) = 105/1.04639 = 100.345$$

$$B(2,0) = 105/1.03915 = 101.044$$

$$B(1,1) = \{0.5[B(2,2) + B(2,1)] + C\}/(1 + r(1,1))$$
$$= \{0.5[99.529 + 100.345] + 5\}/(1 + 0.04704)$$
$$= 100.223$$

$$B(1,0) = \{0.5[B(2,1) + B(2,0)] + C\}/(1 + r(1,0))$$
$$= \{0.5[100.345 + 101.044] + 5\}/(1 + 0.03969)$$
$$= 101.660$$

$$B(0,0) = \{0.5[B(1,1) + B(1,0)] + C\}/(1 + r(0,0))$$
$$= \{0.5[100.223 + 101.660] + 5\}/(1 + 0.04203)$$
$$= 101.668$$

2. The floater is a periodic zero that resets to par at the beginning of the period. Since today is the reset date, the floater is worth 100. The modified duration is the time until reset (or its Macaulay duration), one year in this case, divided through by one plus one period's yield, the annual yield in this case.

$$D_F^* = \frac{D}{(1 + Y)} = \frac{1}{(1 + 0.04203)} = 0.96$$

3. The value and modified duration of the corresponding inverse floater is as follows.

$$B = 0.5[F + IF] \Rightarrow IF = 2 \times B - F$$
$$= 2 \times (101.668) - 100 = 103.336$$

The yield on the sovereign bond, given that the price is 101.668 (from step 1), the annual coupon is 5 and the maturity is three years, is 4.394%. Therefore the duration of the coupon bond is found using the closed form solution for modified duration.

$$D_C^* = \frac{\dfrac{5}{0.04394^2}\left[1 - \dfrac{1}{(1+0.04394)^3}\right] + \dfrac{3\left(100 - \dfrac{5}{0.04394}\right)}{(1+0.04394)^{3+1}}}{101.668}$$

$$= 2.74$$

We find the duration of the inverse floater from the fact that the duration of the coupon bond is a weighted average of the duration of its component securities, the floater and inverse floater in this case. Note that the floater and inverse floater have to be priced in terms of a face value of 50 so the weights add to 100%.

$$D_B^* = W_1 D_F^* + (1 - W_1)D_{IF}^* = \frac{F}{B}D_F^* + \left(\frac{IF}{B}\right)D_{IF}^*$$

$$\Rightarrow D_{IF}^* = \frac{D_B^* - W_1 D_F^*}{(1 - W_1)} = \frac{2.74 - \dfrac{50}{101.668}(0.96)}{\dfrac{101.668 - 50}{101.668}} = 4.46$$

We can check this result by substituting the weights and the duration of the floater and inverse floater into the first equation in this part to see if indeed the weighted average of the duration of the floater and inverse floater equals the duration of the coupon bond.

$$D_B^* = \frac{F}{B}D_F^* + \left(\frac{IF}{B}\right)D_{IF}^*$$

$$= \frac{50}{101.668}(0.96) + \left(\frac{101.668 - 50}{101.668}\right)(4.46) = 2.74$$

4. Actually there is a problem with the above inverse floater. Notice that the payoff on the inverse floater is 5% less the floating rate. At node 2,2 you pay the floating rate of 5.497% but then the inverse floater will have to pay you $5\% - 5.497\% = 0.497\%$. This is not fair to the inverse floater as in effect they have to pay you for investing money in the inverse floater.

The solution is to place a cap on the floater and a floor on the inverse floater such that the cap and floor add to twice the size of the coupon on the underlying bond. That way you never receive anything on a net basis, but then again you never pay anything either. For example, we could set a floor of 1% on the inverse floater and a cap of 9% on the floater. If the floating rate goes to, say, 12%, then the cap is binding and the floater receives 9% of 50 or $4.5. Meanwhile the floor on the inverse floater is also binding so they receive 1% of

50 or \$0.50. Therefore you have to pay \$5 in total, which just equals the coupon you receive from the 5% coupon bond.

Chapter 11

Question 1

As the buyer of credit protection makes payments only when the bond does not default, and the buyer of credit protection receives amounts when the bond does default, we have to work out corporate state securities conditioned upon survival and default. These values are found via the procedure as specified in the text. Specifically the survival contingent values are the sovereign state security price multiplied by the cumulative probability of survival. For example, $C_s(2,2) = S(2,2) \times P_1P_2 = 0.23587 \times (0.99296)(0.98301) = 0.23023$. The default contingent state security prices are the sovereign state security prices multiplied by the probability of default at that state all multiplied by the cumulative probability of survival. For example, $C_d(2,2) = S(2,2) \times (1 - P_2)P_1 = 0.23587(0.01699)(0.99296) = 0.00398$.

State	BDT $S(n,i)$	JT $C(n,i)$	Probability of survival	$C_s(n,i)$ $P \times P \times P \times S(n,i)$	$C_d(n,i)$ $P \times P \times (1-P) \times S(n,i)$
$r(1,1)$	0.48514	0.48377	0.99296	0.48172	0.00342
$r(1,0)$	0.48514	0.48377	0.99296	0.48172	0.00342
$r(2,2)$	0.23587	0.23361	0.98301	0.23023	0.00398
$r(2,1)$	0.47178	0.46727	0.98301	0.46050	0.00796
$r(2,0)$	0.23591	0.23366	0.98301	0.23027	0.00398

The value of the payments are found using (11.1) and the value of receipts are found using (11.2).

The answer for (a) and (b) is contained in the table below. The numbers are calculated according to the equations above. For example, the value of the bond in $C(2,2)$ is 98.52372. The payoff in the event of default is then $100 - B(2,2)\delta = 100 - 98.52372 \times 0.6 = 40.8858$. The value of the receipt in $C(2,2)$ according to the above formula is $0.00398\{40.886\} = 0.1627$. When we add up the value of all the state contingent receipts we find that the credit default swap is worth 0.9272. To find the value of the premiums we apply the payments formula. For example, in $C(2,2)$ the value of the survival contingent payment is $0.23023(0.005)(100) = 0.1151$. Adding up all the products of the premiums formula we find that the value of the payments is 0.9422.

State	Amounts $(100 - d_b)$	Receipts $(100 - d_b) \times C_d(n,i)$	Payments $C_s(n,i) \times Sw \times M$
$r(1,1)$	40.4921	0.1383	0.2409
$r(1,0)$	40.4724	0.1382	0.2409
$r(2,2)$	40.8858	0.1627	0.1151
$r(2,1)$	40.8776	0.3253	0.2303
$r(2,0)$	40.8695	0.1627	0.1151
Value		0.9272	0.9422

(c) Yes they would nearly be the same. This is because Jarrow and Turnbull is calibrated to the credit spread and so given a constant recovery fraction the survival probability will be calibrated to ensure that the replicating portfolios of corporate state security prices replicate the credit spread. Then receipts function is essentially the expected loss rate (one minus the probability of survival times the loss given default). Since credit spread compensates investors for the expected loss, the receipts function will reflect the credit spread. If we then calibrate the swap premium to equal the receipts, then swap premium will closely replicate the credit spread too.

Question 3

A replicating portfolio is a portfolio of securities that has the same cash flow structure and has the same risk as another security that it is supposed to replicate. To prevent arbitrage the replicating portfolio and the security it replicates must have the same price. The replicating portfolio that underlies Jarrow and Turnbull (1995) is the sum of corporate state securities each of which *promises* to pay £1 *if* a particular interest rate occurs, otherwise it pays zero. Notice that there are two sources of uncertainty, interest rate risk (pay offs will only occur *if* a given interest rate state occurs) and default risk (the obligator *promises* to pay £1, but the obligator may be unable to deliver on the promise). If we add up the values of all possible corporate state securities that mature at a given point in time, you will have a portfolio that will replicate the pay off and the risk of a corporate zero coupon bond. That is, the replicating portfolio is *obligated* to pay £1 as for certain one corporate state security that corresponds to the evolved interest rate state is obligated to pay off £1, but still that state security may not pay off as the obligator may default. This is precisely the same cash flow structure and risk as a corporate zero coupon bond. Therefore to prevent arbitrage the replicating portfolio of all corporate state securities that mature at a given point in time must have the same price as a corporate zero that also matures at that same point in time.

Chapter 12

Question 1

To find the value of the embedded option we must first find the value of the underlying straight bond.

The value of the straight bond.

$T = 0$	$T = 1$	$T = 2$	$T = 3$
			100
		99.529	100
	100.223	100.345	100
101.668	101.660	101.044	100

Next we find the intrinsic value of the call option. Note that the strike price is in bold.

$T = 0$	$T = 1$	$T = 2$	$T = 3$
101	**100.5**	**100**	
			0
		0	0
	0	0.345	0
0.668	1.16	1.044	0

Now we need to value the American nature of the embedded call option by taking the higher of the intrinsic value of the value obtained by delaying one more period.

Obviously the value of the call is its intrinsic value for states $S(2,1)$ and $S(2,0)$. For state $S(1,1)$, the value of the embedded call $C(1,1)$ is its delay value of $0.165, for $C(1,0)$ it is the intrinsic value $1.16, as the delay value is lower.

$$C(1,1) = \frac{0.5(0) + 0.5(0.345)}{1.04704} = 0.165$$

$$C(1,0) = \frac{0.5(0.345) + 0.5(1.044)}{1.03969} = 0.668$$

Finally the value of the call today is

$$C(0,0) = \frac{0.5(0.165) + 0.5(1.16)}{1.04203} = 0.636$$

Callable bond price = Straight bond less embedded call option =

101.668 − 0.636 = $101.032.

The OAY is based on the straight bond price of $101.668

The OAY is 4.39%.

The callable bond has a higher yield because its coupon is higher to compensate investors for the embedded call option held to their disadvantage. To determine if the callable bond is priced correctly relative to the straight bond find the value of the call (as above), add its value to the callable market price and then find its option adjusted yield. If the OAY > straight bond yield, buy the callable bond as its yield is 'too rich'. If the OAY< straight bond yield, do not buy the callable bond as it is too expensive.

Question 3
This is not correct because the yield to worst values the embedded call option under only two possible scenarios, that the yield to worst is the yield to maturity and therefore the bond will not be called for certain, or the yield to worst is the yield to call so the bond will be called for certain. Therefore this yield to worst methodology always ignores the optionality of the underlying call option. In other words, whether the bond will be called or not is always subject to some uncertainty that the yield to worst methodology ignores. Therefore the value of the embedded call option is always undervalued by the yield to worst methodology. If the yield to worst is the yield to maturity the option while out of the money is still valuable. The yield to worst treats the value of the call as zero but actually it has some value. Since the callable bond is a straight bond less the embedded call, the callable bond is overvalued as actually the bond is worth less and the actual yield is higher than that suggested by the yield to maturity. Similarly when the yield to worst is the yield to call it is assumed that the bond will be called for certain. However, there is always the possibility that it would be better for the issuer not to call, so again the value of the call feature is greater than the intrinsic value, the callable bond is overpriced and the yield is actually higher than the yield to call. Notice that in both scenarios the yield to worst understates the value of the embedded call option and overstates the value of the callable bond and understates the true callable bond yield. Therefore the yield to worst does not bracket the true yield of the callable bond.

References

Altman, E., D. Cooke and V. Kishore, 'Defaults and Returns on High Yields Bonds: Analysis Through 1998', (1999) New York University Salomon Center.

Altman, E. I. and A. C. Eberhart, 'Do Seniority Provisions Protect Bondholders', *Journal of Portfolio Management*, 20 (1994), 67–75.

Andersson, N., F. Breedon, M. Deacon, A. Derry and G. Murphy, *Estimating and Interpreting the Yield Curve*, Wiley, New York, 1996.

Backus, David, Silverio Foresi and Stanley Zin, 'Arbitrage Opportunities in Arbitrage-free Models on Bond Pricing', *Journal of Business & Economic Statistics*, 16 (1998), 13–26.

Bierman, Harold, Jr. and Jerome E. Hass, 'An Analytical Model of Bond Risk Differentials', *Journal of Financial & Quantitative Analysis*, 10 (1975), 757–773.

Black, Fischer and Piotr Karasinski, 'Bond and Option Pricing when Short Rates are Lognormal', *Financial Analyst Journal*, 47 (1991), 52–59.

Black, Fischer, Emanuel Derman and William Toy, 'A One-Factor Model of Interest Rates and its Application to Treasury Bond Options', *Financial Analyst Journal*, 46 (1990), 33–39.

Bomfim, Antulio, 'Credit Derivatives and their Potential to Synthesize Riskless Assets', *Journal of Fixed Income*, 12 (December 2000), 6–16.

Clare, Andrew, Michalis Ioannides and Frank S. Skinner, 'Hedging Corporate Bonds with Stock Index Futures: A Word of Caution', *Journal of Fixed Income*, 10(2) (2000), 25–34.

Collin-Dufresne, P., R. Goldstein and J. S. Martin, 'The Determinants of Credit Spread Changes', *Journal of Finance*, 56(6) (2001), 2177–2207.

Cox, J. C., J. E. Ingersoll and S. A. Ross, 'A Re-examination of Traditional Hypothesis about the Term Structure of Interest Rates', *Journal of Finance*, 36(4) (1981), 769–799.

Cox, John C., Jonathan E. Ingersoll, Jr. and Stephen A. Ross, 'A Theory of the Term Structure of Interest Rates', *Econometrica*, 53 (1985), 385–408.

Das, R. S. and R. Sundaram, 'A Direct Approach to Arbitrage-free Pricing of Credit Derivatives', (1998) working paper 6635, NBER.

Delianedis, G. and R. Lagnado, 'Recovery Assumptions in the Valuation of Credit Derivatives', *Journal of Fixed Income*, 11 (2002), 20–30.

Diaz, Antonio and Frank S. Skinner, 'Estimating Corporate Yield Curves', *Journal of Fixed Income*, 11(2) (2001), 95–103.

Duffee, Gregory R., 'Idiosyncratic Variation of Treasury Bill Yields', *Journal of Finance*, 51(2) (1996), 527–551.

Duffee, Gregory R., 'The Relation Between Treasury Yields and Corporate Bond Yield Spreads', *Journal of Finance*, 53(6) (1998), 2225–2242.

Duffie, D. and K. J. Singleton, 'Modelling Term Structures of Defaultable Bonds', *Review of Financial Studies*, 12 (1999), 687–720.

Duffie, Darrell, 'Credit Swap Valuation', *Financial Analyst Journal*, 55(1) (Jan/Feb 1999), 73–87.

Dunn, Kenneth B. and Chester S. Spatt, 'A Strategic Analysis of Sinking Fund Bonds', *Journal of Financial Economics*, 13(3) (1984), 399–424.

Elton, E., M. Gruber, D. Agrawal and C. Mann, 'Explaining the Rate Spread on Corporate Bonds', *Journal of Finance*, 56(1) (2001), 247–277.

Estrella, Arturo and Frederic S. Mishkin, 'Predicting U.S. Recessions: Financial Variables as Leading Indicators', *Review of Economics and Statistics*, 80(1) (1998), 45–61.

Estrella, Arturo and Frederic S. Mishkin, 'The Predictive Power of the Term Structure of Interest Rates in Europe and the United States: Implications for the European Central Bank', *European Economic Review*, 41(7) (1997), 1375–1401.

Estrella, Arturo and Gikas A. Hardouvelis, 'The Term Structure as a Predictor of Real Economic Activity', *Journal of Finance*, 46(2) (1991), 555–576.

Fama, Eugene F., 'The Information in the Term Structure', *Journal of Financial Economics*, 13(4) (1984), 509–528.

Fisher, Lawrence and Romand L. Weil, 'Coping with the Risk of Interest-Rate Fluctuations: Returns to Bondholders from Naive and Optimal Strategies', *Journal of Business*, 44(4) (1971), 408–431.

Fong, H. Glifford and Oldrich A. Vasicek, 'Fixed-Income Volatility Management', *Journal of Portfolio Management*, 17(4) (1991), 41–46.

Fons, Jerome S., 'The Default Premium and Corporate Bond Experience', *Journal of Finance*, 42 (1987), 81–97.

Fooladi, Iraj, Gordon S. Roberts and Frank Skinner, 'Duration for Bonds with Default Risk', *Journal of Banking and Finance*, 21(1) (1997), 1–16.

Hardouvelis, Gikas A., 'The Predictive Power of the Term Structure During Recent Monetary Regimes', *Journal of Finance*, 43(2) (1988), 339–356.

Heath, David, Robert Jarrow and Andrew Morton, 'Bond Pricing and the Term Structure of Interest Rates: A New Methodology for Contingent Claims Valuation', *Econometrica*, 60 (1992), 77–106.

Helwege, Jean and Christopher M. Turner, 'The Slope of the Credit Yield for Speculative-Grade Issuers', *Journal of Finance*, 54(5) (1999), 1869–1884.

Hickman, W. B., *Corporate Bond Quality and Investor Experience*, Princeton University Press, 1958.

Ho, Thomas S. Y., 'Key Rate Durations: Measures of Interest Rate Risks', *Journal of Fixed Income*, 2(2) (1992), 29–44.

Ho, Thomas S. Y. and Sang-Bin Lee, 'Term Structure Movements and Pricing Interest Rate Contingent Claims', *Journal of Finance*, 41 (1986), 1011–1030.

Hull, John and Alan White, 'Pricing Interest-Rate-Derivative Securities', *Review of Financial Studies*, 3 (1990), 573–592.

Ioannides, Michalis, 'Testing and Developing Models for the Term Structure of Interest Rates', Ph.D. thesis, ISMA Centre, University of Reading, 2000.

Ioannides, Michalis and Frank S. Skinner, 'Hedging Corporate Bonds', *Journal of Business Finance & Accounting*, 26(7/8) (1999), 919–944.

Jamshidian, Farshid, 'Forward Induction and Construction of Yield Curve Diffusion Models', *Journal of Fixed Income*, 1 (1991), 62–74.

Jarrow, R, D. Lando and S. Turnbull, 'A Markov Model for the Term Structure of Credit Spreads', *The Review of Financial Studies*, 10 (1997), 481–523.

Jarrow, R. and S. Turnbull, 'Pricing Derivatives on Financial Securities Subject to Credit Risk', *Journal of Finance*, 50 (1995), 53–85.

Johnson, Ramon E., 'Term Structures of Corporate Bond Yields as a Function of Risk of Default', *Journal of Finance*, 22(2) (1967), 313–345.

Jonkhart, Marius J. L., 'On the Term Structure of Interest Rates and the Risk of Default: An Analytical Approach', *Journal of Banking and Finance*, 3 (1979), 253–261.

Jordan, J. and S. Mansi, 'How Well Do Constant Maturity Treasuries Approximate the On-the-Run Term Structure?', *Journal of Fixed Income*, 10(2) (2000), 35–45.

Kiesel, R., W. Perraudin and A. Taylor, 'Credit and Interest Rate Risk', in *Risk Management: Value at Risk and Beyond*, M. A. H. Dempster (ed.), Cambridge, 2002.

Kolb, Robert W. and Raymond Chiang, 'Duration, Immunization, and Hedging with Interest Rate Futures', *Journal of Financial Research*, 5 (1982), 161–170.

Litterman, R. and J. Scheinkman, 'Common Factors Affecting Bond Returns', *Journal of Fixed Income*, 1 (1991), 54–61.

Lutz, F. A., 'The Structure of Interest Rates', *Quarterly Journal of Economics*, 55 (1940), 36–63.

McCulloch, J. Huston, 'The Tax-adjusted Yield Curve', *Journal of Finance*, 30 (1975), 811–830.

Merton, R. C., 'On the Pricing of Corporate Debt: The Risk Structure of Interest Rates', *Journal of Finance*, 29 (1974), 449–470.

Mishkin, F. S., 'The Information in the Term Structure: Some Further Results', *Journal of Applied Econometrics*, 3(4) (1988), 307–314.

Nelson and Schaefer, 'The Dynamics of the Term Structure and Alternative Portfolio Immunization Strategies', in *Innovations in Bond Portfolio Management: Duration, Analysis and Immunization*, G. Kaufman, G. Bierwag and A. Tovevs (eds) JAI Press, 1983, pp. 61–101.

Nelson, Charles R. and Andrew F. Siegel, 'Parsimonious Modelling of Yield Curves', *Journal of Business*, 60 (1987), 473–490.

Papageorgiou, Nicolas and Frank S. Skinner, 'Predicting the Direction of Interest Rate Movements', *Journal of Fixed Income*, 11(4) (2002), 87–95.

Papageorgiou, Nicolas and Frank S. Skinner, 'Credit Spreads and the Treasury Zero Coupon Spot Curve', ISMA working paper, 2003.

Sarig, Oded and Arthur Warga, 'Bond Price Data and Bond Market Liquidity', *Journal of Financial and Quantitative Analysis*, 24 (1989), 367–378.

Schönbucher, P., 'Term Structure Modelling of Defaultable Bonds', *Review of Derivatives Research*, 2 (1998), 161–192.

Skinner, F. S. and A. Diaz, 'An Empirical Study of Credit Default Swaps', *Journal of Fixed Income*, 13(1) (2003), 28–38.

Skinner, Frank S., 'Hedging Bonds Subject to Credit Risk', *Journal of Banking and Finance*, 22(3) (1998), 321–345.

Steely, J., 'A Two Factor Model of the UK Yield Curve', *The Manchester School Supplement* (1997), pp. 32–58.

Subramanian, K., 'Term Structure Estimation in Illiquid Markets', *Journal of Fixed Income*', 11(1) (2001), 77–86.

Svensson, L., 'Estimating and Interpreting Forward Interest Rates: Sweden 1992–1994', International Monetary Fund, working paper, D95-1, 1995.

Tuckman, Bruce, *Fixed Income Securities*, John Wiley and Sons, New York, 1995.

Vasicek, O., 'An Equilibrium Characterization of the Term Structure', *Journal of Financial Economics*, 5 (1977), 177–188.

Warga, Arthur D., 'Corporate Bond Price Discrepancies in the Dealer and Exchange Markets', *Journal of Fixed Income*, 1 (1991), 7–17.

Zhou, C., 'A Jump Diffusion Approach to Modelling Credit Risk and Valuing Defaultable Securities', working paper, Federal Reserve Board, Washington, 1997.

Index

Duration gap:
 bank liquidity portfolios, 220
 elimination, 218–20
 maintaining, 220–4
 model, 216–18
Dutch auction, 36, 38–9, 328–9

ECF, see Expected cash flows
Eliminating the duration gap, 218–20
Embedded options, 296–323, 360
Equity holders, default risk, 10–12
Error sum of squares (ESS), 171–2
Eurobond market, 7
European call options, 296, 303
 see also Intrinsic values
 backward induction, 300
 sinking fund bonds, 319–22
European put options, 306–7
Event risk covenants, 14, 325
Evolutionary models, 16, 122–33,
  340–2
Excel spreadsheets, 16, 63–4
Expectations hypothesis, 25–9, 32–3
Expected cash flows (ECF), 240

Falling yields, 211
Fisher effect, 31–2
Fisher Weil duration, 227, 228–31, 233
Fixed income instruments, 15
 see also Bonds
Fixed rate reference bonds, 288–90
Flat price, see Clean price
Floaters, 246–51
 caps and floors, 259–65
 collars, 265–6
 default swaps, 287–8
 duration, 355–6
 inverse floaters, 251–8
 securitization, 252–3
 volatility, 340
Floating rate reference bonds, 287–8
Floors, 253, 258–66
Forward curves, 65–6, 69, 77
Forward induction:
 caps, 262
 floors, 264
 sinking fund bonds, 320–1
 state prices, 96–8
Forward rates:
 bonds, 325–7
 sovereign term structure, 28–32
Frequently traded bonds, 47–52
Full price, see Dirty price
Futures contracts:
 attraction summary, 178
 bonds, 176–9
 hedge ratios, 345–6
 purchase number, 200
Future value of coupon bonds, 52–3

Gamma, callable bonds, 313
Gilt securities, 203–4
Global capital markets, 8–9
Government bond market, 6
 see also Treasury securities

Hazard rate models, 156
Hedge portfolios, 186–9, 288–9
Hedge ratios, 19–21, 227–45
 convexity, 313–14
 duration-based, 174–83
 futures contracts, 345–6
 long swap hedging, 270–1
 N, 169–70
 regression-based, 170–4
 variance curve, 187–8
Hedging objectives, 18–21
Historical data availability, 132
Ho and Lee model, 93–106, 337–8
 calibration, 100–2
 caps, 260–3
 floors, 263–5
 implementation, 102–5
Ho's key rate duration model, 232–7,
  351–3
Hull and White model, 119–20
Hydro Quebec bonds, 7

Immunization, portfolios, 207–14
Inflation:
 Fisher effect, 32
 sovereign interest rates, 33–4
 yield curves, 23
Information:
 asymmetry, 292
 sovereign interest rates, 33–4
Insurance:
 industries, 194–226
 preferred habitat hypothesis, 30–1
Interest instruments, background,
  1–17
Interest rate:
 credit risk correlation, 238
 derivatives, 8–9, 246, 258–66, 278
 measuring structures, 46–73
 methodology, 15–16
 modelling, 78–9, 92–121, 122–58
 payoffs, 263
 risk structure, 18–25, 34–6, 238,
  259, 265–6
 sensitivity, 159–93, 307–14
 sinking fund bonds, 322
 sovereign term structure, 18–34,
  74–91
 swaps, 266–71
 term structure consistent models,
  337–42